Integrating Individual and Ecological Aspects of Crime

Editors:
David P. Farrington
Robert J. Sampson
Per-Olof H. Wikström

BRÅ-report 1993:1

Brottsförebyggande rådet
(National Council for Crime Prevention)
P.O. Box 6494
S-113 82 Stockholm
SWEDEN
Telephone +468-769 84 00
Telefax +468-32 83 64

The National Council for Crime Prevention (Brottsförebyggande rådet), established in 1974, is a government agency under the Ministry of Justice. The purpose of the Council is to promote crime prevention measures in different areas of society and work for the coordination of measures against crime. The Council's activities consist of evaluations, research and disseminating information. Many of the Council's activities are carried out in cooperation with other authorities. The council has an office with a permanent staff.

Additional copies of this publication can be ordered through:
Fritzes Kundtjänst
S-106 47 STOCKHOLM
Telephone +468-690 90 90
Telefax +468-20 50 21

ISSN 1101-2331
ISBN 91-38-12815-2
Cover Göta Glemme, G-*form*
Production Kommentus
Gotab 98006, Stockholm 1993

Integrating Individual and Ecological Aspects of Crime

Preface

Two prominent areas of research within the field of criminology are the study of individual development of offending (sometimes called "criminal career research") and socio-ecological studies of crime (sometimes called "environmental criminology"). These two traditions have largely developed separately as pointed out by Reiss (1986). However, in recent years it has become evident that bridging the gap between theory and research in the two traditions is a necessary step if the understanding and explanation of criminal behavior is to move forward.

Against this background, and my special interest in the topic of integrating these two traditions (Wikström,1991), I proposed in 1991 that the National Council for Crime Prevention (Sweden) should organize a work-shop on the topic of *integrating individual and ecological aspects of crime*. It was so decided, and in 1991 I set up an organizing committee consisting of myself, professor David P Farrington (Cambridge, England) and professor Robert J Sampson (Chicago, USA).

At the 1991 meeting of the American Society of Criminology in San Fransisco I met with both professor Farrington and professor Sampson to discuss issues and presenters for the work-shop. We made a short-list of approximately 60 prominent scholars to be considered for the work-shop. After going through the areas to be included – theory, methodology ,empirical studies, crime prevention – we ended up with a list of thirteen people to be invited. In addition to these thirteen, professor Albert J Reiss jr. was invited to be the general commentator for the work-shop. I was very pleased to find out that all but one of those invited agreed to participate and to produce a paper on the topic he or she was invited to present. Those taking part in the work-shop represents to my judgement the best in contemporary studies of individual developments of offending and socio-ecological studies of crime. Needless to say, there are of course many more equally excellent scholars that was not invited, but as always, time and money put limits to the number of participants.

The work-shop was held at Johannesberg outside Stockholm in the beginning of september 1992. The two first days were devoted to a presentation of the papers and the two final days to comments and detailed discussions of the papers. The final day also included the general work-shop commentary by professor Albert J. Reiss jr. The authors had an opportunity after the work-shop to revise their papers . This book presents the revised papers and a general commentary by professor Reiss.

There is no doubt in my mind that a key issue in criminology in the coming years will increasingly be the integration of individual and ecological aspects of crime. This book attempts to give a "state of the art" description of the problems and prospects facing integrative criminological theory and research.

On the behalf of the National Council for Crime Prevention (Sweden) I wish to thank all those who participated in the work-shop which to me was a memorable occasion both from a scentific and a personal point of view.

Stockholm June 15, 1993

Per-Olof H. Wikström
Director of research

References

Reiss, A.J. (1986). Why are communities important in understanding crime? In A.J. Reiss & M. Tonry (Eds.) Crime and justice 8: Communities and crime. Chicago: University of Chicago Press.

Wikström, P.-O.H. (1991). Urban crime, criminals and victims. New York: Springer Verlag.

Have any Individual, Family or Neighbourhood Influences on Offending been Demonstrated Conclusively?

by David P. Farrington

Introduction

Offending may be influenced by many different categories of factors, including biological, individual, family, peer, school, neighbourhood and demographic ones. The focus in this paper is on individual factors such as high impulsivity and low intelligence, family factors such as poor parental supervision and erratic parental discipline, and neighbourhood factors such as physical deterioration and social disorganisation. In the interests of reducing complexity, biological, peer, school and other factors will be neglected. I will also neglect larger national influences, although cross-national comparisons could be illuminating.

In investigating influences on offending, the major problem is that most allegedly criminogenic factors tend to coincide and tend to be inter-related. For example, adolescents living in physically deteriorated and socially disorganised neighbourhoods disproportionally tend also to come from families with poor parental supervision and erratic parental discipline and tend also to have high impulsivity and low intelligence (e.g. West & Farrington, 1973). The concentration and co-occurrence of these kinds of adversities makes it difficult to establish their independent, interactive or sequential influences on offending. Indeed, the argument in this paper is that no previous researcher has succeeded in demonstrating these independent, interactive or sequential influences conclusively, because no previous researcher has simultaneously measured all the most important individual, family and neighbourhood factors in any research project. As Tonry *et al.* (1991, p. 42) pointed out:

> *... past research has concentrated on either individual- or community-level effects. Almost no research has examined both types of effects... Thus, most individual-level research is inadequate because it neglects variation in community characteristics, while community-level research fails to take account of individual differences.*

My focus is particularly on influences on offending by individuals, rather than influences on offender rates, offence rates or victimization rates of larger units such as neighbourhoods. Wikström (1985) carefully distinguished these three types of neighbourhood rates, based on where offenders live, where offences are committed, and where victims live. Of course, the total number of offences committed by residents of a neighbourhood (conventionally termed the offender rate, although there is sometimes ambiguity about whether this term refers to prevalence) is merely the sum of the number of offences committed by each individual resident, with appropriate adjustment for co-offending (Reiss & Farrington, 1991).

My focus is especially on the most common types of offences that lead to arrests and convictions and that cause the most concern among the general public, namely theft, burglary, robbery, violence, vandalism, drug abuse and minor fraud. I will not attempt to review influences on so-called "white-collar" offending, because of the lack of relevant research. I am concerned with offending from childhood to adulthood, but my focus on family influences means that I will give most emphasis to youthful offending.

It is reasonable to argue that offences arise from the interaction between an individual, with a certain antisocial tendency or criminal potential, and the environment, which provides criminal opportunities. Influences on individual criminal potential are generally long-term, between-individual factors, whereas influences on the commission of offences are generally short-term, within-individual, situational factors. The major influences on criminal potential are energizing, directing and inhibiting factors, whereas the commission of offences involves an individual decision-making process, taking account of consequences, costs and benefits (see Farrington, 1992b, 1993). In the interests of reducing complexity, I will focus here on the longer-term individual, family and neighbourhood influences on criminal potential and neglect immediate situational influences on the commission of offences. Hence, I will neglect features of the physical environment such as opportunities, targets and surveillance (e.g. Clarke, 1992). I am focussing on the development of offenders rather than on the commission of offences.

There are many ways in which individual, family and neighbourhood factors might influence individual offending. All three types of factors could have simultaneous, direct and independent effects. Alternatively, the three types of factors could have indirect or sequential effects. For example, neighbourhood factors might influence family factors, which in turn influence individual factors, which in turn cause offending. If this sequential causal chain applied, neighbourhood and family factors would not predict offending independently of individual factors. Alternatively, there could be interaction effects, so that neighbourhood factors had different effects on different types of individuals, or individual factors had different effects on offending in different types of neighbourhoods. Another possibility is that there are reciprocal or lagged effects, so that an influx of certain types of individuals changes a neighbourhood, which then has different effects on the individuals living there, or if increased neighbourhood offending causes changes in individuals or families (Bursik, 1986).

A key question centres on what are the most important individual, family and neighbourhood factors. Different variables in any given category may have different effects; for example, some neighbourhood factors may have direct effects on offending, while others may have indirect effects mediated by their influence on family factors. Some variables (e.g. poverty, unemployment, social class or race) may be measured simultaneously in individuals, families and neighbourhoods, and may have different effects in the different categories. However, the high correlations between individual, family and neighbourhood variables may make it very difficult to disentangle them. For example, lower-class individuals tend to live in lower-class families and in lower-class neighbourhoods. It is important to investigate the impact of individual, family and neighbourhood variables on the energizing, directing and inhibiting of offending, and on different features of the criminal career, such as onset, persistence and desistance (Farrington, 1992a).

Many criminological theories include statements about individual, family and neighbourhood influences on offending, although it is sometimes unclear if statements in theories, especially about social class, refer to individuals, families or neighbourhoods. For example, Trasler (1962) proposed that the main factor that inhibited offending was conditioned anxiety, which depended on methods of child-rearing, and that methods of child-rearing differed between middle-class and lower-class families and/or neighbourhoods (pp.77–81). Elliott *et al.* (1985, 1989) in their integrated theory proposed that the strain between a person's aspirations and what could be obtained, poor socialization (in families) and social disorganization (in neighbourhoods) produced weak conventional bonding, which in turn produced strong delinquent bonding and ultimately delinquent behaviour. Reiss (1986) argued that slum neighbourhoods produced a concentration of female-headed households, which in turn caused poor parental control, which in turn caused peer influences and delinquent subcultures, which in turn produced delinquency. As illustrated here, most theories propose a sequential chain of influences, with neighbourhood factors having indirect rather than direct effects on offending.

In this paper, I will begin by reviewing the research of Shaw and McKay (1942), which is often quoted as demonstrating neighbourhood influences on offending, and I will go on to consider some more recent research in this tradition. I will then review the research of Glueck and Glueck (1950), which might be regarded as documenting individual and family influences on offending, and then go on to consider some more recent research in this tradition. I will then discuss some more general issues of theory and measurement in investigating individual, family and neighbourhood factors, and then mention some implications for preventing and reducing offending. Finally, I will suggest research that is needed to demonstrate individual, family and neighbourhood influences on offending more conclusively.

The Research of Shaw and McKay

Beginning with *Delinquency Areas* (Shaw *et al.*, 1929) and culminating in *Juvenile Delinquency and Urban Areas* (Shaw & McKay, 1942, 1969), Shaw and McKay documented correlations between juvenile delinquency rates in different areas of Chicago (and other American cities) and census-type rates (e.g. of poor housing, population density, owner occupation, ethnic composition) and rates of social and health problems such as truancy, mental disorder, tuberculosis and infant mortality. The juvenile delinquency rates were based on where offenders lived, not on where offences were committed; most of these rates were obtained by comparing the addresses of male offenders appearing before the juvenile court with the decennial census population figures.

Shaw and McKay concluded that delinquency rates were highest near the centre of a city and decreased with distance out towards the suburban areas. Generally, areas with high delinquency rates tended to have high rates of other social and health problems and tended to be areas of physical deterioration and social disorganisation. One of their results that seems to have attracted rather less attention (but see Wikström, 1991, p. 141) is that a high proportion of all offenders tended to come from a small proportion of areas. This result is somewhat reminiscent of West and Farrington's (1977) conclusion that about 4% of families account for about half of convictions of all family members (fathers, mothers, sons and daughters), and of Sherman *et al.*'s (1989) conclusion that about 3% of places account for about half of all calls to the police. The disproportionality is typically less in the case of areas; for example, Hamparian *et al.* (1978) found that one-third of their cohort of violent juveniles in Columbus, Ohio, lived in 10 (predominantly poor, Black) census tracts containing 8% of the total population.

As Short (1969) noted in his introduction to the revised edition of *Juvenile Delinquency and Urban Areas*, Shaw and McKay's most controversial conclusion was that the pattern of high delinquency rates in inner city areas of Chicago persisted over many years (from the 1900s to the 1960s) despite successive waves of emigration from and immigration into these areas by groups of different ethnic and national origins. In 1900, the residents of inner city areas were predominantly of German, Irish or Scandinavian origin. These groups then moved out and were replaced by immigrants of Eastern European (especially Polish) origin, then Italians moved in as the Polish moved farther out, and then Blacks from the South moved in as the Italians moved father out. Since the relative delinquency rates of different areas stayed fairly consistent over time, it was argued that delinquency was primarily influenced by physical and social characteristics of the neighbourhood, independently of the types of individuals and families living in different areas.

Shaw and McKay (1942, p. 435) concluded that:

> *... the fact that in Chicago the rates of delinquents for many years have remained relatively constant in the areas adjacent to centres of commerce and industry, despite successive changes in the nativity and nationality composition of the population, supports emphatically the conclusion that the delinquency-producing factors are inherent in the community.*

It is hard to overemphasize the importance of this conclusion in the history of criminology. Largely because of it, criminology – which up to the 1920s had been dominated by psychologists and psychiatrists – was captured by sociologists in the 1930s. The sociologist who was most influential in this capture was Sutherland, who was the author of the most influential textbook of criminology (*Principles of Criminology*) between the 1930s and 1970s and arguably the most important sociologist of crime in the twentieth century. As Laub and Sampson (1991, p. 1 421) pointed out:

> *... with the 1939 edition of Principles as a backdrop, criminology became a field closed to the possibility that disciplines other than sociology might have something to contribute... sociology was successful in its attempt to take over the study of crime... Sutherland's leadership role in this action was widely recognised – so much so that Robert Merton even compared Sutherland's* **Principles of Criminology** *to such disciplinary classics as Samuelson's* **Economics** *and Gray's* **Anatomy** *as books that "leave an enduring impress on generations of students"... That Sutherland became the warrior for sociology's coup of criminology was also linked to his social position and rising influence in the sociological discipline... he went on to become president of the American Sociological Association in 1939.*

It is illuminating to see what Sutherland's textbook (1939, pp. 138–142) said about Shaw and McKay's research:

> *... the areas which had high rates in 1930 had high rates, also, in 1900, although in the meantime the national composition of the population of the area had changed almost completely... Two interpretations of the concentration of delinquents near the business and industrial centres of cities have been presented. The first is in terms of the social disorganisation of the neighbourhood. The areas of concentration in American cities and especially Chicago, where the problem has been studied most*

extensively, are areas of physical deterioration, congested population, decreasing population, economic dependency, rented homes, foreign and Negro population, adult criminality, and few institutions supported by the local residents. Lawlessness has become traditional... The second interpretation has been favoured by psychiatrists. The argument is made that the areas in which delinquency rates are high are low-rent areas, and that a population segregated on the basis of rent-paying ability involves a selection of the constitutionally inferior. They interpret the concentration of delinquents therefore in terms of segregation or selective migration... In opposition to this interpretation of delinquency rates in terms of segregation, the most important evidence is Shaw's finding that the delinquency rate remained practically constant over a thirty-year period in spite of an almost complete change in the national composition of the population. This indicates that the delinquency rate is a function of the area rather than of the type of people who reside there.

According to Shaw and McKay (1942, 1969), then, offending depended on neighbourhood features, not individual characteristics. They proposed several explanations of how and why neighbourhoods influenced offending. Perhaps the best known is their linkage of physical deterioration and "social disorganisation": a poor ability of local institutions to control the behaviour of residents, which allowed offending. Examples of community control include questioning people about suspicious activities and admonishing children for unacceptable behaviour (see Bursik, 1988, for a review of the concept of social disorganisation). However, Shaw and McKay (1969) also proposed that, in delinquent areas, traditions of delinquency were transmitted from one generation to the next through differential association (p. 174), families were ineffective (p. 183), there was strain between economic goals and what could be attained (p. 186), and there were gangs and subcultures (p. 171). Generally, they emphasized the cultural transmission of antisocial values and the ineffectiveness of socialization processes in socially disorganised neighbourhoods.

The Current Status of Shaw and McKay's Research

Shaw and McKay's research is still highly cited by American criminologists (see e.g. Cohn & Farrington, 1990). However, it has been subjected to numerous criticisms, including the obvious problem of the validity of juvenile court records as measures of offending and the arbitrariness of their square-mile areas of Chicago as indicators of homogeneous neighbourhoods. Most of these criticisms are included in Gold's (1987) review of Shaw and McKay's contributions to knowledge.

A major issue is the so-called "ecological fallacy". As pointed out in a classic paper by Robinson (1950), valid conclusions about correlations between individuals cannot necessarily be drawn from "ecological correlations" (correlations between rates in neighbourhoods). And yet, Robinson (1950, p. 352), after making explicit reference to Shaw and McKay's work, stated that "in each study which uses ecological correlations, the obvious purpose is to discover something about the behaviour of individuals." For example, Shaw and McKay (1942, p. 435) argued that "local variations in the conduct of children, as revealed in differential rates of delinquents, reflect the differences in social values, norms and attitudes to which the children are exposed". In other words, Shaw and McKay wanted to draw valid conclusions about neighbourhood influences on individual offending, but their use of ecological correlations did not necessarily permit this.

As an example of the problems, Wallis and Maliphant (1967) in London found that delinquency rates in areas were negatively correlated with divorce rates in areas, but that the individual delinquents in their study were more likely to have divorced parents than a representative sample of boys. Part of the problem may be that many census-type rates reflect the behaviour of older people, whereas delinquency rates reflect the behaviour of younger people. Intriguingly, Glaser and Rice (1959) showed that unemployment rates were positively correlated with adult crime rates but negatively correlated with juvenile delinquency rates. Firebaugh (1978) has reviewed conditions when individual-level conclusions can or cannot validly be drawn from aggregate-level correlations.

One problem with Shaw and McKay's research which seems to have gone largely unnoticed, except perhaps by Schmid (1960, p. 675), who carried out a longitudinal study of offender and offence rates in different areas of Seattle, is the comparability of numerators and denominators in calculating rates. The numerator in each of Shaw and McKay's delinquency rate calculations for Chicago areas was the number of different juveniles resident in an area who appeared in the Cook County juvenile court for alleged delinquency during a period of several years (e.g. 1917–23 or 1927–33). The denominator was the number of juveniles resident in the same area on the day of the decennial census (e.g. 1920 or 1930). In an area of high mobility (as the inner city areas were), the number of different juveniles resident in the area at some time during a 7-year period (and hence at risk of delinquency) – even when converted to an annual rate – would be greater than the number resident in the area on the census day (e.g. April 1, 1930). Hence, the delinquency rates in high-mobility areas would be over-estimated.

In assessing neighbourhood influences on offending, I will focus particularly on the issue of the relative consistency of offending rates in different neighbourhoods, irrespective of the types of people living in them. The most damaging criticisms of Shaw and McKay's conclusion about the unimportance of ethnic and national origins were made by Jonassen (1949). He pointed out that it was desirable not only to compare delinquency rates of the same ethnic group in different areas (as Shaw and McKay did) but also of different ethnic groups in the same area. Jonassen argued that Shaw and McKay's published data showed that Northern and Western European groups had lower delinquency rates than Southern and Eastern European groups living in the same areas of Chicago. Jonassen also noticed that Shaw and McKay (1942, p. 440) had found that Orientals had relatively low delinquency rates even when they lived in the most deteriorated areas of a city, whereas Blacks had relatively high delinquency rates in all areas where they lived. Jonassen (1949, p. 613) argued that:

It is difficult to account for such contradictions as are apparent except by hypothesizing the presence of hidden biases which seem to warp inferences from the data in certain directions. The thread of ecological determinism is discernible... Apparent also in the fabric of their reasoning are hints of ideological predilections induced by a reluctance, even under empirical temptations, to sin against the "professional ideology of the social pathologist" or of democracy by entertaining the possibility that all nativity, racial and nationality groups are not equal in their ability to resist the "disorganisation" of juvenile delinquency.

In their reply to Jonassen, Shaw and McKay (1949, p. 617) said that:

It has been charged that there are hints of ideological predilections and for preference of democracy in our studies... It is possibly true... that we have felt some satisfaction over the fact that our data suggest rather consistently that, if circumstances were comparable, the rate of delinquency among devalued groups would not be unlike the rate for favoured groups... The important fact about rates of delinquents for Negro boys is that they, too, vary by type of area. They are higher than the rates for White boys, but it cannot be said that they are higher than rates for White boys in comparable areas, since it is impossible to reproduce in White communities the circumstances under which Negro children live.

After reviewing this exchange between Jonassen and Shaw and McKay, Gold (1987, p. 77) concluded:

... It seems fair to say that Jonassen's challenge is valid. Shaw and McKay had shown that social conditions in an urban area related to delinquency rates, regardless of the ethnicity of the population. But they had not shown that social conditions made all the difference and ethnic culture none. While the correlations between ethnic composition and areal rates declined when socio-economic conditions were partialled out, they did not disappear. Ethnic groups seem to carry different degrees of propensity for delinquency with them, at least over several generations, wherever they settle. This may be due to the more enduring features of their culture, to genetic factors, or, espe-

cially in the case of Blacks, to inescapably bad conditions. Shaw and McKay's data could not identify which.

Later research casts doubt on the relative consistency of delinquency rates over time. In his introduction to *Juvenile Delinquency and Urban Areas*, Short (1969) noted that neighbourhoods which had virtually complete changes in population from White to Black during the late 1940s and 1950s showed the greatest increases in delinquency rates (while the greatest decreases were seen in neighbourhoods which had been predominantly Black for a long time). Interestingly, Jonassen (1949, p. 610) had noted the same increasing tendency much earlier:

> *... examination of the data reveals that in certain areas the correlation, instead of being highly positive, would be highly negative. For example, when comparing Map No.9, indicating the residences of delinquents for the years 1934–1940, with Map No.12, showing residences of delinquents in the period 1900–1906, it would appear that the most dramatic feature of these maps is the difference in delinquency which is apparent in the area between 63rd Street and 31st Street and between Cottage Grove Avenue and State Street. Judging roughly from these spot maps, it would seem that in this case the coefficient of correlation would be highly negative – well above –.90. And this startling change is closely correlated with the entry into this area of persons of the Negro race.*

Hence, Shaw and McKay's research does not prove that neighbourhood factors influence offending independently of individual and family factors.

Because Shaw and McKay were meticulous researchers and their raw data was preserved, Bursik and Webb (1982) were able to test the consistency hypothesis using more sophisticated quantitative methods. They noted that Shaw and McKay had to make all their calculations by hand, and that their conclusions "were primarily based on a visual inspection of the mapped distributions, although some use of correlation coefficients was made" (1982, p. 28). Bursik and Webb concluded that relative delinquency rates were not stable after 1950, and that they reflected demographic changes. Variations in delinquency rates in different areas were significantly correlated with variations in the percentage of Non-Whites, the percentage of foreign-born Whites, and the percentage of overcrowded households. The greatest increases in delinquency rates of areas occurred when Blacks moved from the minority to the majority. Hence, it seems that delinquency rates did vary according to the types of individuals living in different areas of Chicago. It would be interesting to investigate how far these results might be replicable with measures of offending and antisocial behaviour other than official records.

Researchers more interested in individual and family factors have argued for many years that such factors are important. For example, in discussing Shaw and McKay's research, Glueck and Glueck (1950, pp.5–6) stated that:

> *They do not reveal why the deleterious influences of even the most extreme delinquency area fail to turn the great majority of its boys into persistent delinquents. They do not disclose whether the children who did not succumb to the evil and disruptive neighbourhood influence differ from those who become delinquents and if so in what respects... The true significance of the factors dealt with by the area sociologist can be determined only through close study of the points of impact of social forces upon individuals and classes of varying biologic make-up and childhood conditioning. The varieties of the physical, mental and social history of different persons must determine, in large measure, the way in which they will be influenced by social disorganisation, culture conflict, and the growing-pains of the city. To over-emphasize the neighbourhood matrix as a coherent whole and under-emphasize or virtually ignore the biologic make-up and developmental history of the different human beings who themselves contribute to the modification of that matrix is to overlook many of the factors that account for variations in the effect of the culture on the human beings and thereby to distort reality.*

The key problem with Shaw and McKay's (1969) research is that it is impossible to know how far varying delinquency rates of different areas reflect variations in neighbourhood factors such as physical deterioration or social disorganisation and how far they reflect variations in other factors, such as individual characteristics or family influences. The competing hypothesis that neighbourhood delinquency rates depend on population drift or migration or allocation (causing poor, multi-problem, antisocial families to move into low-rent areas or public housing) has never been disproved satisfactorily. For example, in his careful and methodologically sophisticated ecological research in Sweden, Wikström (1985) concluded that violent crime rates were high in inner-city areas primarily because such areas attracted "socially loaded" persons (alcoholics, drug addicts and previously known criminals).

Neither Shaw and McKay nor any subsequent researcher has been able to demonstrate unambiguously that neighbourhood factors have important influences on offending independently of individual and family factors. Nor has any researcher satisfactorily investigated interactions between neighbourhood and individual factors in influencing offending to establish or disprove differential susceptibility of different types of people to neighbourhood influences.

Later Research on Neighbourhood Influences

There has been a great deal of subsequent research, inspired by Shaw and McKay's work, on offender and offence rates in different areas (for reviews, see Baldwin, 1979; Gold, 1987; Bursik, 1988). Much of this has been cross-sectional in nature, although a few researchers have repeated Shaw and McKay's longitudinal method (e.g. Schmid, 1960; Baldwin *et al.*, 1976; Bursik & Webb, 1982; Schuerman & Kobrin, 1986). A recent focus has been on how and why neighbourhood crime rates change over time ("community crime careers": see Reiss, 1986; Bottoms & Wiles, 1986) rather than on the stability of such crime rates.

Very few neighbourhood researchers have tried to study individual, family and neighbourhood influences on individual offending. Such an investigation requires individual-level data, whereas most neighbourhood researchers have followed Shaw and McKay in using neighbourhood-level data and focussing on crime rates (for interesting recent examples, see Sampson & Groves, 1989, and Bursik & Grasmick, 1992). The most relevant multi-level studies of individual offending are probably those carried out by Johnstone (1978), Simcha-Fagan and Schwartz (1986) and Gottfredson *et al.* (1991). Some interesting multi-level studies of individual victimization have been carried out (e.g. Sampson & Lauritsen, 1990), but I will not consider them in this paper. Nor will I consider the statistical issues raised by using neighbourhood-level variables as predictors of individual-level variables.

Johnstone (1978) obtained questionnaires from over 1,100 teenage males and females living in over 200 census tracts in Chicago. He investigated the correlations between self-reported delinquency and four variables, family socio-economic status (education and occupation), neighbourhood poverty (low income and female-headed households), family integration (parental attachment and female-headed households) and delinquent peers. In regression analyses, the neighbourhood variable was significantly related to self-reported delinquency. However, this study included very few variables and, surprisingly, did not even include age, race or gender in the regression analyses.

Simcha-Fagan and Schwartz (1986) began with a neighbourhood design. Noting that census-based variables fell into two clusters, reflecting family disorganisation (one-parent families) and affluence (household income), they studied 12 neighbourhoods of New York City, varying in family disorganisation (high, medium and low), affluence (high or low) and predominantly White or Black ethnic composition. They interviewed over 550 adolescent males and their mothers in these neighbourhoods, and collected neighbourhood data and other information (especially about association with delinquent peers and attachment to school). The neighbourhood variables included in their major analyses were not those in the original design but those derived from their interviews.

In regression analyses, Simcha-Fagan and Schwartz found that the strongest independent correlates of official delinquency were age, family income and community social disorder (which was highly correlated with one-parent families). The strongest independent correlates of self-reported delinquency were age, community residential stability and low community organizational participation (which seemed mainly to reflect parental educational level). However, it seems that other important variables (delinquent peers and low school attachment) were excluded from these analyses, since Simcha-Fagan and Schwartz later concluded that community and family variables had indirect effects on delinquency via their effects on delinquent peers and low school attachment. Hence, "community effects on delinquency are to a large extent mediated by socialization experiences" (1986, p. 695). However, Simcha-Fagan and Schwartz merely showed that one causal model was consistent with their data; it is not clear that they compared the plausibility of radically different causal models. Also, they did not measure any of the individual and family variables that have been found to be most important in longitudinal studies, such as impulsivity, intelligence, supervision, discipline and criminal parents.

Gottfredson *et al.* (1991) collected demographic, family, peer, neighbourhood and self-reported delinquency measures in a school-based questionnaire survey of over 3,700 adolescents. Essentially replicating Simcha-Fagan and Schwartz's findings, the neighbourhood (census) variables fell into two clusters, one ("disorganization") reflecting female-headed households, poverty and welfare dependency and the other ("affluence") reflecting professional/managerial employment and high levels of income and education. Gottfredson *et al.* found that, in multiple regression analyses including demographic, family, peer and school variables, neighbourhood effects were very small. Zero-order correlations with self-reported delinquency were much higher for age, deviant peers, attachment to parents and attachment to school than for neighbourhood variables. Furthermore, the effects were not entirely as predicted, since the only significant result for males was that those living in more affluent neighbourhoods reported *more* delinquency than others. In contrast, males with better educated parents reported less delinquency than others, leading Gottfredson *et al.* to argue that the relationship between social class and delinquency went in opposite directions for neighbourhoods and individuals. They also suggested in their footnotes that there was an interaction between individual and neighbourhood social class.

The major problem with the Gottfredson *et al.* study is that they did not investigate different possible causal models (e.g. sequential versus simultaneous) linking demographic, family, peer, school and neighbourhood variables. In addition, the measures of offending and all non-neighbourhood variables were based on self-reports, raising the possibility that the relationships were inflated by common response biases. Also, the study included a very limited range of variables, and no individual-level characteristics such as high impulsivity or low intelligence.

Also, the study was cross-sectional rather than longitudinal, making it possible to study only between-individual variation.

Gottfredson and Taylor (1986) conducted an interesting study in Baltimore of the effect on recidivism of the neighbourhood context into which a prisoner was released. They found that neighbourhood measures (based on systematic observation) fell into two categories: decay (graffiti, litter, vacant houses, groups of young males hanging about) and land use (commercial, industrial or institutional). After controlling for offender characteristics (criminal history and social background), neighbourhood factors did not help in predicting recidivism, as indeed Reiss (1951a) found many years before. However, there was some evidence of an interaction between types of people and types of neighbourhoods, with the worst (most criminal) offenders doing better if they were released to relatively good neighbourhoods, and vice versa.

It is hard to resist the conclusion that knowledge about individual, family and neighbourhood influences on offending is rather fragmentary.

The Research of the Gluecks

In case it might be thought that I am unduly critical of research on neighbourhood influences, I would like to make it clear that similar problems apply in the study of individual and family influences. Individual and family researchers have generally neglected to study neighbourhood factors. No project has yet demonstrated conclusively that individual and family factors have an influence on offending independently of (or interactively with) neighbourhood factors. It is conceivable that individual and family factors only predict offending because their prevalence varies in different neighbourhoods, and that neighbourhood influences are the most important. It is also conceivable that individual and family factors have different influences on offending in different neighbourhoods.

In illustrating problems of research on individual and family factors, I have chosen to review the work of the Gluecks, who were comparable pioneers in studying individual and family influences to Shaw and McKay in studying neighbourhood influences. All the evidence suggests that the Gluecks were even more meticulous researchers than Shaw and McKay (since more of their raw data and correspondence is preserved: see Laub & Sampson, 1988, 1991) and that they are even more highly cited in the recent criminological literature (Cohn & Farrington, 1990). It was perhaps no accident that the first volume of the prestigious and influential *Crime and Justice* series, which publishes state-of-the-art reviews of the literature on important criminological issues, included one chapter on neighbourhood studies (Baldwin, 1979) that acknowledged the contributions of

Shaw and McKay, and another on longitudinal studies (Farrington, 1979) that acknowledged the contributions of the Gluecks.

The Gluecks primarily advanced criminological knowledge through their longitudinal investigations of criminal careers, and especially in their approximately 15-year follow-ups of 500 reformatory males (Glueck & Glueck, 1930, 1937, 1943), 1000 court delinquents (Glueck & Glueck, 1934, 1940), and 500 institutionalized delinquents and 500 matched non-delinquents (Glueck & Glueck, 1968). However, they are perhaps best known nowadays for their cross-sectional study on *Unravelling Juvenile Delinquency* (Glueck & Glueck, 1950), and I will concentrate on this. In many ways, it is unfortunate that this is their best-known study, since it is not only cross-sectional but also made exaggerated claims about the accuracy with which delinquency can be predicted. Nevertheless, this book contains useful information about almost all conceivable correlates and predictors of delinquency. For example, when I was recently interested in studying the importance of the age of the mother at the time of the birth of her first child, in relation to later offending by her children (see e.g. Morash & Rucker, 1989), I was able to turn to *Unravelling Juvenile Delinquency* and find a – somewhat – relevant table on p. 117.

In *Unravelling Juvenile Delinquency*, the Gluecks attempted to match 500 institutionalized delinquents with 500 non-delinquents in Boston case by case on sex (they were all male), age (within one year), intelligence (within 10 points on the full-scale Wechsler-Bellevue IQ), ethnic origin and also on residence in underprivileged neighbourhoods (in 93% of cases since birth). Based on the backgrounds of parents and grandparents, the ethnic origins were most commonly British (26% of pairs), Italian (25%), Irish (19%) and American (8%); all boys were White. In selecting matched non-delinquents (from specified public schools), undetected persistent minor offenders were excluded, so the delinquent and non-delinquent groups were somewhat extreme. The Gluecks' aim in matching for neighbourhood factors was clearly to investigate whether individual, family and other factors influenced delinquency independently of neighbourhood features.

Unfortunately, their matching for neighbourhood was less satisfactory than their matching for other factors, as one astute young reviewer (Reiss, 1951b) pointed out at the time. As many as 70% of census tracts in the city of Boston (109 out of 156) were classified as underprivileged neighbourhoods, in most cases because of their relatively high juvenile delinquency rates. Hence, it was not surprising that hardly any of the institutionalized delinquents were eliminated from the study because they did not come from underprivileged neighbourhoods. Each non-delinquent was not necessarily resident in the same census tract as his matched delinquent, but only in the same kind of underprivileged area. The matching for neighbourhood seems inadequate, since 55% of delinquents (versus 34% of non-delinquents) lived in blighted slum tenement areas, whereas 49% of non-delinquents (versus 31% of delinquents) lived in interstitial (mixed business and residential) areas.

The Gluecks reported numerous significant differences between delinquents and non-delinquents in individual and family (and other) factors. Based on rather inadequate statistical methods, they concluded that the most important and mutually exclusive family predictors of delinquency that were measurable at age 6 were: erratic or overstrict discipline of the boy by the father, poor supervision of the boy by the mother, hostile or indifferent attitude of the mother and the father to the boy, and low family cohesiveness. According to a psychiatric interview, the most important and mutually exclusive individual-level predictors were adventurousness or risk-taking of the boy, extraversion, suggestibility or the boy being easily led, stubbornness and emotional instability of the boy. However, the possibility remains that their observed individual and family differences between delinquents and non-delinquents were confounded with and a consequence of neighbourhood differences. The delinquents lived in worse areas on average.

The Current Status of the Gluecks' Research

Unravelling Juvenile Delinquency provided basic information about the numerous different correlates of delinquency that any theory needs to take account of and explain. However, this book has of course been subjected to a great deal of criticism, much of which can be found in Hirschi and Selvin (1967). In contrast to the generally uncritical acceptance of Shaw and McKay's conclusions in American criminology, complaints about the Gluecks' research are so numerous and widespread that it is unnecessary for me to detail them here. The greatest difficulties stem from the cross-sectional nature of the research, which raises acute problems of causal order. For example, it is unclear whether the parents of the delinquents became less cohesive and more hostile to the boy as a result of his persistent delinquency, or whether low family cohesiveness and parental hostility preceded and caused the boy's delinquency. Retrospective bias is also a great problem. It is unclear how far measured differences between delinquents and non-delinquents were influenced by the interviewer's knowledge of who had become a delinquent and who had not. Also, the Gluecks should not really have tried to draw conclusions about predictability at age 6 from data collected on average at age 14.

These damaging criticisms of the Gluecks' research inspired a generation of prospective longitudinal studies of offending, focussing on individual and family factors, that aimed to overcome these difficulties, the most important of which are reviewed in Farrington (1979, 1988a). It is perhaps ironic that the widely admired and crucial longitudinal research of Shaw and McKay (1942) inspired a generation of less adequate cross-sectional replications, whereas the widely criticised cross-sectional research of the Gluecks more logically inspired a generation of more adequate longitudinal studies. It is also rather ironic that most of the correlates of delinquency documented by the Gluecks have in fact held up as predictors of offending in the more wide-ranging prospective longitudinal studies. Gottfredson and Hirschi (1987, p. 582) argued that, "despite the myriad criticisms of the Gluecks' work, their findings have proven to be amazingly consistent with subsequent research", and Laub and Sampson (1991, p. 1 433) stated that "major areas of the Gluecks' research... have been shown to be either (a) essentially correct or (b) currently dominating the research agenda in criminology."

Later Research on Individual and Family Influences

Farrington (1992b, 1992c) has reviewed the most important individual, family and other predictors of offending (juvenile and adult, official and self-reported). The most important individual predictors are high impulsivity (hyperactivity, restlessness, poor concentration, daring) and low intelligence and attainment. The most important family predictors are poor parental supervision or monitoring, large family size, erratic or harsh parental discipline, parental conflict, criminal parents or siblings and disrupted families (involving separation of children from biological parents). Any study of the independent and interactive importance of individual, family and neighbourhood factors should include measures of these dimensions at a minimum.

Prospective longitudinal researchers on offending have generally been more interested in individual and family factors than in neighbourhood factors, and consequently have given insufficient attention to neighbourhood influences. As Simcha-Fagan and Schwartz (1986, p. 669) argued, in most cases "no attempt is made to clarify the extent to which the relationship is inherently on the individual-familial level or is moderated by the contexts (neighbourhoods) in which families live." In some studies, the range of variability of neighbourhoods is small. For example, all the children in the Denver Youth Survey (Huizinga *et al.*, 1991) were drawn from high-crime, socially disorganised neighbourhoods. When longitudinal researchers have measured neighbourhood variables, the results have not shown that these variables are very important in comparison with individual and family factors.

For example, Wolfgang *et al.* (1972, 1987) recorded the addresses of each of their cohort males at their 18th birthdays and used the median income of families living in the male's home census tract as a measure of his socio-economic status. However, this measure of neighbourhood affluence was not related to a male's official offending (juvenile or adult) independently of race: "when race was held constant, the original relationship between SES and offender status almost vanished" (Wolfgang *et al.*, 1987, p. 23).

In the Cambridge-Somerville Study (McCord *et al.*, 1959), social workers ranked the neighbourhood of each boy at the time of his entry into the programme, according to area delinquency rates, physical deterioration of buildings, the presence of gangs and the absence of positive community organisations. However, the percentage of boys convicted (up to about age 25) did not vary greatly with neighbourhood ratings: from 38% of boys from the best neighbourhoods to 46% of boys from the worst neighbourhoods. In later research, McCord (1979) found that the neighbourhood did not significantly predict convictions for violence or property crimes up to age 45 (unlike parental child-rearing factors). Of course, it must be remembered that most of these boys were selected for the delinquency prevention programme because they were identified as "difficult" by their schools at about age 10, and none of their neighbourhoods "approached the upper-middle-class standards of some of Boston's suburbs" (McCord *et al.*, 1959, p. 70). Hence, the range of variability of neighbourhoods of boys in the sample may not have been very great.

Similar comments apply to the Cambridge Study in Delinquent Development, which is a prospective longitudinal survey of over 400 London boys from age 8 to age 32. When the boys were first contacted at age 8, the vast majority were living in one of 5 adjacent census wards (see West & Farrington, 1973, p. 119). Official figures for the rate of first convictions of juveniles in each ward showed that the worst ward had a delinquency rate three times that of the best ward. However, the percentage of Study boys convicted as juveniles varied (non-significantly) only from 17% in the best ward to 24% in the worst ward. To put this range of variation into perspective, it might perhaps be noted that 16% of those with non-criminal parents were convicted as juveniles, in comparison with 36% of those with criminal parents. West and Farrington (1973, p. 119) concluded:

> *It seemed that the location of a boy's home in one or other of the wards had a minimal effect upon his likelihood of delinquency. One reason for this may have been that the Study boys were concentrated in unrepresentative sections of the wards. Since the sections in question were located close together, they were probably less different from each other than were the wards as a whole.*

Again, therefore, the neighbourhoods in which the boys were living may have been relatively homogeneous.

There is some evidence from the Cambridge Study that area of residence might have some effect on offending. Osborn (1980) compared males who moved out of London with previously matched males who stayed in London, and found that the males who moved out had significant decreases in their rates of conviction and self-reported offending afterwards. West (1982) speculated that their offending might have decreased because of the breaking up of co-offending groups and because of the lesser opportunities for crime outside London. Most of those who left London moved to better quality neighbourhoods in the leafy "Home Counties" around London. This is an example of how longitudinal data might be used to investigate the effect of neighbourhood, although the numbers were small here and the analytic technique simple.

Wilson and Herrnstein (1985, p. 291) drew rather negative conclusions about the effect of moving people *en masse* to better neighbourhoods:

> *A test of the possibility that people shape neighbourhoods more than neighbourhoods shape people was made possible in Great Britain by the fact that the government there has devoted great energy and large sums to relocating persons from decaying inner-city areas to new public housing in outlying areas, so much so that in many large English cities today as much as half the housing is publicly managed. Yet relocating families to new and better public housing has not reduced levels of delinquency, which have continued to rise.*

However, moving individual families to better neighbourhoods may be more beneficial. Rosenbaum and Popkin (1991) evaluated a programme that subsidized single-parent low-income Black families to move from public housing into private housing in Chicago or its suburbs. They found that mothers who moved to the suburbs were significantly more likely to be employed than those who moved within the city, although both groups were comparable before the move. The suburban mothers mentioned the greater availability of jobs in the suburbs, the greater safety in the streets, and the lesser need to be home to protect their children, as important factors. It would be interesting also to compare the offending of their children in this study.

One of the most extensive investigations of the effect of area of residence by a prospective longitudinal researcher is the comparison of 10-year-old children in Inner London and the Isle of Wight by Rutter *et al.* (1975a, 1975b). This focused on large areas rather than neighbourhoods (it was an urban-rural comparison) and on child conduct disorder rather than delinquency, but it is nevertheless of interest. Rutter and his colleagues found higher rates of conduct disorder in Inner London children, and further showed that these higher rates occurred irrespective of whether the parents grew up in Inner London or moved there later. Hence, the differences were not attributable to the selective migration of problem people into problem areas.

Rutter and his colleagues demonstrated that, compared with

the Isle of Wight, children in Inner London were more likely to suffer severe marital discord, more likely to live in single-parent families, more likely to have psychiatrically disordered mothers, more likely to have criminal fathers, more likely to live in large-sized families, more likely to have fathers with low status jobs, more likely to live in overcrowded housing, more likely to live in Council (public) housing, and more likely to attend schools with a high turnover of teachers. Rutter (1981) concluded that rates of conduct disorder were higher in Inner London primarily because family adversities were more common there; in both areas, about a quarter of the children with a high family adversity score were disordered (Rutter, 1978). To the extent that inner city life had any adverse effect on children's antisocial behaviour, Rutter argued that this was mediated through its effect on families. Interestingly, Robins (1966) in St. Louis also concluded that the neighbourhood did not predict juvenile antisocial behaviour after controlling for antisocial parents. Robins and Hill (1966) showed that the percentage of Black boys becoming delinquent was the same irrespective of the delinquency rate of the census tract in which they lived.

One longitudinal researcher who has simultaneously followed up individuals and neighbourhoods is Shannon (1988, 1991). While his 1988 book did not investigate how far individual offending could be predicted by individual and neighbourhood factors, there was some information about this in his 1991 book. For example, Shannon showed that the type of neighbourhood (inner-city versus other) predicted the future seriousness of offences, but not independently of age, race and gender, which were more important predictors. He also showed that the predictors of offence seriousness differed somewhat according to residence in inner-city or other neighbourhoods.

There is a great need for more detailed longitudinal studies tracking changes in individual, family and neighbourhood variables. However, thinking about such studies raises important issues of measurement and theory. Some of these will be mentioned next.

Measurement and Theory Issues

It seems to me that more is known about individual and family influences on offending than about neighbourhood influences. Research using different data sources is needed to identify key theoretical constructs in neighbourhoods. These might be classified according to whether they reflect the physical or social environment and whether they reflect influences on criminal potential or influences on the commission of crimes. For example, antisocial models and transmitters of deviant values in a neighbourhood might influence criminal potential, whereas criminal opportunities might influence its behavioural manifestation.

In studying neighbourhood influences on offending, there are great problems in defining neighbourhoods. Most prior research has used governmental-defined census units. This has the advantage of permitting the use of officially published census data, but the disadvantage that census units may not be the most theoretically or empirically important and influential neighbourhood units. Future researchers need first to identify the most important theoretical constructs that might mediate neighbourhood influences on offending and then to work out ways of measuring these constructs repeatedly over time. Census variables may not be the most appropriate. It is desirable to measure not only objective features of neighbourhoods but also how individuals perceive neighbourhood characteristics. A number of key neighbourhood measures were proposed by Tonry *et al.* (1991, pp. 46–47), including demographic composition, female-headed families, residential mobility, poverty, housing tenure, recreational resources and neighbourhood decay. They suggested the use of interviews and ethnography, as well as official records, in measuring these factors. Repeated measures are needed to track changes in neighbourhood characteristics over time.

Another problem is that the relevant neighbourhood may be different for each individual. For example,this would be true if the key theoretical construct was a person's close neighbours, who might act as antisocial models, recruiters into offending or co-offenders (see e.g. Reiss & Farrington, 1991), or who might transmit deviant values or methods of committing offences. Any study of neighbourhood influences on offending should seek to investigate the influence of people living in the neighbourhood. These people are also important as potential victims, since many offenders victimize people living close by (see e.g. Wikström, 1991, pp. 213–220).

Further difficulties are caused by the residential mobility and variability of offenders. Many studies show that convicted offenders move more often than non-offenders (e.g. Osborn, 1980). Furthermore, because they are more likely to come from disrupted families, antisocial children are more likely to have variable living arrangements over short time periods, perhaps living with one parent for a time, then with another parent, then with a grandparent, and then with an older sibling. In studying neighbourhood influences, it is important to measure the length of time that each person is exposed to such influences, and hence to measure the population at risk more accurately (e.g. in person-days or person-months, not just persons) and to construct dose-response curves linking exposure time to outcome.

Similar problems arise in defining and measuring families. The number of different possible family configurations is bewildering large, especially in the case of antisocial children (see e.g. Kellam *et al.*, 1977). The idea of following individuals, families and neighbourhoods over time is attractive, but families are likely to change considerably. This is not only because of the instability of marital and quasi-marital relationships but also because of the changes contingent on children growing up, leaving the parental home and forming their own family relationships. The number of relevant families is likely to multiply considerably during the course of a prospective longitudinal study.

In measuring offending, it is of course essential to collect both official records and self-reports, but it is also important to measure different criminal career features such as the prevalence and frequency of offending and the onset, duration and desistance of criminal careers. Neighbourhood and family factors may have different effects on these different features. For example, the density of children in an area might affect onset but not desistance, whereas the availability and quality of organisations such as churches might affect desistance but not onset. Bearing in mind the fact that people's social worlds expand as they grow up, parental influences in general may be more important in regard to onset than desistance, whereas neighbourhood factors in general may be more important in regard to desistance than onset.

It may be unsatisfactory to investigate individual, family and neighbourhood influences on offending only by following up a sample of individuals, because the neighbourhood information obtainable from such a sample may be insufficient. For example, an important question is how far the crucial neighbourhood influence is essentially the sum of influences (independently or interactively) of other individuals in the neighbourhood. This question could only be addressed adequately by collecting data on *all* the individuals living in a neighbourhood, rather than only those included in a sample survey. A population survey would also be required to address questions about the impact of the proportion of antisocial individuals or families in a neighbourhood; for example, there may be a critical mass of antisocial individuals or families which, when exceeded, tips the neighbourhood influence from basically law-abiding to basically criminogenic. Crane (1991) concluded that neighbourhoods had non-linear effects, since there were sharp increases in the prevalence of social problems (teenage pregnancy and dropping out) only in the worst areas of the largest cities.

It would be useful to investigate how neighbourhood features influence some of the key constructs of classic criminological theories, such as the strain between a person's aspirations and what can be achieved by legitimate means (Cloward & Ohlin, 1960), status frustration experienced especially by lower-class boys who fail in school (Cohen, 1955), differential association with delinquent or law-abiding attitudes (Sutherland & Cressey, 1974), the strength of the bond to society (Hirschi, 1969), and the strength of the conscience and patterns of reinforcements for antisocial behaviour (Trasler, 1962). It would also be useful to study the impact of neighbourhood features on key constructs in more modern theories, such as low self-control (Gottfredson & Hirschi, 1990) and the extent to which decisions to offend are influenced by future outcomes as opposed to more immediate ones (Wilson & Herrnstein, 1985).

While the main thrust of this paper is on neighbourhood and other influences on individual offending, it would also be interesting to study individual, family and neighbourhood influences on neighbourhood variables such as the neighbourhood offence rate (based on where offences are committed). Several researchers (e.g. Baldwin *et al.*, 1976; Reiss & Farrington, 1991; Wikström, 1991) have compared where offenders live and where offences are committed, and hence have measured distances travelled by offenders to commit crimes. Measuring neighbourhood offence rates is not easy (for a useful discussion, see Wikström, 1991, pp. 193–198). While the discussion of "community crime careers" is beyond the scope of this paper, it seems to me to be potentially fruitful to apply criminal career concepts at the neighbourhood level, despite the doubts raised by Laub (1987).

It is hard to resist the conclusion that, because of inadequate definitions of neighbourhoods and poor measurement of crucial neighbourhood variables, the importance of neighbourhood effects has been under-estimated up to the present time.

Prevention and Reduction of Offending

Methods of preventing and reducing offending should be based on theoretical and empirical analyses of the causes of offending. Furthermore, experimental tests of the prevention and reduction of offending based on presumed causes of offending could more securely establish the effects of these causes than multivariate analyses of non-experimental data. It might perhaps be argued that existing randomized experiments provide the most compelling evidence of the importance of individual and family influences on offending.

There have been many experimental tests of delinquency prevention techniques based on individual and family influences. For example, Berrueta-Clement *et al.* (1984) in Michigan showed that a pre-school intellectual enrichment programme designed to increase intelligence had long-term benefits in preventing offending. Ross and Ross (1988) in Ottawa showed that a cognitive-behavioural interpersonal social skills training programme designed at least in part to decrease impulsivity led to a decrease in recidivism of adult offenders. Hawkins *et al.* (1991) in Seattle reported that a parent and teacher training programme designed to encourage more consistent reinforcement of socially desirable behaviour led to decreases in aggression, delinquency and alcohol use. Tremblay *et al.* (1991) in Montreal combined parent training with social skills training of boys and succeeded in reducing their burglary, theft and alcohol use.

However, there are very few comparably well designed experimental tests of the effectiveness of neighbourhood influences in preventing offending. As in the evaluation of different policing strategies (e.g. Kelling *et al.*, 1976), areas need to be randomly allocated to different experimental conditions. The lack of experimentation is surprising, in light of the fact that Shaw applied his ideas about social disorganisation to crime prevention in the Chicago Area Project (for reviews of this, see Short, 1969; Schlossman & Sedlak, 1983). However, the effectiveness of this project, based on physically improving neighbourhoods, coordinating community resources and organising recreational facilities, was never properly evaluated. Of course, there are methodological and statistical problems raised by interventions at the neighbourhood level targeted on individuals.

More recent attempts to reduce crime by changing neighbourhood factors have been reviewed by Hope and Shaw (1988). However, most of these projects are targeted on offences, not offenders, and their success is typically evaluated using measures of crimes committed in neighbourhoods (in official records or from victim surveys), rather than crimes committed by residents of neighbourhoods. Hence, these projects do not provide information directly about the effects of neighbourhood features on individual offenders. It might also be noted that most recent crime prevention projects, at least in England, have focused primarily on physical crime prevention by reducing opportunities through increased physical security or increased surveillance (see e.g. Clarke, 1983). For example, Hope and Foster (1992) evaluated the effects of physically improving part of a council housing estate, and found that this tended to displace crime to other parts of the estate.

Conclusions

My paper, like its title, is deliberately provocative. I have spent probably too much time discussing the research of Shaw and McKay (1942) and Glueck and Glueck (1950), because of my concern that generations of criminology students have been taught to revere Shaw and McKay and revile the Gluecks. I wanted to bring out the fact that Shaw and McKay and the Gluecks were comparably important pioneers in criminology, making perhaps the most influential and meticulous contributions to criminological knowledge in the 1930s and 1940s, and that both have long-term relevance up to the present day. However, I also wanted to point out the fact that Shaw and McKay, and "ecological" researchers who have followed them, have not succeeded unambiguously in proving neighbourhood influences on offending, any more than the Gluecks, and the prospective longitudinal researchers who followed them, have succeeded unambiguously in proving individual and family influences on offending. Researchers interested in neighbourhood influences have generally not adequately measured individual and family influences, just as researchers interested in individual and family influences have generally not adequately measured neighbourhood influences.

Nevertheless, there is a surprising degree of theoretical consensus among neighbourhood researchers such as Simcha-Fagan and Schwartz (1986) and Gottfredson *et al.* (1991) and longitudinal researchers such as Rutter (1981) that neighbourhoods have indirect effects on offending via their effects on individuals and families. Despite this consensus, the evidence in favour of it is not convincing. As argued above, with better definitions of neighbourhoods and better measurement of neighbourhood variables, the importance of neighbourhood factors is likely to increase. Researchers need to measure the most important variables in each category (and in other categories, including biological, peer and school factors) and systematically need to compare the relative fit of different theoretical models to the data. Simultaneous and sequential effects, and reciprocal and interaction effects, need to be studied. Criminological theories need to be more wide-ranging and need to include all these different types of variables.

Neighbourhood researchers have generally carried out cross-sectional studies using census-based measures of neighbourhood constructs. More convincing conclusions could be drawn by using several different data sources and by conducting longitudinal and/or experimental studies. Causation can best be demonstrated by studying changes over time within individuals, families and neighbourhoods (Farrington, 1988b). As Tonry *et al.* (1991) and Reiss (1986) have argued, a new generation of longitudinal studies is needed to advance knowledge, in which individuals and neighbourhoods are followed up simultaneously, with wide-ranging measures of key individual, family and neighbourhood factors. These projects should be carried out in large cities with well-defined neighbourhoods and low residential outmigration.

These studies would make it possible to follow up individuals as they moved between different neighbourhoods, and hence to assess neighbourhood influences by using each individual as his or her own control in quasi-experimental analyses. Logically, the best way of establishing neighbourhood influences is to study the same people (or perhaps identical twins) in different neighbourhoods, just as the best way of establishing individual and family influences is to study different people in the same neighbourhoods. The studies could also help to establish the effects of individual, family and neighbourhood factors at different ages and at different stages of criminal careers. They could also investigate interactive effects, for example whether trajectories of within-individual change are different in different neighbourhoods, and whether different types of individuals react differently to the same neighbourhood influences.

In addition, it would be highly advantageous to include experimental interventions in these longitudinal studies, to assess the effects of changing specific individual, family and neighbourhood features. These experiments would have practical implications, in indicating how to reduce offending most effectively. These studies would give us the best chance of disentangling the independent and interactive effects of individual, family, neighbourhood and other influences, and hence of developing more comprehensive theories of offending. In order to advance knowledge about the causes and prevention of offending, they should be mounted in different countries, as speedily as possible.

References

Baldwin, J. (1979). Ecological and areal studies in Great Britain and the United States. In N. Morris & M. Tonry (Eds.) *Crime and Justice,* vol.1 (pp. 29–66). Chicago: University of Chicago press.

Baldwin, J., Bottoms, A.E. & Walker, M.A. (1976). *The Urban Criminal.* London: Tavistock.

Berrueta-Clement, J.R., Schweinhart, L.J., Barnett, W.S., Epstein, A.S. & Weikart, D.P. (1984). *Changed Lives.* Ypsilanti, Mich.: High/Scope.

Bottoms, A.E. & Wiles, P. (1986). Housing tenure and residential community crime careers in Britain. In A.J. Reiss & M. Tonry (Eds.) *Communities and Crime* (pp. 101–162). Chicago: University of Chicago Press.

Bursik, R.J. (1986). Delinquency rates as sources of ecological change. In J.M. Byrne & R.J. Sampson (Eds.) *The Social Ecology of Crime* (pp. 63–74). New York: Springer-Verlag.

Bursik, R.J. (1988). Social disorganisation and theories of crime and delinquency: Problems and prospects. *Criminology,* 26, 519–551.

Bursik, R.J. & Grasmick, H.G. (1992). Longitudinal neighbourhood profiles in delinquency: The decomposition of change. *Journal of Quantitative Criminology,* 8, 247–263.

Bursik, R.J. & Webb, J. (1982). Community change and patterns of delinquency. *American Journal of Sociology,* 88, 24–42.

Clarke, R.V. (1983). Situational crime prevention: Its theoretical basis and practical scope. In M. Tonry & N. Morris (Eds.) *Crime and Justice,* vol.4 (pp. 225–256). Chicago: University of Chicago Press.

Clarke, R.V. (1992). Introduction. In R.V. Clarke (Ed.) *Situational Crime Prevention* (pp. 3–36). Albany, N.Y.: Harrow and Heston.

Cloward, R.A. & Ohlin, L.E. (1960). *Delinquency and Opportunity.* Glencoe, Ill: Free Press.

Cohen, A.K. (1955). Delinquent Boys. Glencoe, Ill: Free Press.

Cohn, E.G. & Farrington, D.P. (1990). Differences between British and American criminology: An analysis of citations. *British Journal of Criminology,* 30, 467–482.

Crane, J. (1991). The epidemic theory of ghettos and neighbourhood effects on dropping out and teenage childbearing. *American Journal of Sociology,* 96, 1226–1259.

Elliott, D.S., Huizinga, D. & Ageton, S. (1985). *Explaining Delinquency and Drug Use.* Beverly Hills, Calif.: Sage.

Elliott, D.S., Huizinga, D. & Menard, S. (1989). *Multiple Problem Youth.* New York: Springer-Verlag.

Farrington, D.P. (1979). Longitudinal research on crime and delinquency. In N. Morris & M. Tonry (Eds.) *Crime and Justice,* vol.1 (pp. 289–348). Chicago: University of Chicago Press.

Farrington, D.P. (1988a). Advancing knowledge about delinquency and crime: The need for a coordinated programme of longitudinal research. *Behavioural Sciences and the Law,* 6, 307–331.

Farrington, D.P. (1988b). Studying changes within individuals: The causes of offending. In M. Rutter (Ed.) *Studies of Psychosocial Risk* (pp. 158–183). Cambridge: Cambridge University Press.

Farrington, D.P. (1992a). Criminal career research in the United Kingdom. *British Journal of Criminology,* 32, 521–536.

Farrington, D.P. (1992b). Explaining the beginning, progress and ending of antisocial behaviour from birth to adulthood. In J. McCord (Ed.) *Facts, Frameworks and Forecasts* (pp. 253–286). New Brunswick, N.J.: Transaction.

Farrington, D.P. (1992c). Juvenile delinquency. In J.C. Coleman (Ed.) *The School Years,* 2nd ed. (pp. 123–163). London: Routledge.

Farrington, D.P. (1993). Motivations for conduct disorder and delinquency. *Development and Psychopathology,* 5, 225–241.

Firebaugh, G. (1978). A rule for inferring individual-level relationships from aggregate data. *American Sociological Review,* 43, 557–572.

Glaser, D. & Rice, K. (1959). Crime, age, and unemployment. *American Sociological Review,* 24, 679–686.

Glueck, S. & Glueck, E.T. (1930). *Five Hundred Criminal Careers.* New York: Knopf.

Glueck, S. & Glueck, E.T. (1934). *One Thousand Juvenile Delinquents.* Cambridge, Mass.: Harvard University Press.

Glueck, S. & Glueck, E.T. (1937). *Later Criminal Careers.* New York: Commonwealth Fund.

Glueck, S. & Glueck, E.T. (1940). *Juvenile Delinquents Grown Up.* New York: Commonwealth Fund.

Glueck, S. & Glueck, E.T. (1943). *Criminal Careers in Retrospect.* New York: Commonwealth Fund.

Glueck, S. & Glueck, E.T. (1950). *Unravelling Juvenile Delinquency.* Cambridge, Mass.: Harvard University Press.

Glueck, S. & Glueck, E.T. (1968). *Delinquents and Non-Delinquents in Perspective.* Cambridge, Mass.: Harvard University Press.

Gold, M. (1987). Social ecology. In H.C. Quay (Ed.) *Handbook of Juvenile Delinquency* (pp. 62–105). New York: Wiley.

Gottfredson, D.C., McNeil, R.J. & Gottfredson, G.D. (1991). Social area influences on delinquency: A multi-level analysis. *Journal of Research on Crime and Delinquency,* 28, 197–226.

Gottfredson, M.R. & Hirschi, T. (1987). The methodological adequacy of longitudinal research on crime. *Criminology,* 25, 581–614.

Gottfredson, M.R. & Hirschi, T. (1990). *A General Theory of Crime.* Stanford, Calif.: Stanford University Press.

Gottfredson, S.D. & Taylor, R.B. (1986). Person-environment interactions in the prediction of recidivism. In J.M. Byrne & R.J. Sampson (Eds.) *The Social Ecology of Crime* (pp. 133–155). New York: Springer-Verlag.

Hamparian, D.M., Schuster, R., Dinitz, S. & Conrad, J.P. (1978). *The Violent Few.* Lexington, Mass.: Heath.

Hawkins, J.D., Von Cleve, E. & Catalano, R.F. (1991). Reducing early childhood aggression: Results of a primary prevention programme. *Journal of the American Academy of Child and Adolescent Psychiatry,* 30, 208–217.

Hirschi, T. (1969). *Causes of Delinquency.* Berkley, Calif.: University of California Press.

Hirschi, T. & Selvin, H.C. (1967). *Delinquency Research.* New York: Free Press.

Hope, T. & Foster, J. (1992). Conflicting forces: Changing the dynamics of crime and community on a 'problem' estate. *British Journal of Criminology,* 32, 488–504.

Hope, T. & Shaw, M. (Eds., 1988). *Communities and Crime Reduction.* London: Her Majesty's Stationery Office.

Huizinga, D., Esbensen, F-A. & Weiher, A.W. (1991). Are there mutiple paths to delinquency? *Journal of Criminal Law and Criminology,* 82, 83–118.

Jonassen, C.T. (1949). A re-evaluation and critique of the logic and some methods of Shaw and McKay. *American Sociological Review,* 14, 608–614.

Johnstone, J.W.C. (1978). Juvenile delinquency and the family: A contextual interpretation. *Youth and Society,* 9, 299–313.

Kellam, S.G., Ensminger, M.E. & Turner, R.J. (1977). Family structure and the mental health of children. *Archives of General Psychiatry,* 34, 1012–1022.

Kelling, G.L., Pate, T., Dieckman, D. & Brown, C.E. (1976). The Kansas City preventive patrol experiment: A summary report. In G.V. Glass (Ed.) *Evaluation Studies Review Annual,* vol.1. Beverly Hills, Calif.: Sage.

Laub, J.H. (1987). Rediscovering the importance of cities, neighbourhoods and crime. *Journal of Quantitative Criminology,* 3, 83–93.

Laub, J.H. & Sampson, R.J. (1988). Unravelling families and delinquency: A reanalysis of the Gluecks' data. *Criminology, 26,* 355–380.

Laub, J.H. & Sampson, R.J. (1991). The Sutherland-Glueck debate: On the sociology of criminological knowledge. *American Journal of Sociology,* 96, 1402–1440.

McCord, J. (1979). Some child-rearing antecedents of criminal behaviour in adult men. *Journal of Personality and Social Psychology,* 37, 1477–1486.

McCord, W., McCord, J. & Zola, I.K. (1959). Origins of Crime. New York: Colombia University Press.

Morash, M. & Rucker, L. (1989). An exploratory study of the connection of mother's age at childbearing to her children's delinquency in four data sets. *Crime and Delinquency,* 35, 45–93.

Osborn, S.G. (1980). Moving home, leaving London and delinquent trends. *British Journal of Criminology,* 20, 54–61.

Reiss, A.J. (1951a). Delinquency as the failure of personal and social controls. *American Sociological Review,* 16, 196–207.

Reiss, A.J. (1951b). Unravelling Juvenile Delinquency. II. An appraisal of the research methods. *American Journal of Sociology,* 57, 115–120.

Reiss, A.J. (1986). Why are communities important in understanding crime? In A.J. Reiss & M. Tonry (Eds.) *Communities and Crime* (pp. 1–33). Chicago: University of Chicago Press.

Reiss, A.J. & Farrington, D.P. (1991). Advancing knowledge about co-offending: Results from a prospective longitudinal survey of London males. *Journal of Criminal Law and Criminology,* 82, 360–395.

Robins, L.N. (1966). Deviant Children Grown Up. Baltimore: Williams and Wilkins.

Robins, L.N. & Hill, S.Y. (1966). Assessing the contributions of family structure, class and peer groups to juvenile delinquency. *Journal of Criminal Law, Criminology and Police Science,* 57, 325–334.

Robinson, W.S. (1950). Ecological correlations and the behaviour of individuals. *American Sociological Review,* 15, 351–357.

Rosenbaum, J.E. & Popkin, S.J. (1991). Employment and earnings of low income Blacks who move to middle-class suburbs. In C. Jencks & P.E. Peterson (Eds.) *The Urban Underclass* (pp. 342–356). Washington, D.C.: The Brookings Institution.

Ross, R.R. & Ross, B.D. (1988). Delinquency prevention through cognitive training. New Education, 10, 70–75.

Rutter, M. (1978). Family, area and school influences in the genesis of conduct disorders. In L.A. Hersov, M. Berger & D. Shaffer (Eds.) *Aggression and Antisocial Behaviour in Childhood and Adolescence* (pp. 95–113). Oxford: Pergamon.

Rutter, M. (1981). The city and the child. *American Journal of Orthopsychiatry,* 51, 610--625.

Rutter, M., Cox, A., Tupling, C., Berger, M. & Yule, W. (1975a). Attainment and adjustment in two geographical areas: I. The prevalence of psychiatric disorder. *British Journal of Psychiatry,* 126, 493–509.

Rutter, M., Yule, B., Quinton, D., Rowlands, O., Yule, W. & Berger, M. (1975b). Attainment and adjustment in two geographical areas: III. Some factors accounting for area differences. *British Journal of Psychiatry,* 126, 520–533.

Sampson, R.J. & Groves, W.B. (1989). Community structure and crime: Testing social-disorganisation theory. *American Journal of Sociology,* 94, 774–802.

Sampson, R.J. & Lauritsen, J. (1990). Deviant lifestyles, proximity to crime, and the offender-victim link in personal violence. *Journal of Research in Crime and Delinquency,* 27, 110–139.

Sherman, L.W., Gartin, P.R. & Buerger, M.E. (1989). Hot spots of predatory crime: Routine activities and the criminology of place. *Criminology,* 27, 27–55.

Schlossman, S & Sedlak, M. (1983). The Chicago Area Project revisited. *Crime and Delinquency,* 29, 398–462.

Schmid, C.F. (1960). Urban crime areas: Part II. *American Sociological Review,* 25, 655–678.

Schuerman, L. & Kobrin, S. (1986). Community careers in crime. In A.J. Reiss & M. Tonry (Eds.) *Communities and Crime* (pp. 67–100). Chicago: University of Chicago Press.

Shannon, L.W. (1988). *Criminal Career Continuity.* New York: Human Sciences Press.

Shannon,, L.W. (1991). *Changing Patterns of Delinquency and Crime.* Boulder, Colo.: Westview.

Shaw, C.R. & McKay, H.D. (1942). *Juvenile Delinquency and Urban Areas.* Chicago: University of Chicago Press.

Shaw, C.R. & McKay, H.D. (1949). Rejoinder. *American Sociological Review,* 14, 614–617.

Shaw, C.R. & McKay, H.D. (1969). *Juvenile Delinquency and Urban Areas* (rev. ed.) Chicago: University of Chicago Press.

Shaw, C.R., Zorbaugh, F., McKay, H.D. & Cottrell, L.S. (1929). *Delinquency Areas.* Chicago: University of Chicago Press.

Short, J.F. (1969). Introduction to the revised edition. In C.R. Shaw & H.D. McKay (1969) *Juvenile Delinquency and Urban Areas* (rev. ed., pp. xxv-liv). Chicago: University of Chicago Press.

Simcha-Fagan, O. & Schwartz, J.E. (1986). Neighbourhood and delinquency: An assessment of contextual effects. *Criminology,* 24, 667–703.

Sutherland, E.H. (1939). *Principles of Criminology* (3rd ed.) Chicago: Lippincott.

Sutherland, E.H. & Cressey, D.R. (1974). *Criminology,* 9th ed. Philadelphia: Lippincott.

Tonry, M., Ohlin, L.E. & Farrington, D.P. (1991). *Human Development and Criminal Behaviour* (with contributions by K. Adams, F. Earls, D.C. Rowe, R.J. Sampson & R.E. Tremblay). New York: Springer-Verlag.

Trasler, G.B. (1962). *The Explanation of Criminality.* London: Routledge and Kegan Paul.

Tremblay, R.E., McCord, J., Boileau, H., Charlebois, P., Gagnon, C., LeBlanc, M. & Larivee, S. (1991). Can disruptive boys be helped to become competent? *Psychiatry,* 54, 148–161.

Wallis, C.P. & Maliphant, R. (1967). Delinquent areas in the county of London: Ecological factors. *British Journal of Criminology,* 7, 250–284.
West, D.J. (1982). *Delinquency: Its Roots, Careers and Prospects.* London: Heinemann.
West, D.J. & Farrington, D.P. (1973). *Who Becomes Delinquent?* London: Heinemann.
West, D.J. & Farrington, D.P. (1977). *The Delinquent Way of Life.* London: Heinemann.
Wikström, P.-O.H. (1985). *Everyday Violence in Contemporary Sweden.* Stockholm: National Council for Crime Prevention.
Wikström, P.-O.H. (1991). *Urban Crime, Criminals and Victims.* New York: Springer-Verlag.
Wilson, J.Q. & Herrnstein, R.J. (1985). *Crime and Human Nature.* New York: Simon and Schuster.
Wolfgang, M.E., Figlio, R.M. & Sellin, T. (1972). *Delinquency in a Birth Cohort.* Chicago: University of Chicago Press.
Wolfgang, M.E., Thornberry, T.P. & Figlio, R.M. (1987). *From Boy to Man, From Delinquency to Crime.* Chicago: University of Chicago Press.

Ecological and Individual Approaches in the Study of Crime and Delinquency

by Carl-Gunnar Janson

Abstract

The relationship between aggregate socioecological variables and associations on the one hand and individuallevel variables and associations on the other, especially in studies of crime and delinquency, is discussed. Non-random clustering of individual-level units to modifiable aggregate units according to spatial proximity prevents consistency between levels. After Robinson's well known paper in 1950 the prevailing notion in sociology became that one could not infer from the ecological to the individual at all without committing the ecological fallacy. This is shown to be an exaggeration. It is claimed that socioecological analysis can have a sociological value of its own besides that of providing contextual variables for individual-level analyses, but that socioecological expectations and interpretations should build on individual-level conditions and associations.

Introduction

"Ecology" is usually defined as the study of the inter-action between the organism and its external environment. Then "human ecology" deals with the interaction between man and his external environment. "Social ecology" is the part of human ecology that falls within sociology.

Since the external environment is distributed in time and space, ecology has been much concerned with spatial organization and with relations among spatially delimited entities. Furthermore, social ecology, as against psychological human ecology, has been dealing mostly with spatial units on an aggregate level, such as neighborhoods, urban places, communities, or regions.

This paper takes a look at the relationship between on the one hand aggregate socioecological variables and associations and on the other individual-level variables and associations, especially in studies of crime and delinquency. A few remarks must suffice on this wide topic, which can be seen as a case of the general problem of non-random aggregation. For short systematic discussions of non-random aggegation, see Blalock 1964, chap.4, Hannan 1971, and Hannan and Burstein 1974.

The Socioecological Approach

Socioecological studies of aggregate spatial variables were prominent within the now semi-classical, i.e. mostly forgotten, Chicago or Ecological School of the 1920s, '30s, and '40s (Hawley 1950, Quinn 1950, Faris 1967). It had a strong interest in social problems and deviance (Faris and Dunham 1939, Shaw 1929, Shaw and McKay 1942). Both theoretically and empirically the focus was on urban spatial structure, neighborhood disorganization, and other socioecological concepts. The same holds for Shevky's and Bell's social area analysis (Shevky and Bell 1955, Anderson and Bean 1961) and the more general factorial socioecological approach (Lander 1954, Van Arsdol, Camilleri, and Schmid 1958, Sweetser 1965, Timms 1971, Janson 1980, Hamm 1982), which developed from the 1950s with strong roots in the Chicago ecological orientation. Later studies have tended to center more on ethnic-racial segregation (Guest and Weed 1976, Van Valey, Roof, and Wilcox 1977, Massey and Denton 1987).

A socioecological analysis may refer to different levels of aggregation. As a first example, on the community or regional level, the level of reported offenses can be seen as functions of characteristics of cities, metropolitan areas, or regions (Land, McCall, and Cohen 1990) or of the police and justice systems with controls for presumably relevant population variables.

Second, on the level of urban areas, neighborhoods, or census tracts, studies of urban spatial structure and of delinquency, crime, and social problems as functions of this structure have old roots. In social ecology the interest is in the spatial structure as such, its dimensions, their changes and distributions. In criminology and the study of deviance the interest is in what way and to what extent rates of delinquency and deviance in urban societies covary with population composition and neighborhood contextual factors. A set of rates may covary strongly, i.e. permit broad interpretations of commonality, or may show specialization.

The studies of urban spatial structure developed very fast both technically and theoretically toward factorial social ecology during the first four post-war decades. Generally, community studies and studies of urban spatial structure do not give the same set of dimensions or factors, even to the extent they use the same variables. For a while this approach was in the forefront of quantitative social sciences, even if one seemed not to have been fully aware of its potential in criminology, its traditions notwithstanding. Since then, although still strong in human geography, the factorial studies appear to have lost much of its impetus. However, the field and the factorial approach, no longer *á la mode*, still may be of interest in social ecology generally as well as in criminology and the sociology of deviance.

Third, a promising field of study could be the distribution and impact of situational factors of the kind discussed in opportunity theory, e.g. the routine activity approach (Cohen and Felson 1979, Felson 1987) and victim-based explanatory strategies (Hindelang, Gottfredson and Garofalo 1979). Such studies may be seen as another case of neighborhood analyses, but mostly they would be on a much smaller area level, focusing on other independent variables, with urban dimensions or their components coming in as controlling variables. Furthermore, area units would probably be sampled rather than covering whole (sectors of) metropolitan areas. Beavon's Vancouver study (1985) of ways to enter or leave blocks but with ample controls of residential and commercial use of the blocks would be an example.

At least to some extent this approach may be micro-ecological, i.e. on the individual level with environmental contextual variables. Such variables measure characteristics of the individual's environment, such as "number of bars on the block" or "percent neighborhood boys known to the police". In a way, this would then be a cross-level study. In a broader criminological field the so-called Stockholm study (Wikström 1990) may be of this type.

However, as already mentioned, the micro-level socioecological study remains exceptional. In fact, in sociology "ecological variable" came, to the disappointment of socio-ecologists such as Hawley (1950) and Duncan (Duncan, Cuzzort, and Duncan 1961), to denote a variable describing spatially delimited aggregate or meso/macro entities. Correspondingly, "ecological correlation" soon took on the meaning of a correlation between variables referring to such fairly large-scale spatial entities.

Socioecological Variables and Corresponding Individual Variables

Ecological variables referring to spatial units usually are percentages or other averages as characteristics of the population or sections of it, such as given age groups, (adult or adolescent) males or females, and the economically active population, of the daytime population or businesses, or of residences or buildings, However, some variables may not be avarages but e.g. sums, dispersions, or measures of skewness or no population characteristic at all, e.g. area size in km^2. The ecological variables describe the aggregate units, but at least if they are constructed as arithmetic means, they also have simple counterparts on the individual level. If two ecological variables are averages over the same individual-level units, e.g. if both characterize the adult male population or both describe dwelling units, their ecological correlation has a corresponding individual correlation. Since the variables average many different kinds of individual-level units, a correlation matrix over these variables may contain few if any coefficients that have individual-level counterparts. However, the corresponding individual correlation (or association generally) was paid much attention in early socioecological studies.

Although the purposes of the studies were socioecological, it was originally often presumed that findings concerning ecological variables that had individual-level counterparts could be generalized to these counterparts also. To use a term from the study of non-random aggregation (Hannan 1971, Lütjohann 1974: 22–31), the early researchers implicitly and somewhat naïvely presumed a general "consistency" between ecological and individual variables, although they were interested in correlations in the first place and only secondarily in regressions. Especially in the field of social problems the parallel interest in individual-level interpretation was keen. Sometimes the primary research interest appears to have been on the individual level, even when an ecological approach was used. Particularly this was the case in some fields, e.g. in studies of voting. There, direct ecological variables were easily available as poll results by election districts and characteristics of districts from censuses or other sources and ready to be used in pseudo-ecological analyses.

Even in criminology, the pseudo-ecological approach held some apparent advantages. At a time when data on offenders were mostly classifications and were almost always taken either from clinical observations or from official crime records, nice graded ecological delinquency variables were put together by just counting the number of the right kind of cases according to place of residence or scene of the crime. Such variables lent themselves easily to quantitative analyses and often gave clear results.

Modifiable Units of Analysis

There were some cautionary statistical voices in this happy world of consistency, as usual. From very early on social ecologists were concerned about an indeterminacy in their ecological variables on top of that for the corresponding individual variables. For the standard ecological variables often constructed as percentages, e.g. percent of juvenile delinquents in a given period of all juveniles under risk, the corresponding individual variables were dichotomies. Given the sample and operational definitions, the dichotomies were determined for all practical purposes. They were subject to sampling errors, in which measurement error played but an unimportant part. Their correlations were phi-coefficients out of fourfold tables, whereas the ecological correlations were ordinary Pearsonian coefficients (for slightly heteroscedastical variables, by the way). Usually this difference was ignored[1], and attention focused on the random component of the ecological variables. Also when the sample was large enough for good stability in the dichotomies, the number of cases in the numerator (sometimes even in the denominator) often became too small for stability in each of n areas. To some degree the same held for other ecological averages than percentages. Perhaps one could expand the period to get more cases. Or one could use larger but fewer areas, since areas were "modifiable".

A kind of unit is modifiable, if collapsing, dividing, or redrawing the borders of such units gives a new set of units of the same kind. For instance, urban areas may be cut in twos, collapsed two by two, or redesigned pairwise into sets of three areas and still be units of the same kind, i.e. urban areas. A person, on the other hand, is a non-modifiable unit, since half a person or a couple is not an individual.

For a spatial average the error term would decrease with the number of observations in the area and increase with the heterogeneity of the area. Given the number of units in which to divide a city, some sets of neighborhoods would conform better than others with the urban spatial structure and thus generally contain more homogeneous neighborhoods. In general, above a certain size, areas tended to be increasingly heterogeneous even in optimal sets. When there was a practical upper bond on the average size of the units, as in studies of urban spatial structure, one might find a set with areas not too small and not too large that gave an optimally low relative error. The correlations between these ecological variables tended to vary correspondingly, increasing with area homogeneity and size (i.e. number of observations). With unit size varying within practical limits in urban-area studies, heterogeneity and size partially balanced each other, but when area size was permitted to grow above such limits, or from units on one level to units on a higher level, the size factor took over and correlations increased markedly (for an early and a late illustration, see Gehlke and Biehl 1934 and Land, McCall, and Cohen 1990, respectively[2]).

In 1938 Herman Wold drew attention to the modifiability of time and spatial entities. Wold as an econometrician was primarily interested in time series, but it was obvious that census tracts and other spatial units also were modifiable. Applying the standard formula for attenuation of correlations due to random variation[3], Wold showed that one should expect aggregate correlations to vary systematically with characteristics of the set of units used. Kendall then applied the same formula on an ecological correlation strongly varying with unit size[4] (Yule and Kendall 1950: 314f). (As is well known, also regressions may be attenuated by random errors in the regressors but not by such errors in the dependent variable.)

Assume now that the corresponding individual variables refer to the same individual units. It then follows that there are many ecological coefficients to pair with this individual-level coefficient. Thus it is not clear which ecological correlation the individual-level correlation is supposed to equal.

Furthermore, in the rather few cases when the corresponding individual correlation was known, it was typically found to be numerically smaller than any of the ecological ones[5]. It was no coincidence that factor analysis was found more useful in ecological studies, pseudo or not, than in micro-sociological studies generally. Even good and valid individual-level matrices seldom produce total communalities over 50 percent, unless one plays the definitional game matching narrow behavioral and propensity measures, whereas ecological communalities can reach 80 percent or more[6], which means that most systematic variation in an ecological data matrix can be reproduced by a considerably smaller factorial matrix.

From the attenuation argument, it may seem reasonable to expect correlations of aggregated variables on reasonably efficient units to be stronger than correlations from corresponding individual variables. However, the argument implicitly assumes a systematic variation, and this presumes the aggregation to be non-random, as in fact aggregation to ecological variables according to spatial propinquity strongly tends to be. As a rule, aggregating by spatial proximity, e.g. by neighborhood, means clustering individuals that are more than randomly similar in many respects (gender being an exception), which makes for a systematic between-units variation, i.e. an ecological variation[7]. As units are made larger parts of the total community studied, clustering becomes less prominemt, i.e. units become more heterogenous.

Thus, not only should one assume the corresponding individual correlations to differ from the set of alternative ecological correlations, in general one should also expect them to be weaker. How the grouping effects came about might not have been clearly understood by most sociologists, but the effects seemed real enough and meant that one had to give up most of the consistency assumption. However, so far, ecological-individual inconsistencies didn't trouble most sociologists the way "aggregation bias" in time series troubled many econometricians; cf Hannan 1971). Most studies, then even more than now, were concerned with ascertaining associations rather than with estimating their strengths. Thus, it didn't matter much if the ecological associations were enlarged, rather the opposite, as long as they could be assumed to have the correct direction.

Next, however, when Robinson's 1950 paper discredited even this assumption, it dealt the fatal blow to pseudo ecological studies and, incidentally, became one of the most frequently quoted papers in sociology.

Robinson's Formula

Robinson derived a simple equation connecting the ecological and the corresponding individual correlations. Let r(exy) be the correlation between two ecological variables x and y in a given set of area units, both variables constructed as arithmetic means of variables x and y, referring to the same set of units on the individual level, the number of undividual units being n(i) in the ith area. Let r(xy) be the individual-level correlation, the "corresponding individual correlation". Furthermore, let r(ixy) be the individual correlation within the ith area and r(oxy) the weighed average of all r(ixy). If r(exy) is calculated with n(i) as weights, the relation between r(exy), r(oxy), and r(xy) is found to be

(1) $$r(xy)=c_1r(oxy)+c_2r(exy),$$

with the c-coefficients between 0 and 1. Actually, c_2 is the product of the correlation ratios for x and y in the set of area units and c_1 a monotonously decreasing function of c_2. Their sum is close to one and has the upper limit one. If r(xy)=r(oxy) and both correlation ratios are equal, then r(xy)=r(exy), but generally the correlations differ from one another. The formula gives good reason why to expect r(exy) to be stronger than r(xy) and to increase with unit size[8]. More important, from the formula follows that the correlations don't necessarily have the same signs. A positive r(exy) can go together with negative r(xy) and r(oxy). It is even possible to have the combination of one positive, one negative, and one zero coefficient. The formula provides a "definite answer as to whether ecological correlations can validly be used as substitutes for individual correlations. They cannot" (Robinson 1950: 357).

It is possible to find actual ecological and corresponding individual correlations with opposite directions, although it takes some search to find them. Robinson found that in the 1930 American census being an immigrant and being illiterate correlated +0.12, whereas the corresponding ecological variables percent immigrants and percent illiterates correlated -0.53 by state. In the early 1950's percent upper-middle class had a weak positive correlation with percent Communists in the Swedish counties, whereas the corresponding individual correlation between being upper-middle class and voting Communist certainly was negative, this being before *radical chic* (Westerståhl and Janson 1958).

Going from Ecological to Corresponding Individual Association

From then on it has been part of the conventional wisdom that one cannot go from ecological to individual correlation or regression. To do so is to commit the wellknown "ecological fallacy" (actually a better name would be the "aggregate fallacy"; cf Alker 1969 for a full treatment). Soon the prevailing notion had it that one could not go from the ecological to the individual level at all. As most received views this conception has its limitations and exaggerations.

An ecological correlation does not exhaust the information contained in an ecological data set. Already in response to Robinson it was pointed out (Goodman 1953 and 1959, Duncan and Davis 1953; cf Cartwright 1968) that, after all, safe individual-level conclusions could sometimes be drawn from ecological data. For dichotomies Duncan and Davis presented a simple and elegant analysis. The ecological variables give the margins in a 2·2 table for the dichotomies in each area. Given the margins, each table has one degree of freedom. Especially its cell frequencies can be filled out in one way so as to make the r(ixy) as negative as possible and in another way so as to make it as positive as possible. Summing over all areas one gets one total frequency 2·2 table with the most negative r(xy) compatible with the ecological variations and another table with the most positive r(xy) possible. If the two extreme correlations are of the same sign, one can safely conclude that the individual r(xy) has that sign. Duncan and Davis used the dichotomies of being black and being in domestic service for the female labor force in a certain city. Using census tracts as area units, they got the lower and upper limits +0.16 and +0.32, respectively, for the correlation between these variables. Thus, the ecological census-tract variation was only compatible with a positive correlation between the corresponding individual variables. In fact, the actual individual correlation was +0.29.

Furthermore, cases with ecological and corresponding individual correlations in opposite directions are the exceptions rather than the rule. The mechanisms they take often are strange enough to be ruled out for theoretical reasons at least tentatively. When the ecological correlation r(exy) is positive, say, then the individual correlations r(oxy) and r(xy) cannot both be zero. For r(xy) to be zero or negative, r(oxy) must be negative. In many cases this would be odd indeed.

Delinquency and Social Class

In the debate, ensuing the 1978 paper by Tittle et al, whether there was any association between social class and criminality, scant attention was paid to ecological evidence, and when it was introduced (Braithwaite 1981), it was mostly dismissed.

Let the ecological variable y be the percentage of offenders in a three-year period of all boys 15–21 years old and x the percentage boys 15–21 years old with a working class origin at the beginning of the three-year period. Let r(exy) be positive. The corresponding individual variables are the dichotomies of offender/non-offender and working-class/middle-class origin. A simple and plausible model would set p(w) and p(m) as the risks among working-class boys and middle-class boys, respectively, to be recorded as an offender in the period. If so, then

(2) $$y=p(w)\cdot x+p(m)\cdot(100-x)+\varepsilon, \text{ i.e.}$$

(3) $$y=[p(w)-p(m)]\cdot x+100p(m)+\varepsilon.$$

If r(exy)>0, then the regression coefficient b(yx)=p(w)-p(m)>0, i.e. the individual correlation is positive. This, in principle, is the model discussed by Goodman (1953 and 1959; see also Duncan, Cuzzort, and Duncan 1961).

In most cases it is an improvement letting the risks vary among areas as increasing functions of x, making the model

(4) $$y_i=p_i(w;x)\cdot x+p_i(m;x)\cdot(100-x)+\varepsilon.$$

On the individual level x is inserted as a contextual variable (cf Scheuch 1969, Valkonen 1969). In one simple model the ps can be seen as average propensities over all areal units. Factors associated with x then generate positive or negative increments, in the simplest form as $a_i[x-m(x)]$, where m(x) is the total average of x. If so, the slopes will take the form (p_i+a_i). An alternative model takes the ps directly as functions of x, in the simplest form $p_i=a_i+b_ix$ with $b_i>0$.

The models are easier to see through, if a graded measure of socioeconomic position x_{ij} for the jth boy in the ith area is substituted for the original social-class variable and assumed to be correlated with delinquency. Then the individual-level models become

(5) $y_{ij}=a+cx_i+px_{ij}+\varepsilon$ and

(6) $y_{ij}=a+[(a+b)x_i]x_{ij}+\varepsilon$, respectively (Valkonen 1969: 56, 67).

The additional slope will increase the difference between the ecological and the total individual correlation, but the latter is still positive. As long as $p_i(w)>p_i(m)$ in enough areas, both individual correlations will be positive, even if the risk function is slightly reversed but the ecological slope still is positive. For r(xy) to be zero or negative, given a positive r(exy), the risk relation must be reversed in enough areas for the average within-area coefficient r(oxy) to be sufficiently negative for the within-area term to overtake the ecological term in Robinson's formula.

Thus, when there is an ecological correlation between male juvenile delinquency and parental working class, formally this correlation can come about in a limited number of ways. First, delinquency may be higher among working-class boys than among middle-class boys in most areas, with the delinquency level in each class more or less the same in all areas. This is the simplest and most straightforward model.

Second, delinquency may be higher among working-class boys than among middle-class boys in most areas, with the delinquency level in one or both classes increasing with the percentage working class in the area. This too is a straightforward, "normal" model, theoretically easy to accept. The increase in delinquency with working class size is either due to heterogeneity of the classes, e.g. leading to an increasing proportion of welfare families in working class and of lower middle class in middle class, or due to some "ecological" process, such as an increase of criminogenic low neighborhood qualities with percentage working class, or interactions within high-risk social strata increasing with their relative sizes. The latter possibilities present an interesting ecological perspective, whereas the first model and the heterogeneity version of the second model mean that an ecological perspective probably would not add much of theoretical interest.

Third, there is no difference in offense rates between working-class and middle-class boys, but the rates increase with percentage working class. This means that the individual average area-wise correlation r(oxy) becomes zero, whereas the total individual correlation remains positive as in the two first models. This third model, however, is more difficult than the earlier ones, because it is hard (although not impossible) to see why the rates should increase with percentage working class, if there is no difference in delinquency among classes within areas.

Fourth, there is less delinquency among working-class boys

than among middle-class boys in most areas, but the levels within classes increase with percentage working class in the area. Now the individual correlation by area is negative, and if it is strong enough, the total individual correlation can be zero or negative. To make theoretical sense of this model seems even more difficult than with the third model.

These are the four alternatives available. There is no way of getting both individual correlations zero at the same time. Either there is a positive total individual correlation or there is also a theoretically intriguing negative areawise individual correlation that should very much make social class a puzzling criminological variable.

Corresponding analyses can be made with other pairs of dichotomies as individual variables and ecological percentages. Furthermore, the extension from dichotomies to graded variables is fairly straightforward. For some pairs of variables the third model and even the fourth one, may make sense.

From Individual to Ecological Association

The discussion so far has tried to establish an individual correlation, specifically that between social class and delinquency, from the corresponding ecological correlation. However, the reverse applications, in which established individual associations are assumed to generate ecological associations in one or the other of the four models above may be more interesting ecologically. In general, given any non-zero ecological association, models beyond the first and the heterogeneity second model may suggest that an ecological perspective would be useful for a better understanding of the phenomena under study.

Thus, in studies of voting with voting Socialist and being working class as variables the second model has been important (Tingsten 1937, Levin, Jansson and Sörbom 1971, Janson 1987). Here the analysis is usually extended in another direction: the individual variables are dichotomies, but the analysis is multivariate with three or more social classes making two or more independent variables. With three social categories the Socialist vote is constructed ecologically in the simplest model as with two social-class regressors as

$$(7) \qquad y=(p_1-p_3)x_1+(p_2-p_3)x_2+100p_3+\varepsilon.$$

This formula often gives p-values outside the permissible range of $0<p<1$, implying that Socialist strength within classes varies with the relative sizes of the classes in the areas. Even with p values within the permissible range the slope may be too steep for the simple model. Obviously, to decide if this is the case, independent p estimates are needed. A main problem here has been to show that the excess slope is not due to the heterogeneity of the social categories used.

The models discussed so far assume that the possible ecological factor at work is associated with the original regressor, which then should be controlled. However, the factor searched for may be at most weakly associated with the regressor. If so, it may not change the slope but lower the correlation. As in the earlier cases the next step should be to find indicators of the presumed factor to insert in the analysis.

In asserting that ecological correlations were always in lieu of the corresponding individual one, Robinson (1950: 392) overstated his case. As Menzel pointed out in a comment (1950) on his paper, in genuine ecological studies corresponding individual correlations generally are not of primary importance. The purpose of ecological associations is not to get at corresponding individual associations. Menzel gives as an example the (presumably) positive ecological correlation between the percent anti-Semitics in the population and the size of the Jewish minority in the area (cf Frisbie and Neidert 1977 on minority inequality as a function of minority size).

Evidently this does not derive from a corresponding individual tendency of Jews to be anti-Semites. Instead the fourth model, which was rejected for the correlation between delinquency and social-class, suggests itself. In each area there can be assumed a strong negative association between being anti-Semite and being a Jew, but the more Jews in the area the stronger the anti-Semitic tendency among the non-Jewish majority. Such a finding has a clear significance in the fields of opinions and ethnic relations.

Furthermore, as pointed out already, substantive ecological interpretations do not presuppose corresponding individual association. Many meaningful and important ecological associciations simply have no corresponding individual association, because their variables average or otherwise build on different individual units.

Linking Individual and Ecological Variables Generally

As illustrated by the above analyses, a corresponding individual association can be estimated from ecological variables only occasionally and on strong assumptions. On the other hand, some conclusions may be possible on a more general and abstract level, concerning their general directions and character. The discussion here has been carried out in terms of correlations and regressions, but the conclusions would have been essentially the same in terms of components of variances.

Ecological variables measure characteristics of aggregate units. In individual-level analyses the dependent variable or its residual may covary with the value for the individual's area on an ecological variable. If so, this value can be inserted as the value of a regressor, a "contextual" variable, in the individual-level analysis ("context" generally referring to "the interrelated conditions in which something exists or occurs"). Such variables describe spatially delimited aggregates or groups (as against categories) of which the individual is or was a member, or settings in which he or she acts or acted. Other variables similarly describe aggregates, groups, or settings that lack or have only implicit spatial character, e.g. family variables, and are used in the same way, but they usually are not thought of as contextual but as background, structural, opportunities/risks etc.

Contextual variables in individual-level analyses can technically be handled quite adequately (cf Bryk and Raudenbush 1991, Raudenbush's chapter in the present volume, and Ringdal 1992). The main difficulty with them is not their statistical analysis. Rather the important problem is finding the right ones.

As regressors contextual variables are treated on the same level as the directly individual ones. Sometimes they are interpreted as providing a baseline for the individual variations, as when Blau (1977) derives probabilities of intergroup relations from group sizes. Usually contextual variables are called upon when individual effects leave a considerable residual correlated with ecological variation. Hauser (1971) is critical of this as a too easy way out of deficient specification. The poorer specification of individual regressors the stronger the contextual effect, the acceptance of which presupposes a (reasonably) complete specification. When without that the found contextual effect is interpreted in terms of group-level mechanisms, the "contextual fallacy" (Alker 1969: 79) is complete.

Perhaps Hauser can be interpreted as claiming that the model discussed earlier in which the deviations from the simple linear regression are due to heterogeneity of the categories is the only plausible model. If so, his position seems too restrictive. The mechanisms behind contextual variables may be selective, compositional, structural, and organizational etc. on the individual level, and one may agree that they should be specified and explored in analyses on that level. In the meantime, the contextual variables may be seen as proxies for the measures of such specifications.

In the ecological approach the purpose of letting one's thoughts alternate between levels is to strengthen and clarify the ecological analysis, not to substitute the latter for individual analysis. The aim is more general, abstract, theoretical, explorative, interpretative, and speculative than actual estimation of parameters.

Conclusions go in both directions, to and from the ecological level. From individual mechanisms, variations, and associations presumed known or assumed, ecological expectations and hypotheses are tentatively derived and ecological measures selected. In the other direction plausible interpretations of ecological findings are looked for in contextual individual-level processes. In both directions easy and obvious reduction to individual and non-contextual mechanisms may indicate that the ecological perspective has not been very profitable. To believe that the ecological outcome can be strictly derived from the individual level is to commit the "individualistic fallacy" (Alker 1969).

The level linkings by no means are restricted to links between ecological associations and their individual counterparts, although the reasoning may be even more tenuous when the corresponding individual variables refer to different sets of units and thus are only indirectly connected. In some cases such variables may be seen as having approximately the same sets, as when variables on familes or households and dwellings may be taken to refer mostly to the families of children described in other variables. However, for many meaningful ecological associations this assumption can't be made. Instead the connection can be that one variable refers to the setting for qualities given by the other variable, or to the environment or situation in which the activities described by the other variable take place.

If juvenile delinquency is seen as a function of, i.a., opportunities offered by events and situations around the teenager's core field of activity, then a measure of juvenile delinquency can be indirectly connected with various variables presumably measuring criminologically relevant aspects of the immediate surroundings: size and structure of the daytime population, retail businesses and other economic activities, building uses and the structure of the built environment, number of cars, household size and employment, age distributions and size of schools etc. Thus, in an equation with individual delinquency as dependent variable these variables can be inserted as contextual regressors or factors.

By imagining an equation of this sort, however vaguely perceived and with no parameters estimated, a social ecologist may use it as support in the research process, from getting expectations and selecting variables to interpreting results (cf Coleman 1990, ch. 1). Doing so, at least implicitly and informally, should come natural to any social ecologist as common sense for research. It also means applying the principle of methodological individualism, which to some extent might be the same thing.

Notes

[1] Another technical difficulty which, however, long remained unnoticed concerned the ecological autocorrelation. Just as variable values of adjacent or nearby units in a time-series may be influenced by the same or related accidental or special circumstances and thus get correlated random or short-wave components, the same may happen to ecological values of adjacent or nearby spatial units. In fact, in both cases an autocorrelation is to be expected. As areas have neighboring areas in two dimensions, the ecological autocorrelation is difficult to handle (cf Ord 1975). In modern socioecological analyses error-term formulas assuming independent observations are almost never used for within-area errors and usually not for between-area variation.

[2] Gelhke and Biehl divided Cleveland in 1930 successively in 252, 200, 175, 150, 125, 100, 50, and 25 areas. In the different series rate of male juvenile delinquents and low median rent correlated 0.516, 0.504, 0.400, 0.475, 0.563, 0.524, 0.579, and 0.621, respectively.

Land, McCall, and Cohen regressed homicide rates for U.S. cities, metropolitan areas, and states on six population variables in 1960, 1970, and 1980. The adjusted R^2 became 0.83, 0.68, and 0.72, respectively, with states as units, whereas cities and metropolitan areas showed little difference with coefficients between 0.50 and 0.59.

[3] The attenuation formula assumed the systematic components to be constant when the error terms were changed, but the ecological variation varied inversely to the heterogeneity of the units, since between-area and within-area variance components together form the total variance. This would tend to strengthen ecological attenuation even further.

[4] In 1936 yields of wheat and potato correlated 0.219 in 48 English counties, 0.296 in 24 pairs of counties, 0.576 in 12 regional areas, 0.765 in 6 areal units, and 0.990 in 3 areas.

[5] In Stockholm rate of males sentenced to prison in 1947 and percent working class among males correlated 0.68 in 84 areas, whereas the corresponding individual correlation was 0.065. In 1948 percent voters and percent working class among males correlated −0.32 in 246 election districts, and −0.26 in 19 parishes but −0.10 individually. Percent blacks and percent illiterates according to the 1930 American census correlated 0.77 in the 48 states, 0.95 in 9 regions, and 0.20 on the individual level (Robinson 1950).

[6] A straightforward analysis of Stockholm urban structure reported a total communality of 90 percent, Janson 1971).

[7] As Blalock (1964) explored and Hannan (1971) and Hannan and Burstein (1974) developed, systematically grouping observations (x,y) according to y or according to x or according to a criterion associated with x or y or both (as in ecological variables) strengthens the xy correlation, whereas random grouping has no systematic effect on the correlation, nor on the regressions. The effect of systematic grouping on regression is more complicated. In grouping according to a criterion affecting both variables, the effect depends on which variable is closest to the criterion.

[8] (a) In the regular case r(oxy) is weaker than r(xy) but of the same sign. Multiplied by a coefficient smaller than one it becomes clearly smaller than r(xy). If so, r(exy) can be expected to be stronger than r(xy) to equal the difference between r(xy) and the r(oxy) term after being multiplied by a much smaller coefficient. (b) If units are grouped, variation is moved from the between-area component (the ecological variable) to the within-area component, which means that the correlation ratio decreases and that r(oxy) tends to be slightly stronger. The former change is usually more important than the latter. Thus, r(exy) usually needs to be stronger to balance the individual terms in the formula.

References

Alker, Jr, H.R. (1969). *A Typology of Ecological Fallacies,* in Dogan, M. and Rokkan, S.(eds), 69–86.

Anderson, T.R. and Bean, L. (1961). The Shevky-Bell Social Areas, *Social Forces,* 40, 119–124.

Beavon, D.J. (1987). *Crime and the Environmental Structures,* 1985, quoted by Felson, M.

Blalock, Jr.H.M. (1964). *Causal Inferences in Nonexperimental Research.* Chapel Hill: University of North Carolina Press.

Blau, P.M. (1977). A Macrosociological Theory of Social Structure. *American Journal of Sociology,* 83, 1, 26–54.

Braithwaite, J. (1981). The Myth of Social Class and Criminology Reconsidered. *American Sociological Review,* 46, 36–57.

Bryk, A.S. & Raudenbush; S.W. (1991). *Hierarchical Linear Models.* Newbury Park etc.: Sage.

Cartwright, D.S. (1969). Ecological Variables, in Borgatta, E.F.(ed): *Sociological Methodology.* San Francisco: Jossey-Bass, 1969, 155–218.

Cohen, L. & Felson, M. (1979). Social Change and Crime Rate Trends. *American Sociological Review,* 44, 588–608.

Coleman, J.S. (1990). *Foundations of Social Theory.* Cambridge, Mass: The Belknap Press of Harvard University Press.

Dogan, M. & Rokkan, S.(eds) (1969). *Quantitative Ecological Analysis in the Social Sciences.* Cambridge, Mass.: The M.I.T. Press.

Duncan, O.D., Cuzzort, R.P. & Duncan, B. (1961). *Statistical Geograhpy.* New York: The Free Press.

Duncan, O.D. & Davis, B. (1953). An Alternative to Ecological Correlation. *American Sociological Review,* 18, 665–666.

Faris, R.E.L. (1967). *Chicago Sociology 1920–1932.* Chicago: University of Chicago Press.

Faris, R.E.L. (1939). *Mental Disorder in Urban Areas.* Chicago: University of Chicago Press.

Felson, M. (1987). Routine Activities and Crime Prevention in the Developing Metropolis. *Criminology,* 25, 911–931.

Frisbie, W.P. & Neidert, L. (1977). Inequality and the Relative Size of Minority Populations. *American Journal of Sociology,* 82, 5, 1007–1030.

Gehlke, C. & Biehl, K. (1934). Certain Effects of Grouping upon the Size of the Correlation Coefficient in Census Tract Material. *Journal of American Statistical Association,* Supplement, 29, 169–170.

Goodman, L. (1950). Ecological Correlations and the Behavior of Individuals. *American Sociological Review,* 15, 351–357.

Goodman, L. (1959). Some Alternatives to Ecological Correlation. *American Journal of Sociology,* 64, 610–625.

Gosnell, H.F. & Schmidt, M.J. (1936). Factorial and Correlational Analysis of the 1934 Vote in Chicago. *Journal of American Statistical Association,* 31, 507–518.

Guest, A.M. & Weed, J.A.: Ethnic Residential Segregation. *American Journal of Sociology* 1976, 81, 5, 1088–1111.

Hamm, B. (1982). *Einführung in die Siedlungssoziologie.* München: C.H.Beck.

Hannan, M.T. (1971). Problems of Aggregation in Blalock Jr, H.M.(ed): *Causal Models in the Social Sciences.* Chicago and New York: Aldine Atherton, 473–503.

Hannan, M.T. & Burstein, L. (1974). Estimation from Grouped Observations. *American Sociological Review,* 39, 3, 374–392.

Hauser, R.M. (1971). Context and Consex: A Cautionary Tale. *American Journal of Sociology,* 76, 645–654.

Hawley, A. (1950). *Human Ecology.* New York: Ronald Press.

Hindelang, M., Gottfredson, M.R., & Garofalo, J. (1978). *Victims of Personal Crime.* Cambridge, Mass.:Ballinger.

Hunter, A.A. (1971). The Ecology of Chicago, 1930–1960. *American Journal of Sociology,* 77, 425–444.

Janson, C-G. (1971). A Preliminary Report on Swedish Urban Spatial Structure, in Berry, B.J.L. (ed): *Comparative Factorial Ecology,* special issue of Economic Geography, 47, 249–257.

Janson, C-G. (1987). Working-Class Segregation in Stockhom and Some Other Swedish Cities, in Bergryd, U. and Janson, C-G. (eds): *Sociological Miscellany.* Stockholm: Department of Sociology, University of Stockholm, 161–195.

Land, K.C., McCall, P.L. & Cohen, L.E. (1990). Structural Covariates of Homicide Rates. *American Journal of Sociology,* 95, 4, 922–963.

Lander, B. (1954). *Toward an Understanding of Juvenile Delinquency.* New York: Columbia University Press.

Levin, L., Jansson, B. & Sörbom, D. (1971). *The Swedish Electorate 1887–1968.* Stockholm: Almqvist & Wiksell.

Lütjohann, H. (1974). *Linear Aggregation in Linear Regression.* Stockholm: University of Stockholm.

Massey, D.S. & Denton, N.A. (1987). Trends in the Residential Segregation of Blacks, Hispanics, and Asians. *American Sociological Review,* 52, 6, 802–825.

Menzel, H. (1950). Comment on Robinson's 'Ecological Correlations and the Behavior of Individuals'. *American Sociological Review,* 15:674.

Ord, K. (1975). Estimation Methods for MODELS OF Spatial Interaction. *Journal of American Statistical Association,* 20, 349, 120–126.

Quinn, J.A. (1950). *Human Ecology.* New York: Prentice-Hall.

Raudenbush, S.W.: *Modeling Individual and Community Effects on Deviance over Time,* chapter in this volume.

Ringdal, K. (1992). Methods for Multilevel Analysis. *Acta Sociologica,* 35, 3, 235–243.

Robinson, W.S. (1950). Ecological Correlations and the

Behavior of Individuals. *American Sociological Review,* 15, 351–357.
Scheuch, E.K. (1969). *Social Context and Individual Behavior,* in Dogan, M. and Rokkan, S., (eds) 133–156.
Shaw, C.R. et al. (1929). *Delinquency Areas.* Chicago: University of Chicago Press.
Shaw, C.R. & Mckay, H.D. (1942). *Juvenile Delinquency and Urban Areas.* Chicago: University of Chicago Press.
Shevky, E. & Bell, W. (1955). Social Area Analysis. Stanford: Stanford University Press.
Sweetser, F.L. (1965). Factorial Ecology: Helsinki, 1960. *Demography,* 2, 372–385.
Timms, D.W.G. (1971). *The Urban Mosaik.* Cambridge: Cambridge University Press.
Tingsten, H. (1937). *Political Behaviour.* London: P.S. King.
Tittle, C.R., Villemez, W.J., & Smith, D.A. (1978). The Myth of Social Class and Criminality. *American Sociological Review,* 43, 643–656.
Valkonen, T. (1969). *Individual and Structural Effects in Ecological Research,* in Dogan, M. and Rokkan, S. (eds), 53–68.
Van Arsdol Jr, M.D., Cammilleri, S.F. & Schmid, C.F. (1958). The Generality of the Shevky Social Area Indexes. *American Sociological Review,* 23, 277–284.
Van Valey, T.L., Roof, W.C., & Wilcox, J.E. (1977). Trends in Residential Segregation; 1960–1970. *American Journal of Sociology,* 82, 4, 826–844.
Westerståhl, J. & Janson, C-G (1958). *Politisk press.* Stockholm: Almqvist & Wiksell.
Wikström, P.-O.H. (1990). The Stockholm Project, in Wikström, P.-O.H. (ed): *Crime and Measures against Crime in the City.* Stockholm: National Council for Crime Prevention Sweden.
Wold, H. (1939). *A Study in the Analysis of Stationary Time Series.* Uppsala: Almqvist & Wiksell.
Yule, U. & Kendall, M.G. (1950). *An Introduction to the Theory of Statistics.* 14th ed. London: Charles Griffin.

Recent Criminological and Social Theory

The Problem of Integrating Knowledge about Individual Criminal Acts and Careers and Areal Dimensions of Crime

by Anthony E. Bottoms

> *Any theory purporting to explain a specific kind of social behaviour such as criminality and delinquency should have two distinct but consistent aspects. First, there should be a statement that explains the statistical distribution of the behaviour in time and space (epidemiology) ... Second, there should be a statement that identifies, at least by implication, the process by which individuals come to exhibit the behaviour in question. Concentration on either the epidemiological segment or the individual conduct segment is sometimes necessary, but it is erroneous and inefficient to ignore [either] segment, to turn it over to another academic discipline, or to leave its solution to a specialized set of workers within a single discipline (Cressey 1964, p.67).*

With these words, Donald Cressey anticipated some of the themes of this conference more than a quarter of a century ago. And another quarter of a century before that, the Chicago empirical sociologists Clifford Shaw and Henry McKay went to considerable pains to ensure that 'their data-gathering net was cast equally for data bearing upon the statistical distribution of delinquency in the urban community over time, and for life-history data depicting in detail the process through which individuals became delinquents' (Finestone 1976, p.24).

These reminders of past endeavours should alert us to two significant points. First, the quotation from Cressey reminds us that there are two ways of seeking to overcome the apparent gap between aggregate statistical patterns (what Cressey calls epidemiology) and explanations of individual action. One way, and perhaps the most natural to modern theorists, aware of the immense complexity of the task of criminological explanation, is to develop some kind of *eclectic approach* or *synthesis*[1], seeking to draw together into an integrated whole the insights from a range of different theoretical approaches and/or empirical studies. The other way, and the one more favoured by Cressey, is to seek to find, if possible, a single explanatory theory which will explain all criminal behaviour (or all of a specific kind of criminal behaviour) in a unitary fashion.

Secondly, reflection on the work of Shaw and McKay reminds us that their overall research strategy resulted in two very different kinds of texts: on the one hand, research reports concentrating on the detailed mapping of areas of delinquent residence at different times and in different cities (most famously, *Juvenile Delinquency and Urban Areas*: Shaw and McKay 1942), and on the other hand, ethnographic studies such as individual life-histories (most famously, *The Jack Roller*: Shaw 1930). Yet one would also have to say that, in the work of these Chicago sociologists, there was little by way of a sustained and coherent attempt to integrate these two different strands of work closely at an overall theoretical level[2]. Hence, Shaw and McKay exemplified in their own work the common social science dilemma of how to integrate, on the one hand, aggregate and (apparently) objective data with, on the other hand, individual and more subjective data, empathetically presented (i.e. in the *verstehen* tradition of sociology). This dilemma, often referred to as the 'structure' versus 'action' debate, remains very much alive in contemporary social theory, and is highly relevant to the themes of this conference. Of course, social scientists subscribing to a fully-blown positivist epistemology would deny the importance of this issue by declining to attach any importance, in explanatory terms, to the subjective perceptions and stated reasons for action of relevant social actors; but for all other social scientists, the question of how to handle the apparent action-structure divide is a very real one, and indeed some introductory textbooks in sociology are predominantly built around precisely this issue.

The preceding paragraphs suggest that we have a range of choices in deciding how to attempt the task of integrating the individual and areal dimensions of criminological knowledge. These choices are presented (in a deliberately simplified dichotomous form) in *Figure 1*.

This essay seeks to discuss some of these problems of integration. It would be as well, therefore, to indicate at the outset the positions that are adopted *vis-a-vis* the choices summarised in *Figure 1*:

First, in my view Shaw and McKay were right to take seriously the life-histories of offenders as seen from their own perspectives; our social science explanations will be incomplete if we fail to take account of, *inter alia*, social actors' perspectives, stated reasons for action, and general understandings of the social world, even though these will rarely if ever constitute a complete explanation of the action in question, because of the actors' limited understanding of themselves and the social context in which they find themselves;

Secondly, I remain an unrepentant advocate of the eclectic or synthesising approach of drawing upon ideas from quite

Figure 1. Schematic Representation of Possible Types of Model for Integrating Knowledge about Individual Criminal Acts and Careers and Areal Dimensions of Crime.

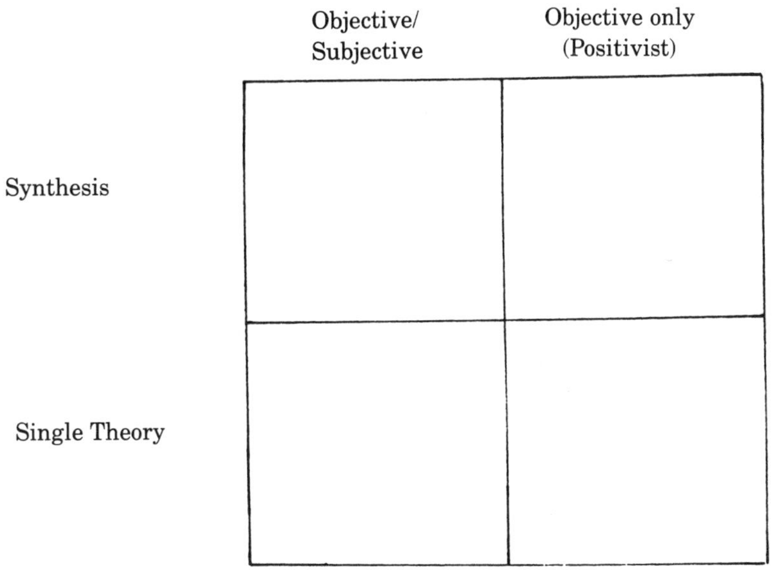

	Objective/ Subjective	Objective only (Positivist)
Synthesis		
Single Theory		

divergent intellectual sources. Scholars from many different intellectual traditions and nationalities have struggled with the explanation of crime; much of what they have written may now be seen as ephemeral or mistaken, but many have left valuable insights of one kind or another. Each of us, as St. Paul put it in another context, tends to 'see through a glass, darkly' (I Corinthians xiii, 12): it would be surprising, therefore, if only one of us (or one particular school) had grasped the whole truth, and it would accordingly seem appropriate to seek to synthesise the valuable findings and insights of various scholars, even those of very different disciplinary backgrounds, or of different political persuasions from our own. As Anthony Giddens (1964, p.xxii) puts it, if ideas or data seem 'important and illuminating, what matters much more than their origin is to be able to sharpen them so as to demonstrate their usefulness, even if within a framework which might be quite different from that which helped to engender them'.

One final preliminary comment needs to be made. Scholars in the field of environmental criminology[3] long ago learned to draw a clear distinction between *area offender rates* (rates of known offenders living in particular localities) and *area offence rates* (rates of offence commission in particular localities) – the reason for the distinction being that the two rates are, in certain areas, by no means always the same (see Morris 1957). This sharp analytic separation between offences and offenders has not always been followed by other criminologists, and of course if pursued too far it carries its own dangers. But in the present context a reminder of the distinction has significant benefits. Most of the research tradition on 'criminal careers' has concentrated very much on *offenders* and their personal and social characteristics (family background, intelligence, area of residence, schooling, etc.), with little specific attention being paid to the offences that the offenders have committed (e.g. why a particular burglary was carried out with co-offenders during a given weekend). By contrast, criminologists from the 'situational crime prevention'/rational choice/routine activities traditions have concentrated their attention very largely on the circumstances of the commission of *offences* (often with special attention to opportunity factors), but with a relative neglect of the offender. [Indeed, in unguarded moments, scholars of this latter sort have even been heard to remark that they have little interest in studying offenders and their characteristics]. I would regard it as self-evident that anyone seriously interested in a synthesising approach to explanation in criminology needs to embrace simultaneously both an explanation of criminal acts and an explanation of who are the offenders – *and to tackle both these projects both at an individual and at an aggregate (including an areal) level.* Hence the perhaps ponderous – but in my judgement necessary – length of the title of this paper: we do indeed need to tackle 'the problem of integrating knowledge about individual criminal acts and careers and areal dimensions of crime'.

The Structure of this Paper

Before proceeding further, it might be helpful at this point to offer a brief 'road-map' to the remainder of this essay. I shall begin by considering two recent attempts at synthesis in criminology – those of Braithwaite (1989) and of Gottfredson and Hirschi (1990) – each of which in my judgement has some merits, but also some defects. The purpose of these analyses is not so much to examine these particular texts for their own sakes, but rather to begin to uncover rather more precisely what is needed for adequate criminological explanation in the synthesising tradition. Since neither Braithwaite nor Gottfredson and Hirschi say much about the importance of *place* in criminological explanation, some recent work on this specific subject (one of the key themes of this conference) is also addressed at this point in the essay.

From these preliminary analyses, I shall then seek to articulate a number of *desiderata for adequate explanatory theories in criminology*. This I regard as a very important short section of the paper: far too many contemporary criminological theories, whatever their merits, simply fail to address some of the listed desiderata.

One key desideratum suggested is an integrated ontological framework, embracing individual action, community and area influences, and the consequences of the distribution of power in a given society. Anthony Giddens's (1984) *structuration theory* is widely regarded in social theory as the most promising available framework of this kind; that theory is, therefore, outlined, and attention is given to some of the key ways in which it might assist the integrative task addressed in this essay. These suggested ways include: (i) structuration theory's analyses of the duality of structure and the varieties of constraint on individual action; (ii) its emphasis on everyday routines; (iii) the centrality of time-space considerations in the theory; and (iv) its complex understanding of unintended social consequences. While considering these topics, a number of criticisms of structuration theory will be mentioned, some of which are thought to be valid. But, overall, it is suggested that this approach to social theory is a rich resource which has remained largely, and unjustifiably, neglected among criminologists. To conclude the essay, therefore, some examples are given as to how the structuration theory approach might enrich future criminological work.

Two Recent General Criminological Theories

I have chosen to focus initially on two recent general theories of crime, those of Braithwaite (1989) and of Gottfredson and Hirschi (1990). These authors have each been bold enough to put forward theories of crime purportedly valid for most crimes in Western societies[4]; and in each case (though perhaps more markedly in Braithwaite's study) there is an important element of synthesis in the work. I should perhaps make very clear that it is the *synthesising* rather than the *general* character of these theories that is of special interest for present purposes. Hence, even if (like Weatherburn 1993) one takes the view that general theories of crime are unlikely 'to deliver any real gains in explanatory power' and that it would be better to pursue detailed explanations for specific patterns of offending, an analysis of the texts of Braithwaite and of Gottfredson and Hirschi may still be a very useful way of beginning to approach the issue of identifying appropriate desiderata for explanations of crime of the synthesising kind, which seek to bring together adequately the individual and the areal levels of explanation.

(a) Braithwaite's Theory of Reintegrative Shaming[5]

John Braithwaite's 'theory of reintegrative shaming' may reasonably be regarded as an extended discussion and attempted correction of labelling theory. Labelling theory, argues Braithwaite, has only modest empirical support in the criminological literature, but few criminologists have seriously investigated under what conditions labelling might amplify initial criminality, and under what conditions it might actually reduce crime. Braithwaite's central ideas in this connection seem to be:

(i) clear moral boundaries are essential for societies which wish to achieve low crime rates. A society without adequate shaming mechanisms for wrongdoers becomes too permissive, and generates high crime;

(ii) but not all shaming is equally effective: the best kind is *reintegrative shaming*, in which the wrongdoer's fault is unequivocally recognised, but at the same time it is made clear that the wrongdoer is not to be ostracised by the communities to which he/she belongs, and which, it is hoped, he/she values (family, school, district etc.);

(iii) the polar opposite to reintegrative shaming is *disintegrative shaming* (or stigmatisation), in which much effort is expended in labelling actors as deviant, but little attention is paid to reintegration, to indicating that the label has been applied to the behaviour rather than the person, and so on. Such disintegrative shaming, postulates Braithwaite, will be more likely to increase than to decrease levels of criminality[6].

The theory is then elaborated in a number of ways, which are summarised in *Figure 2* (taken directly from Braithwaite's book). This diagram shows clearly the synthesising nature of Braithwaite's theoretical work: indeed, as he himself rather modestly puts it, 'with one crucial exception (reintegrative shaming), there is ... no originality in the elements of this theory, simply originality of synthesis' (Braithwaite 1989, p.107).

Figure 2. Summary of Braithwaite's Theory of Reintegrative Shaming.

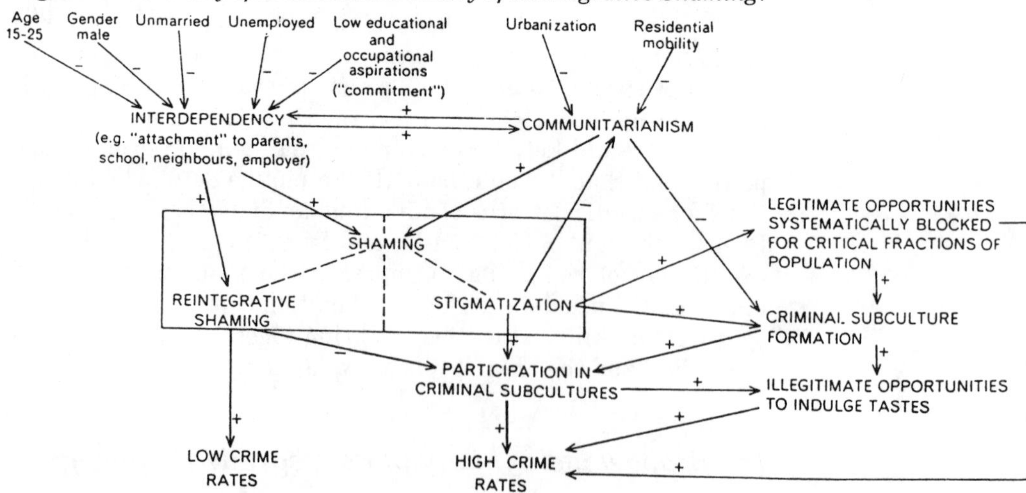

Source: Braithwaite (1989), p.99.

Reprinted with the kind permission of Cambridge University Press.

At the top of *Figure 2* are found the two linked concepts of *communitarianism* and *interdependency*: communitarianism is a concept relating to social groups, and interdependency refers to the individual's degree of attachment to significant others (in families, schools, neighbourhoods, etc.). Braithwaite postulates that where communitarianism or interdependency are strong, crime will usually be low; and vice versa. Various characteristics representing weak communitarianism or interdependency are shown above the boxes at the top of the diagram (e.g. urbanisation = a weakening of communitarianism). This part of Braithwaite's theory obviously draws strongly on control theory.

The next element of the theory – for those who have not been held away from crime by the controls of interdependency – is shaming. This is shown in the box in the middle of the diagram, which incorporates the integrative/disintegrative distinction previously discussed. Braithwaite devotes a whole chapter to the mechanisms of shaming, but it is not possible to elaborate upon these here.

The theory then postulates – as shown at the bottom of the main part of the diagram – that the stigmatisation produced by disintegrative shaming will be more likely to lead to participation in delinquent subcultures. Additionally, as in Cloward and Ohlin's (1960) theory, the social blocking of legitimate opportunities, plus the availability or otherwise of illegitimate opportunities (e.g. drug dealing for gain), is seen as likely to produce high crime rates, *independently* of possible stigmatising processes (see the right hand side of the diagram: also Braithwaite 1989, p.103). In these ways, subcultural theory and opportunity theory make their contribution to Braithwaite's overall framework.

The final theoretical strand of Braithwaite's synthesising approach is learning theory, which is not specifically represented in *Figure 2*, but which in a sense pervades the whole diagram.

This theoretical approach has been widely, and in my view justly, praised as an extremely innovative and stimulating contribution to the criminological literature. Among the virtues of Braithwaite's book is a brief but hard-hitting chapter on 'facts a theory of crime ought to fit', which argues crisply that many of the dominant criminological theories fail to explain thirteen key facts about the distribution of crime in Western societies (for example, the age skew; the gender imbalance; the urban-rural contrast; the importance of attachments to family and school; the sizeable increases in crime in most Western countries since the 1950s, etc.). The theory of reintegrative shaming, argues Braithwaite, copes better with explaining these facts than do most previous theories. Nevertheless, the author freely acknowledges that his theory might require refinement or revision in the light of future research and theoretical criticism.

Despite the theory's many attractions, for the purposes of this essay its weaknesses are also important in helping us to see more clearly the desiderata for an overall theory of crime in the synthesising tradition. It is appropriate, in this connection, to mention four main weaknesses.

The first weakness, picking up an earlier comment in this essay, is that the theory is very *offender-focussed* and says very little about *crimes*. The significance of this point for criminological explanation can be seen in simple practical examples, such as the fact that a sudden quarrel between acquaintances might become murder if there is a gun at hand, but might be no crime at all (or, at most, a minor assault) without the availability of such a weapon. In other words, even motivated potential offenders will not necessarily offend if other appropriate conditions are not present, the most important of such conditions being opportunity[7]. In Britain, this 'crime as opportunity' thesis has been pressed hard by the proponents of so-called 'situational crime prevention', and they have succeeded in demonstrating its importance, even if not quite to the extent that original versions of the approach seemed to want to claim (see generally Clarke 1983, Bottoms 1990).

Braithwaite's theory contains an opportunity dimension, but, as indicated above, this relates solely to the kind of opportunity theory put forward in the 1950s and 1960s in the wake of Robert K. Merton's (1957) *Social Theory and Social Structure* – that is to say, it refers to such matters as the social arrangements which block systematically, for a majority of the population, the routes (or opportunities) to material and career successes; or, in a different vein, the availability or otherwise in a particular locality of illegitimate opportunity structures (e.g. organised crime syndicates). This Mertonian kind of opportunity theory is thus primarily offender-centred, and is significantly different from the offence-oriented opportunity theory referred to in the previous paragraph. As is well known, this latter version of opportunity theory is often called in aid to help to explain the rapid growth of crime in most Western countries since the 1950s, bearing in mind the considerable increase in the availability of mobile or easily-carried consumer goods – such as cars, televisions and videos – during this period (see Cohen and Felson 1979; Netherlands Ministry of Justice 1985, p.10). Braithwaite's explanation of the post-war growth in crime necessarily suffers because of its omission of this point[8].

A second criticism of the reintegrative shaming approach tackles it much more on its own home ground of offender-centred theory. It is clear from much recent research in criminal careers that the distribution of *offences* as between different *offenders* is very skewed: for example, in a British study by the Home Office Statistical Department it was found that nearly 1 in 3 males born in 1953 had been convicted of a 'standard list' offence by the age of 28, but only a small proportion of these (5.5%, or 18% of those convicted), had six or more court appearances before this age, and they accounted for 70% of all the known offences committed by the whole 1953 cohort (Home Office 1985). Similar, although slightly less extreme, results have been found in other cohort studies in the United States, Scandinavia, and Britain, and the conclusions are supported by self-report research as well as by research on official arrests and convictions (Farrington 1987; Balvig 1988). A corollary of this kind of research finding is that explanations of offending might differ as between *occasional offenders* (those who only offend once or twice), *moderate offenders* (those with intermediate levels of criminality who then desist) and *persistent offenders* (cf. Blumstein *et al* 1985). The theory of reintegrative shaming could perhaps be suitably modified to take account of this possibility: but, as it stands, the theory does not adequately confront the empirical challenge presented by the kind of research findings outlined above, and neither does Braithwaite's chapter on 'facts a theory of crime ought to fit' pay sufficient attention to the importance of criminal career research.

A third critical point concerns issues of *place* and of *time*: the staple diet of environmental criminology. Braithwaite rightly and usefully draws attention to some important macro-level differences in crime rates in differing social environments, notably the urban-rural crime contrast, and the low crime rate in Japan. He has, however, much less to say about neighbourhood differences in offender and offence rates[9], an issue to which we must return.

A fourth and final criticism of Braithwaite that I would offer is that the theory says too little about *power*. This is so at several levels. At a *micro* level, it is regrettably the case that some males within high interdependency family contexts nevertheless use their power within the family unit to commit offences of domestic violence or the sexual abuse of children. Female partners, in particular, may attempt to stop this kind of behaviour by intra-family tactics of reintegrative shaming: but the evidence suggests that they are usually unsuccessful, and crimes of this sort often develop into a repeated series of violations[10]. It can be argued that it is a serious weakness of Braithwaite's theory not to discuss crimes of this kind, the issues of physical and social power which are inextricably linked to them, and the implications of these matters for his theoretical position.

Moving to a *meso* level of social organisation, power at this level can be extremely important to criminological explanation, notably as regards the direct and indirect results of various allocative decisions taken by, for example, local government officials concerning the rules for allocating children to schools, land-use and housing choices, etc (on housing, see generally Bottoms and Wiles 1986, and also later sections of this paper). This approach therefore takes one, *as a criminologist*, into issues of power that are not considered within Braithwaite's theory, and which can be shown to be intimately connected with the importance of place in criminological explanation (see further below).

If we turn finally to the *macro* level of social organisation, Braithwaite's theory specifically excludes crimes about the proscription of which there is no social consensus (see footnote 4 above). His own main example of no-consensus crime is victimless crime (e.g. drug offences); but in fact, non-consensuality can extend to more serious crimes than this, linked to overt political struggle, as exemplified by the sectarian murders in Northern Ireland. In a society such as Northern Ireland, crimes of this sort can be of dominating importance – and we need to be aware, in considering a theory like Braithwaite's, that, although it is a general theory of crime, it does not even claim to be able to explain this kind of criminality.

(b) Gottfredson and Hirschi's Theory of Self-control and Hedonistic Choice

Gottfredson and Hirschi's theory is both more individualistic and more offence-oriented than is that of Braithwaite. Its main feature of interest for present purposes lies in its proposed synthesis of offence-based and offender-based explanatory elements[11].

According to Gottfredson and Hirschi (1990), 'criminology once had an idea of crime', but this was an idea that was 'lost with the development of the scientific [i.e. positivist] perspective' (p.14). Crimes are defined as 'acts of force or fraud undertaken in pursuit of self-interest' (p.15), a definition that is linked to the theory of behaviour underpinning eighteenth-century classicism, i.e. the hedonistic principle that 'people pursue self-interest by avoiding pain and seeking pleasure' (p.14). Gottfredson and Hirschi's theory of *crime commission* (as opposed to offender propensity: see below) thus has – as they point out – many similarities to Cohen and Felson's (1979) routine activities/opportunity theory, where a crime is seen as requiring a motivated offender, a suitable target, and the absence of a capable guardian – with the last two of these being regarded as crucial. People pursuing self-interest in a hedonistic calculus will, Gottfredson and Hirschi assert, commit crime *only* if there is a good opportunity to do so, and no 'capable guardian' (such as, in burglary, signs of occupancy or a barking dog) to deter them. The problem, however, is that most modern theories of criminality:

> *take the second and third elements [of Cohen and Felson's theory] as irrelevant, and develop accounts of offender motivation. In fact, in our view, this is the fundamental mistake of modern theory. If we begin to construct our picture of the offender after first understanding the role of guardians and targets, he does not resemble the picture painted by current theories of criminality (Gottfredson and Hirschi 1990, p.24).*

Gottfredson and Hirschi's theory, then, requires an element of *choice at the crime site* by the offender, as contrasted with, as they see it, the many theories of criminality which 'would require burglary by people who tend toward criminality regardless of their assessment of the target' (p.24). In much the same vein, Gottfredson and Hirschi support Bentham's view that 'in every man, be his disposition ever so depraved, the social motives are those which ... regulate and determine the general tenor of his life' (see p.86). In other words, most offenders, even persistent offenders, do not commit offences most of the time; hence Gottfredson and Hirschi complain (I would say correctly) that most positivist criminological theories significantly overstate the distinctions between 'offenders' and 'non-offenders' (cf. Matza 1964).

Gottfredson and Hirschi thus endorse significant elements of classical theory, but it is wrong to see them as uncritical adherents of classicism. Hence, for example, they argue that classicism not only falsely 'presupposes the ready availability of draconian penalties inconsistent with the values of liberal democratic societies'[12] but also 'misapprehends the nature of people with high crime potential' (p.13). On the latter point, it is argued that:

> *classical theory cannot shed much light on the positivistic finding that [individual differences in criminality] remain reasonably stable with change in the social location of individuals and change in their knowledge of the operation of sanction systems* (p.87).

So, Gottfredson and Hirschi argue, there are indeed marked individual differences, of a stable kind over time, as regards people's propensity to commit criminal acts. These differences they ascribe to *low self-control*. People who lack self-control, it is said, 'tend to be impulsive, insensitive, physical (as opposed to mental), risk-taking, short-sighted, and non-verbal' (p.90). Low self-control, however, is not positively learned, but stems primarily from unintentionally defective early socialisation: 'the absence of nurturance, discipline or training' (p.95). Early individual differences such as 'low intelligence, high activity level, physical strength and adventuresomeness' might have an impact on subsequent low self-control, though 'effective socialisation is always possible whatever the configuration of individual traits' (p.96). Hence, socialisation is the key concept in understanding the way in which *potential offenders* are produced; and the family and the school are seen as the main institutions within society which shape effective or ineffective socialisation. But the reduction in criminality levels in adulthood (even among persistent offenders) cannot, Gottfredson and Hirschi claim, 'be explained by change in the person or by his exposure to anti-criminal institutions'; it is consequently ascribed to 'the inexorable aging of the organism' (p.141). As is well known, Gottfredson and Hirschi further argue that the age-distribution of criminality is 'invariant across social and cultural conditions', a position that has been vigorously challenged by others (Blumstein *et al* 1988a, 1988b).

Gottfredson and Hirschi's 'general theory of crime' (to adopt for a moment the title of their book) is therefore most accurately understood as a synthesis between a hedonistic theory of *crime*, and a theory of *criminality* based on low self-control. The probability of a crime occurring in a given situation thus depends partly on the situation itself (understood in terms of opportunity and the absence of capable guardians), and partly on the presence or otherwise of a person with sufficiently low self-control (understood in terms of socialisation processes and aging). This synthesis of a theory of *crime* and a theory of *criminality* is also (and explicitly) linked to an attempted synthesis of *classicism* (re crimes) and *positivism* (re offenders). While Gottfredson and Hirschi are critical of a number of aspects of the work of positivist researchers in criminology, they describe themselves as 'friendly to both the classical and the positivist traditions' (p.86); and these traditions, at least in their own synthesis, are seen as having a 'basic potential complementarity' (p.23).

In my judgement, Gottfredson and Hirschi's innovative attempt to synthesise a theory of crime and a theory of criminality is a major strength of their book, even if (see below) many specific features of that synthesis seem to be flawed. Subsequent theorists who wish to be taken seriously will unquestionably have to follow their lead in this respect: the days of 'offender only' or 'offence only' theories are surely over. By paying central attention to this issue, Gottfredson and Hirschi of course also render themselves immune from the first of the criticisms levelled at Braithwaite's theory in the previous section of this essay.

However, as with Braithwaite's theory, a number of important criticisms of Gottfredson and Hirschi's work can be made. Some of these are by now fairly familiar in the criminological community, and I need spend little time discussing them; these include especially the following:

(i) the age-invariance thesis, and also Gottfredson and Hirschi's stated view that 'the correlates of the prevalence of crime are also correlates of crime incidence' (p.241), neither of which propositions appears fully congruent with the details of research into criminal careers (see Farrington 1992);

(ii) Gottfredson and Hirschi's insistence that their theory covers all crime means that they have to spend considerable effort in debunking conventional accounts of much organised and white-collar crime (chs.9 and 10), an approach which is, on the whole, extremely unconvincing. [To take just two examples from the U.K., it is not at all easy to reconcile Gottfredson and Hirschi's theory with the apparently very significant quantity of thefts of scaffolding from building sites in Britain (Building, Trade and Industry, May 1992), or the many crimes in Northern Ireland associated in one way or another with the para-military organisations involved in the politico-religious conflict in that province].

Moving into less well-trodden territory, six further criticisms of Gottfredson and Hirschi's work may be made, each of which is of relevance to the overall theme of this essay, and the development of desiderata for criminological explanation.

First, as regards the theory of crime, the simple classical pain-pleasure model of choice adopted by Gottfredson and Hirschi seems over-simplified. For example, in an ethnographic analysis of active burglars (which appeared after the publication of Gottfredson and Hirschi's book), Cromwell *et al* (1991) found, congruently with the classicist approach, that offenders weighed potential gain, levels of guardianship and risk of detection at possible crime sites, and that much burglary was relatively opportunistic (though there was variation between individuals in the latter regard: see also Bennett and Wright 1984[13]). On the other hand, these authors also found:

(i) some complex group effects (burglars working in groups are more likely to engage in multiple-offence 'sprees', though at any potential individual site groups tend to perceive more unacceptable risk factors than do individuals);

(ii) some complex drug effects (not only in terms of incentives to burgle, but also in terms of differential risk-taking as between non-drug users, cocaine users, and heroin and marijuana users);

(iii) possible effects on burglary arising from interactive relationships between burglars and fences, the latter often 'amateur or avocational' rather than professional.

Overall, Cromwell *et al* conclude that, to understand active burglars' crime decisions, one needs 'a cognitive behavioral analysis of subroutines, [taking] into account drug and group effects within the larger template model' (p.94). No doubt future research will discover further complexities which will need to be added to this model.

A *second* and linked point of criticism concerns the location of offences – an important topic in environmental criminology. Gottfredson and Hirschi say that criminal acts are predominantly of the kind that:

require little foresight, planning or effort... Thus the carefully planned and executed crime will be extremely rare. The tendency of crime to take place at little remove from the present also implies that crimes will tend to take place at little remove from the offender's usual location....[Among crimes against businesses], it is no accident that 'convenience' stores and gas stations are common targets or that businesses located along major thoroughfares and at freeway offramps are especially attractive (pp.12–13, 18).

Whilst this characterisation is obviously true of many crimes, it runs into difficulty in some respects. For example, the pattern of recorded residential burglaries of high-status homes in Sheffield (Baldwin and Bottoms 1976, p.63) and Stockholm (Wikström 1991, ch.8) cannot be fully squared with Gottfredson and Hirschi's assumptions. Moreover, nothing in Gottfredson and Hirschi's theory easily explains Sherman *et al*'s (1989) finding of a highly skewed spatial distribution of offence locations, even *within* high crime areas. Once again, there seems to be more going on here than a simple hedonistic calculus, allied to low self-control (see further discussion in the following section of this paper).

Thirdly, there is the issue of offence specialisation. An important element in Gottfredson and Hirschi's theoretical approach is that specialisation is a myth: the crucial individual differences in self-control are relevant to all kinds of crime, so offenders are 'versatile', i.e. they commit 'a wide variety of criminal acts, with no strong inclination to pursue a specific criminal act or a pattern of criminal acts to the exclusion of others' (p.91). Anyone who has struggled (as I had to in my first research job: see Bottoms and McClintock 1973 ch.2) to classify the crime patterns of a group of typical incarcerated young offenders, is bound to agree, to a large extent anyway, with this point of view – for that kind of offender. But, again, the empirical world is more complex than Gottfredson and Hirschi allow for. For example, crimes within the home (domestic violence or child sex abuse) may well be perpetrated on a repeated basis by some men who do not offend at all in other contexts, but within the socio-spatial situation of the family are less inhibited (see footnote 10 above). Once this point is grasped – and it is obviously congruent with the psychological evidence about the situation-specific nature of a good deal of human behaviour – it becomes apparent that similar comments can be made about, for example, some white collar crime, drink-driving behaviour, etc. In which case, the *generality* of Gottfredson and Hirschi's 'low self-control' theoretical model of *criminality* is to some extent compromised, just as is their simple version of the hedonistic calculus as regards *crime*.

Fourthly, and in some ways as a follow-up to the previous point, it has to be said that Gottfredson and Hirschi's appreciation of gender and victimisation is seriously inadequate. They repeatedly stress evidence about the similarity of the characteristics of (male) offenders and victims, while largely ignoring female victimisation, and the methodological issues surrounding this debate. These matters are of considerable importance for a criminological theory which seeks adequately to take account of spatial issues, not least because there is empirical evidence of substantially greater harassment of women (especially younger women) than of men in public space (see e.g. Anderson *et al* 1990, pp.23–4; Painter 1992), harassment which is not unnaturally regarded by many women as threatening potential victimisation.

There is also considerable evidence of women taking preventive action to avoid these perceived threats by deliberately not going to certain areas, or specific places within certain areas, especially at night; or by going to such places only with a companion (see e.g. Ramsay 1989, pp.6–8). Environmental criminology has not yet fully researched or theorised these issues, but it can surely be argued that a criminological theory interested in self-control and self-policing should not ignore the potential 'self-policing' element in the behaviour of potential *victims*, as well as of offenders; e.g. the extent to which aggregate victimisation patterns are affected by differential risk-taking or place-avoidance behaviour across different groups (in this case males and females), and why.

A *fifth* criticism would be that, in developing a theory of criminality primarily based on individual differences in low self-control (linked to socialisation processes in the home and the school), Gottfredson and Hirschi seem extraordinarily blind to the socialisation and social control potential of *communities*. They are of course aware of, for example, the substantial urban-rural crime rate difference, but say very little about it, somehow wanting to relegate it to the perceived inadequacies of what they generally call 'the disciplines', in this case specifically 'sociological positivism' (p.123). But this is surely inadequate: there is no sensible reason that I can think of to believe that, while the family and the school can contribute powerfully to processes of socialisation and social control, wider communities cannot[14]. By 'blanking out' this element, Gottfredson and Hirschi make it very difficult for their theory adequately to explain the low Japanese crime rate (despite their chapter 7), the important urban-rural issue (a topic unduly neglected by too many criminological theorists), or significant offender rate differences in socially similar urban sub-areas (see further below). The same criticism could be made as regards explaining the rise in crime in most Western societies since the 1950s, an issue not directly raised by Gottfredson and Hirschi, but which they would presumably – and implausibly – have to try to explain on the basis *only* of new opportunities for crime and changes in family and schooling processes. In all these respects, Gottfredson and Hirschi's theory may be regarded as in some ways the obverse of Braithwaite's: while Braithwaite is strong on 'community' and 'interdependency' issues but says very little about criminal opportunities or stable individual differences in criminal careers, the reverse is true of Gottfredson and Hirschi. This difference highlights the importance of attempting to integrate these various traditions of work, as is a main aim of this conference. Moreover, the introduction of a wider 'community' dimension into criminological theorisation (over and above the family/school level considered by Gottfredson and Hirschi) inevitably alerts us again to the issue of *social power*, previously discussed in the context of Braithwaite's theory. In relation to Gottfredson and Hirschi's theory, the introduction of a more macro-level social power dimension also produces a crucial reminder that aspects of social organisation, political decision-making etc. in the wider society may in a number of subtle (or even not-so-subtle) ways have an important influence on the everyday lives of families (especially those with lower incomes) and schools (especially those in poorer areas).

A *sixth* and final point concerns Gottfredson and Hirschi's overall classicist/positivist framework of explanation. As previously noted, Gottfredson and Hirschi regard these traditions as potentially complementary; indeed, they explicitly state that 'on inspection, the two approaches turn out to contain no inherently contradictory assumptions' (p.23). However, there is no sustained attempt in Gottfredson and Hirschi's book to substantiate this assertion. Given that classicism works within an ontological framework of freewill, and positivism is explicitly determinist (see e.g., Taylor Walton and Young 1973, chs.1 and 2), some elaboration of the 'no contradictory assumptions' thesis seems clearly necessary if Gottfredson and Hirschi's theory is to be taken at all seriously at this level.

On a related point, one should also note one very strange feature of Gottfredson and Hirschi's work. Their assumption that what they call 'the disciplines' in criminology (i.e. anything except classicism, and embracing biological, psychological, economic and sociological approaches to explanation) *are all necessarily positivist* would make no sense to anyone in the mainstream of British sociological criminology[15] – or indeed European sociology in general. Of course, there are some sharply conflicting theoretical voices within these realms of scholarship, but Anthony Giddens (1984) is surely right to emphasise also some key *common features* of recent European sociology –

> *'One is that most of the schools of thought in question ... emphasise the active, reflexive character of human conduct. That is to say, they are unified in their rejection of the tendency of the [previous] orthodox consensus to see human behaviour as the result of forces that actors neither control nor comprehend. In addition ... they accord a fundamental role to language, and to cognitive faculties in the explication of social life. Language is embedded in the concrete activities of day-to-day life and is in some sense partly constitutive of those activities. Finally, the declining importance of empiricist philosophies of natural science is recognised to have profound implications for the social sciences also'. (p.xvi).*

There is no space here to develop these issues in detail, though it is worth commenting that the points raised by Giddens are highly congruent with recent psychological research approaches emphasising 'the individual as a productive processor of reality' (see Hurrelmann 1988). For the purposes of this paper, I shall however assume that the 'new consensus' referred to by Giddens is correct, especially in its emphasis on reflexivity and on language and cognitive faculties; and hence that positivism, whatever its virtues (and it has some), is ultimately both epistemologically and ontologically inadequate as a framework for research in the social sciences. Such a conclusion, of course, raises all the more starkly the issue of providing an adequate ontological framework of explanation, as we seek to integrate the insights of research work on individual criminal acts and careers, on the one hand, and areal dimensions of crime and criminality on the other.

Explaining Offence Locations and Offender Residence Patterns

Since neither Braithwaite nor Gottfredson and Hirschi have succeeded fully in explaining the distribution of either offence locations or offender residence patterns, and since these matters are of central significance for this conference, some discussion of these topics seems essential before proceeding with the remainder of the argument.

Gottfredson and Hirschi are of course right to emphasise that *opportunity* is an important variable in relation to *offence location*. For example, Liddle and Bottoms (1993), drawing on raw data collected by a local crime prevention team concerning car crime in multi-storey car-parks in Croydon, England, found that parks used on a long-stay basis by commuters (mainly working in London) had a much higher victimisation rate than short-stay car parks used mainly by shoppers. (In the latter, there was much more of an element of natural guardianship created by the regular comings and goings of car park customers and their families and friends). This example, of course, is highly congruent with *routine activities theory*, as previously discussed, and emphasises also the close link between routine activities theory and opportunity theory in relation to the opportunities created by the routine activities of victims or potential victims (cf. also Cohen and Felson's (1979) own claim as to a link between increases in the daytime residential burglary rate in the post-World War II period and the number of houses unguarded as more women went out to work).

As previously noted, routine activities theory as developed by Felson and others is centrally concerned with the interaction between a motivated offender, a suitable target and the absence of capable guardians. Perhaps surprisingly, however, as actually developed by its proponents the theory has taken the motivated offender as essentially a given; hence, researchers have concentrated all their analytic attention on the other two stated features. Nevertheless, within environmental criminology a parallel strand of work has been developed, emphasising the

Figure 3. Brantinghams' Model of Intersection of Criminal Opportunities with Offender's Cognitive Awareness Space.

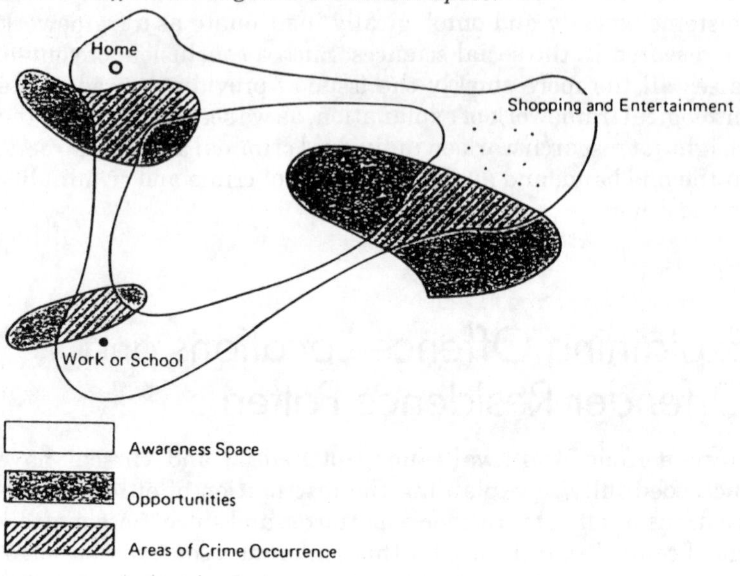

Source: Brantingham and Brantingham (1984), p.362

routine activities of *offenders* and the relevance of their activities for offence location analysis, and this work can be seen as a very useful complement to routine activities theory.

It is self-evidently the case that there are some purely *opportunist* crimes, where a person responds 'there and then' to a set of attractive environmental cues[16] (e.g. a teenage boy calls at a friend's house, finds the back door open and £20 unguarded on the table); and also some *affectively spontaneous* crimes, where a person commits, say, an assault in the course of a sudden heated argument with an acquaintance. These offences, by definition, must occur in the place where the offender already happens to be, as a result of his/her daily life-choices. More than a decade ago, however, Patricia and Paul Brantingham (1981) proposed that the offender's daily life patterns might influence the location of offending behaviour even where the offender was engaging, to some degree, in a search pattern for a suitable target, having already decided in principle to commit an offence (as, perhaps, in burglary). All of us, it was argued by these authors, carry in our heads 'cognitive maps' of the cities where we live. Some parts of the city we will know extremely well (e.g. the areas immediately around our home, near our workplace, and in the city centre where we go for shopping and entertainment purposes); and we will also tend to know well the roads linking these various areas, or out of the city into the surrounding countryside. By contrast, there will be some areas of the city which we hardly know at all, such as residential areas (away from main roads) in which we have no social acquaintances. Brantingham and Brantingham innovatively postulated that most offenders will not commit offences in poorly-known areas; hence offences, even 'search pattern' offences, were, they argued, most likely to occur where *criminal opportunities* interacted with *cognitively-known areas* – a hypothesis schematically illustrated in *Figure 3*. Subsequent empirical work in the ethnographic tradition, while not extensive, has supported these claims (see e.g. Rengert and Wasilchick 1985, ch.3).

A more recent and extensive statistical analysis of offence locations in Stockholm by Wikström (1991, ch.8) has demonstrated major differences in the geographical distributions of different offences, strongly related *inter alia* to the *types of activities* occurring in different parts of the city (e.g. number and types of places of entertainment such as bars) and the *composition of the population in the area at any given time* (including in this regard both residents and visitors). These findings led Wikström (1990) to postulate a tentative model for explaining variations in the crime rate and types of crime in different districts, taking also into account issues such as opportunity, Brantingham and Brantingham's insights, etc. This model by Wikström is shown in *Figure 4*[17]. Subsequently, Bottoms and Wiles (1992), while broadly endorsing Wikström's model, argued that, *inter alia*[18]:

(i) the model paid inadequate attention to the changes (as opposed to the continuities) in the use by social actors of different districts within the city, or (at the more micro-level as highlighted, for example, by the work of Sherman et al. 1989) to the constantly evolving character of particular streets or particular bars in city centre locations;

(ii) Wikström's work, arising as it did solely from a quantitative analysis of crime patterns in Stockholm, was in danger of paying too little attention to the perceptions and daily life choices of individual actors within the city, and the way in

Figure 4. Wikström's Tentative for Explaining Variations in Crime and Types of Crime in the Urban Environment.

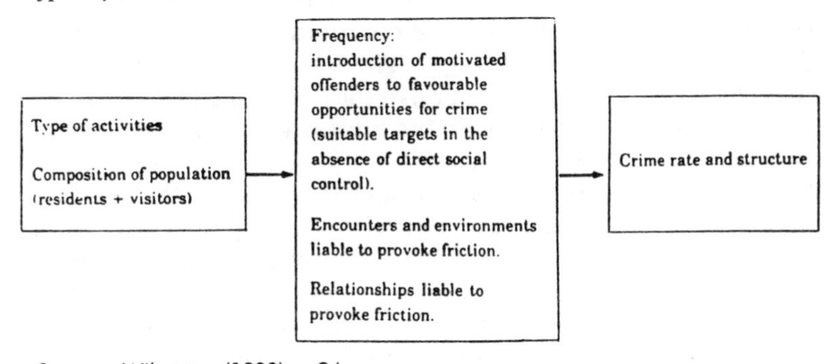

Source: Wikström (1990), p.24

which these came together to build up the aggregate patterns displayed in the statistical data.

One might further suggest (elaborating a point hinted at but not fully developed by Bottoms and Wiles) that both the above issues are likely to be strongly influenced by the *symbolic* meaning of particular locations. To real-life actors, places are often not just neutral locations for social interactions. They are pregnant with meaning (e.g. perhaps the decor indicates clearly that this is a place only for the young, or only for the rich), and very often, intimately linked to aspects of actors' personal biographies. Such matters are often very subtle and nuanced, but they can crucially affect (in an interactive way), the kinds of variables shown in *Figure 4*, and they need to be incorporated into any full model for explaining offence locations.

We may now turn, equally briefly, to the problem of explaining *offender residence patterns*. With admirable precision and brevity, Wikström (1991, p.130) has explained that there are two main reasons why area of residence and aggregate offender rates might be statistically related; they are[19] -

(i) Area of residence and offender rates might be related because more crime-prone individuals and groups are distributed (by the operations of the local housing market) to certain areas – however, the area itself does not, in this type of correlation, affect the criminality levels of the residents;

(ii) Area of residence *might however also in itself influence criminal motivation*, through the impact of area contextual characteristics on the social life and social control of an area, where this influence may be divided into, *first*, short-term situational influences on criminal motivation[20], and *secondly*, longer-term influences on the development of personality and modes of living which might affect the individual's propensity to commit crime.

Wikström himself subsequently developed, in the same book, a statistical path model of offender rates in different districts of Stockholm. In this analysis, each district was first assigned to one of three major housing types (on the basis of the predominant type of housing in the area), and a linkage was then made to three aspects of population composition previously found to be important (in a factor analysis) in distinguishing different areas of the city according to social type. These housing and population variables were brought together in a composite model explaining about half the area variation in the total offender rate in Stockholm (see *Figure 5*). As Wikström is at pains to point out, it is not clear from this (purely statistical) analysis how far the offender rate variation by district has been influenced by the 'contextual characteristics' he had earlier identified as potentially influencing offending in particular areas; however, what is clear from this work is that area variation in offender rates is a very complex issue, and is by no means simply explicable (as some

Figure 5. Wikström's Path Model of Housing, Population Composition, and Total Offender Rates in Different Districts of Stockholm.

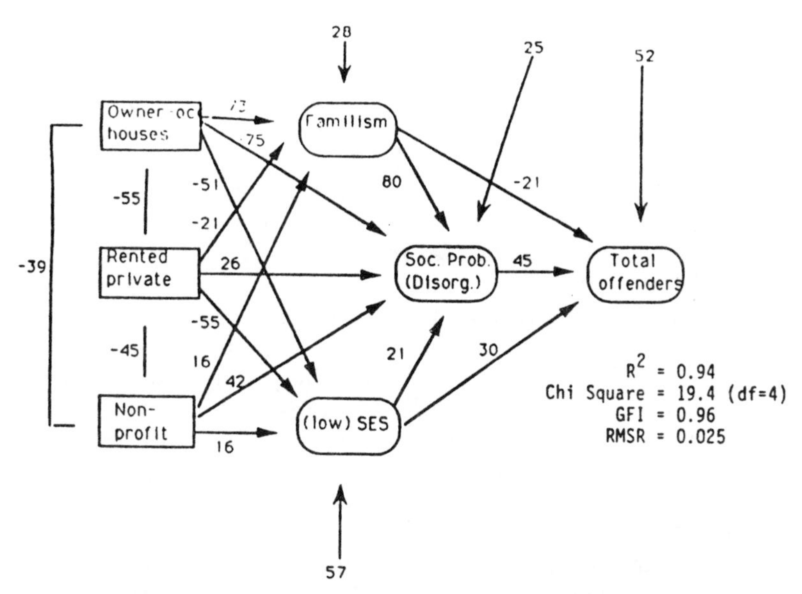

Note: Numbers on arrows linking boxes show path coefficients multiplied by 100. Floating numbers show proportion of unexplained rate variation for the relevant variable.

Source: Wikström (1991), p.182

have at times wanted to assert) by, for example, social class differences between areas.

Wikström's emphasis, in his path model, on the predominant housing type of a geographical area was directly derived from research in which I have been involved in Sheffield, England (see Wikström 1991, pp.149–53; Baldwin and Bottoms 1976). From the experience gained in the Sheffield project, my colleagues and I have argued (see especially Bottoms and Wiles 1986) that the local housing market is of central importance in influencing the area 'contextual characteristics' that might affect offender rates; in the present context, some brief explication of this apparently bold claim therefore seems necessary.

Before the Sheffield study on crime and the city was begun, Rex and Moore (1967) had published an influential sociological analysis of Commonwealth migration to Britain, centred on empirical work in Birmingham. These authors were struck by the importance of the housing market in shaping the potential access of Commonwealth migrants to different districts within Birmingham[21], and from this observation they developed a generalised theory of 'housing classes'[22]. In carrying out an overall statistical study of the relationship between offender rates and census data in the whole of Sheffield (Baldwin and Bottoms

1976) we tried to operationalise some of the thinking of Rex and Moore – necessarily a little crudely, given the nature of our data – by classifying each census enumeration district on the basis of its predominant housing type, and then seeing whether the resulting 'predominant housing' variables were of importance in explaining the offender rates of urban sub-areas, when population data were also considered. The answer was emphatically in the affirmative, and indeed a different regression model had to be fitted for predominantly public (or 'council') areas and for private housing areas[23]. It was also found, however, that there were major variations in offender rates *within* the range of areas that shared a predominant housing type – for example, some council housing areas had very high offender rates, and some very low rates. It was decided to attempt some further investigation of these issues – and especially the possible role of the housing market in influencing offender rate differences between areas – by more on-the-ground work in specific areas, using a variety of research methods including surveys and participant observation.

It was out of this line of thinking that there emerged the intriguing study of two adjacent council housing areas known as Gardenia and Stonewall, first researched in the mid-1970s (see Bottoms, Mawby and Xanthos 1989; for a follow-up study in the 1980s see Bottoms, Claytor and Wiles 1992). Briefly, the original research problem was that these two areas (population 2500–3000 each, and separated only by a main road), had (i) a 300% difference in recorded offender rates, and a 350% difference in recorded offence rates against individual residents and households, but (ii) no statistically significant differences at all on a set of key demographic variables (namely – sex; age; social class; ethnic origin; mean household size; % single; % male unemployment; age of termination of full-time education; and length of stay in current dwelling). Preliminary research (victim and self-report studies) established that the crime rate differences could not, for the most part, be regarded as artefactual. A further point of interest was that both areas had been built at approximately the same time (in the first quarter of the twentieth century), and both had, it seemed clear, begun as 'good', crime-free areas. Stonewall had retained this characteristic, but Gardenia had 'tipped' sometime in the 1940s.

The research team were unable to discover retrospectively exactly why Gardenia had tipped (though some speculative suggestions were made). But through detailed analysis of records in the local authority's housing department, plus ethnographic work in the areas, we were able to show that, once Gardenia had tipped, the local rules of housing allocation had the unintended effects of maintaining the difference between the two areas[24], and of ensuring that Gardenia attracted, as new tenants, predominantly (i) those in severe housing need, and (ii) those who had prior affective links with the area (relatives living on the estate etc.). To some extent, therefore, housing allocative processes were drawing to the two estates new residents with a differential propensity to offend (i.e. the first of Wikström's two suggestions as to how offender rates and area of residence can be related was to an extent in operation). On the other hand, ethnographic work also showed that what Wikström has called 'contextual characteristics' were certainly very much in evidence, and helped to influence the differential offender rate. These 'contextual characteristics' were very complex, and interactive, but included (in addition to the housing market context) certain physical geographical features; a mild criminal sub-culture in one part of the more criminal estate (Gardenia); the effects of the negative reputation of Gardenia on its residents and on potential residents; possibly a difference relating to the main schools serving the two areas; and some important differences in parental and peer socialisation processes (see Bottoms, Mawby and Xanthos 1989, pp.67–75, esp. p.74). Criminologists such as Gottfredson and Hirschi would no doubt be particularly interested in the last of these points, and also in the Addendum to the Gardenia-Stonewall paper, in which is described an interlocking family network on Gardenia, with obviously low self-control in many of its members (Bottoms, Mawby and Xanthos 1989, pp.75–79). The Sheffield researchers, however, would want to insist that these socialisation practices (and the very different ones being practised in Stonewall, a demographically very similar area) can be understood only *within the total social context of Gardenia*, and that some aspects of individual children's socialisation (e.g. the degree of parental supervision exercised) would probably have been different in a different social milieu (cf. Hurrelmann 1988, p.92: 'the social and material environment that members of a family confront functions as a framing condition for the child's process of education and socialisation').

It must be re-emphasised, at this point, that in the analysis of offender rates in Gardenia and Stonewall – as in other residential areas studied in Sheffield – the researchers have identified the local housing market as a key sifting mechanism (within which choices are made by a number of social actors, including potential residents). The operation of the local housing market, however, can have crucial secondary effects in terms of, for example, the nature of the relationships which subsequently develop in the area, or responses by outsiders (including social control agents, potential residents, etc) – some of which effects might themselves then affect the housing market context of the area, e.g. by altering the area's perceived desirability, and perhaps escalating the number or residents wishing to leave. This complex interactive model is set out in *Figure 6* (taken from Bottoms, Claytor and Wiles 1992). This model has recently received significant implicit support from Hope and Foster's (1992) analysis of changes in crime over time in a council area in

Figure 6. Diagrammatic Representation of the Relationship Between the Potential Effects of the Housing Market and Residential Community Crime Careers.

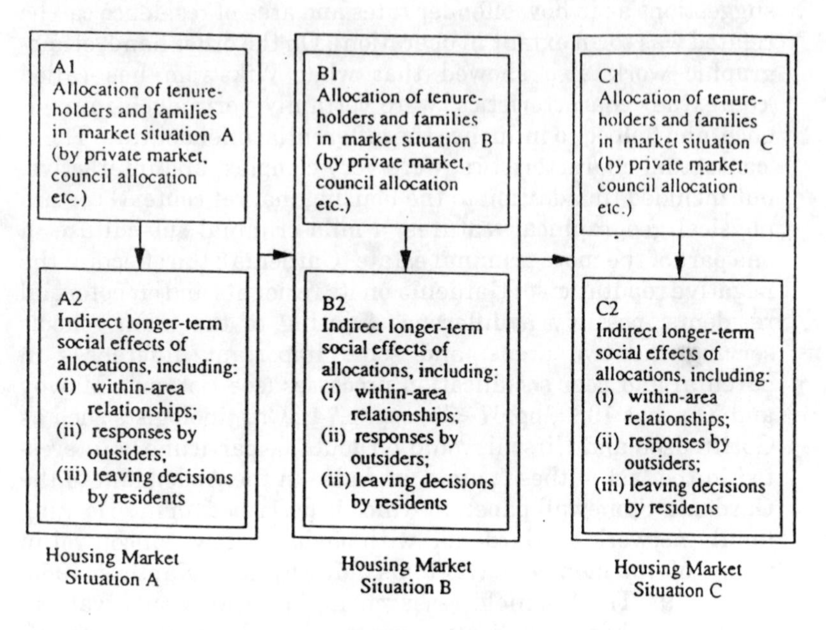

Source: Bottoms, Claytor and Wiles (1992), p.120

Reprinted with the kind permission of Routledge.

another city in the North of England; the model also has some marked similarities to the work of Taub, Taylor and Dunham (1984) in Chicago[25], a point of particular interest since the latter researchers were, of course, working in areas dominated by private housing markets, rather than the public housing context of Gardenia-Stonewall and the estate studied by Hope and Foster. As prefigured earlier in this paper, then, *meso-level allocative mechanisms* in society (such as housing markets and school allocations) emerge from this strand of research as having an independent explanatory role in the criminological explanation of offender location. The research also emphasises – as, in a different way, did the conclusions from the research on offence location - the intimate interconnection of individual choices and social processes in the generation of particular social effects. These various lessons need to be borne in mind as we now seek to build on the preceding argument by trying to identify desiderata for criminological explanation.

Desiderata for Criminological Theory

As previously emphasised, a main reason for the nature of the preceding discussion – i.e. the careful analysis of two general theories of crime, plus some special attention to aspects of place in the explanation of crime – has been to attempt to derive a worthwhile set of desiderata for criminological explanation in the synthesising tradition, with a *verstehen* element (see *Figure 1* and discussion thereof).

It would be wearisome, in the light of previous sections, to explain in detail the reasons for the choice of the various axioms suggested. It is hoped, therefore, that readers will be able to make the connections between earlier parts of this paper and the following suggested desiderata.

It seems, then, that criminology needs an explanatory theoretical approach that will, at least:

1. Provide an integrated ontological framework, embracing individual action, family/school/community/peer/area influences, and the consequences of the distribution of power in a given society;

2. Embrace modern (post-empiricist) social science perspectives emphasising reflexivity, cognitive processes, and the 'individual as a productive processor of reality';

3. Distinguish clearly between *crimes* and *offenders*, but provide a theory which can account for both;

4. As regards *offenders*, provide a theory which can explain *both* the main aggregate differentiating variables (age; sex; urban-rural differences; inter-societal differences; and, for street crimes, social class) *and* variations connected with these variables (e.g. differential desistance of different individuals or groups at the same age; differential offending levels of individuals or groups from similar social class backgrounds, brought up in different contexts);

5. Be willing to accept that there are some stable individual differences between offenders and non-offenders (and between persisters and desisters) linked to low self-control, but, at the same time, to insist that these differences (i) can be produced by different communities as well as by different family and school processes; and (ii) even when produced by family socialisation, they may be at least in part the result of community/areal influences (see the Gardenia-Stonewall study) or broader macro-social processes such as the distribution of power or resources in society;

6. As regards *crimes*, provide a theory which will set these incidents in the context of offenders' everyday lives (not overemphasising the amount of time they spend committing offences), and be willing to see many of these crimes as choices made within the context of those everyday lives (which offenders will be able, at least to some extent, to explain). This approach

will embrace, *inter alia*, issues of opportunity; the routine activities of potential victims; the routine activities and 'cognitive maps' of potential offenders; and group and drug effects plus interactions between property offenders and fences (Cromwell *et al* 1991);

7. Be willing to consider crimes with considerable degrees of organisation, as well as unplanned crime, as part of the total explanatory task;

8. Be willing to recognise the situation-specific nature of some offences, whilst also (where appropriate) linking this feature to broader social processes (e.g. the link between macro-socially created patriarchal social structures and attitudes and situation-specific repeated domestic violence);

9. Recognise that, in the case of some crimes at least, potential victims may exercise a degree of self-policing to avoid being offended against, and that this behaviour itself needs to be understood in social science terms as part of the overall criminological enterprise;

10. Recognise the importance of *the activities taking place in particular areas* in relation to explanations of offence location, and the potential relationship of this point to *symbolic meanings of place*;

11. Recognise the importance of *power* and its consequences in many criminological contexts, from the micro level (e.g. gender relations in the home) to the macro level (the overall distribution of political, economic and social power in society). Relevant corollaries of the importance of power include: (i) the potentially considerable indirect role of meso-level allocative processes in the production of offending (at both areal and individual levels); and (ii) the constraints on choice for those lacking power in any particular situation, which may in the longer term enhance offending levels[26];

12. Recognise the potential importance of *societal reaction to crime* (through the criminal justice system or through other processes) in affecting crime levels, and recognise also that this variable might have differential effects according to different types of societal reaction, and/or in different social contexts;

13. Provide a theory that can explain *changes over time* as well as contemporary distributions of crime: in particular, it is vital to be able to explain the secular growth in crime in most Western societies since the 1950s.

Structuration Theory

In previous sections of this essay, including the first desideratum listed above, it has been emphasised that there is a need for: (i) a synthesised theoretical approach that will knit together individual and aggregate levels of analysis, including the subjective dimensions of individual experience; and (ii) an overall ontological framework that will be more coherent and convincing than Gottfredson and Hirschi's attempted classicist-positivist synthesis.

I would suggest that, in seeking to meet these goals, criminologists should consider very carefully the claims of Anthony Giddens's *structuration theory*, an approach to social theory that he developed over a decade from the mid-1970s, and which has found its fullest statement in *The Constitution of Society* (Giddens 1984). John Urry, a leading British sociologist who – as we shall see – is not uncritical of structuration theory in certain respects, has nevertheless claimed that it is:

> *the most systematic, interesting and sustained attempt so far found to develop an approach to social theory that transcends the dichotomies of determinism and voluntarianism, society and the individual, and object and subject (Urry 1986).*

If that is true, then clearly structuration theory might have something to say in respect of the problems of integration addressed in this paper.

What, then, is structuration theory? The very name tells us something about it, for the term 'structuration' combines connotations of structure and of action (or process). But what Giddens argues is not simply that social science explanations need to be adequate at both the individual level and the level of social totality (as for example Max Weber long ago insisted), but rather that it is, ultimately, a fundamental mistake to conceive of these 'levels' as truly separate. Instead, Giddens proposes that:

> *The basic domain of study of the social sciences, according to the theory of structuration, is neither the experience of the individual actor, nor the existence of any form of societal totality, but social practices ordered across space and time* (Giddens 1984, p.2).

Elsewhere, Giddens, emphasising that structuration theory is only one part of his sociological writing, describes the approach in the following way:

> *... it is the label I attach to my concern to develop an ontological framework for the study of human social activities. By 'ontology' here, I mean a conceptual investigation of the nature of human action, social institutions and the interrelations between action and institutions (Giddens 1991, p.201).*

By now, structuration theory has generated a sizeable secondary literature (see, for example, Held and Thompson 1989; Cohen 1989; Clark, Modgil and Modgil 1990; Bryant and Jary 1991; Craib 1992). It is not possible or appropriate, in the present context, to enter into many of the issues involved in these debates. Rather, what I shall attempt is *first*, to give a brief summary of some of the main features of structuration theory (for the benefit of readers unfamiliar with it), and then *secondly* to indicate four ways in which, in my view, the theory would be helpful as an overall 'ontological framework' (as Giddens puts it) within which criminologists can work at producing explanations which might meet the desiderata outlined in the previous section.

At the risk of oversimplification, structuration theory may be summarised in the following way[27]:

1. Human subjects are knowledgeable agents, though this knowledgeability is bounded on the one hand by the unconscious, and on the other hand by unacknowledged conditions and/or unintended consequences of action.

2. The study of day-to-day life is integral to the analysis of the reproduction of institutionalized social practices (consider, for example, the daily reproduction of the social institution of the school, and the way in which the everyday lives of pupils, teachers and parents both help to reproduce the school and are influenced by its existence and practices).

3. Human subjects largely act within a domain of 'practical consciousness' which often cannot be expressed in terms such as 'motives' or 'reasons' but which 'consist of all the things which actors know tacitly about how to "go on" in the context of social life without being able to give them direct discursive expression' (Giddens 1984, p.xxiii). In research contexts, the 'practical consciousness' of relevant actors must be understood and made plain by the empirical researcher in explanation. Practical consciousness must be distinguished from 'discursive consciousness' which is 'what actors are able to say, or to give verbal expression to, about social conditions, including especially the conditions of their own action' (Giddens 1984, p.374).

4. Structuration theory seeks to escape from the traditional dualism in social theory between 'objectivism' and 'subjectivism'. Thus the theory accepts concepts of 'structure' and 'constraint', normally associated with 'objective' social science, but insists that they be understood only through the actions of knowledgeable agents; on the other hand it believes that 'subjectivist' social science has overemphasized the degree to which everyday action is directly motivated (i.e. it has considerably underemphasized the importance of practical consciousness).

5. Structuration theory uses the term 'structure' in a somewhat different sense from most previous usage in sociology. While most sociology is content to use the two terms 'structure' and 'system' more or less interchangeably, to refer to the descriptive analysis of the relations of interaction which 'compose' organizations or collectivities, structuration theory conceptualises structure and system as sharply different (see Bryant and Jary 1991, p.7). 'Structure' is defined as '*rules and resources*, recursively implicated in the reproduction of social systems' (Giddens 1984, p.377, emphasis added)[28]; it is a 'virtual order', which does not exist in time-space, but only 'as memory traces, the organic basis of human knowledgeability, and as

instantiated in action' (*ibid*). Hence, 'structure is what gives *form* and *shape* to social life, but it is not *itself* that form and shape, [and] nor should 'give' be understood in an active sense here, because structure only exists in and through the activities of human agents' (Giddens 1989, p.256, emphasis in original). The term 'system', by contrast, refers to 'the patterning of social relations across time-space, understood as reproduced practices' (Giddens 1984, p.377).

6. Structures may act as constraints on individual actions but they are also, and at the same time, the medium and outcome of the conduct they recursively organise – what Giddens refers to as the 'duality of structure', a central concept in structuration theory. As he put it in an early work: 'to enquire into the structuration of social practices is to seek to explain how it comes about that structures are constituted through action, and reciprocally how action is constituted structurally' (Giddens 1976, p.161). Structures, therefore, do not exist outside of action, and they do not only constrain, but also enable social action.

7. 'Routine' is a predominant form of agents' day-to-day social activity. Most daily practices are not directly motivated, and routinised practices are a prime expression of the 'duality of structure' in respect of the continuity of social life. Routine is psychologically linked to the minimization of unconscious sources of anxiety (i.e., to the maintenance of what Giddens calls 'ontological security').

8. The dimensions of the duality of structure are shown in *Figure 7*, linked to the institutional orders of social systems. This diagram shows a threefold structural differentiation between signification, domination and legitimation, and the institutional orders associated with these concepts (i.e. symbolic orders/modes of discourse; political and economic institutions; legal institutions). In any concrete empirical situation, all aspects of this differentiation need to be investigated. The diagram further shows the close connection between structure and system, and indeed:

> *one of the main propositions of structuration theory is that the rules and resources drawn upon in the production and reproduction of social action are at the same time the means of system reproduction (Giddens 1984, p.19).*

9. The study of power cannot be regarded as a second-order consideration in the social sciences; rather, power is one of several primary concepts, all clustered around the relations of action and structure.

10. No unitary meaning can be given to the concept of 'constraint' in social analysis. Rather, there are three types of constraints on action (Giddens 1984, pp.174–179; Giddens 1989, p.258): (i) physical constraints, deriving from the human body and the material environment; (ii) constraints involved with the operation of power (i.e. relating to the resource/sanction aspects

Figure 7. Dimensions of the Duality of Structure with Corresponding Institutional Orders in Social System.

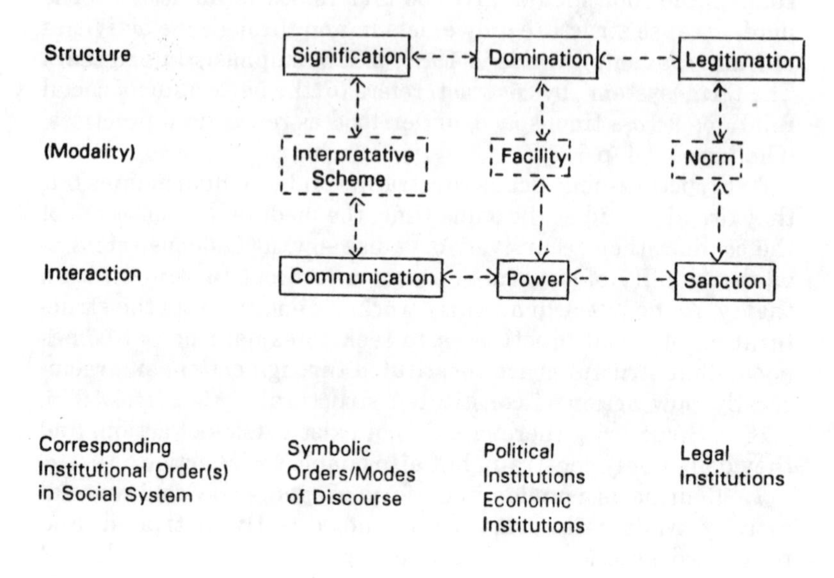

Source: Giddens (1984), pp.29 and 31

of social systems); and (iii) structural constraints, originating in the perceived 'fixity' or 'objectivity' of social systems in relation to the individual agent. The latter two types 'constrain' the actor by setting limits on the feasible range of options that he/she can follow, rather than by physical impossibility.

11. Structuration theory accepts and tries to elaborate Marx's famous dictum that human beings 'make history, but not in circumstances of their own choosing'. This is part of the duality of structure, and emphasises that social change and social process, linked to the reflexivity of human action, is an intrinsic part of human social life, even though that social life also has considerable continuities. However, the reflexive nature of human social life prohibits the explanation of social change in terms of any simple and sovereign set of causal mechanisms.

12. It follows from all of the above that the study of *context* (or the situated character of all human interaction) is inherent in social analysis. The study of contextuality involves an understanding of the *setting* of the interaction, the *co-presence* of actors, and the *reflexive communication* between them.

It will be apparent from the above why Giddens refers to structuration theory as a general 'ontological framework'. In the preface to *The Constitution of Society* (Giddens 1984, p.ix) he further (and disarmingly) says that 'the vague term "approach" to social science actually conveys very well what I take to be the methodological implications of structuration theory'. More recently, he has pointed out explicitly that structuration theory 'is not intended to be a theory "of" anything' (a fact that had 'infuriated some critics'), but that precisely this characteristic was 'quite necessary to any attempt to provide an ontology of social activity in the sense noted previously' (Giddens 1991, p.204).

Those who have followed the argument of this paper this far will now perceive something of an apparent difficulty. I began with some concrete problems of criminological explanation, attempting some constructive criticisms of the work of Braithwaite and of Gottfredson and Hirschi, introducing some aspects of the literature on crime and place, and providing (a little boldly, perhaps) thirteen desiderata for criminological explanation. While it is true that the first of those desiderata referred to the need for an ontological framework, many of the others were much more specific and practical. How, then, can structuration theory, which 'is not intended to be a theory "of" anything' (see above), help us to take forward the explanatory tasks of criminology?

My reply to this question has to return to the idea of structuration theory as an *approach* or *framework*. It gives us, I would suggest, a *way of seeing* social interactions in a manner which transcends the old subject/object, aggregate/individual dichotomies, and treats as its 'basic domain' of study *social practices ordered across space and time* rather than individuals or societal totalities (Giddens 1984, p.2). My central claim is that this different way of seeing the empirical world should assist us in the integrative task of criminological explanation – which, as previously indicated, needs to make *overall* sense of, for example, the explanation of both specific criminal acts and the development of criminal careers, and of working at 'levels' as different as (i) the choices made by a group of potential burglars at a particular crime site and (ii) the reasons for the difference in crime rates between Japan and most Western countries.

It is obviously not possible, in a single paper, to try to take forward all the thirteen suggested desiderata for criminological theory within a framework of structuration theory. Rather, what I shall now seek to do is to select four important features of structuration theory, and to try to show how these could be of importance in trying to develop criminological explanations. The four features of structuration theory on which I shall concentrate for this purpose are: *first*, the concept of the duality of structure, and the varieties of constraint on individual action; *secondly*, the importance of routines in structuration theory; *thirdly*, structuration theory's understanding of the centrality of *space* and *time* in social practices; and *fourthly*, the role played by unintended consequences within the structuration approach. In each case, I will try to show, by means of examples, how the particular concept taken from structuration theory might enhance our development of an integrated criminological theory, in the sense previously described.

(a) The Duality of Structure and the Varieties of Constraint on Individual Action

It can be argued that the concept of 'duality of structure' (note: *not* 'dualism of structure and agency') provides exactly the kind of framework within which major systematic continuities of behaviour (e.g. sex ratios or inter-societal differences in offending), and variations from those continuities, can be analyzed, without either (i) reducing human actors to implicitly inanimate states, or (ii) over-reifying the role of social structures in modern societies.

As an example of this point, we may take a British ethnographic research study (discussed in some detail by Giddens himself) which is by no means irrelevant to criminologists. Paul Willis's (1977) *Learning to Labour* set out to explain 'how working class kids get working class jobs', roundly asserting on the first page of the book that 'it is much too facile simply to say that they have no choice ... there is no obvious physical coercion, and a degree of self-direction' (p.1). Empirically, the book is based on a participant observation study concentrating upon twelve non-academic working class boys during their last year at school and into their first six months at work, with some comparative case studies of different kinds of comparison-group youths (e.g. a group of more conformist, academically-oriented youths from the same school). The book's twelve central characters ('the lads') are described by Willis as belonging to a 'counter-school culture', the most basic and explicit dimension of which was an 'entrenched general and personalised opposition to authority' (Willis 1977, p.11); perhaps not surprisingly, therefore, there is plenty of evidence of delinquency in their lives (e.g. pp.26, 33, 41). As Giddens (1984, p.291) points out, it is not too difficult to see how officials in society could view 'the lads' as '"louts" or "wreckers" unable to appreciate the importance of the educational opportunities the school offers', and social scientists might similarly characterise them in the language of 'imperfect socialisation'. Through detailed ethnographic research, Willis provides a different and more subtle account of the motivation of these young men, from their own perspective; for example, he shows that in certain respects they have very real skills (e.g. in knowing how to use the language of 'pisstakes'; or in knowing how far school staff can be pushed, and in manipulating formal school rules to the lads' own advantage). In developing this complex oppositional culture, 'the lads' draw on a fund of experience built into their lives outside the school, and developed historically over many years in general working class culture: in other words, they draw on general structural 'rules and resources', which they then adapt for their own purposes in a specific situation (see Giddens 1984, p.297ff). Membership of a group, however, is vital to this achievement: 'it is impossible to form a distinctive culture by yourself' (Willis 1977, p.23).

Willis shows that 'the lads' very much want 'to escape from school ... and the lure of the prospect of money and cultural membership among "real men" beckons very seductively as refracted through their own culture' (p.100). They are aware that their more conventional schoolmates might well, in the longer term, have better careers ('they're thinking about the future ... they'll have 'ouses and everything before us ... they'll be the civil servants, toffs, and we'll be the brickies and things like that': p.98); but this does not affect their worldview:

> *We wanna live for now, wanna live while we're young, want money to go out with ... I don't say it's wise, I say it's better for us ... we just like it too much (pp.97–8).*

So the world of manual work is entered, willingly, though also with some awareness of its true nature (what Willis calls 'partial penetration': see ch.5). But, in summary:

> *The astonishing thing which this book attempts to present is that there is a moment – and it only needs to be this for the gates to shut on the future – in working class culture when the manual giving of labour power represents both a freedom, election and transcendence, and a precise insertion into a system of exploitation and oppression for working class people (Willis 1977, p.120).*
>
> *In this text, therefore, we find a complex interweaving of: (i) the worldview of 'the lads', empathetically portrayed to reveal skills that many observers might fail to notice; (ii) the structures of the school (discussed in some detail in the book, but only touched on here); (iii) the lads' drawing on and reworking of the structures of working class culture; and (iv) the system reproduction of manual working class labour. It is not difficult to see how, from this core set of analyses, one might also address questions such as how all this links with the earlier socialisation experiences of 'the lads', how they view the area in which they live, and how, in detail, they behave in a given delinquent episode.*
>
> *A further empirical example, which links more directly with the earlier part of this paper, would be to reconsider the striking Gardenia-Stonewall contrast of the 1970's through the eyes of structuration theory and the 'duality of structure.' Such an analysis would include features such as:*

(i) the way in which the council's housing allocation system was understood and responded to by potential tenants trying to relate their own circumstances, aspirations and cultural understandings to the official rules, and to the interpretations of official rules made by housing officials (sometimes this interaction could have surprising results: see the example given from another Sheffield estate in Bottoms and Wiles 1992, p.27; see also, for Gardenia and Stonewall, Xanthos 1981); also the system consequences of such understandings and interactions;

(ii) the way in which residents on Gardenia responded to the negative reputation of the area (remembering that signification is one of the dimensions of the duality of structure: for empirical evidence on this issue see Xanthos 1981; Bottoms Mawby and Xanthos 1989).

The Gardenia-Stonewall example also directly links the preceding discussion to the concept of *power*, which was previously highlighted in the discussions of the work of Braithwaite and Gottfredson and Hirschi (for example, in relation to domestic violence and crimes arising from the political conflict in Northern Ireland). The concept of power was of direct relevance for some prospective tenants of Gardenia in the 1970's, who were unwilling to become residents of an estate that they perceived as potentially very damaging to the long-term future of their children, but who perceived themselves as having very little alternative given their economic resources and a weak formal position in the official housing allocation system: i.e. they were, as they saw it, 'forced' to accept a Gardenia tenancy. This example highlights the point, made in the summary statement of structuration theory, that constraints on individual action can be of various types (physical; power-based; structural); once again, however, it is important that the issues are seen through the eyes of all the relevant parties (e.g. the prospective tenants as well as the housing officials).

(b) Routines

As indicated above, it is probably the case that the concept of duality of structure is of most relevance to criminology in considering differences in *offender rates* between social groups (e.g. gender differences; differences between residents of different areas or countries; differences between school non-conformists and conformists). By contrast, the concept of *routines* seems at first sight most immediately relevant to explaining specific offences, and the places in which they are committed, and indeed earlier sections of this paper have commented on the importance of routines in this regard, both as regards victims and as regards offenders.

It is certainly of very great interest that, in a single decade (the 1980s), two different sub-fields of criminology (routines activities/opportunity theory; the Brantinghams' work in environmental criminology) should have been *separately* developed, but each with the concept of daily routine at its heart. These North American developments, however, took place completely independently of structuration theory, which was concurrently being elaborated by a leading British sociologist, and which gave to a number of apparently humdrum concepts ('social practices ordered across space and time'; 'the study of day-to-day life'; 'routines') a hitherto undreamt-of prominence in social theory.

In this intriguing convergence of interest around the theme of 'routines', there is obvious scope for further development, not least since those (different kinds of) criminologists who have emphasised routines have not done so with anything approaching Giddens's understanding of the centrality of routines to general social structures and to system reproduction. That understanding surely opens up the possibility of greatly enriched empirical investigations of routines, in a criminological context, in the future. It also shows us, however, that – contrary to first impressions – it would in fact be wrong to restrict the study of routines in criminology to the *offence commission* dimension of the subject. For Giddens, 'routinized practices are the prime expression of the duality of structure in respect of the continuity of social life' (Giddens 1984, p.282), and we have seen above that the duality of structure is potentially of great importance for the understanding of systematic differences in offender rates. It follows, then, that the systematic study of routines will need to become much more central to the *offender-focussed* criminology of the future, as well as to the study of crime commission.

Giddens has surely done social scientists (including criminologists) a great service by bringing the concept of routines into the heart of social theory. That is not to say, however, that his analysis of routines is beyond criticism. In the first place, Giddens's emphasis is always on routines as a way of fending off ontological insecurity. It is perfectly true that psychological research supports this proposition (those not allowed to settle into any kind of routine quickly become very insecure), but there is a danger that this particular emphasis will cause theorists to ignore alternative perspectives which highlight also the deadening, stultifying effect of repeated routines, at least in certain social contexts. This alternative perspective might well sometimes be criminologically relevant: for example, in the case of some crimes committed primarily for excitement against the background of a very routinised existence.

Secondly, John Urry (1991, p.168) complains that:

> *Giddens's conception of human activity is too routinized, too boring, and it is difficult in his framework to conceptualise pleasure-producing activities such as travel, leisure, holidaymaking ... and so on. Much social activity indeed involves semi-routines in which travel is an important element. What are involved are disruptions to everyday patterns that are nevertheless recognizably acceptable.*

Again, this is an important point with some potential criminological significance, e.g. as regards crimes on holiday, or football hooliganism.

Both these criticisms therefore seem to have some merit, but it is important to see that both could be accepted as qualifications to the basic view of routines in structuration theory. Neither criticism, in my judgement, affects the central conclusion that – in the wake of criminological developments concerning routines, and structuration theory's emphasis upon them – this is an area requiring much more systematic attention in mainstream criminology.

(c) The Centrality of Space and Time in Structuration Theory

Giddens is quite explicit about the importance of space-time issues in structuration theory:

> *[Most] social scientists have failed to construct their thinking around the modes in which social systems are constituted across time-space ... investigation of this issue is one main task imposed by the 'problem of order' as conceptualized in the theory of structuration. It is not a particular type or 'area' of social science which can be pursued or discarded at will. It is at the very heart of social theory, as interpreted through the notion of structuration, and should hence also be regarded as of very considerable importance for the conduct of empirical research in the social sciences* (Giddens 1984, p.110).

The reason for the centrality of space-time issues in structuration theory is not hard to discern. As we have seen, the structuration approach insists that the basic domain of study of the social sciences is 'social practices', rather than the experiences of individual actors or 'any form of societal totality'. If one is, as an 'objectivist' social scientist, studying (say) class structures or the educational system, it is easy to see how space/time issues can appear largely irrelevant; and the same would be true for a 'subjectivist' social scientist analysing, for example, the life histories of a group of prisoners. But if, in attempting to overcome the objectivist/subjectivist divide, one concentrates attention upon 'social practices', it is impossible to avoid space-time issues, *since social practices must necessarily take place in space and time*. Once again, Giddens is here moving social theory closer to everyday lived experience: in day-to-day life, time and space issues are of continual (sometimes of central) importance, and certainly much more central than they appear in most existing macro-social or micro-social research studies.

In developing this topic, I must straight away make clear that 'space', as a concept, is different from 'place' (see below on time-space distanciation). But, as most previous environmental criminology has been about place (or 'locale' as Giddens puts it)[29], and as place is included within space-time issues[30], let us begin with structuration theory's view of place.

Giddens (1984, pp.366–7) asserts that sociologists need to

learn from geographers the importance of a 'sense of place' in social interaction: and here he draws on the work of Allan Pred (1981, p.46), who has said that the 'situated' or 'contextual' character of social interaction can be adequately fleshed out empirically only if we grasp how the 'reproduction of particular cultural, economic and political institutions in time and space are continually bound up with the temporally and spatially specific actions, knowledge build-up and biographies of particular individuals'. Pursuing the argument, Giddens goes on:

> *The co-ordination of the daily paths of individuals within a given range of locales, plus what some researchers have called a 'sense of place', are concretized aspects of the duality of structure. The dialectic of 'daily path' and 'life path' is the way in which the continuity of the biography of the individual is expressed in, and also expresses, the continuity of institutional reproduction. A sense of place seems of major importance in the sustaining of ontological security precisely because it provides a psychological tie between the biography of the individual and the locales that are the settings of the time-space paths through which that individual moves (Giddens 1984, p.367).*

The empirical corollary of this view is, of course, that we need to research, in localised contexts, 'just how the life processes of individuals, including their daily, weekly and monthly paths, are linked to the *longue durée* of social institutions' (Urry 1991, p.163).

In research procedures of this sort, I would argue, are to be found the way to overcome the apparent disjunction to be found at the heart of Shaw and McKay's work (see the introduction to this paper), i.e. the disjunction between analyses of aggregate statistical data and individual life histories.

In a similar vein, we have noted in an earlier section the finding by Sherman *et al.* (1989) of a highly skewed spatial distribution of offence locations, even *within* high crime rate areas. From their data, Sherman *et al.* posed the following question (not answerable with the kind of research data they had available):

> *whether the routine activities of places, given their physical environment, are actually criminogenic. Do places vary in their capacity to help* **cause** *crime, or merely in their frequency of* **hosting** *crime that was going to occur some place inevitably, regardless of the specific place? Are the routine activities of hot spots criminogenic* **generators** *of crime, or merely more attractive* **receptors** *of crime? (Sherman et al. 1989, p.46, emphasis in original).*

From the point of view of structuration theory, of course, the terms in which this question is posed are unsatisfactory, because they reify the concept of place. But it is not difficult to see how research procedures could be developed which would allow one to unravel the ways in which the routines, daily practices and perceptions of individuals interact with the pre-existing structures associated with particular micro-locations (including symbolic structures), and how these matters might vary as between different micro-locations.

John Urry (1991) has criticised Giddens's writings on space-time issues, on the grounds that they do not fully comply with structuration theory's own basic presuppositions:

> *No real account is provided [by Giddens] as to how human agency is chronically implicated in the very structuring of time and space. They are viewed as essential to the context of human actions, but as such they channel or structure such actions from the outside. By contrast, I shall argue that time and space should be seen as produced and producing, as contested and determined and as symbolically represented and structurally organized (p.160).*

Inter alia, it is specifically argued by Urry that Giddens pays too little attention (i) to the ways in which aspects of space and place are, over time, structured, reproduced and re-structured by human agency; and (ii) to the symbolic meaning of place. These matters are certainly important for criminological research (see, for example, the several earlier remarks in this paper about the symbolism of place; see also the Gardenia study (Bottoms, Mawby and Xanthos 1989), for some understanding of the structuring and reproduction of a 'problem' housing estate). Whether Giddens's own writings on space-time are or are not open to criticism on the grounds suggested by Urry is perhaps debatable; but in any case there seems little doubt that structuration theory as such is readily able to encompass these points.

I indicated earlier that it was important to distinguish the concept of 'place' from that of 'space'. That is particularly so in the modern world, since recent communications technology has made it possible for people to interact with one another easily across vast distances (by telephone, fax, air travel etc); and, concomitantly, it has become easier to move capital around the globe, so increasing the effective independence of large multinational corporations from direct control and regulation by single nation states, and increasing also the power of these corporations to outmanoeuvre local labour resistances. These changes have had a number of important consequences for daily life in particular local areas, including (i) a decline in the importance of 'regional economies' in which economic, social and political relations in a particular region are distinctively shaped by specifically local industries or trades; and (ii) an increased 'disembedding' of social relations from specifically neighbourhood contexts, as mobility renders it possible to build affective ties across distances – and, often enough, on the basis of individual choice rather than (as often in the past) upon membership of an identifiable and well-understood traditional group such as an extended family or a church[31]. All these phenomena can be regarded as effects of the process referred to by Giddens as the radically increased time-space distanciation of the modern social world, i.e. 'the stretching of social systems across time-space'. There is, by now, a considerable literature on such matters (to take three very different examples, see e.g. Lash and Urry 1987, Harvey 1989, Giddens 1990), but it would stretch this paper beyond its limits to discuss such issues in any detail here. Suffice it to say, therefore: (i) that the issues very briefly touched upon here can have very profound consequences for social life – including crime and criminality – in specific local places, and that these consequences are researchable;[32] and (ii) that the issues mentioned are obviously crucially related to the centrality of time-space, and also of social practices, in the conceptual apparatus of structuration theory. For these reasons, those who wish, within a structuration framework, to carry out local studies seeking to integrate individual and areal levels of analysis on crime and criminality will find that, ultimately, they cannot afford to turn away from these much more macro-level processes.

(d) Unintended Consequences

According to Giddens (1984, pp.11–12), in the social sciences 'it is hard to exaggerate the importance of the unintended consequences of intentional conduct'. He goes on to identify three analytically separate research contexts in which the influence of unintended consequences can be discerned; each of these, as we shall see, is relevant to the kind of integrated research analysis (mixing individual and aggregate concerns) which is the subject of this paper.

The *first* of the three types is 'a pattern of unintended consequences initiated by a single event'. An amusing criminological example of this was the 1973 British statute that, for reasons of road safety, required motor-cycle riders to wear a protective helmet, but which had the unintended yet welcome consequence of a significant reduction in motorcycle theft, 'no doubt because few potential thieves have a helmet with them at the opportune time and place, and without one they run a high risk of being stopped by the police' (Clarke 1983, p.244). More complex versions of this type of 'single event' unintended consequence often arise in local neighbourhood contexts, and an interesting example occurred in the Five Towns crime prevention initiative studied by Liddle and Bottoms (1993). In one town, against a background of some previous lack of consultation between two different levels of local government (county and district), the county council planned, *inter alia*, a major crime prevention initiative focussed on one specific housing area. Unconnected with these events, the local newspaper published an article about crime in part of the relevant housing area, entitled 'Flats of Fear'. Though the crime figures did not in fact really support the press's interpretation of the situation, the newspaper report had the unintended consequence of escalating friction between the county and district levels of government, leading to the district in effect vetoing a proposal for a particular course of action proposed by the county. Local politics the world over could multiply such stories; the important point, however, is that such events could potentially have consequences for local criminality, and therefore require examination when assessing the context of such criminality in specific areas. As regards structuration theory, the significant feature of this kind of unintended consequence is that it emphasises the knowledgeability of human agents, able to think reflexively about events that are occurring around them. Since the initiator(s) of a single event (in this case, those responsible for the newspaper story) often cannot know, in all respects, how their action will be received and reacted to by all relevant others, the scope for unintended consequences arising from single intended actions is huge.

The *second* type of unintended consequence occurs where, instead of a series of consequences being initiated by a single event, there is an aggregate pattern resulting from a complex of individual activities. An example given by Giddens (1984, p.10) is as follows:

> *A pattern of ethnic segregation might develop, without any of those involved intending this to happen, in the following way, which can be illustrated by analogy. Imagine a chessboard which has a set of 5-pence pieces and a set of 10-pence pieces. These are distributed randomly on the board, as individuals might be in an urban area. It is presumed that, while they feel no hostility towards the other group, the members of each group do not want to live in a neighbourhood where they are ethnically in a minority. On the chessboard each piece is moved around until it is in such a position that at least 50 per cent of the adjoining pieces are of the same type. The result is a pattern of extreme segregation. The 10-pence pieces end up as a sort of ghetto in the midst of the 5-pence pieces. The 'composition effect' is an outcome of an aggregate of acts – whether those of moving pieces on the board or those of agents in a housing market – each of which is intentionally carried out. But the eventual outcome is neither intended nor desired by anyone. It is, as it were, everyone's doing and no one's (Giddens 1984, p.10).*

It is possible to show (see Taub *et al.* 1984) that the 'tipping' of housing areas – for example, from low-crime to high-crime, as happened in Gardenia in the 1940s – often follows similar patterns of aggregate individual decisions producing unintended consequences. In a situation of potential 'tipping', it might seem rational for any given individual or family to try to leave the area as soon as possible; but an aggregate of such individual decisions might (depending upon other surrounding circumstances) actually accelerate the tipping process, since they will be perceived by relevant others as confirming the area's accelerating decline.

It is for precisely these reasons, as Taub *et al.* show very clearly, that corporate actors committed to a local area (such as a university, a hospital or a residents' or retailers' association) are much better placed than individuals ever can be to halt tipping processes. Corporate actors can achieve this because they may be able to influence the way individual residents take their 'stay or leave' decisions, in a way that no single other resident could reasonably do. Perhaps, for example, a corporate actor could put money into an area and promote various initiatives to make people feel safer in public space (as the University of Chicago did in the Hyde Park area of that city); or perhaps (as might be the case with residents' or retailers' associations) the corporate actor could give individuals the courage and support to act in pursuance of collective rather than individual goals.

Given the apparent centrality of housing processes in the creation of offender rates in local areas (see earlier section of this paper), it is not hard to see how this kind of analysis of unintended consequence might be of great criminological importance.

The *third* type of unintended consequence concerns unintended system reproduction. We have already seen an example of this in Willis's study: an unintended consequence of the actions of 'the lads' is that they help to reproduce the class structure. Of course, functionalist sociologists had also previously analysed this kind of social consequence, with their talk of 'latent functions' and so on; but Giddens is at pains to distance structuration theory in this regard from what he sees as functionalists'"reified", "quasi-biological" and teleological references to functions, dysfunctions and system needs' (Bryant and Jary 1991, p.8; see also Giddens 1984, pp.14, 294f). Rather, structuration theory, as always, can conceptualise system reproduction as occurring only through the actions of knowledgeable human subjects. However, in the specific case of unintended system reproduction, it might be the largely routinised character of social practices, and the prominence of practical rather than discursive consciousness in daily life, that may especially promote the relevant unintended consequences.

The examples given under all the above three types of unintended consequences (the Five Towns 'single event'; aggregate individual decisions in housing market contexts; the Willis example of unintended system reproduction) should sufficiently indicate the considerable potential importance of this concept for criminologists interested in integrating individual and aggregate approaches to the study of crime.

Concluding Remarks: Pointers for Future Criminological Work

To conclude this essay, I shall offer a few brief pointers as to how the structuration theory approach might enrich future criminological work. I shall mention just three topics in this regard: *first*, the relevance of structuration theory for empirical research; *secondly*, its potential relevance as regards the 'social disorganisation' debate; and *thirdly*, its relevance for integrating work on *crimes* and on *offenders* into an integrated overall framework.

(a) Structuration Theory and Empirical Research

Gregson (1989) has argued that structuration theory is not particularly relevant to empirical researchers; it operates, she claims, at too high a level of abstraction to be of much use in concrete research; and in any case, since its concern is primarily ontological, 'to transfer structurationist concepts directly into research analysis is misconceived' (p.246). These criticisms are mostly not accepted by Giddens (1989, p.293ff).

I do not wish here to enter into the details of the debate between Gregson and Giddens. I would however agree with Gregson that Giddens's (1984, ch.6) chapter on empirical research in *The Constitution of Society* is not of much direct assistance to those proposing to conduct empirical research; but then it seems a little hard to expect a major social theorist, who does not conduct empirical research, to provide such guidance. On the other hand, Gregson seems mistaken in arguing that because Giddens's concerns are ontological, they are essentially irrelevant for social research: for example, structuration theory's emphasis on *social practices*, which is absolutely central to its ontological claims, also surely provides a clear pointer for the empirical researcher to consider certain kinds of observation or certain kinds of interview question, as he/she plans a research strategy for a particular empirical project.

To elaborate this point: the empirical researcher, I believe, cannot simply 'read off' from structuration theory a particular set of empirical concerns or strategies. However, a thorough understanding of the world-view presented by structuration theory should sensitise the researcher to particular issues which are capable of empirical analysis in a specific context. It is precisely for this reason that I have highlighted above four particular aspects of structuration theory (duality of structure and constraint; routines; unintended consequences; and space-time issues, including the contextual understanding of place and time-space distanciation); for each of these aspects of the theory is, in my view, capable of sensitive translation into empirical research contexts. Certainly, for example, I can see ways in which the Gardenia-Stonewall study could have been empirically enriched had the researchers been fully aware of theoretical apparatus of structuration theory at the appropriate time. Equally, it is not hard to see that most existing criminal career research in criminology has taken the four highlighted issues to heart to only a very limited extent (if at all). These are, therefore, issues for a future research agenda as we seek more fully to integrate criminological analyses of individual acts and careers, on the one hand, and the areal dimensions of crime, on the other.

(b) Social Disorganisation

Since the days of Shaw and McKay, criminology has had a long struggle with the concept of 'social disorganisation' (for a review, see Bursik 1988). Many recent writers have accepted Kornhauser's (1978, p.63) definition of the term: 'social disorganisation exists in the first instance when the structure and culture of a community are incapable of implementing and expressing the values of its own residents'. On the other hand, Robert Faris (1964), a member of the Chicago School of Sociology, provided a rather different definition: 'social disorganisation denotes a breach of social organisation ... it is any kind or degree of weakening or disruption of the pattern of social relations which constitutes a society, an association or any social system'.

It is not hard to see that, in Giddens's terms, Kornhauser's definition is focussed upon the *structures* of a given community, and upon a potential conflict of these structures with the surrounding local system of social relations. Faris's definition, on the other hand, is straightforwardly about aspects of the *social system*. It would not be appropriate here to elaborate these issues – that would need another paper – but it should be apparent, even from these brief remarks, that Giddens's distinction between *structure* and *system* provides at least a possible framework within which some of the issues and confusions of the social disorganisation debate might be clarified.

(c) Integrating Criminological Work on Crimes and Offenders

This paper has placed a good deal of emphasis on integrating criminological knowledge about crimes and about offenders; and Gottfredson and Hirschi's attempt to achieve this was seen as one of the major strengths of their theory. As a final comment, therefore, it seems appropriate to consider how the framework of structuration theory applies to this particular issue.

As we have seen, there is good evidence that offenders often think actively at potential crime sites – moving elsewhere, for example, if there are signs of occupancy or obvious surveillance when a burglary is contemplated. This evidence fits well, therefore, with structuration theory's emphasis on the knowledgeability and reflexivity of human subjects. At the same time, the evidence also suggests that offenders do not make fully rational choices about crime sites, being for example much more likely than not to confine their search patterns to geographical areas within their 'cognitive awareness space'. Again, this is congruent with the propositions of structuration theory about routines and about ontological security.

Crimes, however, are committed by individuals, and it is vital that, in a properly integrated theory, we shall be able coherently to link evidence about the committing of offences with evidence about such matters as criminal careers or aggregate patterns of offending (gender-differences, differences between countries, etc). It has been argued in a preceding section that the concept of the duality of structure is of special relevance to these broad offender-based issues; and that is true both as regards the overall structural principles of a given society (re gender roles, etc), and as regards the development of specific patterns of behaviour by individuals (cf. the discussion of the behaviour of 'the lads' in Willis's study). Hence, analysis of offenders' reflexivity at crime sites, and relatively routinised search patterns, ultimately has to be linked also to these broader social mechanisms concerning the individual's own biography and relevant structural principles, interactively understood through the duality of structure. But all the concepts in play here – reflexivity, routine, structural principles, duality of structure – are, as we have seen, clearly linked in structuration theory within an overall ontological framework. In a very real sense, therefore, a structuration theory approach can be seen to transcend the classicist-positivist tension at the heart of Gottfredson and Hirschi's theory[33].

Notes

[1] In this paper, I have hereafter adopted the language of 'synthesis' rather than 'eclecticism', because of the tendency of many scholars to apply the term 'eclectic' especially to 'systems that make no strenuous effort to create intellectual harmony between discrete elements' (Flew 1979, p.94).
[2] Of course, this remark should not be seen as in any way detracting from the enormous intellectual contribution and achievements of Shaw and McKay.
[3] Though it is not without its problems, especially in an era of 'green' issues, I have used this concept throughout this paper as the most convenient generic description of analyses of the relationship between place, crime and offending. Other such descriptions include 'the geography of crime', 'the ecology of crime', etc.
[4] Gottfredson and Hirschi are the more ambitious; they claim 'to explain all crime, at all times, and, for that matter, many forms of behavior that are not sanctioned by the state' (1990: 117). Braithwaite describes his theory as 'a general theory of crime' (1989: vii), but restricts his attention to economically advanced societies, and specifically excludes from the theory 'the small minority of criminal laws that are not consensually regarded as justified' (1989:3).
[5] This section of the paper draws heavily on my earlier discussion of Braithwaite's work in a conference organised by the Indonesian Society of Criminology (see Bottoms 1992: note however that in that text the author's footnotes have been editorially integrated into the text in parentheses, sometimes with confusing results).
[6] It is worth noting the subsequent empirical support for Braithwaite's propositions in Lawrence Sherman's (1992) overview of domestic violence policy experiments in the United States: 'arrest increases domestic violence among people who have nothing to lose, especially the unemployed; arrest deters domestic violence in cities with higher propositions of white and Hispanic suspects' (p.247).
[7] The concept of 'opportunity' is however itself a complex one. The concept can include, for example, the ready availability of potential criminal targets; the availability of adequate means to accomplish a particular crime; the absence of capable guardians or adequate surveillance; and so on. For a full discussion see Clarke (1983).
[8] Braithwaite's explanation focusses on 'a decline of interdependency and communitarianism and a progressive uncoupling of punishment and shaming' (p.106). The first of these points is widely accepted by many criminologists (including the Netherlands Ministry of Justice report referred to in the text); the second is much more controversial.
[9] It should be noted that one of Braithwaite's 'facts a theory must fit' is that 'crime is ... committed disproportionately by people ... who live in areas characterised by high residential mobility' (p.47). The author is apparently not aware that the evidence from the Sheffield study suggests a more complex relationship between crime, area and mobility (see Baldwin and Bottoms 1976, pp.169–71; Bottoms, Mawby and Xanthos 1989).
[10] See the comment by Lorna Smith (1989, p.16): 'despite disagreement over many aspects of domestic violence by various researchers, one of the few things about which there is almost universal agreement is that it escalates in frequency and intensity over time. Numerous studies have exploded the myth that serious injuries seldom occur or that weapons are seldom used. *If violence happens once it is likely to happen often*' (emphasis added).
[11] I should like to express my gratitude to Carl-Gunnar Janson for sharing with me his helpful unpublished summary of Gottfredson and Hirschi's argument: I have to some extent drawn on this in what follows.
[12] This view is actually highly questionable: Beccaria, for example, argued for the abolition of the death penalty, and contended that certainty of punishment was more important than severity of punishment in producing deterrence.
[13] Note, however, that Cromwell and his colleagues used a different (and wider) definition of 'opportunistic' than did Bennett and Wright – see Cromwell *et al.* (1991, p.48).

[14] Reflection on the socialisation potential of well-integrated religious communities might be helpful in understanding this point. Cf. also Giddens (1984, p.283): 'among the structural properties of social systems, structural principles [i.e. factors involved in the overall institutional alignment of a society or type of society] are particularly important, since they specify overall types of society'.

[15] Or indeed to some American sociological criminologists: see e.g. Matza (1969).

[16] This uses Bennett and Wright's (1984) definition of 'opportunist': see note 13 above.

[17] In the central box of *Figure 4*, a distinction is drawn by Wikström between, on the one hand, Cohen and Felson's familiar formulation (at the top of the box), which is seen as most appropriate for instrumental crimes such as theft, robbery and rape; and, on the other hand, expressive crimes such as assault and criminal damage which are thought to be more related to relationships, encounters and environments liable to provoke friction (see the foot of the box). See generally Wikström (1990, pp.21–24).

[18] Bottoms and Wiles (1992, p.33) also argued that Wikström's formulation paid too little attention to issues of design and spatial form.

[19] This is not an exact quotation from Wikström, but rather my paraphrase and elaboration of his very helpful formulation.

[20] 'Situational' here has a broad meaning, and not the specific 'opportunity-reduction' definition used by advocates of 'situational crime prevention' such as Clarke (1983).

[21] For example, because building societies treated mortgage applications by immigrants with some suspicion (p.30), and because the City Council operated a five-year waiting period before one could qualify for a council tenancy, even if housing need was otherwise established (p.24).

[22] The specific concept of 'housing classes' has subsequently proved controversial, and has been dropped by most writers – see e.g. Bottoms, Mawby and Xanthos (1989, p.75, note 43).

[23] It should be noted, for those unfamiliar with British social policy, that public housing has been much more extensively developed in Britain than in many countries. At the time of the analysis reported in Baldwin and Bottoms (1976), 64 (31%) of the 204 census enumeration districts in Sheffield consisted predominantly of public housing (p.108).

[24] Subsequently, however, there was some convergence between the two areas – but again this could be explained by housing market changes: see Bottoms, Claytor and Wiles (1992).

[25] See especially these authors' conclusion (ch.9) that three types of social and ecological pressures interactively determine overall patterns of change in urban neighbourhoods: namely (i) ecological facts, (ii) corporate and institutional decisions and (iii) decisions of individual neighbourhood residents.

[26] This refers to both (i) the kind of issues mentioned in Braithwaite's theory (stigmatization, blocking of social opportunities) and (ii) the possible longer-term influences on socialisation patterns created by chronic powerlessness of certain groups.

[27] This summary owes much to Giddens's own summary (1984, pp.281–284) of the 'aspects of structuration theory which impinge most generally upon problems of empirical research'; it also draws upon, and develops, the summary in Bottoms and Wiles (1992, pp.18–19).

[28] An analogy sometimes used by Giddens is that structure resembles language: on the merits of this analogy, see the essay by Thompson and the reply by Giddens in Held and Thompson (1989).

[29] Giddens's (1984, p.375) definition of 'locale' is 'a physical region involved as part of the setting of interaction, having definite boundaries which help to concentrate interaction in one way or another'. Urry (1991, p.172) prefers the concept of 'place', and argues that Giddens views what he calls locale as 'the context for action rather than as the outcome of action'.

[30] 'Time', incidentally, is a much-neglected topic in criminology, but should properly be of great importance within the field of environmental criminology. For an interesting study see Cohn (1991).

[31] See, in this connection, Giddens's (1990, p.102) extremely interesting (if

perhaps oversimplified) contrast between the main 'environments of trust' in pre-modern and in modern societies. In pre-modern societies, he suggests, these are: (i) kinship relations, (ii) the local community as a place, (iii) religious cosmologies, and (iv) tradition; in modern culture, they are (i) personal, intimate friendship relationships, (ii) abstract systems, and (iii) counterfactual thought.

[32] For a small-scale exploratory study in this vein, of a primarily ethnographic character, see Breed (1992).

[33] A number of the themes of this paper were first addressed in a joint chapter with Paul Wiles (Bottoms and Wiles 1992). The present elaboration of these themes is my own; but, as in all my writing on environmental criminology in recent years, this paper owes much to my continuing discussions, intellectual partnership and friendship with Paul Wiles.

References

Anderson, S., Grove Smith, C., Kinsey, R. & Wood, J. (1990). *The Edinburgh Crime Survey: First Report,* Edinburgh: Scottish Office Central Research Unit Papers.

Baldwin, J. & Bottoms, A.E. (1976). *The Urban Criminal,* London: Tavistock.

Balvig, F. (1988). *Delinquent and Not-Delinquent Youth: A Study on Self-Reported Delinquency among Youth in a Metropolitan Suburb in Denmark* (Kriminalistisk Instituts Stencilserie No.43), Copenhagen: Institute of Criminal Science, University of Copenhagen.

Bennett, T. & Wright, R. (1984). *Burglars on Burglary,* Aldershot: Gower.

Blumstein, A., Farrington, D.P. & Moitra, S. (1985). Delinquency careers: innocents, desisters and persisters, in M. Tonry and N. Morris (Eds.), *Crime and Justice: An Annual Review of Research,* vol.6, Chicago: University of Chicago Press.

Blumstein, A., Cohen, J. & Farrington, D.P. (1988a). Criminal career research: its value for criminology, *Criminology, 26, 1–36.*

Blumstein, A., Cohen, J. & Farrington, D.P. (1988b). Longitudinal and criminal career research: further clarifications, *Criminology, 26,* 57–74.

Bottoms, A.E. (1990). Crime prevention facing the 1990s *Policing and Society, 1,* 3–22.

Bottoms, A.E. (1992). Concluding reflections, in H. Strang and J. Vernon (Eds.) *International Trends in Crime: East meets West,* Australian Institute of Criminology Conference Proceedings Series No.12, Canberra: Australian Institute of Criminology.

Bottoms, A.E., Claytor, A. & Wiles, P. (1992). Housing markets and residential community crime careers: a case study from Sheffield, in D.J. Evans, N.R. Fyfe and D.T. Herbert (Eds.), *Crime, Policing and Place: Essays in Environmental Criminology,* London: Routledge.

Bottoms, A.E., Mawby, R.I. & Xanthos, P. (1989). A tale of two estates, in D. Downes (Ed.), *Crime and the City,* London: Macmillan.

Bottoms, A.E. & McClintock, F.H. (1973). *Criminals Coming of Age,*London: Heinemann Educational Books.

Bottoms, A.E. & Wiles, P. (1986). Housing tenure and residential community crime careers in Britain, in A.J. Reiss and M. Tonry (Eds.), *Communities and Crime,* Chicago: University of Chicago Press.

Bottoms, A.E. & Wiles, P. (1992). 'Explanations of crime and place, in D.J. Evans, N.R. Fyfe and D.T. Herbert (Eds.), *Crime,*

Policing and Place: Essays in Environmental Criminology, London: Routledge.

Braithwaite, J. (1989). *Crime, Shame and Reintegration*, Cambridge: Cambridge University Press.

Brantingham, P.J. & Brantingham, P.L. (1984). *Patterns in Crime*, New York: Macmillan.

Brantingham, P.L. & Brantingham, P.J. (1981). Notes on the geometry of crime, in P.J. Brantingham and P.L. Brantingham (Eds.), *Environmental Criminology*, Beverly Hills, California: Sage Publications.

Breed, K. (1992). Fear, Censure and Crime: Social Aspects of Modernity, unpublished Ph.D. thesis, University of Cambridge.

Bryant, C.G.A. & Jary, D. (Eds.) (1991). *Giddens' Theory of Structuration: A Critical Appreciation*, London: Routledge.

Bursik, R.J. (1988). Social disorganisation and theories of crime and delinquency: problems and prospects, *Criminology, 26*, 519–551.

Clark, J., Modgil, C. & Modgil, S. (1990). *Anthony Giddens: Consensus and Controversy*, London: Falmer Press.

Clarke, R.V.G. (1983). Situational crime prevention: its theoretical basis and practical scope, in M. Tonry and N. Morris (Eds.) *Crime and Justice: An Annual Review of Research*, vol.4, Chicago: Chicago University Press.

Cohen, I. (1989). *Structuration Theory: Anthony Giddens and the Constitution of Social Life*, London: Macmillan.

Cohen, L.E. & Felson, M. (1979). Social change and crime rate trends: a routine activities approach, *American Sociological Review, 44*, 588–608.

Cohn, E. (1991). The Effects of Weather and Temporal Variables on Calls for Police Time, unpublished Ph.D. thesis, University of Cambridge.

Craib, I. (1992). *Anthony Giddens*, London: Routledge.

Cressey, D. (1964). *Delinquency, Crime and Differential Association*, The Hague: Martinus Nijhoff.

Cromwell, P.F., Olson, J.N. & Avary D'A.W. (1991). *Breaking and Entering: An Ethnographic Analysis of Burglary*, Newbury Park, California: Sage.

Faris, R.E.L. (1964). Social disorganisation, in J. Gould and W.L. Kolb (Eds.) *A Dictionary of the Social Sciences*, London: Tavistock Publications.

Farrington, D.P. (1987). Early precursors of frequent offending, in J.Q. Wilson and G.C. Loury (Eds.), *From Children to Citizens, Volume III: Families, Schools and Delinquency Prevention*, New York: Springer-Verlag.

Farrington, D.P. (1992). Criminal career research: lessons for crime prevention, *Studies on Crime and Crime Prevention: Annual Review*, vol.1, Stockholm: Scandinavian University Press.

Finestone, H. (1976). The delinquent and society: the Shaw and

McKay tradition, in J.F. Short, Jr. (Ed.) *Delinquency, Crime and Society*, Chicago: University of Chicago Press.

Flew, A. (Ed.) (1979). *A Dictionary of Philosophy*, New York: St. Martin's Press.

Giddens, A. (1976). *New Rules of Sociological Method*, London: Hutchinson.

Giddens, A. (1984). *The Constitution of Society*, Cambridge: Polity Press.

Giddens, A. (1989). A reply to my critics in D. Held and J.B. Thompson (Eds.), *Social Theory of Modern Societies: Anthony Giddens and His Critics*, Cambridge: Cambridge University Press.

Giddens, A. (1990). *The Consequences of Modernity*, Cambridge, Polity Press.

Giddens, A. (1991). Structuration theory: past, present and future, in C.G.A. Bryant and D. Jary (Eds.), *Giddens' Theory of Structuration: A Critical Appreciation*, London: Routledge.

Gottfredson, M.R. & Hirschi, T. (1990). *A General Theory of Crime*, Stanford: Stanford University Press.

Gregson, N. (1989). On the (ir)relevance of structuration theory to empirical research, in D. Held and J.B. Thompson (Eds.) *Social Theory of Modern Societies: Anthony Giddens and His Critics*, Cambridge: Cambridge University Press.

Harvey, D. (1989). *The Condition of Postmodernity*, Oxford: Basil Blackwell.

Held, D. & Thompson, J.B. (1989). *Social Theory of Modern Societies: Anthony Giddens and His Critics*, Cambridge: Cambridge University Press.

Home Office (1985). Criminal careers of those born in 1953, 1958 and 1963, *Home Office Statistical Bulletin*, No.7, London: Home Office.

Hope, T. & Foster, J. (1992). Conflicting forces: changing the dynamics of crime and community on a "problem" estate, *British Journal of Criminology, 32*, 488–504.

Hurrelmann, K. (1988). *Social Structure and Personality Development: The Individual as a Productive Processor of Reality*, Cambridge: Cambridge University Press.

Kornhauser, R.R. (1978). *Social Sources of Delinquency*, Chicago: University of Chicago Press.

Lash, S. & Urry, J. (1987). *The End of Organized Capitalism*, Cambridge: Polity Press.

Liddle, M. & Bottoms, A.E. (1993). *The Five Towns Crime Prevention Initiative: Key Findings and Implications from a Retrospective Research Analysis*, London: Home Office.

Matza, D. (1964). *Delinquency and Drift*, New York: John Wiley.

Matza, D. (1969). *Becoming Deviant*, Englewood Cliffs, New Jersey: Prentice Hall.

Merton, R.K. (1957). *Social Theory and Social Structure* (revised edition), Glencoe, Illinois: Free Press.

Morris, T. (1957). *The Criminal Area*, London: Routledge.

Netherlands Ministry of Justice (1985). *Society and Crime: A Policy Plan for the Netherlands*, The Hague: Ministerie van Justitie.

Painter, K. (1992). Different worlds: the spatial, temporal and social dimensions of female victimization, in D.J. Evans, Fyfe N.R. and D.T. Herbert (Eds.), *Crime and Policing: Essays in Environmental Criminology*, London: Routledge.

Pred, A. (1983). Structuration and place: on the becoming sense of place and structure of feeling *Journal for the Theory of Social Behavior*, *13*, 45–68.

Ramsay, M. (1989). *Downtown Drinkers: The Perceptions and Fears of the Public in a City Centre*, Home Office Crime Prevention Unit Paper No.19, London: Home Office.

Rengert, G. & Wasilchick, J. (1985). *Suburban Burglary*, Springfield, Illinois: Charles C. Thomas.

Rex, J. & Moore, R. (1967). *Race, Community and Conflict: A Study of Sparkbrook*, London: Oxford University Press.

Shaw, C.R. (1930). *The Jack Roller*, Chicago: University of Chicago Press.

Shaw, C.R. & McKay, H.D. (1942). *Juvenile Delinquency and Urban Areas*, Chicago: University of Chicago Press.

Sherman, L.W. (1992). *Policing Domestic Violence: Experiments and Dilemmas*, New York: Free Press.

Sherman, L.W., Gartin, P.R. & Buerger, M.E. (1989). Hot spots of predatory crime: routine activities and the criminology of place, *Criminology*, *27*, 27–55.

Smith, L. (1989). *Domestic Violence: An Overview of the Literature*, Home Office Research Study No.107, London: H.M.S.O.

Taub, R., Taylor, D.G. & Dunham, J.D. (1984). *Paths of Neighborhood Change*, Chicago: University of Chicago Press.

Taylor, I., Walton, P. & Young, J. (1973). *The New Criminology*, London: Routledge.

Urry, J. (1986). Book review of *The Constitution of Society* by Anthony Giddens, *Sociological Review*, *34*, 434–437.

Urry, J. (1991). Time and space in 'Giddens' social theory, in C.G.A. Bryant and D. Jary (Eds.) *Giddens' Theory of Structuration: A Critical Appreciation*, London Routledge.

Weatherburn, D. (1993). On the quest for a general theory of crime, *Australian and New Zealand Journal of Criminology*, *26*, 35–46.

Wikström, P-O.H. (1990). Delinquency and urban structure, in P-O.H. Wikström (Ed.) *Crime and Measures against Crime in the City*, Stockholm: National Council for Crime Prevention.

Wikström, P-O.H. (1991). *Urban Crime, Criminals and Victims: The Swedish Experience in an Anglo-American Comparative Perspective*, New York: Springer-Verlag.

Willis, P. (1977). *Learning to Labour*, Farnborough: Saxon House.

Xanthos, P. (1981). Crime, the Housing Market, and Reputation: A Study of Some Local Authority Estates in Sheffield, unpublished Ph.D. thesis, University of Sheffield.

An Ecological Model of Socialisation in Explaining Offending

by Peter L. Martens

Background

The family occupies a central position in the lives of children and adolescents. The family's way of life, the problems confronting parents at work and during their leisure, and parents' personal problems, all leave their mark on the child's behaviour. The social situation of the family provides the foundations of children's upbringing and goes quite a long way towards explaining their intellectual and social accomplishments. By the same token, the situation of the family can, up to a point, account for antisocial and criminal behaviour on the part of children and adolescents.

Criminological research into criminal behaviour among children and adolescents, using a socialisation perspective, is a part of traditional socialisation research. Criminology, then, has at its service a relatively advanced and theoretically based conceptual apparatus for both individual processes and family relations. This also gives it access to proven instruments for measuring different aspects of individual characteristics and inter-personal processes with the family. On the other hand, traditional socialisation research lacks a more detailed conceptual apparatus for describing the environment in which the family lives. The social position of the parents in the community - their socio-economic status, in other words – has been made to serve as an indicator of, among other things, standard of housing and residential environment.

A family lives in a geographically defined area. The *field of activity* of the members of the family (Janson, 1968, p. 227) centres on the home. For parents, the *field of activity* also centres on the workplace, while for children it centres on the day nursery, school, leisure centre etc. The housing area especially plays a central social and psychological role in the life of a family. The neighbourhood can be termed one of the foundations of everyday family life. The socio-ecological tradition of criminology specialises in describing similarities and dissimilarities between communities in terms of different characteristics which can conceivably influence criminal behaviour among the inhabitants. In this tradition the communities are often described in sweeping terms, using data for example from official statistics of population structure (age, sex, percentage of foreign birth, percentage of single parents and so on), in- and out-migration to and from the area (residential mobility), social welfare inputs (the percentage on social security), crime rate and so on. Obviously, community descriptions of this kind supply important information about fundamental social conditions in the communities, but they tell us absolutely nothing about who becomes or does not become a criminal. Nor is this the purpose of the traditional ecological approach in criminology, which is aimed rather at trying to identify the factors in neighbourhoods (or whatever geographical unit one is using) which generate criminal behaviour.

Traditional socialisation research, then, can be said to have equipped criminology with a well-developed conceptual apparatus for describing the psychological and socio-psychological processes within the family. But socialisation research lacks instruments for visualising the housing conditions of the family. Putting it drastically, research into the importance of the family for children's and adolescents' criminal behaviour at individual level lacks a socio-ecological context. The socio-ecological approach in criminology has the important task of describing geographically defined areas in which people live and of accounting for various ecological processes which contribute (independently) towards the development of criminal behaviour among residents of the area. But the socio-ecological perspective cannot accommodate the social life of communities. It is a perspective in which people living in the areas investigated are not given a hearing.

What is needed in order to integrate the individual and socio-ecological perspectives is a frame of reference for the socialisation process which is capable of accommodating both perspectives. Here I believe that Bronfenbrenner's *ecology of human development* frame of reference can be of great assistance (Bronfenbrenner, 1980). The ecology of human development socialisation model is based on the notion of social networks. Adults living in a municipality or neighbourhood develop a social network consisting of contact with next-of-kin (e.g. parents and siblings), other people at work or other people in the neighbourhood. Children develop social networks in their everyday dealings with co-evals and adults in the neighbourhood, at the day nursery, at school, at the leisure centre and so on. These networks can be expected to influence children's and young people's social development and adjustment over and above the influence of the family. Neighbourhoods can differ with respect to the occurrence of social problems and services for parents, such as child supervision. Family policy in different communities can show varying degrees of responsiveness to the needs of parents and children. Even if a community has high political ambitions of giving parents the support they need, the structure of the area may, e.g. due to palpable instability (disorganisation), preclude a realisation of the political/ideological intentions. Bronfenbrenner's ecology of human development provides a theoretical frame of reference which takes in all the aspects or levels I have now mentioned. Before going any further on the subject of the ecology of human development perspective and how it can account for antisocial and criminal behaviour among children and adolescents, however, I propose to summarise a number of important theoretical viewpoints in this context, from both traditional socialisation research and from socio-ecological research.

Traditional Socialisation Research

The situation of the family can be characterised at various levels or from various viewpoints, *viz sociological*, *socio-psychological* and *psychological*. The sociological view observes the importance of the family's social status and structure – social background factors, in other words – as an influence, say, on children's behaviour. The socio-psychological viewpoint discusses the character of personal contact within the family and what it means for the child's development, i.e. socialisation factors. The psychological approach deals with individual characteristics of children, e.g. personality character, intelligence and school achievement.

Sociological Factors

The sociological factors referred to in literature on this subject as important for explaining juvenile crime are the socio-economic status of the family, family size and broken families. Family ethnic background is also included.

Socio-economic status

The socio-economic status of the family is the sociological variable to which criminological research has referred most when seeking to explain deviant and criminal behaviour among young people. The consensus view is that a powerful negative connection exists between social class and criminal behaviour where young people are concerned, with working-class youngsters being more predisposed to crime than young people from the middle class. The results of empirical studies in this field are not unambiguous.

Some studies point to significant relations in the above sense, while others have not revealed any such relations worth mentioning. There is a pattern to be discerned in the research findings. Studies measuring crime in terms of *reported offences* have yielded significant differences between social classes, with a correlation between r= -0.20 and -0.30 at most, while those based on *self-reported* crime have not yielded any appreciable class differences. The debate occurring in criminology on differences in findings concerning the connection between social class and crime, e.g. by Tittle et al. (1978) and Braithwaite (1981), has been summarised in Swedish by Wikström (1983). Tittle and Meier (1990), reviewing research on the SES/delinquency relationship published since 1977, have concluded that, no matter whether the data used are official or self-reported, no pervasive relationship exists. "*It appears, on the basis of the recent evidence, that SES may not be nearly so important as many seem to think (Braithwaite, 1981; Kleck, 1982; Nettler, 1978, 1985), but it may well be more important than others have concluded (Tittle et al, 1978). But the circumstances under which individual SES plays a role in delinquency production remain elusive. Sometimes SES does appear to predict delinquency; most of the time it does not. ... One response to this reality is to continue to try to find conditions under which SES predicts delinquency. ... A second approach ... would reconceptualize the problem in terms of interactions among SES and other variables that ultimately have import for delinquency. ... A third strategy would be to rethink the whole idea of SES and its potential effects on delinquency. After all, SES, no matter how conceptualized, is no more than a configurative concept, presumably amalgamating many specific attributes (Loeber & Dishion, 1983)." (Tittle & Meier, 1990, p. 294).*

Family size

Among the more stable results of criminological research are those relating to connections between family size and criminal behaviour among children and adolescents. Studies have consistently shown a positive connection between family size and juvenile criminal tendencies. The larger the family, the greater is the risk of young people committing criminal acts (Gottfredson & Hirschi, 1990, p. 102). This is partly explained by the weakening of social control in large families. As the number of children in the family increases, parents have less chance of devoting attention to each child individually. Children can take relatively great liberties in their social relations outside the family, and are therefore more liable to get into bad company and commit crimes. Even if the relationships have been found to be statistically significant, they tend to be less than r=0.20.

Broken families

Families are broken by divorce, illness, bereavement etc. One fundamental thesis concerning the connection between broken families and criminal behaviour among children is that the break-up of a family aggravates the risk of deviant and criminal behaviour among the children (Loeber & Stouthamer-Loeber, 1986). This result recurs in the majority of surveys comparing criminality among children and adolescents from, respectively, broken and complete families, Swedish studies included (Martens, 1992). However, the strength of the observed relationships are moderate (RIOC being between 0.10 to 0.30).

Immigrant background

The Nordic countries do not yet have any systematic criminological research into criminal behaviour among young persons with immigrant backgrounds. The ethnic minorities discussed by American criminological research do not really correspond to the immigrant concept employed by Western European and Swedish immigrant research. One widespread view in Western European research literature in this field is that young persons with immigrant backgrounds have a higher crime rate than youngsters from the majority population (Sveri, 1966; Sveri, 1973, 1980, 1987; Suikkila, 1983; Bundeskriminalamt, 1989; Loll & Friedrichs, 1983; Walter, 1987; Killias, 1989; Junger, 1989, 1990; Martens, 1990, 1992).

However, looking at results from studies using self-report measures of crime, we find only slight differences between immigrant and native boys (Junger, 1990; Martens, 1992). In a study of children in the ninth grade in Stockholm, boys with an *immigrant background* (with at least one parent born in a foreign country) were found to have a higher participation rate only in acts of violence than boys with a Swedish background. Among girls, those with an immigrant background had a considerably lower crime participation rate than the native girls (Martens, 1992). A marked difference was found, however, between boys *born in a foreign country* and boys born in Sweden: the former had a higher participation rate than the latter, in particular regarding more serious offences like assault, burglary and car theft (Martens, 1992).

Socio-psychological Factors

The socio-psychological aspect of the family characterises the parent-child relationship. In socialisation research, various concepts have been developed for describing different aspects of this relationship. They refer to parents' emotional relationship to the child, their control of the child and their general treatment of the child (patterns of upbringing).

Emotional relation

One basic prerequisite of "successful" socialisation of the family is for parents to relate well to the child emotionally. The parent-child relationship must be *affectionate*, which among other things means the parents being responsive to children's needs and wishes in matters concerning the child and the family. Control theories speak here of "attachment to parents" (cf. Bahr, 1979). Hirschi (1969; ref.: Bahr, 1979, p. 621) maintain: "... *the more a child was attached to and identified with his parents the lower were his chances to delinquency ... this attachment tends to bind the child to parental expectations and therefore to the norm of the larger system.*"

Parental attachment also affects the parents' possibilities of controlling the child, especially when the child grows older. The closer the relationship, the better the communication between parents and child and, hence, the better informed the parents tend to be about the child's doings. Conversely, the more distant the relationship, the less informed the parents tend to be. When the relationship is close, and communication between the parties open, the parents receive the necessary information directly in their daily interaction with the child.

Control of the child

Parental control of the child's behaviour is fundamental in order for the child to learn the rules and norms prevailing in the community. Parental supervision, then, is an important precondition for the child to become self-controlling. Thus, through external control, internal control is developed in the child. Deficiencies in internal control can lead to various kinds of deviant behaviour.

Parental *monitoring* of the child's doings is an aspect of control which has proved to be especially important when accounting for deviant and criminal behaviour among young people (Snyder & Patterson, 1987; Martens, 1992). Parental knowledge of the child's whereabouts when he is not at home, the friends he goes around with and of what he does in his spare time (and together with his friends) becomes particularly important when the child begins looking for contacts outside the family.

Another aspect of control concerns the *demand* which parents make of their children, e.g. regarding homework, achievement in school or deadlines for coming home in the evening.

Snyder and Patterson (1987) maintain that the methods of control counteracting children's antisocial behaviour are characterised by

- parents being able to indicate clearly to the child which forms of behaviour are undesirable,
- parents reacting consistently when undesirable forms of behaviour occur,
- reactions not being unduly strict or harsh.

Similar thoughts are propounded by Gottfredson & Hirschi (1990, pp. 97–100). Loeber & Stouthamer-Loeber (1986) pay special attention to the risk associated with parental neglect of children: when the child is neglected by its parents, this aggravates the risk of deviant behaviour.

Children need a clearly structured existence, so as to be able to relate themselves to the world at large and develop an identity of their own. Parental control can be looked on as a way of helping the child to structure the world around it. Weak control can mean parents giving excessively vague clues to the rules and norms which apply. Excessively powerful control inhibits the child's own initiative and limits its prospects of satisfying its own needs. The possibilities of a child testing its skills and fulfilling its own ambitions can be restricted by rigid parental demands.

Patterns of upbringing

Parents can control a child in a variety of ways. Control can show various degrees of allowance for the child's needs and preferences. Most socialisation researchers have tried to characterise the parent-child relation in terms of control and affection as two basic dimensions (cf. Martens, 1976). Strong and weak control of the child, combined with – respectively – a chilly and affectionate parent-child relationship make it possible to characterise various methods of child education (see Maccoby & Martin, 1983).

Strong control combined with consideration for the child's needs and wishes (i.e. affection) is called an *authoritative* attitude to the child. It is the authoritative pattern which is considered to be the ideal parent-child relationship. An authoritative parent tends, according to Baumrind (1971), to make age-adequate demands of the child concerning mature behaviour, independence and clarity of communication. This parent respects the child's individuality and its capacity for coping with various situations. Maximum scope is then provided for the child's development of social ability and competence.

Strong control of the child combined with little or no allowance for its needs and wishes describes an *authoritarian* relation to the child. Control of the child takes place entirely on the parent's premisses. If the child's wishes differ from the parent's, the child has to give way. Authoritarian parental behaviour can, in its most extreme forms, lead to *physical maltreatment* of children (LaRose & Wolfe, 1987; Wolfe, 1987).

Parents are deemed *permissive* when they exercise weak control of the child and at the same time show a palpably considerate attitude to its needs and wishes.

Weak control of the child combined with lack of interest in catering to its needs implies parental *neglect* of the child.

Psycho-analytical theory (Cederblad, 1984, pp. 164–175) tells us that authoritarian parental behaviour results in children either becoming *cautious* and developing neurotic symptoms or *revolting* against the limits imposed by the norms of the world around them and against the authorities setting those limits. Children whose parents fail to define clear limits for them (permissiveness) or whose parents are very slack in matters of upbringing (neglect) develop *insufficient impulse control*. When contact between the child and its parents is very poor or superficial, there occurs *deficient identification* with the parents. This also happens if the relation is one of conflict and is full of aggressive feelings towards the parents. Lack of identification with the parent results in the child not properly internalising the external limits defined by parents in the form of feelings of shame and guilt. The small child then continues living by *the desire principle* as opposed to the reality principle. Later on in life too (as an adult), the child will want immediate satisfaction of its desires and will be incapable of deferring the gratification of its impulses.

Conflict management in the family

The members of the family are constantly coming up against everyday problems and annoyances of various kinds, both within the family and outside it. This can lead to stress both in the home and outside it. The stressors can be of a minor nature, such as incidents at work (quarrels with other employees) or they may be of a more serious character and precipitate personal crises, as for example in the case of unemployment and divorce. The favourable resolution of crises requires the members of the family to be equipped with a certain amount of problem-solving capacity and to have acquired strategies for sorting out problems.

Children and youngsters who do not have the opportunity of acquiring – and themselves practising – effective strategies for solving everyday problems are more liable to develop antisocial behaviour. Longitudinal studies have shown (see Snyder & Patterson, 1987) that conflict-ridden relations between parents and between the child and its parents co-vary with deviant behaviour among children. This seems to apply both to self-reported and officially reported deviant behaviour. Children who grow up in families with perpetual quarrels, conflicts and bad relationships between their parents are in the risk zone for becoming deviant and criminal when they grow older.

Similar results have been obtained in cross-sectional studies (see Snyder & Patterson, 1987). A low level of intimacy in the interaction of parents and children, lack of give and take in the solving of problems and a minimum of time for discussing various problems with the child are more often characteristics of parents with problem children than of other parents. Deviant families are distinguished by the more frequent occurrence of outbursts of temper, defence, reproach, an unfriendly tone of voice, less assumption of responsibility and no discussion of decisions in matters affecting the family. Both parents and child in the socially less well-adjusted family take it for granted that the opposite number has objections and level accusations against the others before an attempt has even been made to solve the problems.

A similar argument is stated by Loeber & Stouthamer-Loeber (1986) in "the conflict paradigm", which says that in families where the parents themselves and/or the parents and the child are in a perpetual state of conflict with each other, there is a great likelihood of the child developing deviant or criminal behaviour. In the course of their interaction, parents and children involve each other in escalated conflicts. The conflicts may be due to the child (who is disruptive and disobedient) and to the parents having difficulty in setting clear limits for the child. The parents are unable to correct the child by psychological means, and instead they resort to physical methods of punishment. Parents using physical punishment teach this method of resolving conflicts to their children, who later, in their turn, resort to physical violence as a means of resolving conflicts outside the home.

In extreme cases, the parent-child relationship can become so conflict-ridden that interaction breaks down and both sides develop aggressive feelings towards each other, which exacerbates the conflicts even further.

The relationship between the conflict rate and children's deviant behaviour tends in general to be rather high, with RIOC reaching about 0.60 according to calculations by Loeber and Stouthamer-Loeber (1986). According to Snyder and Patterson (1987), measures of family conflict-solving methods are capable of explaining, at most, 20 per cent of the variance in deviant juvenile conduct and delinquency, which indicates a medium-strength correlation.

Parents' criminal behaviour

In families where the parents are deviant or criminal or have positive attitudes to such actions, there is a relatively great likelihood of children also developing deviant or criminal behaviour. Loeber & Stouthamer-Loeber (1986) call this the deviant behaviours and attitudes paradigm. Parents themselves can be deviant in a variety of ways, may have a criminal record or have deviant attitudes which influence the child in the same direction. Children can learn deviant behaviour by witnessing the deviant behaviour of their parents (model learning). Even if the parents themselves are not deviant, through their attitudes towards criminal acts they can condone their child's behaviour or actually encourage the child to commit criminal offences.

Only a small number of studies have been made of the relationship between parental deviant behaviours or attitudes on the one hand and children's deviant behaviour on the other, and the results are anything but unequivocal. This makes it difficult to indicate the degree of correlation with any confidence.

Individual (psychological) Factors

Antisocial behaviour versus criminal behaviour

Criminological research lacks a developmental perspective on the individual and his actions. This, according to Farrington (1992), is because attention has been one-sidedly concentrated on criminal actions, which do not become apparent until later during childhood and achieve their peak during adolescence. Criminal actions are a form of antisocial behaviour. Antisocial behaviour develops already in early childhood or can be partly congenital. Under certain conditions, antisocial behaviour can develop into criminal behaviour. Criminal behaviour, then, has to be related to a wider context. According to Farrington (1992), it is important that we should in future try to obtain a more detailed insight into the connection between antisocial behaviour and criminal behaviour, and also into the development process undergone by criminal behaviour from early childhood to adult age. A child can commit a criminal offence spontaneously and never repeat it. But some children commit criminal offenses on several occasions, and a number of those children escalate their criminal activity by including elements of progressively more serious types of crime. The active criminal curtails his criminal career but can switch to other forms of antisocial behaviour instead of crime.

By saying that criminological research lacks a development perspective on the individual and his actions, we do not mean to imply that research into antisocial behaviour has been adequate in this respect, any more than the study of antisocial personality.

Early character disturbances

Antisocial behaviour among children and adults is partly based on early character disturbances. Cederblad (1984, pp. 164–167) distinguishes between disturbances of the ego functions (ego weakness) and disturbances of the superego functions (superego weakness) when describing early character disturbances.

Disturbances of the ego functions: the commonest disturbances of the ego functions are disrupted contact capacity, poor self-control, lack of perseverance, poor emotional stability and weak ego identity.

a. *Disturbed contact capacity* means that a person has difficulty in developing lasting and profound contacts with others, which is one of the main preconditions of social participation. There is a lack of empathy – that is, the capacity for sensing and understanding other people's feelings. Children with disturbances of this kind can give the impression, in their contacts with others, of being cold and calculating.
b. Children with *poor self-control* have little control of their impulses; this applies to both feelings and actions. Often they

vent their aggressive and sexual impulses in a manner which is not socially permitted, and in doing so they are liable to harm both others and themselves.

c. To be able to get on well and make progress in society, one must have the perseverance to pursue certain objectives, even in the face of setbacks. Thus the individual must be able to tolerate a certain degree of frustration. A child with an early character disturbance can have a low frustration tolerance or *lack of perseverance*.
d. Good relations with other people require the individual to be emotionally stable, i.e. to preserve a basic tone of feeling over a considerable period of time. Children with early character disturbances have *poor emotional stability*. They are often unstable and erratic in their feelings, fluctuating between aggression and calm, cheerfulness and misery, and so on.
e. Persons with *poor ego identity* have a poor view of their value in relation to others and do not have a holistic image of their personality.

Disturbances of the superego functions: The superego comprises internalised norms and values and is thus concerned with inner (moral) control. Cederblad (1984) distinguishes between two types of disturbance of the superego functions, namely disturbances of the formation of ideals (the ego ideal) and of the conscience functions.

a. The image a person has of the sort of person he or she wants to be is called *ideal formation*. This can be a question of personal characteristics such as being industrious, tolerant or committed, or of norms and values such as honesty, dependability, truthfulness and so on. Character-disturbed persons often have an unclear ideal formation or an asocial ego ideal.
b. Normally a person experiences feeling of guilt and shame when acting contrary to his ideal formation. Persons with disturbances of *functions of conscience* do not experience their antisocial acts as being antisocial. They do not have any feelings of shame or guilt when violating commonly accepted norms and values.

Persons with character disturbances have difficulty in putting up with monotony. They have a great need of variety, excitement and vivid sensory impressions. They can expose themselves to dangerous situations, for example by getting intoxicated on alcohol and other drugs which have a powerfully heightening effect on experience. Biochemical studies have shown that persons with character disturbances display low levels of repose for the stress hormones adrenalin and nonadrenalin. EEG examinations have shown character-disturbed persons to have a low level of brain activation. This can partly explain why such persons look for powerful sensory experiences. Within criminology, more and more interest has begun to be taken in biological factors underlying antisocial and criminal behaviour (see Tonry, Ohlin & Farrington, 1991).

Multivariate Analyses

Multiple regression analyses in which structural (sociological), socio-psychological and individual variables are introduced block by block to explain criminality among young people have shown the individual variables to have the highest explanatory value, followed by the socio-psychological variables. The structural variables have the lowest explanatory power (Loeber & Dishion, 1983; Snyder & Patterson, 1987; Loeber & Stouthamer-Loeber, 1986; Smith, 1991; Martens, 1992), accounting as they do for only a small percentage of the total variance in self-reported delinquency. Introducing socialisation variables increases the explained variance by between 10 or 20 per cent, and the introduction of individual variables, including association with delinquent peers, increases the explained variance by another 20 or 30 per cent.

Path analyses using structural variables as exogenous variables and socialisation variables as endogenous variables for explaining juvenile crime show the structural variables to affect criminal behaviour via the socialisation variables (Snyder & Patterson, 1987; Laub & Sampson, 1988; Martens 1992).

In connection with an extensive review of literature in this field, Snyder & Patterson (1987, p. 231) discussed findings with regard to the direct effect of socio-economic status on children's and adolescents' criminal behaviour and came to the conclusion that *"the association of social class and delinquency is mediated, in part, by the quality of the parenting or family interaction."*

Laub & Sampson (1988), who carried out a re-analysis of Glueck and Glueck's data in the form of a causal model with structural background data as exogenous variables and socialisation variables as endogenous variables for explaining serious crime, concluded (p. 375) that "*... none of the structural background factors had a significant, direct effect on delinquency. Instead, family processes mediated some 80 per cent of the effect of structural background on delinquency."*

Similar conclusions can be drawn from analyses of the influence of structural variables and socialisation variables on children's intellectual development and school achievement (Martens, 1982, 1984).

There seems to be a general pattern indicating that, when socio-economic status, family structure and socialisation in the family are included in multivariate analyses, it is the character of *interaction in the family* which best explains the social adjustment of children and adolescents.

Interaction effects between structural variables, between socialisation variables or between structural and socialisation variables have not been discussed that thoroughly in the research literature. A study of juveniles in Stockholm (Wikström, 1990) has revealed that (self-reported) delinquency is particularly high among boys from broken homes and where the family has an immigrant background (Martens, unpublished). McCord (1982 ref.: Loeb & Stouthamer-Loeber, 1986) found that split family in combination with parental conflict or parental delinquency increases the risk of juvenile delinquency. Weintraub and Gold (1991) have found that the interaction between the child's sex and parental monitoring and between parental monitoring and mother's affection both had an independent effect on the child's delinquent behaviour, with beta-weights in the region of 0.20. The interaction between sex and monitoring indicates that lack of monitoring is more closely related to delinquent behaviour for boys than for girls. The interaction between monitoring and affection shows that delinquency tends to be lower where monitoring and maternal affection are higher.

Some studies have focused upon *combinations of various "risk factors"* such as low income, broken homes, parental conflicts, parental rejection, parental criminality etc. It has been found that the more such risk factors are present in a family, the more likely it is that the child will later develop delinquent behaviour (Loeber & Stouthamer-Loeber, 1986; Snyder & Patterson, 1987). To quote Snyder and Patterson (1987, p. 233): *"In reviewing predictors of delinquency, Loeber and Dishion (1983) found that single family variables improved prediction over chance on the order of 20 percent, while the use of multiple family variables improved prediction by 50 to 80 percent over chance levels. Using parent criminality, poor parenting practices, low income, and large family size as risk factors, West and Farrington (1977) found that the probability of delinquency was about 25 percent for those adolescents with one risk factor, but was 70 percent for those with three risk factors."*

The multivariate analytical studies call attention to the fact that antisocial and delinquent behaviour among children and juveniles might develop differently in different combinations of structural variables and socialisation variables, i.e. in different *socialisation contexts*. Future research on the relationship between family socialisation and juvenile delinquency should focus more systematically upon family contexts associated with delinquent behaviour.

The Socio-ecological Perspective

Crime rates are higher in urban than in rural communities, and they tend to increase with the size of the urban community. Certain crimes occur more often in big cities than in smaller towns (Wikström, 1987, p. 8). The higher crime rate of big cities can be partly put down to life there being easier for social deviants, to the existence there of a soil in which criminal subcultures can take root, to the smaller risk of discovery, to the existence of variegated amusements, and to the greater pressure of temptation. The two commonest explanations for the higher crime rates of urban communities are *the structure of opportunities* and *weaker social control* (Wikström, 1987, pp. 10–11).

The criminality of urban communities can be explained in terms of the form of housing which predominates in those communities and the structure of their population (residentially speaking) as per the following model (Wikström, 1991, Chap. 7):

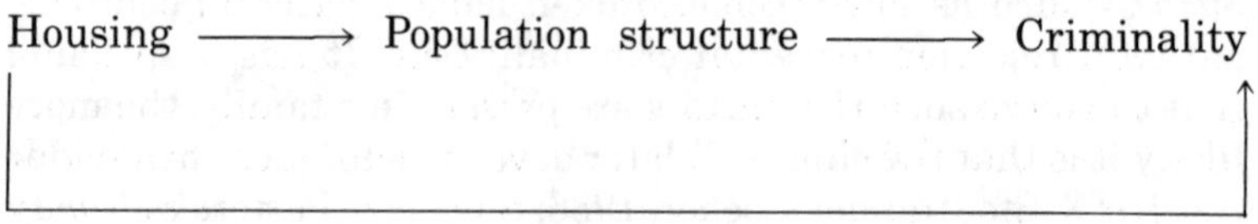

Housing ⟶ Population structure ⟶ Criminality

Different housing areas in, say, Stockholm, have different structures of population and housing development (multi-family dwellings, terrace houses or detached houses). Form of housing and type of tenure are related to socio-economic status. Living in public utility homes is associated with low socio-economic status. Owning one's home (tenant-owner flat, terrace house or detached house) is related to higher status. The preconditions of criminal behaviour among young persons depend partly on the type of area in which they live, the people who live there and what problems they have.

A housing area is more than just the sum total of the individual persons or homes etc. in it. Instead it is a context which, in addition to individual and socio-psychological factors, can influence the behaviour of its residents. Tonry, Ohlin and Farrington (1991, p. 24) have put forward the hypotheses that "*community structure has contextual effects on criminal behavior that are independent of individual characteristics and peer networks*" and that "*individual characteristics, family process, and life course transitions interact with community characteristics to explain patterns of criminal behavior over time.*"

Wikström (1991a) gives two possible reasons why population structure should be capable of influencing the local offender rate: "*(a) More crime-prone social groups are segregated to certain types of areas, and (b) social life and control in an area (area contextual effects) may influence the offending of the residents through situational inducements to offend or through long-term influences on the development of personality and modes of living (the latter only for youths).*" (Wikström, 1991, p. 180).

Different residential environments present different risks of young persons coming into contact with crime. The greater the number of people in the area with social problems or criminal records, the greater is the risk of young persons in the area coming into contact with deviant and criminal behaviour. Violence among young people varies from one community to another. Exposure to the threat of violence may change the individuals' behaviour: some people, in particularly elderly persons and women, become more cautious and avoid going out in the evenings (cf. Wikström, 1990, pp. 56–57). In European cities, the inner-city or downtown area attracts young people living in the suburbs. "*There is a lot that happens and a lot to do. Youth are also freed from adult control since the likelihood that they will come across family members, school teachers, neighbours etc. is quite small.*" *Furthermore,* "*Since there is a significant segregation in the city, e.g. between neighbourhoods dominated by immigrants and others, between affluent and less affluent neighbourhoods etc., this means that when youth commute to the central city they are confronted with youth from other types of neighbourhoods and with social backgrounds different to their own, which may cause friction and develop into fights and violence*". (Wikström, forthcoming)

In this socio-ecological approach, it is presumed that different communities offer preconditions for different living patterns among both adults and children, naturally within the frames of the total community (the macrosystem). This makes it conceivable that different communities can develop different specific socialisation patterns, as regards not only the family but the peer group and school as well. (Dolmén & Lindström, 1991)

An Ecological Socialisation Model

Like most other socialisation theories, Bronfenbrenner's ecology of human development focuses on the development of "normal" behaviour. Hence, the model does not specifically explain antisocial behaviour in children such as criminality. The model nevertheless has potentialities for shedding further light upon previously obtained relationships between family socialisation and criminal behaviour by adding an ecological dimension.

Bronfenbrenner developed his ecological approach as a response to the traditional socialisation research, which he conceived as being too narrow for describing children's daily life. He himself had actually contributed to the development of traditional socialisation research, specifically to the discussion of the relationship between social class and socialisation (Bronfenbrenner, 1958).

The Basic Idea

The child's *interaction* with the environment and the child's cognitive and emotional *development* are two important ingredients in Bronfenbrenner's ecological model. But the model is by no means the only theory to emphasise these two aspects. Most theories explaining social behaviour and behavioural change (e.g. social learning theories, psychoanalytic theories, symbolic interactionistic theories) point to the importance of the interaction between the child and its environment. Even the psychological theories of development, such as the theories of the Piagetian tradition, emphasise the interaction between the human organism and the environment in psychological growth.

However, what is specific to Bronfenbrenner is his emphasis on the child's development in its *everyday context*. Bronfenbrenner focuses less strongly than Piaget and the psychoanalytically oriented researchers on psychological processes during the child's development. He is more interested in with *whom* the child *interacts* in day-to-day situations, the character of these interactions and in what way persons outside the family can enhance or inhibit the quality of parent-child interaction. Hence, the focus is on the environment, or to put it in Bronfenbrenner's own words: "*the actual environments in which human beings live and grow*" (Bronfenbrenner, 1979, p. xiv). The environment consists both of the persons whom the child interacts with face-to-face in different social settings (such as the family, the day care centre, school etc.) and the settings indirectly influencing the child, such as the parents' workplace, the parents' social networks and the community. The inclusion of the environment as an important component in explaining individual behaviour makes Bronfenbrenner's approach *ecological*.

The Structure of the Model

The ecological environment is conceived as "*a nested arrangement of concentric structures, each contained within the next. These structures are referred to as the micro-, meso-, exo-, and macro-systems, ...*" (Bronfenbrenner, 1979, p. 22).

The microsystem

The developing person, the *child*, is the core of the system. *Microsystems* comprise the individual environments, or contexts, of which the child is a constituent part. These are the child's *immediate settings* which form the basis of its everyday life. It is the people with whom the developing person interacts on a face-to-face basis. A microsystem is made up of people, objects and events which either influence or are themselves influenced by the child.

Important concepts in the analysis of microsystems are the child's *relationship* with other members of the system, *activities*, and *roles*. Examples of such microsystems or settings are the family, the child's group at day nursery, its school class, any associations or clubs of which the child may be a member, the neighbourhood in which it lives, etc.

Children undergo continuous physiological, physical and psychological development. A child's relationship with its immediate environment changes constantly. Among other things, the interaction radius increases as the child develops. In consequence, the child's settings or microsystems will change accordingly and the child's relationships within any one system will be constantly modified. As the child is itself an active participant in a given setting, it will both shape and be shaped by the system, and the set of standards and values governing the interaction of the members of the system will become those of the child itself (internalisation). "*The individual child constructs the microsystem as much as he or she is shaped by it*" (Garbarino, 1982, p. 35).

The microsystem has an inhibitive effect on the development of the child if there are deficiencies in the system itself or if such deficiencies should arise. The child's microsystem becomes inhibiting if for some reason it is cut back or reduced – the number of persons making up the system may be diminished (by divorce, for example), there may be an imbalance in the mutual interaction between the members of the setting, interaction may display a high degree of (psychological) destructiveness, or there may be a combination of all three of these factors.

The mesosystem

> *A mesosystem comprises the interrelations among two or more settings in which the developing person actively participates (such as, for a child, the relations among home, school, and neighborhood peer group; for an adult, among family, work and social life).*
> (Bronfenbrenner, 1979, p. 25)

A child is a constituent part of several microsystems at once. The older the child grows the more its social environment expands, i.e. its "set" of microsystems tends to become more and more complex with age. The individual environments are perceived by the child itself as an integrated whole, and taken together comprise the *mesosystem*. "*Mesosystems are relationships between contexts or microsystems in which the developing person experiences reality*" (Garbarino, 1982, p. 23), although it is unlikely that the child actually draws any clear lines of demarcation between the various systems of which it is a part. To quote Andersson (1982, pp. 46–47, in Swedish):

"When the child leaves home and sets off for school, it is obviously unable to erase the experience of home but brings it along to school. Similarly, when the child returns home in the afternoon the experiences of the school day, whether good or bad, will not magically disappear but will remain with the child and may also have an impact on its situation at home."

The nature of the mesosystem will depend on the relationships between the various immediate settings of which the child is a member. A strongly knit mesosystem whose overall influence is beneficial for the child will also be beneficial for its general development. If, for example, school is seen by the family as something positive, the child will find it easier to adapt to academic standards and values, and this, in turn, will facilitate its school work and stimulate an appetite for academic achievement.

The exosystem

An exosystem refers to one or more settings that do not involve the developing person as an active participant, but in which events occur that affect, or are affected by, what happens in the setting containing the developing person.
(Bronfenbrenner, 1979, p. 25).

The exosystem lies outside the child 's immediate setting but is nevertheless the supporting framework of the child's day-to-day life. The child's immediate setting is coloured by the social and financial status of the parents and the conditions they experience at work, the economic, social and physical nature of the district in which the child lives, the ethnic make-up of the neighbourhood, and a number of other factors. The exosystem influences the child through the mesosystem and microsystem.

For example, a child may be inhibited in its association with its parents in that the parents are overworked or are encountering problems at work – when they come home from work they may be physically or mentally exhausted and simply too tired to involve themselves as much as they would like. The availability of support for the parents in their role as child rearers may vary considerably from one district to another.

"The landscaping of a residential district may help to make it easier or more difficult – both objectively and subjectively – for the parents to create the climate in which they would prefer their children to be brought up. The district may house resources, both formal and informal, which families, if they know them at all, may turn to their own advantage; or it may offer potential development opportunities and thus enable the families themselves to create the resources they consider necessary for their support. Likewise, the district may also display features actually tending to inhibit good parenting. In addition, local conditions may be experienced and exploited in many different ways depending on the background and general situation of the individual in question: some may regard them as

supportive, others may see them as more of an obstruction." (Andersson & Rydén, 1979, p. 2, in Swedish).

A child's development benefits from an exosystem making it easier for the parents to live up to their own expectations and ambitions as raisers of children. Such systems help to liberate resources, enabling parents to play an active role as social partners of their children.

The potential support available to parents depends among other things on how far the municipal authorities are prepared to provide backing for parents and children in the form of, for example, day nurseries, pre-schools and regular schools, leisure centres, youth centres, facilities for children with special needs etc.

The macrosystem

> *"The various microlevel, mesolevel and exolevel systems of a culture or sub-culture are an expression of its overall ideological, historical and political values and conditions, meaning that the conditions of one particular culture may appear to be relatively alike as compared with those of another. Their more general patterns are outlined in the macrosystem model."* (Andersson, 1982, p. 40, in Swedish).

Seen from the ecological perspective, it is the influence of the macrosystem on the microsystem which is the most relevant to socialisation – it is not the macrosystem in itself (i.e. the overall ideological "superstructure" of society) which is of importance, but rather the implications for the interaction between the child and the people with which it is involved at the micro-system level. It is, of course, difficult to make comparisons between macrosystems, i.e. between different cultures, for a single culture may sometimes comprise subcultures differing widely enough to affect conditions at the microlevel, e.g. the family. Sweden has developed into a multi-cultural society since the Second World War. It is reasonable to assume that a child from an immigrant group professing a faith other than the Christian/Protestant religion (of the Church of Sweden), and taking a different view from the average Swede of the relationship between men and women or between parents and their children, would develop a pattern of family interaction differing from that found in a "normal" Swedish household.

Figure 1 shows a schematic representation of the various ecological structures. The ecological structure of the child is defined by three concentric circles, the innermost showing the contexts in which the child is involved at any one time. These contexts represent the child's entire set of microsystems – parents, siblings, friends, the home, teacher, school class etc. - which together make up the mesosystem (the entire inner circle). The middle circle is the exosystem, which includes all those circumstances which have an indirect influence on the development of the child, such as professional or working status of the parents, local residential conditions, etc. The outer circle represents the macrosystem, which embraces public political attitudes to socio-political issues, family policies, and legislation on parenthood, children and the family etc.

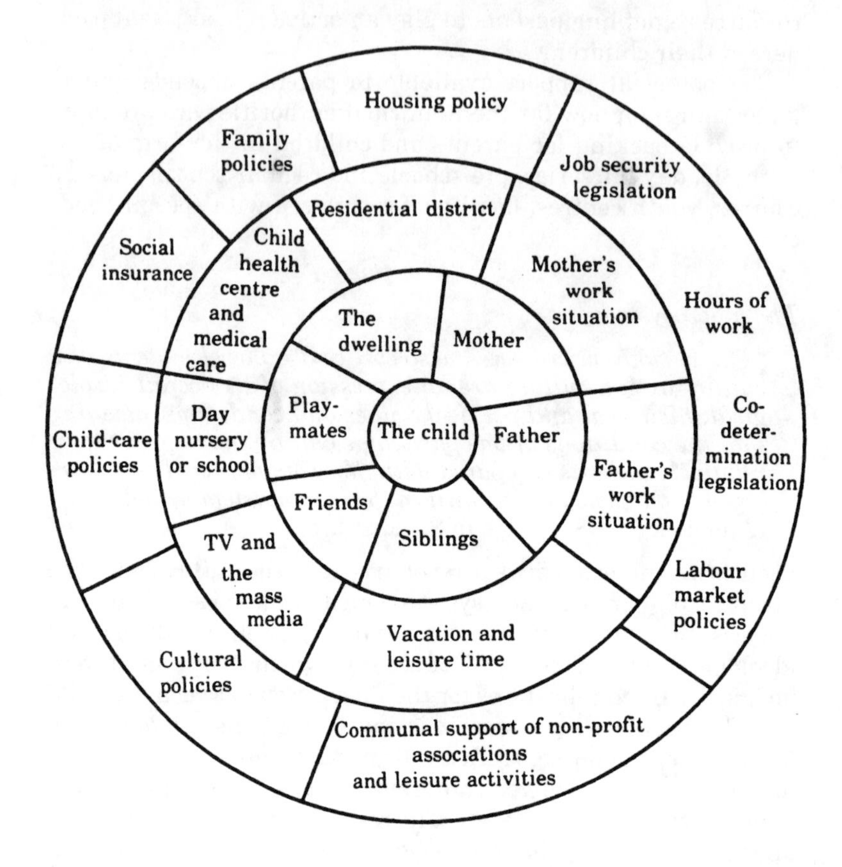

Figure 1. Schematic representation of the concepts of micro-, meso-, exo- and macrosystems. (Source: Sandquist, 1979, Figure 1).

A Word About Dynamics

The basic unit for analysing the microsystem is the *dyad*, which is a relationship between two parties – between the developing person, i.e. the child, and above all the child's parent or custodian. These two parties affect each other: the parent affects the child and the child affects the parent. When the child develops mentally and physically, the interaction between the two parties also changes character.

Bronfenbrenner distinguishes between three types of dyad: *observational* dyad, *joint activity* dyad and *primary* dyad.

The observational dyad is a more superficial form but is still very important, especially during early socialisation. Even if the child cannot communicate verbally itself, association with the mother in various everyday situations, with the mother at the same time explaining to the child what it can see or what is going on, is an important prerequisite of the child's conceptual development. In the theory of social learning, reference is made to learning by observation (Bandura and Walters, 1965). This occurs, for example, when the mother moves about the kitchen with the baby on her arm and prepares food while explaining to the child what she is doing.

In the joint activity dyad, the two parties do something together. Their actions dovetail in a wider pattern of action. When parent and child do something together in their leisure hours, the child's learning is stimulated and it is made more motivated for further achievement.

The joint activity dyad can be described in terms of *reciprocity*, *balance of power* and *emotional relation* between the parties.

Reciprocity means the two parties exerting reciprocal influence, with A influencing B and vice versa. The reciprocity of the relationship stimulates the child's social skills and its development of independence. Reciprocity provides a point of reference for the meaning of "independence of parents". It provides motivation for and a guarantee of continuity in the social dealings between the two parties. Reciprocity has a positive impact on learning by helping to increase the speed and complexity of learning.

In all social relations there is an inherent power relation. In the joint activity dyad, the child learns the meaning of power relationship as a social phenomenon. Here the child learns to cope with power relation differences in social interaction. When the child develops, then "normally" the balance of power between parent and child shifts gradually in the child's favour. As the child matures, both mentally and physically, the parent relinquishes his claims to power and allows the child to decide for itself how it is to act in various situations. In the course of its development, the child acquires progressively greater opportunities of exercising control over the situation. This, at all events, is what happens in an optimum learning and development situation.

In the interaction of the parties in a dyad, there also develops an emotional relationship between them. This emotional relationship can be mutually positive, mutually negative, mutually ambivalent or asymmetrical (with one party positive and the other negative). A mutual positive relation between the child and parent has a beneficial influence on the child's development. A positive reciprocal relationship between two parties influences the formation of a "primary dyad".

The primary dyad is highly reminiscent of the concepts of "primary group" and "significant others" – accepted terms of sociology and social psychology. The parties in the primary dyad are important to each other. They often think of each other. The dyad is characterised by the parties' strong positive feelings for each other. They also influence one another in various social contexts when they are not together. There are (emotional) forces in the primary dyad which play a very important part in motivating the developing party (the child) for learning and in steering the child in the course of its development, in both the presence and the absence of the adult. The dyad as a primary relation can be viewed as a development system with its own inherent forces which stimulates and stabilises various learning processes within the child.

The relation between two parties in a dyad can be indirectly influenced by the relation to a third party. Contact between a child and its mother is influenced, for example, by the mother's relations with her husband or the child's father. If the relationship between the mother and father is positive, this has a beneficial effect on mother-child contact. If, on the other hand, the relationship is conspicuously bad, this has a negative impact on contacts between mother and child. The same goes for the child-father dyad. A father having poor contact with the mother will have greater difficulty in establishing good contact with the child. This indirect influence is called the *second-order effect.*

Mother-child contact is also influenced by the mother's relation to other persons outside the family. Positive and supportive contact from various persons in the mother's surroundings, such as parents, siblings, friends and colleagues and bosses at work can facilitate the mother's relation to the child. If various supportive persons in the immediate surroundings are lacking, this can lead to various forms of stress in contact with the child and thus have a negative impact on the mother-child relation and, consequently, constrict the frames for the child's development. This reasoning is in line with the research work of Wahler (1990) and Wahler & Dumas (1986, 1989), specifically regarding their work on the social networks of troubled mothers. Mothers with constant coercion difficulties in their relationship with their children also tend to have other problems in their day-to-day lives. Mothers experiencing "chronic coercion difficulties" with their children tend to report "*significantly higher levels of depression ..., more coping problems in social exchanges with spouses and other adults ..., a greater number of daily crises in life management issues ..., and socioeconomic disadvantage ...*" (Wahler, 1990, p. 47).

The Ecology of Development and Offending

Even though the development-ecological frame of reference is above all concerned with discussing factors in the immediate setting which affect the normal behaviour of children and young persons, it is of course also potentially capable of explaining anti-social and criminal behaviour. With its heavy emphasis on the interaction of the child and its immediate setting in everyday situations, it offers a different perspective from that referred to by traditional socialisation research for interpreting the social background factors and the socio-psychological processes.

Structural Background Variables

One general criticism levelled at traditional socialisation research by the ecology of development approach is that social background variables are regarded as linear (and additive) variables. As a consequence of the mainly phenomenological approach of the ecology of human development, the background variables should be placed in an ecological context. This calls for a closer investigation of the settings referred to in the definitions of the background variables (Bronfenbrenner, 1980 p. 245). Bronfenbrenner, however, provides no satisfactory examples of how this is to be done, and he admits that such analyses can be very hard to carry out in practice.

Social class

As an example of contextual analysis of the social class of the family, Bronfenbrenner raises Kohn's theory, according to which it is parental employment or profession which leaves a certain imprint on children's socialisation. A person's occupation is more than a position in the social hierarchy. In his discussion of occupation as an indicator of social class, Bronfenbrenner refers to Kohn's theoretical argument that occupation reflects the complexity of work and the demands made by work on individual initiative (Kohn, 1969). Parents practising a profession which is of a complex nature and requires personal initiative (e.g. explaining different tasks to subordinates and giving them instructions) transmit these requirements to dealings with their children in the home. Parents whose occupation makes little demands on their personal initiative (e.g. an occupation which involves carefully complying with various regulations or working at a predetermined pace on an assembly line) and requiring obedience and compliance (without question), transmit this attitude to their interaction in the home, and especially their dealings with their children. Thus children of middle-class families are socialised for personal initiative and children of working-class families for obeying those in authority. The former children develop a higher degree of self-control, while the latter are more attuned to outward control (told what to do). Children's attitudes to inward and outward control, in their turn, have a bearing on their social behaviour in general and, not least, on antisocial and criminal behaviour.

Family structure

Bronfenbrenner maintains that any change in the family constellation, be it the birth of a new child and the growth of the family or the parents getting divorced, implies an ecological transition *within the family.*

An increase in the family means stricter interaction within the family and more attention being paid to the new arrival than to the others. "*The addition of another child in the family tends to reduce the warmth and contact between the parent and other children and to result in a more restrictive but less effective home.*" (Baldwin, 1947; ref.: Bronfenbrenner, 1980, p. 72). Traditional socialisation research has actually found that a conspicuously strict attitude to the children on the parents' part augments the risk of criminal behaviour among the children.

Bronfenbrenner devotes a great deal of scope to the situation of *single parents* as upbringers of children. Referring to the study by Hetherington, Cox & Cox (1977), he concludes among other things that "*It is the boy from a divorced home who is more likely to be impulsive, unable to delay immediate gratification, inconsiderate, aggressive, or delinquent.*" (Bronfenbrenner, 1980, p. 75). It is worth mentioning that one of the few occasions on which Bronfenbrenner mentions antisocial behaviour and crime among children is in fact when discussing the situation of divorced mothers as parents.

A divorce between parents is a situation of crisis for the children. Things are most difficult for children who are under five years old at the time of the divorce. The divorce is also in the nature of a crisis for the mother, impeding her everyday relation to the child. To children, the crisis means greater dependence on the mother and heavier demands on her. The mother, in her crisis, is less disposed to accommodate the child's demands. Thus there are great risks of the relationship between the mother and children breaking down. "*The disruptive effects of separation on parents, children, and their relations with each other reached their peak one year after the divorce and declined through the second year although the divorced mothers never gained as much control as their married counterparts.*" (Bronfenbrenner, 1980, p. 74). If, however, the mother is still on good terms with the children's father after the divorce and the father is always available to the children, this facilitates her parental role. Supportive persons outside the family (her own parents, siblings, close friends, a new boyfriend) can also make things easier for the mother, so that she can relate more effectively to the children. In families where the mother-child relation has been good from the outset, where the mother, following the divorce, has been available when needed by the children and where the mother has preserved her authoritative attitude to the child, children have not had such great problems.

Immigrant background

Immigrant background is usually referred to as a background factor with a negative effect on socialisation, but Bronfenbrenner sees an advantage to the child in growing up in different contexts such as different cultures. This diversity, however, is beneficial to the developing child only so long as its other conditions are good. In unsatisfactory living conditions, the confrontation with two different cultures can have a negative effect and actually retard the child's intellectual and emotional development. If conditions at home are bad, diversity can create problems of identity on the part of the child, which augments the risk of antisocial behavioural tendencies.

Socio-psychological Aspects

Parental behaviour

One important prerequisite of a child's development into an independent person is for the parents gradually to relinquish their claims to power over the child. As the child matures, physically and mentally, he is increasingly allowed to decide things for himself. This is a description of the democratic parent, and it fits in well with the *authoritative* parent as described previously. That parent's antithesis is the *authoritarian* parent, who is insensitive to the child's demands and possibilities. Other parental attitudes prejudicial to children's social development are *permissiveness* and *neglect*. Parents' relations to their children are to quite a large extent a reflection of their own personality and degree of social adjustment. The authoritative parent can be expected to function well, not only in the family context but also in his other social settings. He (or she) is a responsible, co-operative person, generally well-integrated with the community. There is harmony in the parent's social settings (his or her mesosystem). In connection with various stress situations, such as passing conflicts at work or within the family, this parent acts in a balanced manner and resolves the situations constructively.

We may presume that an authoritarian pattern of upbringing is rooted to a certain extent in a dominant or authoritarian personality structure on the parents' part. An authoritarian person tends among other things to think in clearly defined categories, i.e. stereotypes. He or she is a person who is "*moralis-*

ing, rigid and intolerant, suspicious of new ideas and hostile to strangers" (Psykologisk uppslagsbok, 1976, p. 491). A person of this kind has difficulty in developing affectionate contact with the child. The parent is incapable of gradually relinquishing his claims to power as the child develops. Instead the child has to assert itself, which the parent has difficulty in accepting. A conflict can very easily occur between child and parent. Family relations in general are probably bad. The parent's relations with his other social settings, presumably, are also tense. There is suspicion of outsiders, and social contacts are strained. The parent has difficulty in developing more intimate social relations with people outside the family, and this leads to social isolation. The parent also has difficulty in coping with stressful situations. In conflicts with persons in different social contexts, he or she reacts by asserting himself, and previously unresolved conflicts are constantly flaring up again.

Permissiveness as a *pattern* of upbringing is presumably connected with a weak ego identity on the parent's part. The parent has difficulty in making clear to the child what it may and may not do. The parent has difficulty in *gradually* giving the child more power over the situation. In his "benevolence", he (or she) gives the child more say in things than the child can really cope with. Within the family, conflicts are avoided as far as possible and when they break out they are never entirely resolved. Parents with a poor ego identity are introverts and develop a limited social network.

Parents' *general* neglect of their children can be due to a variety of circumstances: the parent may have a disturbed capacity for contact, may harbour feelings of hate towards the child, may abuse alcohol and other drugs, may be self-centred on account of extensive emotional and social problems, and so on. Parents who do not bother about their children can be expected to be generally indifferent about trying to maintain very close social contacts with other people. If they lead an asocial life, they associate with others of a similar disposition. If so, their social network exists partly in the antisocial sub-culture. In extreme cases, parents are taken in charge by the social and legal authorities, during which time their children are placed with other families or in institutions.

Parental Behaviour and Ecological Context

Kornhauser (1978, p. 63) defines a socially unstable community as "*a community that cannot supply a structure through which common values can be realised and common problems solved.*" Socially unstable communities are characterised by high residential mobility and a high level of ethnic heterogeneity.

One of the basic ideas of the ecology of human development frame of reference is that the success of parenting can depend on the support parents receive in their community in the form of social networks (relatives, neighbours, friends etc.) or social services such as day nurseries and leisure centres. Parents living in a socially stable community have better outward conditions for their role than parents living in a socially unstable (socially disorganised) community.

The prospects of monitoring one's child's actions outside the home vary with the social stability of the community. Parents can gain insight into their child's doings by variously involving themselves in the child's different microsystems (outside the family). The more parents involve their children and the children's peers in the daily social activity of the home, the greater their control over the children will be. Parents who have good contact with their children acquire, in the course of daily conversations with them, information about their doings away from home (monitoring). By allowing their children to associate with their peers in a natural manner in the home (e.g. by letting them play with their friends at home, have parties to which their friends and the friends's parents are invited, do their homework together with friends in the home), the parents acquire a good insight into the child's social circle. Parents can also keep a close watch on their children's actions through their contacts with people outside the family, such as neighbours, parents of the children's friends, and the children's teachers. The ability of parents to develop an extensive social network in the neighbourhood community is for the same people to live in the community, i.e. for the community to be socially *stable*. The institutions frequented by the children, i.e. day nurseries, schools and leisure centres, should also be stable in the sense of having a low personnel turnover and of children and parents having continuous contact with the personnel. The staff of these institutions are also in a position to start and develop various educational programmes to stimulate children's development. Teachers can also monitor the children's development and progress and inform parents of their observations concerning the children's development of various skills.

For parents who are well-integrated in society, living in a socially stable community is ideal. Those parents have every chance of succeeding in their parental role. Parents who are socially less well-adjusted and live in a socially stable community should feel a certain security in their parental role. That security could be expected to have a positive effect on the parent-child relation. Children from inferior home conditions but living in a stable community have a good chance of obtaining support and stimulus in their psychological and social development through efficient child supervision and schooling.

In contrast to the community described above, we have the socially *unstable* neighbourhood. High residential mobility reduces the prospects of parents building up a stable social network. There is also a high turnover of personnel at the local day nurseries, schools and leisure centres etc., with the result that there is no continuity in the monitoring of children's development. Nor is there any scope for educational activity in these institutions. People there are perhaps more preoccupied with recruiting temporary staff so that teaching can at least take place. This type of community is also distinguished by a high rate of social problems, crime and gang formation among young people etc.

Parents who are well-adjusted in society and live in a socially unstable area presumably cope quite well with parenthood in these circumstances. They are presumably under stress and afraid of their children "getting into bad company". They have more difficulty in gaining an insight into their children's doings away from home through their social networks, because the networks are difficult to build up and keep going. Parents therefore have to monitor their children's actions more closely. Children and their families have to put up with conditions at day nursery, school and leisure centre, and the parents themselves must try and make up the intellectual and social stimulus which school is not capable of providing. If the parents can afford it, they will send their children to a day nursery and school with better conditions (e.g. a day nursery or school run privately), perhaps in another community. Less well-adjusted parents living in an unstable community have special difficulty in parenting their children effectively. In fact, the parents' bad sides may be accentuated in this environment. They are not in a position to keep an eye on their children themselves, especially when the children grow older. Great personal resources are needed to build up a social network in an unstable area, and the less well-adjusted parents seldom have such resources at their disposal. As parents they are vulnerable. Presumably a relatively large number of them have jobs which are physically strenuous and home relationships which are more burdensome (due, for example, to perpetual conflicts with the partner) than inspiring or supportive. These parents think more about themselves than about their children's development and future. The conflict between parents and children is escalated and can easily develop into the vicious circle described by Snyder & Patterson (1987), especially if the parent is of a generally authoritarian disposition. Personal shortcomings and problems are projected on to outside groups, i.e. ethnic minorities or immigrants. Parents with a poor ego identity and a permissive relation to the child lose control of the child's actions away from home.

There are several kinds of caretakers in a neighbourhood who in one way another supervise or monitor the child. In other words, there is a multiple monitoring of a child in a neighbourhood. It is the cumulative effect of the monitoring across the caretakers that counts. The cumulative effect of good monitoring in the neighbourhood might compensate for poor parental monitoring. When several caretakers in a neighbourhood fail in supervising the children, the parents' possibilities of monitoring their children diminish. Cumulative poor monitoring across caretakers in a neighbourhood can reach a point at which community surveillance breaks down.

The Mesosystem and the Child's Behaviour

Rejection mechanisms

The child's behaviour affects the way in which the rest of the world reacts to it. Some children are greatly liked by other children and adults, while others arouse antipathy. The child's behaviour, or rather the reactions of other people to its behaviours, influence the structure of the child's meso-system.

In day nursery and play-school, some children behave disruptively and aggressively and have difficulty in adapting to the rules issued by adults. They cannot wait their turn when taking part in games and play. They may also have a craving for attention and be demanding in their dealings with adults. When they start school, their antisocial behaviour becomes more visible: the children then present problems of discipline, show destructive tendencies and have outbursts of aggression (keep getting into fights). They are unhappy at school and play truant. Some of them display criminal tendencies: shoplifting, theft, wanton damage and substance abuse.

Snyder and Patterson (1987) have developed a two-stage model of deviant behaviour among children. The *first stage* refers to the relationship at home. Neglect of the child during early socialisation causes the child to become poorly adjusted, which among other things results in it becoming generally disruptive and quarrelsome. The *second stage* concerns other people's reactions to the child's behaviour.

Parents usually adjust their demands for independence and correctional behaviour the child's level of maturity, but some children are very difficult to handle from early on, due to hyperactivity, impulsiveness or attention problems etc. The parents' attempts to change the child's behaviour result in oppositional behaviour by the child, which can be stressful for the parents. These parents may reach a point in their relationship to the child where they give up their responsibilities as socialisers for the sake of domestic peace. They let the child do practically whatever it wants to. The parents' relation to a problem child can finally reach the point where they begin to dislike the child and wish it to leave the home permanently (Loeber & Stouthamer-Loeber, 1986, pp. 109–112). A poor relationship with the parents certainly helps to push a child into socialising with peers outside the home, thereby avoiding the domestic hassle.

Children and youngsters who behave disruptively run into counter-reactions in all social settings. Peers find them unpleasant to associate with and avoid them. The peers's parents urge their children to avoid those children who behave disruptively. Because they upset organised activities, they have problems in their groups at day nursery and in school. Teachers find their disruptive behaviour a cause of stress, and children who disrupt activities are referred to "sin bins". Because these children lack the concentration and perseverance for tackling problems of a more complicated nature, they fall down on their schoolwork.

Disruptive children and youngsters are excluded from the society of their peers. They also drop out of school and education. Many of them can be expected to leave school early. The children and youngsters who are constantly rejected by the mainstream community turn to other children and youngsters in a similar situation for companionship. They can be captured by an antisocial sub-culture or become involved in an antisocial setting.

In microsystems with antisocial opposite numbers, these youngsters experience fellowship with others who are like-minded and are accepted by virtue of their deviant values and behaviour. The likelihood of coming together with antisocial peers is greatest in communities with a high proportion of social problems and crime. Perhaps these areas already have an antisocial tradition, i.e. a network of persons leading an asocial life. These persons are incapable of assuming the responsibility which an ordinary job demands – partly due to character disturbance and partly because, as a result of their lifestyle, they are both mentally and socially run down. Children and youngsters who, during their formative years, have constantly been rejected from the company of their peers and school, are easily attracted by the antisocial sub-culture, which then forms part of the young individual's meso-system.

The antisocial setting becomes more important to the youngster than school and the family. In this setting the child learns the norms and values which apply in that particular setting. Parents and other socially well-adjusted persons are kept out, and there is nobody to reproach the youngster for his shortcomings. On the contrary, in this setting one achieves high status by being antisocial. Thus the antisocial setting bestows a certain security on the youngsters included in it. Here they also learn various techniques, e.g. techniques of criminal behaviour. The antisocial microsystems also include monitoring to ensure that the individual youngster lives up to the agreed norms. Since many of the members probably have poor self-control, control within the system is maintained by means of threats, i.e. through aggression and violence. It is threats of violence and exclusion from the group which keep the members of the antisocial setting in their places.

Speaking theoretically in terms of labelling, one might say that, through his constant failures in school and in his peer relationships, the youngster has been labelled asocial, and this labelling is something which is confirmed and which he can live up to in the antisocial setting. In that setting he can actually achieve high status through success in the behaviours which the setting values highly. In a perspective of strain theory, one might say that it is not only a conflict between means and ends but also frustration at not being accepted by the general community which starts the youngster off on an antisocial, criminal career.

A child identified as disruptive and badly behaved can easily get caught up in a vicious circle. In the words of Cederblad (1984):

> *"Once the child has begun to be looked on by people around him, his family, school, the day nursery or neighbourhood groups, as antisocial, rowdy or an abuser of thinner, beer, hashish etc., the mechanism of social rejection comes into play. The identified deviant attracts more attention when acting his part. People observe him more and so, if he steels things, breaks things or abuses substances, he gets caught more often than other peers who may possibly experiment with the same actions. His behaviour can lead to suspension from the leisure centre, transfer to a remedial class at school, other children being forbidden by their parents to have anything to do with him, and eventually placement in various caring institutions where he comes together with others identified by the community as deviants of the same kind."* (Cederblad, 1984, p. 173, in Swedish).

Youngsters can get involved in antisocial contexts more or less by chance, through a peer who moves regularly in antisocial circles. If they have then begun practising criminal behaviour, they can be retained in the setting (the microsystem) through addiction (abuse of alcohol and other drugs) or through social control, e.g. threats of what will happen to them if they leave the group. (Withdrawal is a betrayal to the group and can be a threat to it, e.g. through the possibility of the group's secrets being revealed.)

Not all children on bad terms with their parents become deviants and criminals. Some of them become timid and keep themselves to themselves. Their superego is so strongly developed that the thought of committing a criminal act would never enter their minds.

Support from outside the family

Research into the causes of criminal behaviour, using the individual perspective, is preoccupied with factors *leading to crime.* The ecology of human development approach can also take into account factors (above all) in the child's surroundings which can have a preventive effect.

Children and youngsters with bad home conditions can obtain help and support from people outside the family. A very good relationship with an outside person whom the child is continuously in touch with (perhaps a relative, a neighbour, classmate's parent, day nursery staff member, recreation leader etc.) can neutralise a bad home environment. The link with a supportive adult of this kind can occur spontaneously, through the development of mutual sympathy and understanding between the adult and child. This, however, requires mental stability on the part of the child, social receptiveness and perhaps a certain self-perception of his own situation. If outsiders take a positive attitude to the child, this can help the child to cope with tension in the home. Support of this kind requires the area where the child lives to be relatively stable. A socially unstable community makes a poor foundation for relating to adults in the child's setting.

The community where the child lives can show a varying degree of awareness concerning deficient home relations and willingness to provide young families and children with social and psychological support, e.g. in the form of various social training programmes for parents and the family.

Transformation of the mesosystem

As we saw earlier, the structure of the child's microsystem (the meso-system) changes character as the child develops. During the initial period of development, the mother is the most important person to the child, followed by the other members of the family. When the child is out playing or in day nursery, playmates and adults from outside the family enter the picture. At school, classmates and teachers are important persons, while during leisure hours out of school and away from home is peers in the same or a neighbouring community. At first it is mainly peers of the same sex as the child who count, but those of the opposite sex also become important during adolescence.

During late adolescence there occurs a restructuring of the ranking order of reference persons. Peers become more important in relation to parents. This is the beginning of the child's emancipation from its parents. The end of compulsory schooling also comes during this emancipation process, and this too is the age at which a certain type of criminal behaviour peaks (cf. Wikström, 1989).

For some children the restructuring of the ranking order of the reference persons comes at a much earlier age. This deviant timing may well affect the children's future development. They might be pushed into various situations which they are not prepared to handle psychologically.

The ecology of human development frame of reference calls for a longitudinal approach. This underlines, for example, the importance of Farrington's (1992) theory that criminal behaviour is a form of antisocial behaviour and that the definition of criminal behaviour varies according to the developmental status of the child or adolescent. To quote Tonry, Ohlin & Farrington (1991, p. 143):

> *"For example, we might suspect a developmental sequence exists involving hyperactivity between ages 2 and 5, conduct disorder between ages 8 and 10, shoplifting between ages 13*

and 15, robbery between 19 and 21, and family violence and alcohol abuse between ages 20 and 25."

The ecology of human development frame of reference could also be used as a basis for investigating more closely which factors in the environment (the meso-system) contribute towards the commencement of criminal behaviour by children and adolescents and what factors cause some of them to repeat their criminal acts and drift into a career of crime. This frame of reference can also be used for explaining why a criminal abandons his criminal activity. Here is an illustration from Farrington (1992):

> "*On my own theory, the onset of offending depends partly on an increase in antisocial tendency (e.g. caused by a change in social influence from parents to peers)* and partly on changes in situational factors, opportunities, benefits, and costs. Similarly, desistance occurs when there is a decrease in antisocial tendency (e.g. *caused by a change in social influence from peers to spouses or girlfriends*) and changes in situational factors." (Farrington, 1992, p. 279; my emphasis).

Bronfenbrenner's View of Criminal Behaviour

According to Bronfenbrenner, criminal behaviour among children and adolescents is a reaction to *alienation* in the community. Home and school, for example, have become divorced. Schools close down and are moved away from the child's community. Small schools are amalgamated to form bigger units with bigger classes, and larger numbers of pupils and teachers. Staff and pupils never get to know each other, and school becomes more faceless. The teachers are recruited from various communities and seldom live near the school. It is quite common for parents and teachers not to be personally acquainted. The school is not naturally integrated with the neighbourhood. One of the important functions of school is to bring up children and adolescents to be responsible members of society, but school and society, having no concrete links with each other, fail to discharge this role.

The reason why children and adolescents become increasingly alienated is that their social life becomes more and more segmented. The family is a thing apart, school is a thing apart and so too are peer groups and leisure. Children's and adolescents' microsystems become more or less watertight compartments. Criminal behaviour reflects "*a breakdown of the interconnections between various segments of the child's life – family, school, peer group, neighborhood ...*" (Bronfenbrenner, 1980, p. 231).

Bronfenbrenner's argument puts one in mind of a discussion by Coleman & Husén (1981), remarking that the socialising function of the family has been increasingly taken over by other, specialised institutions in the community and that different socialisation agents often convey contradictory messages, causing fragmentation in the minds of children and adolescents.

There are also clear parallels here to the theory of social control and its view of crime as a consequence of the individual's deficient bonding with society (Hirschi, 1969) and also parallels to the argument of social disorganisation as an explanation for criminal behaviour (Kornhauser, 1978). From a social control perspective, this "breakdown of the interconnections" can be seen as *a breakdown of controls.*

Empirical Studies

Empirical studies conceptually based on the ecology of human development are very few in number. A cross-national project initiated by Bronfenbrenner, with Sweden, Germany, Wales, Israel and the U.S. taking part, has reported some results from their respective studies (see Cochran, Larner, Gunnarsson & Henderson, 1990; Kihlbom, 1991). These studies give some hints as to the methodological and analytical approaches generated or active when the human developmental ecology is used as a theoretical base.

The studies employ a *longitudinal* approach. Families and their children are followed up and studied during a longer time period. Observational studies of the child at home and outside home (in the play-group, at the pre-school or school), structured and semi-structured interviews with the family about various activities, in-depth interviews, diaries, psychological testing of the children etc. have been used to get the needed information about the families and the children.

The ecological dimension has been of central importance when *sampling* the families participating in these studies (Andersson & Rydén, 1979; Cochran, Gunnarsson, Gräbe & Lewis, 1984). However, the further data analyses hardly take into account the differences in the character of the neighbourhood areas where the families reside. To the extent they do, it is rather superficially. For example, the Swedish study differentiated between low-resource and medium-resource neighbourhoods, thereby combining the data for Stockholm and Göteborg (Gothenburg) in Sweden (see Sandqvist, 1982). The empirical analyses carried out have used the data on the individual level, combining the subjects from all the neighbourhood areas.

The consequence of the ecological-developmental approach to socialisation is that a lot of data are gathered about each family in the study. This data collection is time-consuming and generates a great deal of information. This is why the studies performed so far have had small sample sizes (n varies between 76 for Wales and 281 for the U.S.). Furthermore, the families chosen for the study have not been representative for the neighbourhood area in which they reside. Generalisations on the neighbourhood level can therefore not be made on the basis of these studies.

In a study designed to analyse ecological and socio-psychological factors influencing antisocial and criminal behaviour among children and young people, one has to complete with community measures relevant to criminological studies, such as demographic structure, family structure, residential mobility, socioeconomic variables, school variables, social service resources, housing structure, recreational resources, formal organisational participation by residents, health resources and services, information on friendship and kinship networks, crime and justice indicators, opportunity structures for crime etc. (see further Tonry, Ohlin & Farrington, 1991 pp. 46–77). Furthermore, in order to identify more specifically the resources and limitations of the neighbourhood area for a family, one has to develop adequate measurement instruments.

The following can be said regarding future empirical research in this field. To arrive at a more complete and general picture of the neighbourhood areas under investigation, we need larger samples than in the cross-national studies mentioned above. Working with larger samples and with more detailed, ecologically oriented variables in addition to the kind of information usually collected in the ecology of human development approach, one will quite soon obtain what may be an embarrassingly large volume of data. Of course, not all the available data can be analysed at once. Attention must be made to focus on one or two limited aspects at a time, and the volume of data reduced accordingly. So far in their cross-national study, for example, Bronfenbrenner's colleagues have mainly analysed the construction of social networks among parents and their children.

Discussion

The ecology of human development model describes all levels in the child's environment, from its immediate setting via settings which indirectly influence the child (the exo-system) to the more abstract general level of the macrosystem.

The model discusses processes of interaction and the way in which the child forms a subjective view of its surroundings in this interaction, but it lacks a theory of the child's internal (mental) processes. Nor does the model have any detailed array of concepts for characterising the child's interaction with, for example, its parents. The ecology of human development model could be enhanced by drawing on the knowledge available from traditional socialisation research.

The neighbourhood community, according to the ecology of human development, is one of the child's most important exosystems. The model says, in so many words, that the neighbourhood indirectly influences the child, but it has not developed any method or conceptual apparatus for describing communities and processes influencing the behaviour of their populations. The socio-ecological tradition of criminology could assist the ecology of human development model here by visualising neighbourhood factors by which criminal behaviour is influenced.

The ecology of human development model does, however, contain perspectives which are lacking in the other two traditions, namely *perspectives of everyday life*. The model focuses attention on practical problems confronting children and parents in their everyday lives, and it also includes the question of how to solve those problems. The way in which parents, for example, cope with parenthood without coming under stress due to a conflict with other roles they have in the community depends on the flexibility of their working hours, what childminding arrangements they are able to make, the extent to which health and support are forthcoming from neighbours, friends or people at work in emergencies, and so on.

The inclusion of perspectives of everyday life in socialisation research has methodological implications. The methods of investigation and analysis by which traditional socialisation research and socio-ecological research in criminology are dominated have to be supplemented by elements of qualitative methods. Questions should be more systematically asked concerning everyday life in a community. Furthermore, the usual descriptions of communities need to be supplemented with elements of observation methods (as developed, for example, in social anthropology) and key person interviews (i.e. informant interviews).

Another consequence of the emphasis placed on everyday life by the ecology of human development is that the child's development has to be studied in a context. The relation between a child's behaviour and the environment it grows up in is less linear than the traditional theories of socialisation most often imply. Even if a child lives in a broken home or is on poor terms with its parents, this need not necessarily mean the child developing antisocial or criminal behaviour. A divorced mother with young children can have a social network which backs her up in the parental role. Furthermore, through social intercourse in its various social settings (through its own devices), the child can develop a protective social network which will more than make up for deficient home conditions.

The focus on everyday life also gives the model a social policy dimension, i.e. what is included in the macrosystem. An attempt is made to answer questions of the following kind: What is the reason for families in, say, a community or neighbourhood encountering a certain problem? How can conditions in the community be changed so as to eliminate or alleviate the problems of these families? Once suitable changes have been made, has this had any discernible effect on the families? This political/practical dimension has long been something of a hot potato to researchers in the social and behavioural sciences.

The political dimension, however, has become more "respectable" among researchers in these sciences as evaluation research has been developed and gained an increasingly firm foothold. In criminal research, a discussion has long been in progress concerning various possibilities of crime prevention (e.g. Burchard & Burchard, 1987). Hitherto, a fair degree of success has been achieved in preventing crimes like burglary and theft by purely technical measures. But supportive and other measures to prevent children in the risk zone embarking on a career of crime have been less conspicuously successful. With the aid of deeper research into the causes of antisocial and criminal behaviour among children and adolescents, let us hope that various strategies can be evolved in future for preventing crime more efficiently. But, to quote Tonry, Ohlin and Farrington (1991, p. 3): "*If ... we want in the next 20 years to know more than we do now and we want to see established improved public policies that both reduce crime and improve the lives of the least well-off among us, we require new research strategies.*"

The ecology of human development is to a great extent based on the idea of social networks. We have observed here that the model is compatible both with traditional socialisation research and with the socio-ecological tradition of criminology. The social network perspective seems to have an inherent potential for accommodating several scientific approaches. It is interesting to see that the integrative capacity of this perspective has also been discovered by other researchers:

> "*An advantage of a network approach is that it can integrate several theoretical perspectives on crime. Elements of social control theory (Hirschi 1969), learning theory (Akers et al., 1985), differential association theory (Sutherland 1939), and subcultural theory (Cloward & Ohlin 1960) can be incorporated into it.*"
> (Tonry, Ohlin & Farrington, 1991, p. 157).

The study of children's behaviour in a developmental perspective is fundamental to the ecology of human development frame of reference. Accordingly, criminal behaviour must also be viewed in this perspective (cf. Farrington, 1992; Loeber & LeBlanc, 1990). Criminal behaviour in children does not just begin on a given occasion. It develops out of antisocial tendencies which are already apparent during early childhood. A criminal act can be spontaneous and non-recurrent, in which case it was opportunity and circumstances more than anything else which induced the child to do what it did. But if children commit crimes on repeated occasions and drift into a criminal career, then more often than not there is a previous history of various behavioural problems in early childhood (aggressiveness, mendacity, generally disorderly behaviour, truancy, running away from home and so on). What, though, are the special circumstances causing a child to begin committing crimes? Why do some individuals persist with their criminal activity and indeed escalate it with more numerous and serious crimes? What factors help to induce a criminally active person to desist entirely from further crime? Some of those who terminate their criminal career develop other types of antisocial behaviour. The whole of the process described, with its intra-individual and inter-individual variations, will have to be studied and explained more closely in future (Farrington, 1992), and this, I believe, is where the ecology of human development model can be of some assistance. Here the longitudinal approach is the only conceivable possibility. This conclusion contradicts Hirschi and Gottfredson (Hirschi & Gottfredson, 1983; Gottfredson & Hirschi, 1986, 1987, 1988, 1990), who have argued that most research using the longitudinal design can be studied just as well or even better with a cross-sectional design. Cross-sectional studies are certainly sufficient when, for example, describing the circumstances at a specific point in time. However, the cross-sectional design is based on a mechanistic view and therefore it is not all that much help to us in getting closer to the dynamics behind the processes we want to grasp. The development of antisocial and criminal behaviour is an integral part of the development of human behaviour in general (Piaget, 1948; Kohlberg, 1968, 1969). What is needed in the future is to put antisocial and criminal behaviour in the general context of the development of human behaviour (such as emotional and intellectual development).

References

Akers, R. L., Krohn, M. D., Lanza-Kaduce, L. & Radosevic, M. (1985). *Deviant behaviour: A social learning approach.* Wadsworth, Belmont, Calif.

Andersson, B.-E. (1982). *Utvecklingsekologi.* En teoretisk referensram till studiet av mänsklig utveckling. Fast-projektet 15. Högskolan för lärarutbildning i Stockholm, institutionen för pedagogik.

Andersson, B.-E. & Rydén, L. (1979). *Urvalet av bostadsområden i FAST-projektet.* Fast-projektet 3. Högskolan för lärarutbildning, Institutet för pedagogik. Stockholm.

Bahr, S. J. (1979). Family determinants and effects of deviance. In Burr W R, Hill R, Nye F I & Reiss I I (eds): *Contemporary theories about the family,* Chap 2. Macmillan, New York.

Baldwin, A. L. (1947). Changes in parent behavior during pregnancy. *Child Development,* 1947, 18, 29–39.

Bandura, A. & Walters, R. H. (1963). *Social learning and personality development.* Holt, Rinehart and Winston, New York.

Baumrind, D. (1972). Some thoughts about childrearing. In Bronfenbrenner, U. (ed): *Influences of human development,* pp 396–409. The Dryden Press, Inc.,Hinsdale, Ill.

Braithwaite, J. (1981). The myth of social class and criminality reconsidered. *American Sociological Review,* vol 46, s 36–57.

Bronfenbrenner, U. (1979). The ecology of human development. Experiments by nature and design. Harvard University Press, Cambridge.

Bronfenbrenner, U. (1958). Socialization and social class through time and space. In Maccoby, E E et al (eds.): *Readings in social psychology* Pp. 400–425. Holt, Rinehart and Winston, New York.

Bundeskriminalamt (1989). *Ausländerkriminalität in der Bundesrepublik Deutschland.* Band 34. Bundeskriminalamt Wiesbaden, BKA-Vortragsreihe, Wiesbaden.

Burchard, J. D. & Burchard, S. N. (ed) (1987). *Prevention of delinquent behavior.* SAGE Publications, Beverly Hills.

Cederblad, M. (1984). *Barn och ungdomspsykiatri.* Barnet i familjen – familjen i samhället. Esselte Studium, Uppsala.

Cloward, R. & Ohlin, L. (1960). *Delinquency and opportunity.* The Free Press, New York.

Cochran, M., Larner, M., Riley, D., Gunnarsson, L. & Henderson, C. R. (eds.) (1990). *Extending families.* The social networks of parents and their children. Cambridge University Press, Cambridge.

Cochran, M. & Gunnarsson, L. with Gräbe, S. and Lewis, J. (1990): The social networks of coupled mothers in four cultures. In: Cochran, M, Larner, M, Riley, D, Gunnarsson, L, and Henderson, C R (eds.) (1990): *Extending families.* The social networks of parents and their children. Cambridge University Press, Cambridge, Chap. 6.

Coleman, J. S. & Husén, T. (1985). *Becoming adult in a changing society.* OECD, Centre for Educational Research and Innovation (CERI), Paris.

Dolmén, L. R. & Lindström, P. (1991). *Skola, livsstil och brott.* BRÅ-rapport 1991:3. Allmänna Förlaget, Stockholm.

Farrington, D. P. (1992). Explaining the beginning, progress, and ending of antisocial behavior brom birth to adulthood. In: McCord, J (ed.): *Facts, frameworks, and forecastst.* Advances in criminological theory, Vol. 3, pp 553 – 286. Transaction Publishers, New Brunswick (USA).

Garbarino, J. (1982). *Children and families in the social environment.* Aldine Publishing Company. New York.

Gottfredson, M. R. & Hirschi, T. (1986). The true value of lambda would appear to be zero. *Criminology,* 24 (2), 213–234.

Gottfredson, M. R. & Hirschi, Tm (1987). The methodological adequacy of longitudinal research on crime. *Criminology,* 25(3), 581–614.

Gottfredson, M. R. & Hirschi, T. (1990). *A general theory of crime.* Stanford University Press. Stanford.

Hetherington, E. M., Cox, M. & Cox, R. (1977). *The development of children in mother-headed families.* Paper presented in the Conference of Families in Contemporary America. Washington, D.C. George Washington University. Referred to in Bronfenbrenner (1979).

Hirschi, T. (1969). *Causes of delinquency.* University of California press. Berkley.

Hirschi, T. & Gottfredson, M. R. (1983). Age and the explanation of crime. *American Journal of Sociology,* 89(3), 552–584.

Janson, C.-G. (1968). Socialekologiska metoder. In Karlsson, G: *Sociologiska metoder.* Svenska Bokförlaget, Scandinavian University Books. Stockholm.

Junger, M. (1989). Ethnic minorities, crime and public policy. In Hood, R (ed.): *Crime and criminal policy in Europe.* Proceedings of a European colloquium 3–6 july 1988, 142–173. Centre for Criminological Research, Oxford.

Junger, M. (1990). *Delinquency and ethnicity.* An investigation on social factors relating to delinquency among Moroccan, Turkish, Surinamese and Duch boys. Kluwer law and taxation publishers, Deventer-Boston.

Kihlbom, U. (1991). *Barns utveckling och mödrars arbete.* En longitudinell studie av barns utveckling i relation till deras mödrars arbetsförhållanden. FAST- projektet nr 80. Almquist & Wiksell International, Stockholm.

Killias, M. (1989). *Criminality among second generation immigrants in Western Europe: A review of the evidence.* Paper presented at the VIIth international workshop on juvenile criminology "The future of the juvenile justice system" in May 29–31, 1989 at Leeuwenhorst, Holland.

Kleck, G. (1982). On the use of self-report data to determine the class distribution of criminal and delinquent behaviour. *American Sociological Review,* Vol. 47, pp 427–433.

Kohlberg, L. (1968). Stage and sequence: The cognitive-developmental approach to socialization. In Goslin, D A (ed.): *Handbook of socialization theory and research.* Rand McNally and Company, Chicago, Chap. 6.

Kohlberg, L. (1969). *Stages in the development of moral thought and action.* Holt, Rinehart & Winston, New York.

Kornhauser, R. R. (1978). *Social sources of delinquency.* An appriasal of analytic models. The University of Chicago Press, Chicago.

LaRose, L. & Wolfe, D. A. (1987). Psychological characteristics of parents who abuse or neglect their children. In Lahey B B och Kazdin A E (eds): *Advances in clinical child psychology* (Vol 10). Plenum. New York.

Laub, J. H. & Sampson, R. J. (1988). Unraveling families and delinquency: A reanalysis of the Glueck's data. *Criminology,* Vol 26, nr 3, 355–379.

Loeber, R. & LeBlanc, M. (1990). Toward a developmental criminology. In Tonry, M and Morris, N (eds): *Crime and Justice: A review of research,* Vol. 12, pp 375–473. University of Chicago Press, Chicago.

Loeber, R. & Stouthamer-Loeber, M. (1986). Family factors as correlates and predictors of juvenile conduct problems and delinquency. In Tonry, M & Morris, N (red): *Crime and Justice,* Vol 7. University of Chicago Press. Chicago.

Loeber, R. & Dishion, T. (1983). Early predictions of male delinquency: A review. *Psychological Bulletin, 93, 69–99.*

Loll, B.-U. & Friedrichs, J. (1983). *Jugendkriminalität von Ausländern der zweiten und dritten Generation.* Studie im Auftrage des Bundeskriminalamtes; Endbericht. Universität Hamburg. Forschungsstelle vergleichende Stadtforschung. Arbeitsunterlage für das Prognose-Gremium beim Bundeskriminalamt "Entwicklung der Kriminalität".

Maccoby, E. E. & Martin, J. A. (1983). Socialization in the context of the family: Parent-child interaction. In Hetherington E M (red): *Handbook of child psychology,* Vol IV, pp 1–101. John Wiley. New York.

Martens, P. L. (1976). Patterns of child rearing ideology. Project Metropolitan, Research report no 5, Stockholm University, Department of Sociology.

Martens, P. L. (1981). Socioeconomic status, family structure, and socialization of early adolescent children. Project Metropolitan, Research report no 16, Stockholm university.

Martens, P. L. (1982). Achievement related behavior of early adolescents. Project Metropolitan, Research report no 18. Stockholm university, Department of Sociology.

Martens, P. L. (1990). Brottslighet bland ungdomar med invandrarbakgrund. In Wikström, P-O H (red): *Brott och* *åtgärder mot brott i stadsmiljö.* BRÅ-rapport 1990:5, kapitel 6. Allmänna Förlaget, Stockholm.

Martens, P. L. (1992). *Familj, uppväxt och brott.* BRÅ-rapport 1992:1. Allmänna Förlaget, Stockholm.

McCord, J. (1982). A longitudinal view of the relationship between parental abscence and crime. In Gunn, J. and Farrington, D.P (eds): *Abnormal offenders, delinquency, and the criminal justice system.* Wiley, Chichester, England. Pp. 113–128.

Nettler, G. (1978). Social status and self-reported criminality. *Social Forces,* 57, 1477–1486.

Nettler, G. (1985). Social class and crime, one more time. *Social Forces,* 63, 1076–1077.

Piaget, J. (1948). *The moral judgement of the child.* The Free Press, Glencoe, Ill. (Originally published in 1932).

Psykologisk uppslagsbok (1976): Ed.: Johannesson, I. Natur och Kultur, Stockholm.

Rollins, B. C. & Thomas, D. L. (1979). Parental support, power, and control techniques in the socialization of children. In Burr, W R, Hill, R., Nye, I F, and Reiss I L (eds): *Contemporary theories about the family.* Vol 1, 317–364. The Free Press, New York.

Sandquist, K. (1979). *Föräldrars upplevelse av stress och stöd.* Teoretiska utgångspunkter och utveckling av ett intervjuformulär. ST-projektets rapport 5. Högskolan för lärarutbildning i Stockholm, Institutionen för pedagogik. Stockholm.

Smith, W. R. (1991). *Social structure, family structure, child rearing, and delinquency: Another look.* Project Metropolitan. Research report no. 33. Stockholm: Stockolm university.

Snyder, J. & Patterson, G. (1987). Family interaction and delinquent behavior. In Quay H (ed): *Handbook of juvenile delinquency.* John Wiley & Sons. New York. Chap 8.

Suikkila, J. (1983). Några synpunkter på alkoholbruk och brottslighet bland ungdomar i Sverige och Finland. In: Eriksson U-B and Tham H (eds): *Utlänningar och brottsligheten.* Rapport 1983:4, Brottsförebyggande rådets forskningsenhet, 190–214. Allmänna Förlaget, Stockholm.

Sutherland, E. (1939). *Principles of criminology.* Lippincott, Philadelphia.

Sveri, K. (1966). Kulturkonflikt och brottslighet. In: Schwarz, D (ed.): *Svenska minoriteter.* Aldus, Stockholm. Pp. 107–119.

Sveri, B. (1973). *Utlänningars brottslighet.* En kriminalstatistisk jämförelse mellan svenska och utländska medborgare. Svensk Juristtidning, 1973, 279–310.

Sveri, B. (1980). *Utlänningars brottslighet.* En jämförelse mellan om grövre brott övertygade personer 1967 och 1977. Kriminalvetenskapliga institutet vid Stockholms universitet. Stockholm.

Sveri, B. (1987). *Återfall i brott bland utländska medborgare.*

Kriminalvetenskapliga institutet vid Stockholms universitet. Stockholm.

Tittle, C. R. & Meier, R. F. (1990). Specifying the SES/Delinquency relationship. *Criminology,* 28, 271–300.

Tittle, C. R., Villemez, W. J. & Smith, D. A. (1978). The myth of social class and criminality. *American Sociological Review,* vol 43, s 643–656.

Tonry, M., Ohlin, L. E. & Farrington, D. P. (1991). *Human development and criminal behavior.* New ways of advancing knowledge. Springer-Verlag, New York.

Wahler, R. G. (1990). Some perceptual functions of social networks in coercive mother-child interactions. *Journal of Social and Clinical Psychology,* 9 (1), 43–53.

Wahler, R. G. & Dumas, J. E. (1986). Maintanance factors in coercive mother-child interactions: The compliance and predictability hypotheses. *Journal of Applied Behavior Analysis,* 19 (1), 13–22.

Walter, M. (1987). Kriminalität junger Ausländer. Forschungsstand und offene Fragen. *Bewährungshilfe,* 34 (1), 60–82.

Wikström, P.-O. H. (1983). *Social klass och brottslighet.* BRÅ-APROPÅ, Vol 9, s 4–12.

Wikström, P.-O. H. (1987). *Brott och stadsmiljö.* Storstadskriminalitet. Del 1. Rapport 1887:3, Brottsförebyggande rådets forskningsenhet. Allmänna Förlaget, Stockholm.

Wikström, P.-O. H. (1989). Ålder och brott.En undersökning av brottslighetens utveckling i en ålderskull stockholmare från 13 till 25 års ålder. In BRÅ-rapport 1989:3: *Brottsutvecklingen 1988,* 133–171. Brottsförebyggande rådet och Allmänna Förlaget. Stockholm.

Wikström, P.-O. H. (1990). The Stockholm project: An introduction. In Wikström, P-O H (ed.): *Crime and measures against crime in the city.* BRÅ-Report 1990:5. Allmänna Förlaget, Stockholm.

Wikström, P.-O. H. (1991a). *Urban crime, criminals, and victims.* Springer Verlag, New York.

Wikström, P.-O. H. (1991b). *Sociala problem, brott och trygghet.* En intervjuundersökning med vuxna i åtta förortsområden i Stockholm. BRÅ-rapport 1991:5. Allmänna Förlaget, Stockholm.

Wikström, P.-O. H. (forthcoming). Preventing city-center street crimes. In Tonry, M & Farrington, D P: *Preventing crime, Crime and Justice,* vol. 19. University of Chicago Press, Chicago.

Wolfe, D. A. (1987). *Child abuse.* Implications for child development and psychopathology. SAGE Publications, Beverly Hills.

Family and Community-Level Influences on Crime: A Contextual Theory and Strategies for Research Testing

by Robert J. Sampson

As evidenced by this conference, recent work in criminology has begun to challenge the bifurcated mode of traditional research that separates the individual and community levels of analysis. Indeed, criminologists are now recognizing that the two levels of analysis are not incompatible – both individual *and* community factors are important in understanding crime (Reiss 1986a; Bursik and Grasmick 1993). Of course, recognizing the need for multilevel integration and implementing it are two different things. Methodological and theoretical disputes abound, and few studies have demonstrated a unified approach to the individual and community dimensions of crime.

This paper confronts the challenge of multilevel integration by proposing a theoretical and methodological perspective on families, informal social control, and delinquency. Drawing largely on social disorganization theory linked with the concept of social capital, I focus on the embeddedness of families and juveniles in the social networks of local communities. I specifically argue that both community and family social capital contribute to the inhibition of delinquency and crime. In this regard, I extend the idea that family management practices – especially the monitoring and supervision of youth – are intertwined with dimensions of community social organization (Sampson 1992; Furstenberg 1993). I also discuss the operationalization of key constructs and new research designs that are being implemented to test core hypotheses. I focus in particular on studies of delinquency, adolescent development, and community social organization in Chicago and Denver, USA.

Theoretical Background

Shaw and McKay (1942, 1969) posited that low economic status, ethnic heterogeneity, and residential mobility led to the disruption of community social organization, which in turn accounted for variations in crime and delinquency rates. As recently extended by Kornhauser (1978), Bursik (1988), and Sampson and Groves (1989), social disorganization may be seen as the inability of a community structure to realize the common values of its residents and maintain effective social controls. The structural dimensions of community social disorganization refer to the prevalence and inter-dependence of social networks in a community, and in the span of collective supervision that the community directs toward local problems. Social organization is reflected in both informal networks (e.g., the density of acquaintanceship; intergenerational kinship ties; mutual guardianship) and formal institutions (e.g., organizational density; institutional stability).

This social disorganization approach is grounded in what Kasarda and Janowitz (1974: 329) call the systemic model, where the local community is viewed as a complex system of friendship and kinship networks, and formal and informal associational ties rooted in family life and on-going socialization processes (see also Bursik and Grasmick 1993). From this view, social organization and social disorganization are seen as different ends of the same continuum with respect to systemic networks of community social control. When formulated in this manner, the concept of social disorganization is clearly separable not only from the processes that may lead to it (e.g., poverty, mobility), but from the degree of criminal behavior that may result (see Bursik 1988; Bursik and Grasmick 1993).

Both Bursik (1988) and Sampson and Groves (1989) have explicated the intervening dimensions of community social organization that bear on adolescence and the control of delinquency. Among others, these include local friendship ties, density of acquaintanceship, organizational density, and local participation in formal and voluntary organizations. Perhaps the most important construct, however, is the ability of a community to supervise and control teenage peer-groups – especially gangs. Delinquency is primarily a group phenomenon (Thrasher 1963; Shaw and McKay 1942; Reiss 1986b), and hence, the capacity of the community to control group-level dynamics is a key theoretical mechanism linking community characteristics with crime (see Sampson 1992). Indeed, a central finding underlying Thrasher's research was that the majority of gangs developed from unsupervised, spontaneous play-groups (1963: 25). Shaw and McKay (1969) argued that residents of cohesive communities were better able to control these and other teenage behaviors that set the context for group-related crime (see also Short 1963: xxiv). Examples of such informal social controls include supervision of leisure-time youth activities and breaking up the street-corner congregation of youth (Thrasher 1963: 339; Maccoby et al. 1958: Shaw and McKay 1969: 176–185; Skogan 1986: 217).

A related dimension of a general conceptualization of social organization is social cohesion. Like friendship networks or organizational participation, social cohesion is a macro-level concept that has a parallel at the individual level in the form of estrangement and alienation (or "anomie"). Still, the cohesion of the social order is not merely the aggregation of individual properties. For example, the individual-level experience of alienation and isolation is conceptually distinct from community-level variations in the proportion of people who engage in collective helping behavior. Social cohesion ultimately refers to the extent to which communities are able to achieve a stable moral and social order. Social cohesion thus refers more to the dimension of moral or social integration than networks of affiliation and association.

Like social disorganization, an abstract concept like cohesion is perhaps best conceptualized on a theoretical continuum. At the social cohesion end, communities are characterized by helping/caring functions, mutual guardianship and trust, and collective socialization of the young. By contrast, disintegration is reflected in the social cleavages that rend a community (e.g., racial/ethnic), social disorder and predatory morality (e.g., hustling, "conning"), alienation (mutual mistrust and estrangement), disengagement from political participation (e.g., nonvoting), and the public incivilities that may signal a decline in cohesion (e.g., broken windows; graffiti). Even the breakdown of commercial trust as reflected in prohibitive lending practices and symbolic and real barriers between businesses and residents (e.g., a "city of iron gates") may forecast the social disintegration of a community.

Assessing and Measuring Social Disorganization

Prior research largely supports the core hypothesis of Shaw and McKay (1942) that the structural antecedents of poverty, residential mobility, and heterogeneity explain variations in crime and delinquency rates (see Bursik and Grasmick 1993; Sampson and Lauritsen 1993). In addition, recent research has established that crime rates are positively linked to community- level variations in family "disruption" (e.g., percent single-parent households; divorce rate), and rates of community change (see also Reiss 1986a; Byrne and Sampson 1986; Bursik 1988). As hypothesized by Sampson and Groves (1989), family disruption, urbanization, and the anonymity accompanying rapid population change all undercut the capacity of a community to exercise informal social control, especially of teenage peer groups in public spaces (e.g., parks, streets, recreation areas).

Although it is difficult to measure directly the intervening mechanisms of social disorganization, two recent studies provide empirical support for the theory's structural dimensions. First, Taylor et al. (1984) examined variations in violent crime (e.g., mugging, assault, murder, rape) across 63 street blocks in Baltimore in 1978. Based on interviews with 687 household respondents, Taylor et al. (1984: 316) constructed block-level measures of the proportion of respondents who belonged to an organization to which co-residents also belonged, and the proportion of respondents who felt responsible for what happened in the area surrounding their home. Both of these measures were significantly and negatively related to variations in crime rates exclusive of other ecological factors (1984: 320). These results support the social-disorganization hypothesis that increases in organizational participation and informal social control – especially of public activities by neighborhood youth – reduce community-level rates of violence.

Second, Sampson and Groves' (1989) analysis of the British Crime Survey in 1982 and 1984 showed that the prevalence of unsupervised teenage peer-groups in a community had the largest effect on rates of robbery and violence by strangers. The density of local friendship networks – measured by the proportion of residents with half or more of their friends living in the neighborhood – also had a significant negative effect on robbery rates, while the level of organizational participation by residents had significant inverse effects on both robbery and stranger violence (1989: 789). Moreover, variations in these structural dimensions of community social (dis)organization transmitted in large part the effects of community socioeconomic status, residential mobility, ethnic heterogeneity, and family disruption in a theoretically consistent manner. For example, mobility had significant inverse effects on friendship networks, family disruption was the largest predictor of unsupervised peer groups, and socioeconomic status had the largest inverse effects on organizational participation.

Although not extensive, there is also an empirical literature on social cohesion that we can draw upon to inform measurement strategies. For example, a well-known study by Angell (1942) some five decades ago provides an empirical base for measuring the moral integration of communities (e.g., helping/caring functions). Voting records and contributions to social-service agencies are two such indicators of cohesion. Sampson (1991) studied community-level variations in social cohesion as measured by the proportion of residents who were willing to help one another. Similarly, Skogan (1986) reports on research showing the ways in which neighborhood incivilities influenced aspects of social cohesion and helping behavior. Turning to empirical research of an ethnographic design, Rieder's (1985) study of *Canarsie* and Anderson's (1990) recent portrayal of two neighborhoods in *Streetwise* focused on the social cleavages that disrupted community-wide trust, social integration, and more generally, the search for moral order.

When the findings of Taylor et al. (1984), Sampson and Groves (1989), and Sampson (1991) are considered along with ethnographic research that points to the salience of social cohesion (Rieder 1985; Anderson 1990) and informal community structures in controlling the formation of gangs (e.g., Suttles 1968;

Sullivan 1989), support emerges for the theoretical notion that structural elements of social organization and cohesion have relevance for explaining macrolevel variations in crime.

Integrating the Micro-Macro Levels: Families and Community

The importance of the family in understanding crime and delinquency has been well established. Based on a recent meta-analysis of existing research, Loeber and Stouthamer-Loeber (1986: 29) found that socialization variables, such as lack of parental supervision, parental rejection, and parent-child involvement, were among the most powerful predictors of delinquency. Similarly, Hirschi (1983) and Patterson (1982) describe a set of parenting skills that revolve around the monitoring and supervision of youth behavior, consistent punishment, and the formation of close social bonds among parents and children. These three dimensions of informal social control – discipline, supervision/monitoring, and attachment – are consistently related to delinquency according to existing research (see also Laub and Sampson 1988).

When considering the role of families and crime, however, criminologists tend to mirror developmental theorists in viewing childrearing as a dyadic or mostly interpersonal activity that takes place within individual families or "under the roof" (Sampson 1992). Although this viewpoint is not incorrect, it is incomplete and ignores the fact that parenting styles are an adaptation to considerations outside the household, especially the social organization of the community (Furstenberg 1993: 233). Exactly how parents perceive and manage their children's involvement in the world outside the household is a topic that has not received much research attention. This is unfortunate, for as Furstenberg (1993: 233) notes, family management strategies tied to the community may be no less consequential for children's development than the more direct, proximate controls observed inside the home. Therefore, in this section I extend a community-level approach to what is usually treated as a purely "familial" or within-household fact – childrearing.

Central to my integration of families and community is the concept of *social capital* (see also Sampson 1992). As Coleman (1990: 302) argues, the distinguishing feature of social capital lies in the structure of interpersonal relations. Social capital is created when relations among persons facilitate action, "making possible the achievements of certain ends that in its absence would not be possible" (Coleman 1988: 98). By contrast, physical capital is embodied in observable material form, and human capital is embodied in the skills and knowledge acquired by an individual. Social capital is even less tangible, for it is a social good embodied in the relations among persons (1990: 304). A core idea, then, is that social capital facilitates effective family management, independent of the physical and human capital of families (e.g., income).

Coleman's notion of social capital can be linked with social disorganization theory in a straightforward manner – lack of social capital is one of the primary features of socially disorganized communities as defined earlier (see also Coleman 1990: 307). The theoretical task is to identify the characteristics of communities that facilitate social capital available to families and children. One of the most important factors according to Coleman (1990: 318–320) is the closure (i.e., connectedness) of social networks among families and children in a community. In a system involving parents and children, communities characterized by an extensive set of obligations, expectations, and social networks connecting the adults are better able to facilitate the control and supervision of children. This notion helps to understand parent-child relations that are not just "under-the-roof." For example, when closure is present through the relationship of a child to two adults whose relationship transcends the household (e.g., friendship, work-related acquaintanceship, etc.), the adults have the potential to "observe the child's actions in different circumstances, talk to each other about the child, compare notes, and establish norms" (1990: 593). This form of relation can also provide reinforcement for disciplining the child, as found when parents in communities with dense social networks and high stability assume responsibility for the supervision of youth that are not their own (Coleman 1990: 320; Sampson and Groves 1989). Closure of local networks can thus provide the child with norms and sanctions that could not be brought about by a single adult alone, or even married-couple families in isolation.

Since the mere presence of a relationship among adults is not sufficient to produce social capital, the idea of social capital goes beyond the notion of density of acquaintanceship (Sampson 1991). That is, cross-generational closure of networks among parents and children that are tied to the parents or guardians of childhood friends in a community proves most effective in norms and supervision imposed on children. A simple example is where the parents' friends or acquaintances are the parents of their children's friends. By contrast, a parent who has many friends or acquaintances – even within the community – is constrained in social capital if the friends do not include parents or relatives of his/her own children's friends. One can extend this model to closure among networks involving parents and teachers, religious and recreational leaders, businesses that serve youth, and even the police (Sampson 1992).

The foregoing conceptualization leads to a theoretical distinction between social capital at the individual and community levels. At the individual level, social capital inheres in informal social controls (e.g., monitoring and supervision; intergenerational ties) provided by families. The analog at the community level is aggregate patterns of informal social control and cohesion (e.g., collective supervision, neighborhood monitoring) found in areas with high levels of social organization. Integrating social disorganization theory with the literature on delinquency, social capital, and family management, I thus derive two general sets of hypotheses: (H1) at the macro (community) level, the effect of structural disadvantage and concentrated urban poverty on delinquency rates is accounted for by intervening dimensions of social disorganization, and (H2) at the micro (individual) level, both neighborhood social cohesion and family social capital inhibit delinquent outcomes independent of individual-level constructs and family background (e.g., income, broken homes). From Furstenberg's (1993) work a more specific hypothesis is also suggested: social cohesion has indirect contextual effects on the control of delinquency by facilitating social capital available to families – especially the establishment of adult-child-peer networks and effective parental monitoring.

Community-level Ethnographic Evidence

A recent ethnographic study by Furstenberg (1993) of family management practices in two inner-city neighborhoods of Philadelphia supports the hypothesis that the lack of social capital among adults and children is an important component of ineffective child rearing and problematic child development. Whether highly skilled as a parent or not, residents he studied in a poor, unstable, and socially disorganized neighborhood in North Philadelphia tended to adopt an individualistic style of parental management. Families usually isolated themselves and their children from the surrounding community, and were not part of neighborhood institutions. They distrusted local schools, regarded local services suspiciously, and, to the extent they used supportive services at all, they took their business outside the community (Furstenberg 1993: 237–243). The family system was thus largely disconnected from the community, and parents were left to "manage on their own" (1993: 243). The result was not only that children suffered greater risks associated with attenuated supervision and monitoring, but they also missed out on positive opportunities to be connected to the wider society through job, school, and friendship ties. This concept of individualistic strategies is similar to Wilson's (1987) notion of the *social isolation* prevalent in areas of concentrated urban poverty and racial segregation.

In contrast was a poor but nonetheless socially cohesive neighborhood in South Philadelphia labeled "Garrison Heights." Although Furstenberg found the same range of parenting skills as in North Philadelphia, what differed was the form of social networks among families – even those with poor parenting skills. As such, despite similar backgrounds (e.g., poverty, family structure), the youth in South Philadelphia faced quite different structural constraints than youth in the North Philadelphia neighborhood. For example, parents in Garrison Heights participated in shared parental responsibility, informal social control of youth in public space, and were bound together by kinship and friendship bonds that connected local institutions with the family. Youth could not easily escape the scrutiny of the neighborhood, and the task of parents inside the home was reinforced by mutual support of other neighborhood parents.

In short, parenting was viewed as a "collective activity" that "contrasts to the individualistic mode of family management forced upon parents in more anomic neighborhoods" (Furstenberg 1993: 249). The density and intergenerational closure of social networks in Garrison Heights made it possible for children in the community to be socialized not just by parents, but friends, relatives, and neighbors as well. This form of social cohesion was especially useful to families with problems in the daily management and supervision of their children. Indeed, Furstenberg's research (see especially his description of "Meg," pp. 243–249) suggests that even marginal families without the benefit of human capital (e.g., skilled and knowledgeable parents) or physical capital (e.g., material resources) may have counterbalancing sources of support in communities of dense social networks and social capital.

Family Disruption and Social Capital

A theoretical framework combining social disorganization theory with the idea of social capital also helps us to make sense of the effects of community family structure on crime. It is fairly well established in individual-level research that broken homes do not have much influence on delinquency (Loeber and Stouthamer-Loeber 1986). However, the *structure* of family relationships in a community may have important contextual or threshold influences (Sampson 1992). For example, high levels of family "disruption" (e.g., divorce rates; single-parent families with children) may facilitate crime by decreasing community networks of informal social control (e.g., taking note of or questioning strangers, watching over others' property, assuming responsibility for supervision of youth activities, intervening in local disturbances).

This conceptualization is similar to Coleman's idea of social capital (e.g., facilitation of action such as supervision) and does not assume that it is the children of divorced or separated parents that are engaging in crime. Rather, I suggest that youth in stable family areas, regardless of their own family situation, have more controls placed on their leisure-time activities, particularly with peer groups (see also Sullivan 1989: 178; Anderson 1990: 91). Because of the common occurrence of group delinquency, neighborhood family disruption is likely to influence the extent to which neighborhood youth are provided the opportunities to form a peer-control system free of the supervision or knowledge of adults (Reiss 1986a).

The empirical support for this notion is indirect but nonetheless fairly consistent. As reviewed in Sampson and Lauritsen (1993), several recent studies report a large positive relationship between neighborhood family disruption (usually percent female-headed families or divorce rate) and rates of crime. For example, Sampson (1985) found that rates of victimization were 2–3 times higher among residents of neighborhoods with high levels of family disruption compared to low levels, regardless of alternative predictors of victimization such as percent black and poverty. The percentage of female-headed families also helped to explain the relationship between percent black and crime. Namely, percent black and percent female-headed families are positively and significantly related; however, when percent female-headed families is controlled, percent black is not significantly related to violent victimization (1985: 27). Similarly, Smith and Jarjoura (1988) report that family structure, especially percent single-parent families, helps account for the association between race and violent crime at the community level: racial composition was not significantly related to violent crime in multivariate models once percent single-parent families was included.

Assessing Contextual Theories of Social Disorganization

The data requirements to assess the multilevel theory of social disorganization presented above are strict, explaining why the theory has been rarely, if ever, tested in previous research. First, and most obvious, one must collect extensive data spanning the individual, family, and community levels. Second, there must be sufficient variation in key theoretical constructs at the community level. The sampling designs of most delinquency studies, especially national surveys, preclude the examination of individuals nested within communities that vary on key social characteristics. Third, there must be a sufficient number of macro-level units to sustain an aggregate (between-community) analysis. Fourth, even with a nested design and a sufficient number of communities, serious methodological constraints have plagued the estimation of prior multilevel models (e.g., nonindependence of observations within units, biased standard errors, unreliable indicators). Statistical models designed for multilevel data are called for (see Bryk and Raudenbush 1992).

Finally, and probably most important, data are needed to measure directly the constructs of community social organization. Traditional (e.g., census) studies are not well suited to such an examination; instead, extensive and original data collection is required within each of the communities in the analysis (Heitgerd and Bursik 1987: 785). Ethnographic research (e.g., Suttles 1968, Furstenberg 1993) is an exception by providing rich descriptive accounts of community processes central to theoretical concerns. However, ethnographies are constrained in their ability to test theories because they focus on a single community, or, at most, on a cluster of neighborhoods where community properties do not display sufficient variation (Reiss 1986a: 27). There are some excellent studies that have examined quantitative dimensions of informal social control (see e.g., Maccoby et al. 1958; Simcha-Fagan and Schwartz 1986), but they too have been limited to relatively few communities, precluding multivariate analysis. Inner-city neighborhoods and minority groups have been especially neglected.

Two studies-in-progress counteract these past trends and hence promise to shed new light on the multilevel sources of crime and delinquency in urban environments. One study already in the field is the "Neighborhoods Project" of the Research Network on Successful Adolescent Development, directed by Richard Jessor and sponsored by the John D. and Catherine T. MacArthur Foundation. This collaborative project on adolescent development involves ongoing studies in Chicago and Denver, USA. The Chicago Neighborhood Project (CNP) is being directed by William Julius Wilson at the University of Chicago, and the Denver Youth Study (DYS) is being carried out under the direction of Delbert Elliott at the Institute of Behavioral Science.

The CNP is based on data collected from over 500 black families living in Chicago neighborhoods in 1990. The sample was selected so that there would be variation in key community-level constructs, especially poverty. Although "neighborhoods" were defined operationally by census boundaries, inspection of city maps combined with other knowledge of Chicago neighborhoods suggests that most of these areas have natural boundaries with distinct geographical features (e.g., parks, major streets). An average of 15 mothers and 22 children live in each of over 30 neighborhoods under study. The Denver site of the Neighborhoods Project is analyzing variations in community characteristics for both block groups and census tracts. Importantly, identical survey items were administered in both Chicago and Denver that tap neighborhood-level constructs such as informal social control, density of local networks, organizational participation, social cohesion, value and normative consensus, criminal opportunities, and other dimensions of community social organization.

Global ratings by each respondent can be aggregated to form neighborhood-level indicators.

Overall, then, the Neighborhoods Project (1993) in Chicago and Denver will permit examination of variations in community social organization – especially informal social control – and how they are related to variations in adolescent delinquency and other problem behaviors. The project is specifically assessing the hypothesis that informal social controls mediate the effect of structural disadvantage on delinquency rates in the direction specified by social disorganization theory. The Denver and Chicago studies are exploring new ground in another respect. Namely, they were designed to allow a detailed investigation of African-American (Chicago) and Hispanic (Denver) neighborhoods – disadvantaged urban poor as well as urban middle-class.

The Program on Human Development and Criminal Behavior (1993) is a second and even larger project that aims to substantially increase our understanding of how community-level and individual-level factors interact in the development of criminal behavior and substance abuse. Also supported by the MacArthur Foundation in addition to the National Institute of Justice, the Program on Human Development and Criminal Behavior PHDCD) is directed by Felton Earls and Albert J. Reiss Jr. To study variations in community organization a large number of neighborhoods (70–80) will be selected from Chicago. Changes in these areas will be monitored over an eight year period by drawing probability samples of community residents and interviewing them in cross-sectional surveys that will be repeated on three occasions over an eight year period.

Embedded in the study of communities is an accelerated longitudinal design incorporating nine overlapping age groups and 11,000 subjects. The starting points of the nine age groups will begin with prenatal development and include subjects at 3, 6, 9, 12, 15, 18, 21, and 24 years. Individuals will be tracked and developmental change examined for eight years, yielding results that will approximate what would be learned from tracking a single birth cohort for some three decades (32 years). Subjects will be obtained through a probability sample of children, adolescents, and young adults who represent the ethnic and socioeconomic class structure of each neighborhood. Cohort samples will be followed over the same eight year period that is used to monitor community change. The complete design thus aims to link the dynamic changes in urban community contexts with developmental change within individual subjects. This objective has not been attempted before in a study of this size and scope (for further details see Program on Human Development and Criminal Behavior 1993).

In brief, the PHDCB design proposes to follow subjects not only over time, but also through environmental contexts. A unique feature of the proposed study is the plan to sample individuals from approximately 75 communities within the city of Chicago, stratified by race/ethnicity and socioeconomic status. The study of individual variation will be nested within the study of community variation, so that one can examine individual-level variables in statistical interaction with aspects of neighborhood context. At least three types of community comparisons can thus be made: subjects who live in different types of communities may differ, subjects may change as their communities change over time, and subjects may change when they move from one type of community to another. Measures of social disorganization, resources and services, criminal activity, community demographics, and other factors will be collected repeatedly to track each communities' changing characteristics over the eight years of the study. This proposed design moves beyond traditional longitudinal studies of crime and development through the multiple cohort (accelerated) design and the degree of detail characterizing community-level influences through time.

Conclusion

Theories of communities and crime generally ignore family management and aspects of child development, whereas theories of the family tend to ignore community ecology (Bronfenbrenner et al. 1984). For example, the dominant perspectives on community emphasize structural characteristics thought to influence motivations to crime such as economic deprivation and inequality (see the review in Sampson and Lauritsen 1993). Aspects of family management such as the daily monitoring and supervision of children are usually ignored. By contrast, those who study child development usually neglect community context and focus instead on individual families "under the roof" (see Sampson 1992).

The Neighborhoods Project (1993) and the Program on Human Development and Criminal Behavior (1993) represent new steps in counteracting this trend by integrating individual, family, and community effects on antisocial and criminal behavior across stages of the life course. Of course, these efforts will face formidable analytical challenges. The analyses will have to consider both individual and community change. To date, criminological analyses have not yet considered individuals as they move from one community context to another, and communities as they differentially change over time. Only by studying both individuals and communities as they are simultaneously changing are we likely to unravel causal sequences of social development and crime in a definitive fashion.

Furthermore, until recently contextual analyses in criminology have relied on ordinary least-squares methodology even though the cluster design of the multilevel sampling calls for hierarchical linear models (see Bryk and Raudenbush 1992).

Combined with potential confounding effects arising from self-selection (Tienda 1991) and reciprocal effects from crime itself (Skogan 1986), future analyses will be difficult to implement.

Nevertheless, the two main hypotheses developed earlier in this paper seem worthy of further consideration by these and other projects attempting to wrestle with multilevel influences on delinquency. The first is that variations in community social organization – especially informal social control – appear to mediate the effect of structural disadvantage (e.g., concentration of poverty, welfare dependency, family disruption) on crime and delinquency rates. Urban poverty in racially segregated environments (see Wilson 1987) may thus have important consequences for understanding the negative effect of community-level informal social control on crime rates.

Second, community-level variations in social cohesion and informal social control in all likelihood have indirect effects on individual-level variations in delinquent outcomes as mediated by family management and social capital. In particular, the monitoring of youth activities and time spent with peers, networks between parents and their children's friends and parents, and the effective and consistent discipline of children are hypothesized to be fostered in neighborhoods characterized by high levels of social cohesion and informal social controls. In turn, strong family social controls reduce the probability of delinquent outcomes.

This multilevel theory sheds light on the perplexing finding in prior research that community characteristics have few contextual effects on individual delinquency (see Bursik 1993). The reason may be that most studies search for direct effects of context on delinquency, even though on theoretical grounds this may be unwarranted. Perhaps because of this focus on direct effects, contextual influences have been prematurely rejected. Supportive of the general thrust of Furstenberg's (1993) argument, it may be that community social control finds its expression in individual-level outcomes largely through the mediating influence of peers, school, and the family (see also Simcha-Fagan and Schwartz 1986; Sampson 1992). Research designed to uncover the direct and indirect influences of family and community on delinquency – especially over time – thus represents an important agenda for the future.

References

Anderson, E. (1990). *Streetwise: Race, Class, and Change in an Urban Community.* Chicago: University of Chicago Press.

Angell, R. (1942). The Social Integration of American Cities. *American Journal of Sociology* 47: 575–592.

Bronfenbrenner, U., Moen, P. & Garbarino, J. (1984). Child, Family, and Community. Pp. 283–328 in *Review of Child Development Research,* Volume 7: The Family, edited by R. Parke. Chicago: University of Chicago Press.

Bryk, A. & Raudenbush, S. (1992). *Hierarchical Linear Models.* Newbury Park, CA: Sage.

Bursik, R.J. Jr. (1988). Social Disorganization and Theories of Crime and Delinquency: Problems and Prospects. *Criminology* 26: 519–552.

Bursik, R.J. Jr. (1993). Contextual Models in Delinquency Research. In *Current Theories of Crime and Delinquency,* edited by J. David Hawkins. Newbury Park, CA: Sage, forthcoming.

Bursik, R.J. Jr. & Grasmick, H. (1993). *Neighborhoods and Crime: The Dimensions of Effective Community Control.* New York: Lexington.

Byrne, J. & Sampson, R.J. (1986). Key Issues in the Social Ecology of Crime. Pp. 1–22 in J. Byrne and R.J. Sampson, eds., *The Social Ecology of Crime.* New York: Springer-Verlag, Inc.

Coleman, J. (1988). Social Capital in the Creation of Human Capital. *American Journal of Sociology* 94: S95-S120.

Coleman, J. (1990). *Foundations of Social Theory.* Cambridge: Harvard University Press.

Furstenberg, F. (1993). How Families Manage Risk and Opportunity in Dangerous Neighborhoods. Pp. 231–258 in *Sociology and the Public Agenda,* edited by W. J. Wilson. Newbury Park, CA: Sage.

Heitgerd, J. L. & Bursik, R.J. Jr. (1987). Extracommunity Dynamics and the Ecology of Delinquency. *American Journal of Sociology* 92: 775–787.

Hirschi, T. (1983). Crime and the Family. In *Crime and Public Policy,* edited by J.Q. Wilson. San Francisco: Institute for Contemporary Studies.

Kasarda, J. & Janowitz, M. (1974). Community Attachment in Mass Society. *American Sociological* Review 39: 328–339.

Kornhauser, R. (1978). *Social Sources of Delinquency.* Chicago: University of Chicago Press.

Land, K., McCall, P. & Cohen, L. (1990). Structural Covariates of Homicide Rates: Are There any Invariances across Time and Space? *American Journal of Sociology* 95: 922–63.

Laub, J. & Sampson, R. (1988). Unraveling Families and

Delinquency: A Reanalysis of the Gluecks' Data. *Criminology* 26: 355–380.

Loeber, R. & Stouthamer-Loeber, M. (1986). Family Factors as Correlates and Predictors of Juvenile Conduct Problems and Delinquency. In M. Tonry and N. Morris, eds., *Crime and Justice: An Annual Review of Research* (Vol. 7). Chicago: University of Chicago Press.

Maccoby, E., Johnson, J. & Church, R. (1958). Community Integration and the Social Control of Juvenile Delinquency. Journal of Social Issues 14: 38–51.

Neighborhoods Project. (1993). *Network on Successful Adolescence, Collaborative Work-in-Progress*. Chicago: Center for the Study Urban Inequality; Denver: Institute for Behavioral Science.

Patterson, G. (1982). *Coercive Family Process*. Eugene, Oregon: Castalia.

Program on Human Development and Criminal Behavior. (1993). Boston: Harvard School of Public Health.

Reiss, A. J., Jr. (1986a). Why are Communities Important in Understanding Crime? Pp. 1–33 in *Communities and Crime,* edited by A.J. Reiss, Jr. and M. Tonry. Chicago: University of Chicago Press.

Reiss, A. J., Jr. (1986b). Co-offender Influences on Criminal Careers. Pp. 121–160 in *Criminal Careers and "Career Criminals",* edited by A. Blumstein, J. Cohen, J. Roth, and C. Visher. Washington, D.C.: National Academy Press.

Rieder, J. (1985). Canarsie: *The Jews and Italians of Brooklyn Against Liberalism.* Cambridge: Harvard University Press.

Sampson, R. J. (1985). Neighborhood and Crime: The Structural Determinants of Personal Victimization. *Journal of Research in Crime and Delinquency* 22: 7–40.

Sampson, R. J. (1991). Linking the Micro and Macrolevel Dimensions of Community Social Organization. *Social Forces* 70: 43–64.

Sampson, R. J. (1992). Family Management and Child Development: Insights from Social Disorganization Theory. Pp. 63–93 in Facts, Frameworks, and Forecasts, Vol. 3 of *Advances in Criminological Theory,* edited by Joan McCord. New Brunswick: Transaction.

Sampson, R.J. & Groves, W. B. (1989). Community Structure and Crime: Testing Social-disorganization Theory. *American Journal of Sociology* 94: 774–802.

Sampson, R.J. & Lauritsen, J. (1993). Violent Victimization and Offending: Individual, Situational, and Community-level Risk Factors. In *Understanding and Preventing Violence* (volume 3). Washington, D.C.: National Academy Press, forthcoming.

Shaw, C. & McKay, H. (1942). *Juvenile Delinquency and Urban Areas.* Chicago: University of Chicago Press.

Shaw, C. & McKay, H. (1969). *Juvenile Delinquency and Urban*

Areas (Revised Edition). Chicago: University of Chicago Press.

Short, J. F. Jr. (1963). Introduction to the abridged edition. Pp. xv-liii in F. Thrasher, The Gang: *A Study of 1,313 Gangs in Chicago*. Chicago: University of Chicago Press.

Short, J. F. & Strodtbeck, F. (1965). *Group Process and Gang Delinquency*. Chicago: University of Chicago Press.

Simcha-Fagan, O. & Schwartz, J. (1986). Neighborhood and Delinquency: An Assessment of Contextual Effects. *Criminology* 24: 667–704.

Skogan, W. (1986). Fear of Crime and Neighborhood Change. Pp. 203–229 in *Communities and Crime,* edited by A.J. Reiss, Jr. and M. Tonry. Chicago: University of Chicago Press.

Smith, D. R. & Jarjoura, G. R. (1988). Social Structure and Criminal Victimization. *Journal of Research in Crime and Delinquency* 25: 27–52.

Sullivan, M. (1989). *Getting Paid: Youth Crime and Work in the Inner City*. Ithaca, N.Y.: Cornell University Press.

Suttles, G. (1968). *The Social Order of the Slum*. Chicago: University of Chicago Press.

Taylor, R., S. Gottfredson, and S. Brower. 1984. Block Crime and Fear: Defensible Space, Local Social Ties, and Territorial Functioning. *Journal of Research in Crime and Delinquency* 21: 303–331.

Thrasher, F. (1963). *The Gang: A Study of 1,313 Gangs in Chicago* (Revised Edition). Chicago: University of Chicago Press.

Tienda, M. (1991). Poor People and Poor Places: Deciphering Neighborhood Effects on Poverty Outcomes. Pp. 244–262 in *Macro-Micro Linkages in Sociology,* edited by J. Huber. Newbury, CA: Sage.

Wilson, W. J. (1987). *The Truly Disadvantaged: The Inner City, the Underclass, and Public Policy*. Chicago: Univ. of Chicago Press.

Individual Pathways to Crime in Different Types of Neighborhood

by Rolf Loeber and Per-Olof H. Wikström

Introduction

There is a large body of theory and research in the field of socio-ecological studies of crime. There is also a large body of theory and research in studies of individual aspects of offending. But the monumental task of integrating the two has just begun.

Although there seem to be agreement for the need of integration (e.g. Reiss,1986; Tonry, Ohlin & Farrington,1991), so far, very few empirical studies have attempted this. Most studies that have tried to take into account the influence of both neighborhood context and individual characteristics of offending have been cross-sectional. A pioneering study in this field is Reiss & Rhodes (1961) "*The Distribution of Juvenile Delinquency in the Social Class Structure.*" There is a great need to examine the interaction between individual characteristics and neighborhoods over time. As Tonry, Ohlin, and Farrington (1991:42) have expressed;

> "*...there are strong theoretical reasons to expect that individual characteristics, family processes, and life transistions interact with community characteristics to explain criminal careers. In particular, trajectories of within-individual longitudinal change may differ by community context.*"

In this paper we will present a preliminary analysis of the relationship between individual developmental pathways in offending and neighborhood characteristics. Two basic pathways will be considered; pathways in overt and covert offending. The basic question is whether or not the developmental pathways are invariant by type of neighborhood.

The steps in the analyses are;

(1) The neighborhoods are classified into types of neighborhoods on the basis of a factorial social ecological analysis of population variables,
(2) The individual subjects are categorized according to the type of neighborhood of residence.

(3) The neighborhood classification potential in picking up neighborhood variation in offending is validated by studying how prevalence in offending varies by neighborhood type.
(4) The subjects are classified according to their individual development in overt and covert pathways of offending.
(5) Finally, the individuals' penetration in each pathway is related to neighborhood type.

Although the neighborhood classification is cross-sectional the pathways classification is based on longitudinal data. In a later stage of this research we will attempt to relate the pathways (and other individual developmental characteristics of offending) to other aspects of neighborhoods and to neighborhood change.

City Neighborhoods and Offending

The overall environment of a large town or city is characterized by a form of social life which is influenced by its heterogeneity and the size and density of the population. There is also considerable variation in the social life of its constituent parts. Sites are put to a wide variety of uses; the various urban districts display a multitude of combinations of housing types, industry, shops, public entertainments, etc., and may range from purely residential areas to downtown districts with few permanent inhabitants.

Patterns of urban land use appear to have not only certain universal similarities but also unique characteristics associated with the country and city in question. It is beyond the scope of this paper to review the reasons for these variations in detail, although "market forces" and the degree and structure of urban planning appear to be two important factors (se e.g. Harris & Ullman, 1974; Johnston, 1984). For the present purpose, however, it will be sufficient to note that the use to which city land is put differs considerably from district to district.

As land is used for widely differing purposes, human activities (home life, work, leisure, entertainment, etc.) will vary considerably form neighborhood to neighborhood. Since the frequency of different types of activities varies with both the day of the week and the time of day, there is not only a spatial variation in human activities but also a temporal one – variations occur over time in any given area. Together with the street layout and the structure of the public transport system, spatial and temporal differences in human activities affect patterns of human movement throughout the city at different times of the day. This, in turn, influences the frequency and types of encounters between people of differing backgrounds and relationships and the circumstances in which they meet in different parts of the city at different times of the day. As to criminal activities, the opportunties to delinquent acts and the conditions for social control are likely to vary between areas of a city depending on its land use pattern and its consequences for social life. (Wikström, 1991).

Housing and residential segregation

Housing is a specialized form of land use. It is well known that segregation by social grouping is common (see e.g. Timms, 1971; Schwirian, 1974). This is especially of importance in any study of big-city crime, since delinquency is unevenly distributed across the population and within different social classes and age groups. Studies of differential housing in urban environments have shown that three factors are of particular importance to segregation: familism (type of family), socio-economic status, and, in an ethnically heterogeneous community, ethnicity (see e.g. Timms, 1971, p. 85; Schwirian, 1974, pp. 8–10; Janson, 1980, p. 447; Wikström, 1991). In addition, the segregated accommodation of "problem housholds" has become an increasing focus of interest in urban structure studies over the last number of years (see Walldén, 1985, pp. 191–192; Wikström, 1991).

A major cause of urban segregation is regional variation in types of housing (e.g. detached houses, multi-family blocks, etc.) and right of tenure (rented, privately owned) (see Bottoms, Claytor & Wiles, 1992; Wikström, 1991). Different types of households have different preferences as to accommodation. Families with children, for example, will often prefer to live in a single family house (if they can afford it), while single persons may prefer a flat in a multi-unit dwelling. The financial strength of a household is a predominant factor in its choice of accommodation. Households with meagre economic resources (and especially the socially marginalized households of criminals and drug abusers) are often limited to a rented flat, mostly in slum areas and in buildings belonging to and administered by public authorities, since they usually acquire their accommodation through the Public Housing Authority (often on the grounds that they have social priority).

The mechanisms through which flats and houses are allocated give rise to different combinations of local populations as defined by type of family, socio-economic status, ethnic status, and social problems. This, in combination with the type of housing characteristic of the district, influences the social life of any particular neighborhood. The heterogeneity of the population (in terms of age, ethnic origin, etc.) may vary strongly from one district to another. There must also be other differences in social life,for example, between the inhabitants of a highrise district and those living in a suburb of detached houses, which can be attributed at least in part to the actual type of buildings. Physical design characteristics of buildings and housing estates often influence social life and social control in neighborhood by their effects on *social space, privacy and surveillance opportunities.*

Residential segregation and offending

The offender distribution in urban populations is highly skewed, and the offender rate varies significantly among different age and social groups . Moreover, it is also well established that there is a significant residential segregation of different social groups in urban areas, but this differs from country to country (see, e.g., Theodorson. 1961; Timms, 1971; Schwirian, 1974; Wikström, 1991). Therefore, one is to expect that the offender rate should vary among different residential areas of a city – perhaps more so in more segregated cities than in others – and covary with the social group patterns of residential segregation within the city. At one extreme, one can view all of the residential area variation in offender rates as caused by the social group segregation in the city. But of course, it is also possible to view it from the other extreme – that all social group variation in offending is due to contextual effects resulting from differential patterns of residence for different social groups . The truth is probably somewere in between these two extremes.

Neighborhood differences in offending

It is a well-established fact that offender rates vary significantly between urban neighborhoods (see, Brantingham & Brantingham, 1984 p. 297–331). There are two main reasons why area of residence and offending may be related (Wikström,1991):

1. Neighborhood and offending may be related because more crime-prone social groups are segregated to certain types of neighborhoods.
2. Neighborhood may also, in itself, influence criminal motivation through the impact of area contextual characteristics (social and built environment) on social life and social control in an area.

This latter influence may be divided into (a) short-term situational influences on criminal motivation, and (b) long-term influences on the development of personality and modes of living affecting the individual's propensity to commit crime.
Contextual effects may be defined as "*macro processes that are presumed to have an impact on the individual actor over and above the effects of any individual-level variables that may be operating* " (Blalock, 1985, p. 354).

The question as to what degree individual characteristics, and social life and control in area of residence, respectively, influence individuals' propensity to commit crime is still a key issue in criminology. There are few studies with suitable data to fully examine this issue. One major difficulty lies in not being able to separate and weigh the relative importance of individual, social and psychological characteristics and area contextual influences, especially in light of the fact that these influences are likely to interact and that their relative impact may change over the individuals' life span.

For children and adolescents, the relationship between area of residence and offending is likely, at least partly, to reflect residential segregation patterns (i.e., families with more crime-prone children tend to be segregated in certain types of areas). In addition to possible short-term situational influences on offending, area of residence in childhood and adolescence may also have a long-term influence on offending through its impact on socialization processes as depending on neighborhood differences in social life and social control. This may then foster a delinquent way of life that might persist into adulthood. Timms (1971) has stressed the great importance of neighborhoods in the socialization process:

> "*For much of the first ten or eleven years of life much of the individual's activity is confined to an area within a relatively small radius of his home. In this area he obtains most of his extra-familial social relationships, notably in play-groups. It is more likely than not that his school will be in close proximity and most of his school peers will be neighbours.*" (pp. 31–32)

In summary, for children and adolescents, variations in offender rates by area may reflect segregation patterns and long- and short-term area contextual influences. Since juvenile offending is not static but often changes with time, we also have to ask to what extent such changes takes place in an orderly fashion and whether it is possible to discern pathways to serious forms of offending.

Pathways

Traditional quantification of deviant behavior of juveniles has concentrated on measures of prevalence, frequency or seriousness, usually at a particular point or interval of time. These measures, although useful, do not indicate the position of the individual on a developmental trajectory or pathway of deviance over his/her life time. In order to achieve this, one would like to quantify how far an individual has progressed on a conceptual pathway from less to more serious forms of deviance. Research on pathways (Loeber, 1991) first determines the nature of the deviancy dimension which constitutes the basis of a developmental pathway, and then establishes whether most individuals' temporal development of deviance best fits a given pathway model. Given that this is the case, then individuals' position on the pathways at a given time can be established.

In the area of aggression and violence, for example, the first step is to determine the temporal development of aggression and violence in order to formulate and test a developmental pathway toward serious violence. The second step is to determine individuals' position on that pathway. The major advantage of the use of pathways in quantifying individuals' deviance is that it can take into account past history of deviance, speed of deviancy development, and identification of the next step in development which the individual has not yet attained (which is useful for prevention).

Disruptive child behaviors are known to be heterogeneous, and distinctions have been made between overt (or aggressive) and covert (or concealing) problem behaviors (Loeber & Schmaling, 1985a; Frick et al., in press). Therefore, youths can be conceptualized as developing within each domain, with some advancing to more serious overt problems, others advancing to more serious covert problems, and a third group advancing in both domains. This is akin to the concept of developmental lines as conceived by Anna Freud (1965). In order to establish the development of pathology, an entire profile of developmental lines or pathways needs to be examined with an eye on establishing discrepancies between actual and normal development for each line of functioning.

Age of onset, and temporal order of behaviors are some of the basic elements of pathways (Loeber, 1991). Researchers (Farrington et al., 1990) have debated whether ages of onset of delinquency, like ages of onset of substance use, develop in an orderly and predictable manner (Blumstein, Cohen, Roth, & Visher, 1986). Findings on the development of substance use show that the first stage includes the use of beer or wine; the second stage concerns marijuana use; while the final stage involves the use of hard drugs (Hamburg, Kraemer, & Jahnke, 1975; Kandel, 1980).

In order to test whether developmental stages exist for delinquent behavior, a developmental sequence must be formulated and its predictive utility tested. The first test is to examine the distribution of disruptive boys at each stage of a pathway; a majority should begin their course of disruptive behavior at the first stage, a smaller number should begin at the intermediate stage and a minority should begin with behaviors typical of the later stage. The second test is whether the majority of those who advance to a serious outcome have actually displayed intermediate stage(s) within the sequence. In that sense, the quest is for intermediate stages which are a "necessary" condition for the progression to more serious stages of behavior. For instance, in substance use, most of those who use hard drugs will have initially sampled beer or wine, cigarettes or liquor, and marijuana, in that order (Kandel, 1978). The existence of a common developmental sequence, however, does not mean that all individuals will go through the full sequence. Instead, it is likely that a large proportion advances through the early stage in the sequence, a smaller proportion of individuals reaches the intermediate stage, while an even smaller proportion of individuals eventually travels the full sequence.

Findings on the utility of the age of onset of disruptive behavior problems have been a matter of controversy. Interpretations of results has depended on the type of behavior studied and whether the subjects were clinic-referred or a community sample (Barkley, 1989; Behar & Stewart, 1982; Jacobson, 1985; Loeber, Stouthamer-Loeber, & Green, 1991; Stewart, Copeland, & deBlois, 1988). Some research findings have hinted at developmental sequences in delinquency. For example, Le Blanc and Fréchette (1989) plotted youngsters' self-reported age of onset of delinquent acts in a three-panel longitudinal study. They found that larceny tended to have an earlier age of onset than shoplifting which, in turn, had an earlier age of onset than petty theft, burglary, or motor vehicle theft. Similarly, a re-analysis of Belson's (1975) retrospective interview with London boys, aged 13 to 16, provided evidence for a developmental sequence in theft, with minor theft occurring at an earlier age than major theft (Loeber, 1988). The retrospective reports, however, leave open the possibility that recall biases may have operated. Also, comparisons between ages of onset for different theft behaviors referred to group data rather than to within-subject changes over time.

There is a scarcity of prospective studies which have addressed developmental sequences in delinquency. Le Blanc, Côté, and Loeber (1981), in their analysis of a follow-up of boys from Montreal, were able to outline specific *behavioral* sequences over time, such as minor theft to vandalism, and minor theft to selling and using drugs. These analyses, however, were limited to two points in time. Moreover, few studies have classified *individuals* according to their development of deviant behavior over time.

Single vs. multiple pathways

Another unresolved issue is whether there is a single pathway representing all different types of disruptive behavior (such as stealing, violence, and truancy) or whether the development of these behaviors can be best captured by multiple pathways or developmental lines for each separate domain of behavior. A literature review of the developmental studies on disruptive behavior (Loeber, 1988) concluded that there was evidence for several pathways of disruptive child behavior. A first pathway, called the Aggressive/Versatile Pathway was characterized by youngsters who developed aggressive *and* concealing or covert conduct problems. Hyperactivity was thought to be most linked to this pathway. A second pathway, labelled the Nonaggressive Antisocial Pathway was largely confined to youth who developed nonaggressive, covert acts only. Both the Aggressive/Versatile and the Nonaggressive Paths appeared closely tied to the development of substance (ab)use. However, a third pathway, called the Exclusive Substance Abuse Path, concerned those youth who advanced to serious levels of substance use in the absence of substantial involvement in disruptive behaviors. Other researchers have recently proposed a division of disruptive youths based on age of onset in childhood or adolescence (Moffitt, 1992; Tolan & Guerra 1992).

A dynamic classification of disruptive youngsters according to pathways, however, should be considered in the context of the results from concurrent classification studies. Meta-analyses of parent and teacher ratings of disruptive child behavior (Loeber & Schmaling, 1985a, Lahey et al., 1992) showed that one major dimension of disruptive behavior had overt problem behavior on one pole (e.g., temper tantrums, attacks people), and covert problem behavior on the other pole (e.g., theft, sets fires).

Overt and covert problem behaviors appear to have different correlates (Kazdin, 1992; Loeber & Schmaling, 1985b). Several studies have demonstrated that youngsters can be meaningfully classified according to the overt and covert dimensions of disruptive behavior (Loeber & Schmaling, 1985b; Frick et al., 1993) with the proviso, however, that some youth engage in both types of behavior (called versatiles). The distinction between overt and covert disruptive behavior largely corresponds to the distinction between person-related and property-related offenses. The difference lies in that the overt-covert distinction also incorporates minor delinquent problem behaviors.

Meta-analyses have not specifically focused on disobedience. Disobedience, defiance, truancy and running away differ from most other disruptive behaviors since they usually do not inflict the same degree of distress on others as do overt and covert crimes. Instead, we see these problems as various expressions of conflict with authority, often but not always occuring at an early age, which frequently overlap with overt and covert problem behaviors (in the meta-analyses, however, they were interspersed with these behaviors).

For these reasons, we hypothesize the existence of three basic but overlapping pathways in the development of disruptive child behavior: (a) Authority Conflict Pathway; (b) Covert Behavior Pathway; and (c) Overt Behavior Pathway. In the latter two pathways the assumption is that less serious disruptive behaviors tend to precede the onset of moderately serious behaviors which, in turn, precede the onset of very serious acts.

Neighborhoods and Pathways

Most ecological studies on crime have focused on exploring and explaining differences in *rates* of offending (crime, and victimization). There are good reasons to believe that neighborhood characteristics influences variation in motivation to offend. It is also likely that neighborhood characteristics can influence the *patterns* of development of offending. In some areas social control may be stronger and opportunities for crime less, while in others the reverse may be true. For instance, criminal behavior may in some neighborhoods develop more easily into serious forms than in other areas due to differences in levels of social control. Opportunity structures may also differ between neighborhoods and, thereby, possibly influencing types of offending patterns. Demographic characteristics, such as number of youth, may influence peer group formation and interactions. The presence in neighborhood of a lot of adult criminals and abusers may influence youth behavioral patterns. And so forth.

The study of the pattern of individual development of offending in different ecological contexts (e.g., urban-rural areas and different neighborhoods of cities) is a largely neglected field in criminological research. Most studies of relevance for this are either concerned with either ecological influences on offending or the individual development of offending but seldom with the relationship between the two (but, see Shannon, 1988). Hence, we know quite little about the influence of the ecological context on the pattern of the individual development of offending.

Data and Measures

In this section we will present the individual and ecological data, the individual and ecological measures, and the classifications of pathways and neighborhoods to be used in the analysis of the relationship between the two.

Ecological Data

The data for the ecological analyses are taken from the 1980 census of Pittsburgh (Pennsylvania). Pittsburgh is traditionally divided into 88 neighborhoods which will form the basic unit in the urban structure analyses. However, a single neighborhood (Bluff) needed to be excluded because inspection of graphs of variable distributions showed that one of the included variables (mean household size) had an extreme value for this area. This value distorted the whole urban population structure analyses and it was therefore judged to be best to exclude the Bluff area. The probable reason for the extreme value was identified as the presence in this neighborhood of a large number of student dormatories and the ways in which the residents of these were counted as "households". However, the Bluff area was re-entered into the pathway analysis by classifying it on basis of its values on all other included neighborhood variables except mean household size.

Individual Data

Subjects were boys enrolled in the city's public schools . Subject selection and measures have been described in detail by Loeber, Stouthamer-Loeber, Van Kammen and Farrington (1991), and are only briefly summarized here. The present study concerns the middle and oldest of three samples in this study. Schools provided the names of all boys in grades 4 and 7, from whom a random sample was drawn. Interviewers then went to the subjects' homes to enroll the boys and their principal caretaker (usually the mother) in the study.

An initial screening (called phase S) was used to generate retrospective data on the boys' distruptive and delinquent behavior. This information was used to develop a sample with an overrepresentation of boys who had already demonstrated disruptive behavior. For that purpose the top 30% of the most antisocial boys in each grade were selected and an equal number of the remaining 70% were randomly selected which resulted in a total sample of about 500 boys in each of the two grades (N=508 for middle sample, N=506 for oldest sample). In this study the data have been weighted in order to be representative of the population of boys in public schools in Pittsburgh.

The demographic characteristics of the sample have been reported in detail by Van Kammen, Loeber and Stouthamer-Loeber (1991). Approximately half of the boys (56.2 % in the oldest sample, 53,7 % in the middle sample) were African-American and half were Caucasian; 36.4% of the families in the oldest sample and 40.6 % in the middle sample received welfare, and 44.0% of those in the oldest and 36,7 in the middle sample lived in single households. The attrition rate was very low, with 89.5% of the oldest sample and 93.9 % of the middle sample completing the sixth assessment (phase E).

Ecological Measures

On basis of the findings from previous studies of the factorial social ecology of cities (e.g. Janson, 1980, Wikström,1991) – showing familism (i.e. family type), socioeconomic status and ethnic status to be the important segregational dimensions – nine variables from the census data were selected for the ecological analysis:

1. Mean household size.
2. Percent youth (ages 10–19)
3. Percent living in same residence the last 5 years or more.
4. Percent broken families (of families with children).
5. Median household income
6. Percent families below poverty level.
7. Percent households on public assistance.
8. Percent unemployed.
9. Percent African-Americans.

Individual Measures

The primary caretaker completed an extended version of the Child Behavior Checklist (MCBC) at phases S through E (Acenbach & Edelbrock, 1983; Loeber, Stouthamer-Loeber, Van Kammen & Farrington, 1991). At the second phase of data collection (A), primary caretakers were also administered a revised form of the Diagnostic Schedule for Children (DISC) (Costello, Edelbrock, Dulcan, Kalas, & Klaric, 1984). The interview assessed lifetime symptom manifestation in a variety of areas including oppositional defiant behavior and conduct problems. This interview made it possible to ascertain DSM-III-R diagnoses of Disruptive Behavior Disorders, of which the diagnosis of Attention-Deficit Hyperactivity Disorder will be considered here. In phases S through E, the boys responded to a revised version of the Self-Reported Delinquency Scale (SRD) (Elliott, Huizinga, & Ageton, 1985). The SRD used a six-month reference period. In addition in phase A, life-time questions, including questions about the age of onset of delinquency were asked.

Thus, for the analyses, retrospective data on the onset of disruptive child behavior was based on the lifetime question in the DISC, and the SRD questionnaire administered at either phases S or A. Prospective information on onset of child behaviors was measured using the MCBC, the YSR, and the SRD questionnaire at six month intervals at phases B through E. When possible, information was pooled across mother and child reports, so that a symptom's presence could be determined by a positive report by either of the two informants. MCBC or YSR items with low base rates regarded as serious forms of disruptive behavior were considered positively endorsed if either the child or mother reported that the were "somewhat true" or "very true" (e.g., shoplifting, gang fights, fire setting). MCBC or YSR items with high base rates regarded as less serious forms of disruptive behavior were considered positively endorsed if either the child or mother reported that they were "very true" (e.g., stubborn, lying, staying out late). This restriction was implemented in order to avoid the inclusion of oppositional behaviors other than those which were very distinct.

Moreover, prior research indicated that parents compared to children are better informants on childhood oppositional behaviors (Loeber, Green, & Lahey, 1990; Loeber, Green, Lahey, & Stouthamer-Loeber, 1989). Parents therefore were the principal informants about the onset of those behaviors. For most of the other behaviors considered here, the report of onset by both parent and child was used. If the parent and child reported different ages of onset for a particular behavior, the age of onset selected was the earliest reported age. As indicated in Table 1, the availability of different informants for particular disruptive behaviors varied, depending on the nature of the instruments.

Table 1. Items used to generate onset information for covert and overt behaviors.

		Instrument used; Retrospective	Prospective
COVERT BEHAVIOR			
Minor Covert Behavior	Lying	DISC	MCBC, YSR
	Shoplifting	SRD	MCBC, SRD
Property Damage	Setting fires	SRD	MCBC, SRD
	Vandalism	SRD	SRD
Moderate Delinquency	Joyriding	SRD	SRD, MCBC
	Pickpocketing	SRD	SRD
	Stealing from car	SRD	SRD
	Fencing	SRD	SRD
	Illegal Checks	SRD	SRD
	Illegal credit cards	SRD	SRD
Serious Delinquency	Stealing a car	SRD	SRD
	Selling drugs	SRD	SRD, MCBC
	Breaking/Entering	SRD	SRD
OVERT BEHAVIOR			
Minor Aggression	Annoying others	DISC	MCBC
	Bullying	DISC	MCBC
Fighting	Fighting	DISC	MCBC, YSR
	Gang fighting	SRD	SRD, MCBC
Violence	Attacking someone	SRD	SRD
	Strongarming	SRD	SRD
	Forcing sex	SRD	SRD

Note: DISC = Diagnostic Interview Schedule for Children – parent version; MCBC = Modified Child Behavior Checklist; YSR = Youth Self Report; SRD = Youth Self-Reported Delinquency Scale.

Classifications

Neighborhood Classification

The classification of neighborhoods into types was done in two steps. First a principal component factor analysis (varimax rotated) was preformed. Two factors with an eigenvalue above one were extracted. The first one was interpreted as (low) Socio-economic status, and the second as (high) Familism (Table 2) i.e. stable residential communities dominated by child-rich families. The total variance explained by the two factors was 77 %. The first (SES) factor explained 55 % and the second (Familism) factor explained 22 % of the variance. Also an oblique rotation was preformed (not shown) to test whether factors were significantly correlated or not. The result showed a weak, non-significant correlation (r=0.12).

Table 2. Principal components. Varimax rotated. Pittsburgh neighborhoods (N = 87).

Variables	Fact 1 (SES)	Fact 2 (Familism)	h_2
Household size	0,14	*0,90*	0,84
Youth in population	*0,48*	*0,73*	0,76
Res. stability	–0,22	*0,73*	0,58
Split families	*0,95*	–0,04	0,91
Median income	*–0,86*	0,33	0,84
Fam. below poverty	*0,93*	0,09	0,87
Public assistance	*0,93*	0,11	0,88
Unemployed	*0,69*	0,25	0,55
Afro-American	*0,85*	0,16	0,75
Explained variance;	0,55	0,22	

Note: Loadings 0.40 or higher in Italics.

The second step of the neighborhood classification was to calculate factor scores for each of the two factors. The resulting scores was divided into the neighborhoods with the 25 % highest values (upper quartile) and the neighborhoods with the 25 % lowest values (lower quartile) and the 50 % rest (middle values). The neighborhoods in the upper SES quartile are primarily poor areas and those in the lower quartile are primarily wealthy areas. The distributions of the factor scores in these classes were plotted on maps of Pittsburgh neighborhoods. The map of the SES neighborhood distribution shows a tendency for low SES areas to be located near the city centre – although there are more distant pockets of low SES neighborhoods – and the high SES neighborhoods to be located on the outskirts of Pittsburgh (Map 1). The map of the distribution of familism scores by neighborhood shows that high familism areas tends to be located on the outskirts of Pittsburgh, and that low familism areas tends to be located near the city centre or in some of the east parts of Pittsburgh (Map 2).

The neighborhoods included in each of the nine groups are shown in table 5. Individual subjects participating in the study resided in all of the Pittsburgh neighborhoods except five: North shore, Allegheny West, Allegheny Center, the CBD and North Oakland. After the classification of the neighborhoods was completed the individual subjects were assigned to neighborhood type on the basis of their area of residence SES and familism scores (Table 3).

Table 3. Individual subjects by neighborhood SES and familism. No and per cent. Middle & oldest sample.

	Familism: High	Medium	Low
High SES	98 (6.9)	99 (7.0)	56 (3.9)
Medium SES	79 (5.5)	462 (32.5)	86 (6.0)
Low SES	167 (11.7)	321 (22.6)	53 (3.7)

Note: Weighted data. N = 1.530 , Missing data = 109.

MAP 1. Factor 1 (SES). Factor scores

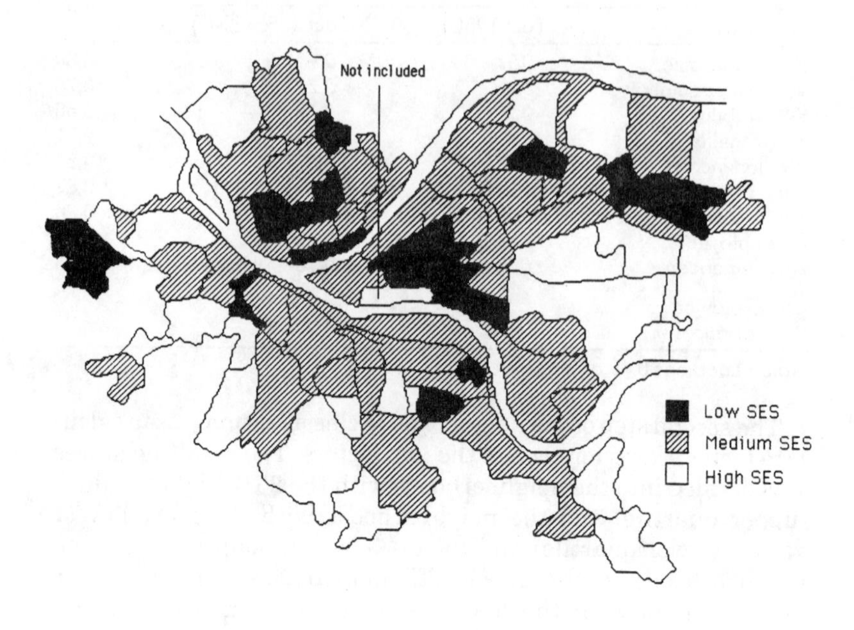

MAP 2. Factor 2 (Familism). Factor scores

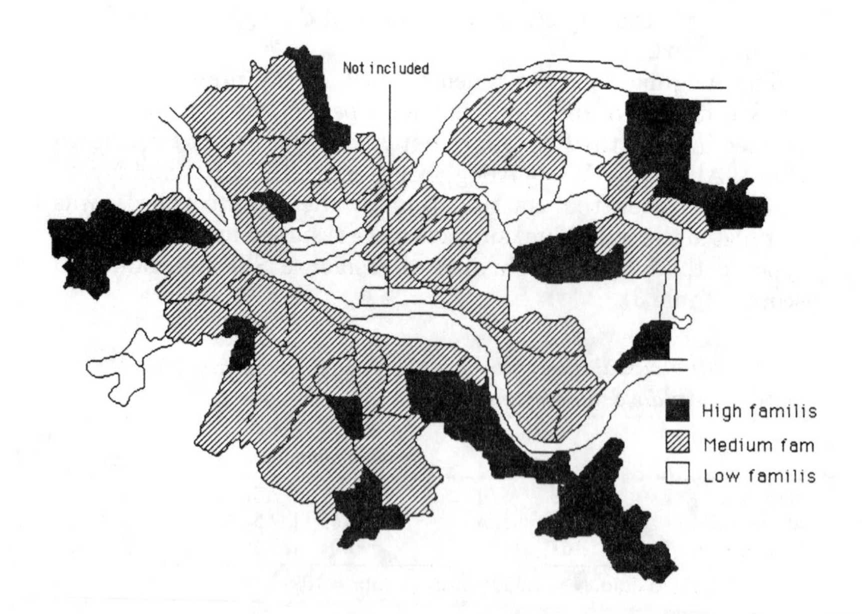

Validation of neighborhood classification

The ninefold neighborhood classification resulting from the factor analysis was validated against the *City of Pittsburgh Neighborhood Classification* (City of Pittsburgh 1992–1997 Development Policies, pages 53–54).

Table 4. The city of Pittsburgh classification.

Group/No of neighborhoods	Characterization of neighborhoods in group
Group 1 (N=31)	The most stable and prosperous neighborhoods in the city.
Group 2 (N=3)	A small group of wards described as having a tremendous store of architecturally and historically significant structures. During the 1950s and 1960s much abandonment of this housing stock took place, and the conditions in these neighborhoods deteriorated as a result. In the 1970s and the 1980s a gentrification process started resulting in a higher than average increase in property values and resident's incomes.
Group 3 (N=17)	Moderate income neighborhoods with high rates of home ownership.
Group 4 (N=19)	Moderate income neighborhoods with low rates of home ownership.
Group 5 (N=6)	The city's poorest neighborhoods with widespread physical deterioration and vacant properties.
Group 6 (N=8)	Neighborhoods with concentrations of publicly assisted housing.

The comparison of the neighborhood grouping made for this study and the Pittsburgh neighborhood classification show overall a good correspondence (see Table 5). For instance, all neighborhoods (except Bluff) classified in the Pittsburgh neighborhood classification as slums or public housing areas (groups 5 and 6) belonged to those classified in the low SES groups by the factor analysis.

Table 5. Neighborhoods included in different groups of neighborhood types.

Group on basis of 1980 cencus factor analysis	Group according to city of Pittsburgh Neighborhood classific
High SES, High Familism	
Summer Hill	1
Square Hill North	1
Swisshelm Park	1
Mount Oliver	3
Bon Air	1
Sheraden	1
Ridgemont	1
Windgap	1
Overbrook	1
Lincoln Place	1
New Homestead	1

Group on basis of 1980 cencus factor analysis	Group according to city of Pittsburgh Neighborhood classific
High SES,Medium Familism	
Brighton Heights	1
Stanton Heights	1
Pt Breeze South	1
Brookline	1
Banksville	1
Westwood	1
High SES, Low Familism	
Highland Park	1
Square Hill South	1
Regent Square	1
Oakwood	1
Medium SES, High Familism	
Lin-Lem Belmar	4
Arlington	3
Chartiers city	1
Hays	3
East Hills	4
Medium SES, Medium Familism	
Upper Hill	3
Chateau	Unclassified
Perry North	3
Marshall-Shadela	3
Spring Hill	3
Spring Garden	3
Troy Hill	3
Perry South	4
Bluff	5
Stripp	Unclassified
Polish Hill	3
Central Lawrence	4
Hasel-Glen-Gh	4 & 5*
Greenfield	1
South Side Slope	3
Mount Washington	1
Allentown	3
Beltzhoover	4
Duq Heights	1
Beechview	1
Esplen	4
Crafton Heights	1
Carrick	1
Knoxville	3
Morningside	1
Medium SES, Low Familism	
East Allegheny	4
Lower Lawrence	4
Central Oakland	4
Shadyside	1
Bloomfield	3
Friendship	4
East Liberty	4
Point Breeze North	1
South Side Flats	3
East Carneige	1

Group on basis of 1980 cencus factor analysis	Group according to city of Pittsburgh Neighborhood classific
Low SES, High Familism	
Homewood North	4
Carlifornia-Kirkb	4
Northview Heights	6
St Clair	6
Fairywood	6
Low SES, Medium Familism	
Lower Hill (Crawford Roberts)	4
Bedford Dwell	6
Terrace Village	6
Homewood West	5
Homewood South	5
Manchester	2
Fineview	4
West Oakland	5
South Oakland	3
Garfield	4
Larimer	5
Arlington Heights	6
West End	4
Low SES, Low Familism	
Middle Hill	5
Central North side	2

* Divided into two separate neighborhoods in the Pitt. Neigh. Classific.

The Neighborhood Classification and Offending

As stated in the introduction, previous reserach have shown that offending rates differ by type of neighborhood. Relating the distribution of (life-time self-reported) serious delinquency to the Pittsburgh neighborhood classification shows that neighborhood SES, but not neighborhood familism, is related to serious delinquency (Figure 1). The SES – serious delinquency relationship is highly statistical significant. ($p = 0.000$). Serious delinquency is defined as acts of car theft, breaking and entering, strongarming, attempting to seriously hurt or kill, forced sex or selling drugs.

Interestingly, caretakers' view of crime in the neighborhood was more strongly related to the neighborhood SES than the subjects self-reported serious delinquency. Furthermore, within each SES group the highest per cents of caretakers' negative view of neighborhood crime were found for the high familism areas and the lowest for the low familism area (figure 2). This may indicate that the presence of a lot of youth in area in some ways are related to caretakers view of the neighborhood crime problem. It was also found that peer delinquency varied

Figure 1. Per cent with serious delinquency by neighborhood SES and familism. Middle and oldest sample combined.

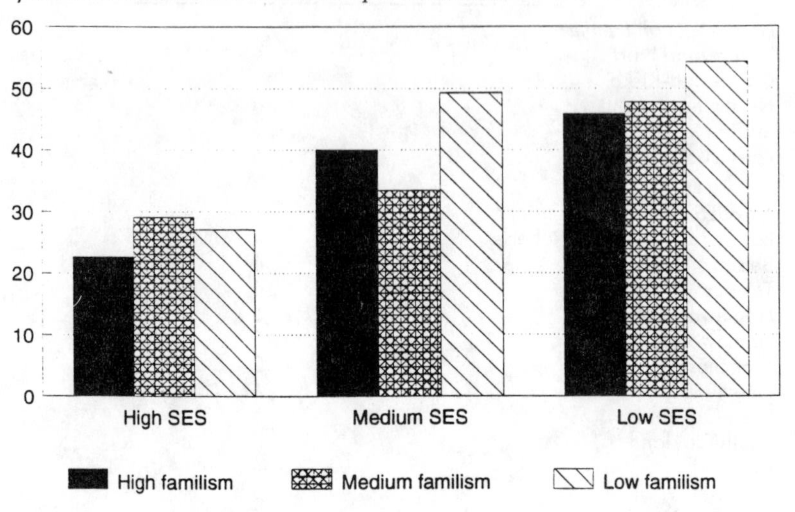

Figure 2. Caretakers reporting of high crime levels in neighborhood by neighborhood SES and familism. Middle and oldest sample combined. Per cent in upper quartile of scale based on 10 questions.

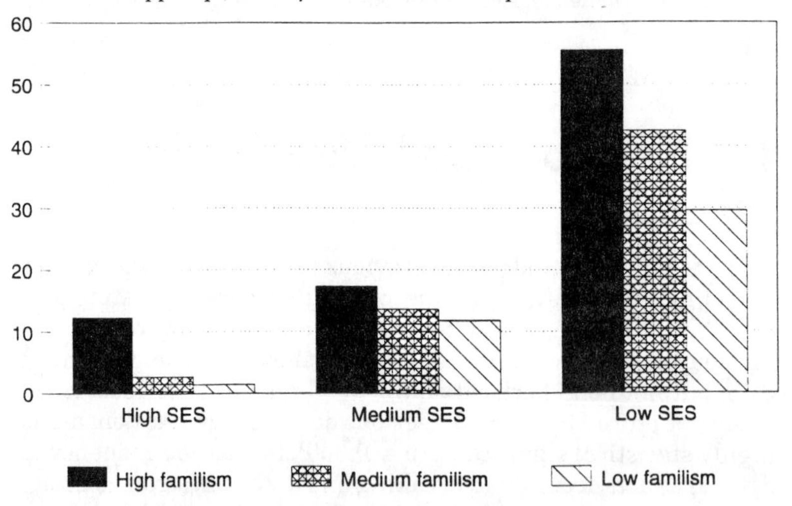

significantly by neighborhood SES, but not by neighborhood familism (figure 3).

These findings are interesting in themselves because they replicate with self-report data the significant neighborhood variations in the rate of offending by area SES reported in many studies using police recorded data (see Wikström,1991 130–141). In fact, there are only a limited number of previous studies using

Figure 3. High peer delinquency (upper quartile) by neighborhood SES and familism. Middle and oldest sample combined.

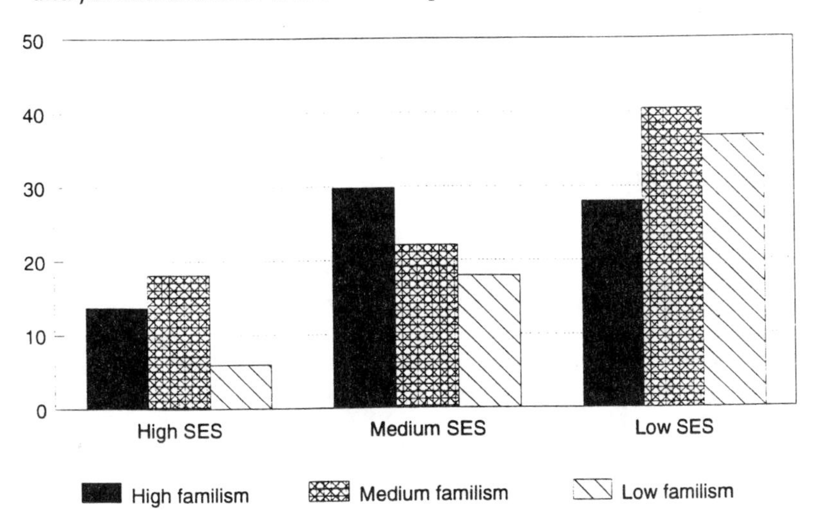

self-reported data showing offending rates by types of city neighborhoods (see Braithwaite,1979). However, it is out of scope of the present study to discuss them here. It was sufficient for the present study to conclude that the neighborhood classification reflect significant variation in the boys' offending rates between the neighborhoods. The results also show that the SES dimension of neighborhood is the most important element in this relationship.

Classification of Pathways

The formulation of pathways has been described in an earlier paper (Loeber et al., 1993). Two analytic steps were first distinquished, i.e., the detection of the most common sequence (called developmental sequence), and the identification of the proportion of individuals who travel part of the full sequence (called pathways) (Loeber & Le Blanc, 1990). Thus, the analyses initially focus on the relation between variables (the developmental sequences) and then on within-subject change over time (the developmental pathways).

The most parsimonious model of developmental pathways consists of three parallel pathways: (a) an Authority Conflict Pathway, consisting of a sequence starting with stubborn behavior, followed by defiance, which in turn can be followed by authority avoidance; (b) Covert Pathway, consisting of a sequence starting with minor covert behaviors, followed by property damage, and followed by moderate to serious forms of delinquency; (c) Overt Pathway, starting with minor aggression, followed by physical fighting, and followed, in turn, by violence.

Table 6. Major steps in overt and covert pathways to be used in analyses.

OVERT PATHWAY

(1) No overt behavior.
(2) Minor aggression only,
(3) Aggression-fighting (including fighting only).
(4) Aggression-fighting-violence (including fighting-violence, aggression-violence and violence only)

COVERT PATHWAY

(1) No covert behavior.
(2) Covert behavior only (i.e. lying,shoplifting)
(3) Covert behavior-property damage (including property damage only)
(4) Covert behavior-property damage-delinquency (including property damage-delinquency, covert behavior-delinquency and delinquency only).

Thus, a given individual could occupy a position on all three of the pathways, but would have rarely travelled each pathway to the same degree.

In this study we shall consider only the overt and the covert pathways. Moreover, we shall analyze only these pathways for the four major steps shown in table 6. An additional class are called non-fitters, i.e., those who started an overt (or covert) behavior but not in the predicted order. For example, those who started with violence and then went on to fighting were considered non-fitters.

Table 7. Distribution of subjects by major steps in overt and covert pathways. Weighted data.

		Middle Sample		Oldest sample		Total*	
		N	%	N	%	N	%
OVERT PATHWAY							
(1)	No overt behavior	222	31.8	194	29.4	416	30.7
(2)	Minor aggresion only,	114	16.3	108	16.4	222	16.4
(3)	Aggr.-fighting	220	31.5	149	22.6	369	27.2
(4)	Agg.-fight.-violence	88	12.6	108	16.4	196	14.4
(5)	Non-fitters	54	7.7	100	15.2	154	11.3
	Missing data:	69		104		173	
	TOTAL;	767		763		1530	
COVERT PATHWAY							
(1)	No covert behavior	190	27.2	113	16.2	303	21.7
(2)	Covert behavior only	126	18.1	62	8.9	188	13.5
(3)	Cov. beh.- damages	150	21.5	62	8.9	212	15.2
(4)	Cov. beh.-damge.-delinq	139	19.9	258	37.0	397	28.5
(5)	Non-fitters	93	13.3	202	29.0	295	21.1
	Missing data:	69		66		135	
	TOTAL:	767		763		1530	

* Middle + Oldest sample.

The distribution of the individual subjects by major steps of the overt and covert pathways are shown in Table 7. Most subjects fitted the developmental steps, although some may have entered at a later step, or skipped the middle step.

It should be noted that the middle sample had reached the age of 13 while the oldest sample has reached the ages of 16. Therefore it is not surprising that more of the subjects in the oldest sample had reached the highest stage of the covert development steps. That this difference between the two samples is not the same for overt behavior is likely to be due to that violent behavior , as defined here (see table 1 above) , not is likely to have reached its peak at age 16.

Comparing the middle and the oldest sample, the proportion non-fitters was significantly higher for the oldest sample, and the proportion non-fitters was higher for covert than for overt behavior in both samples. This may be a result of the longer retrospective period for the oldest sample, for whom it may have been more difficult to time-order early events.

Overt Pathways by Neighborhood SES and Familism

The basic questions to be raised in this section is whether the distribution of individual subjects who have reached different development steps in each of the pathways are the same in different types of neighborhood , i.e. whether they are invariant by neighborhood SES and familism. First we will show the results for the combined middle and oldest sample. Thereafter the findings will also be shown separately for the middle (age 13) and the oldest sample (age 16). Because the number of boys were too small in some combinations of neighborhood SES and familism we will show the distribution of steps within pathways separately for SES and familism.

Neighborhoods classified by SES

The analyses showed that neighborhood SES was significantly related to steps in the overt pathway (Figure 4). Fewer boys in high SES than other areas are involved in overt behavior, but this only held for the middle sample when the two samples were considered separately (Figure 5). This difference between the two samples is likely to be due to a later age of onset in overt behavior in high SES compared to other areas.

The proportion of boys who advanced to higher developments steps was higher in low SES areas (Figure 4). This difference was stronger for the middle than the oldest sample (Figure 5) but the analysis may be a bit distorted by the fact that the low SES

Figure 4. Distribution of steps in the overt pathway development by neighborhood SES. Middle and oldest sample combined. Per cent.

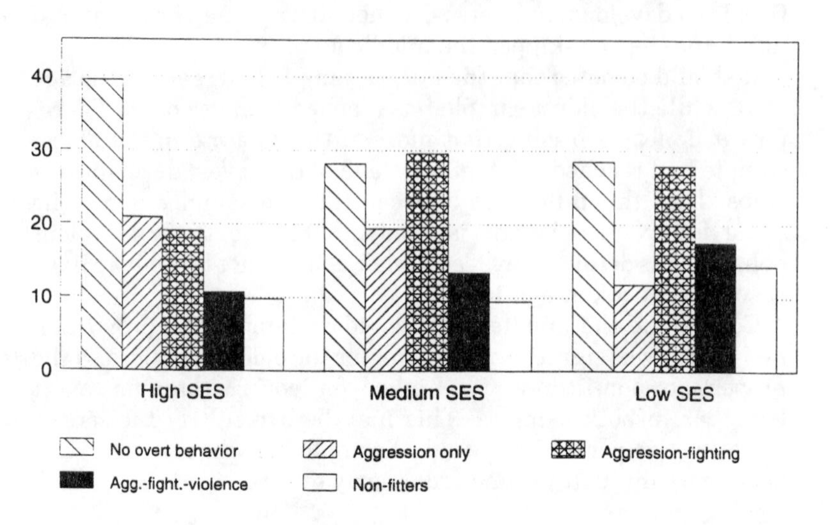

Chi-square 37,3 (df=8) prob.=0.000)

subjects in the oldest sample had a significantly higher proportion of non-fitters than in the remaining two neighborhood groups.

In summary, the findings indicate that more boys in low than in high SES areas, especially at younger ages, were involved in overt behavior. A higher proportion of the boys living in low SES areas tended to penetrate into the overt pathway and engage in violence than those living in high SES neighborhoods.

In addition we divided the low SES neighborhoods into those located near the Central Business District (CBD) and those located more at the outskirts of the city. The reason for doing this is that it has been claimed that living in poor neighborhoods located close to areas of extensive commerce, due to the proximity to good opportunities for crime, is likely to have a positive influence on boys offending. This argument has been put forward primarily as regards to crimes against property (Brantingham & Jeffery,1981), but we will do this analysis also for the overt behaviors since it can be argued that the city-centre environment is the public space with the highest rate of frictions between people (Wikström,1993).

The concentration of low SES neighborhoods just to the east of the CBD was classified as inner-city low SES (i.e. Lower hill, Middle hill, Bedford dwellings, Terrace village, West Oakland, South Oakland) and the rest of the low SES areas as outer-city low SES neighborhoods (see Map 1 above).

The findings show (figure 6) that the low SES inner-city neighborhoods have more boys' involved in overt behavior than the rest, and moreover, that the proportion having reached the

Figure 5. Distribution of steps in the overt pathway development by neighborhood SES. Top figure;middle sample. Bottom figure; oldest sample. Per cent.

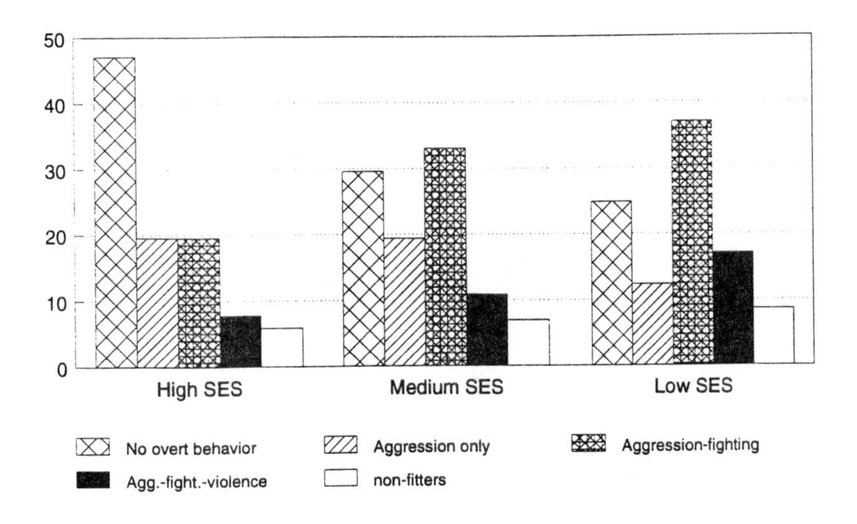

Chi-square 30,5 (df=8) prob.=0.000)

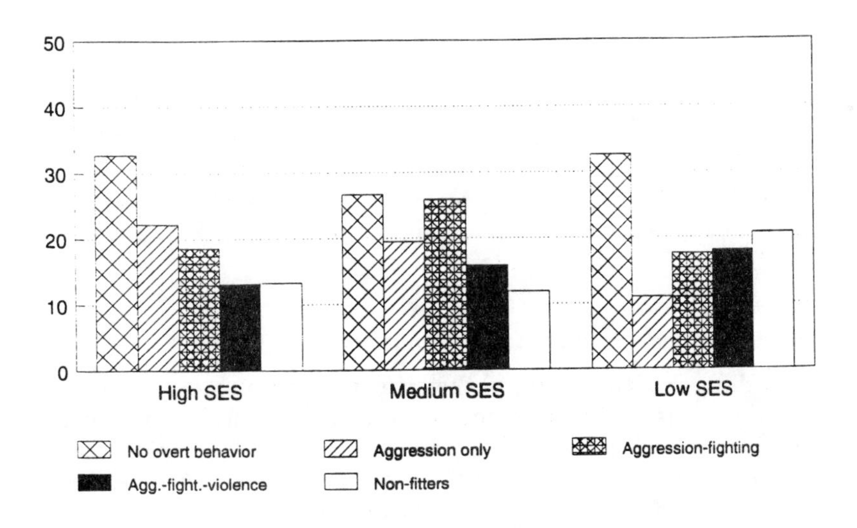

Chi-square 21,8 (df=8) prob.=0.005)

Figure 6. Distribution of steps in the overt pathway develop- ment by neighborhood SES. Low SES areas divided in to inner-city and outer-city areas. Middle and oldest sample combined. Per cent.

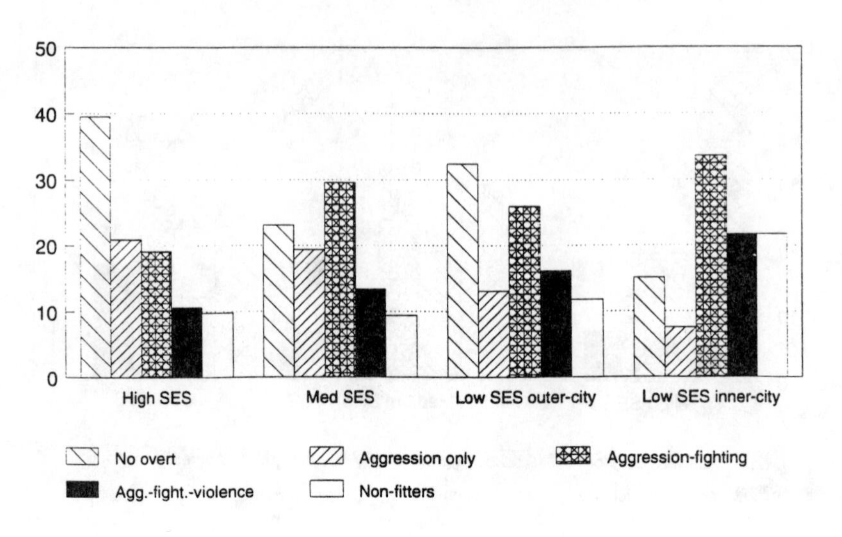

Chi-square 60,3 (df=12) prob.=0.000)

highest development step of the overt pathway is significantly higher than in other neighborhood types. This relationship held better for the middle than the oldest sample (figure 7), but it should be noted that the proportion non-fitters in the oldest sample was especially high among the boys' living in the inner-city low SES neighborhoods.

Neighborhood classification by familism

The differences in overt pathway development steps by area familism was statistically non-significant both for the combined samples as well as for the middle and the oldest sample taken separately (no figures shown). We may therefore conclude that neighborhood familism was neither significantly related to proportion involved in overt behavior or to subjects degree of penetration into the pathway.

Figure 7. Distribution of steps in the overt pathway development by neighborhood SES. Low SES areas divided in to inner-city and outer-city areas. Top figure;middle sample. Bottom figure; oldest sample. Per cent.

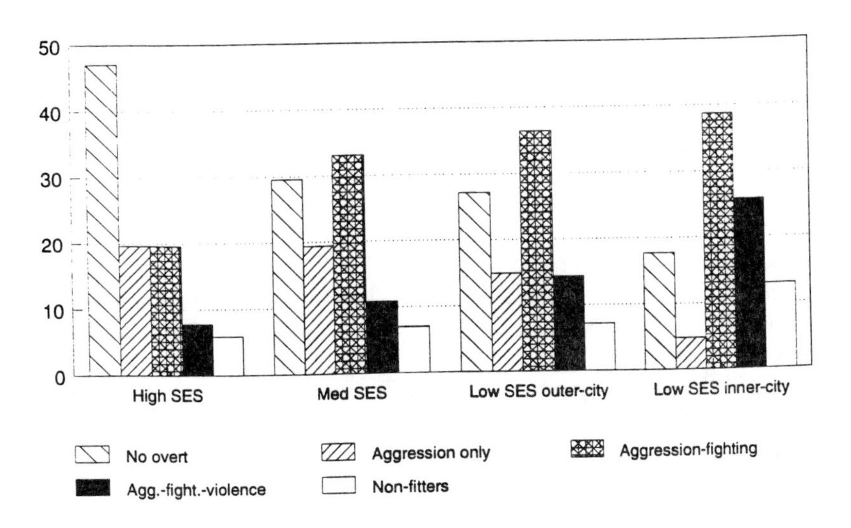

Chi-square 41,6 (df=12) prob.=0.000)

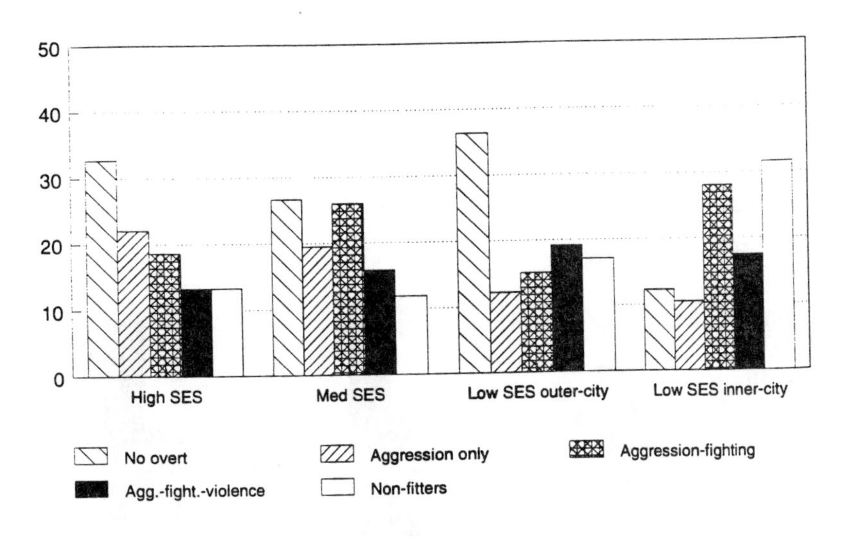

Chi-square 42,0 (df=12) prob.=0.000)

Covert Pathways by Neighborhood SES and Familism

In the previous section we focused on how aggression and violent behavior was related to the major dimension of neighborhood population differentiation. In this section we will performe the same analysis for the covert pathway.

Neighborhood classification by SES

Just as for the overt pathway, the distribution of steps in the covert pathway was significantly related to neighborhood SES (Figure 8). More boys in low SES areas have been involved in covert behaviors. This held for the middle but not for the oldest sample (Figure 9). Again this may indicate a tendency for boys' in low SES area to have an earlier age of onset in delinquency than boys in other areas of the city.

As to boys' penetration into the covert pathway the results show a significant difference by neighborhood SES (just as for the overt pathway) . More boys' living in low SES areas had reached the highest step (Figure 8). This held better for the middle than for the oldest sample (Figure 9), but again the proportion of non-fitters was markedly higher among the low SES neighborhood boys'.

Figure 8. Distribution of steps in the covert pathway by neighborhood SES. Middle and oldest sample combined. Per cent.

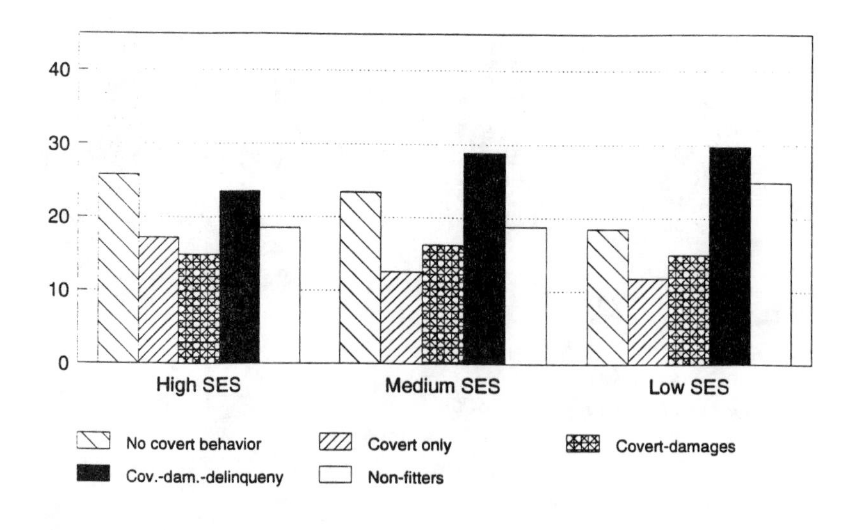

Chi-square 16,7 (df=8) prob.=0.033)

Figure 9. Distribution of the steps in the covert pathway by neighborhood SES. Top figure;middle sample. Bottom figure; oldest sample. Per cent.

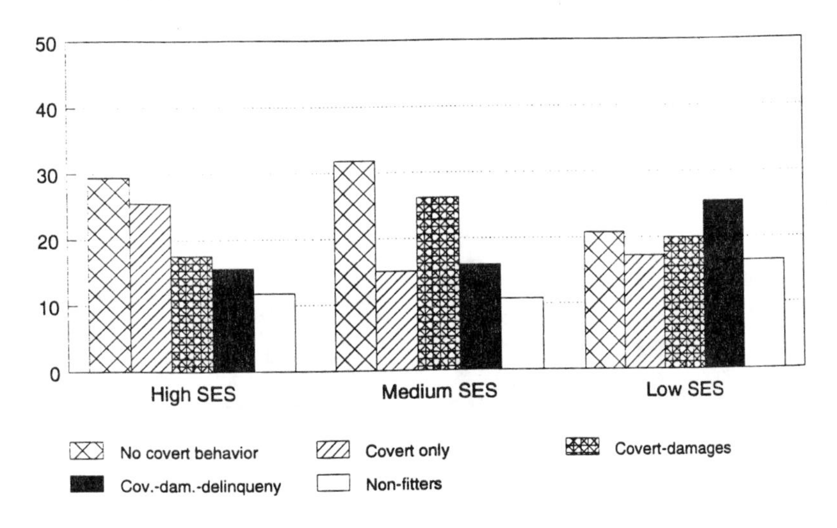

Chi-square 25,0 (df=8) prob.=0.002)

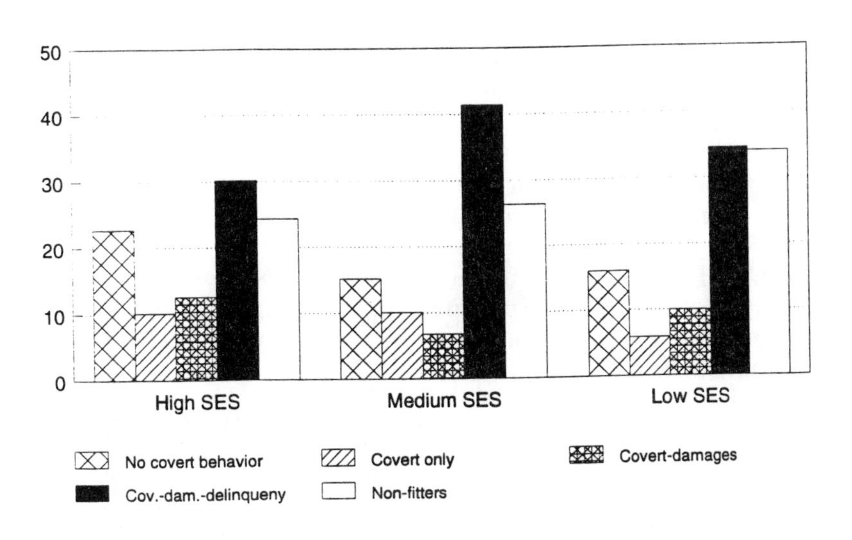

Chi-square 16,7 (df=8) prob.=0.034)

Figure 10. Distribution of steps in the covert pathway development by neighborhood SES. Low Ses areas divided into inner-city and outer-city areas. Middle and oldest sample combined. Per cent.

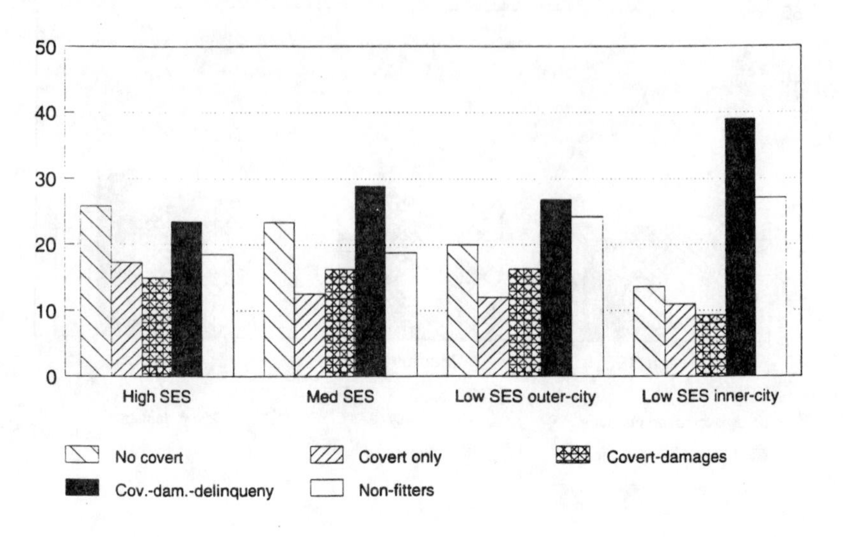

Chi-square 26,6 (df=12) prob.=0.009)

For boys' living in low SES neighborhoods, distinguishing between those living in the inner-city and those living in the outer-city (Figure 10), the results show that a much higher proportion of the boys' living in the inner-city low SES neighborhoods have penetrated the full pathway up to moderate to serious delinquency. This held for the middle sample, were the difference was even greater, (Figure 11) but not for the oldest sample. However, the proportion in the oldest sample of non-fitters is very high for low SES inner-city boys' (close to 50 %).

In summary, the basic pattern of relationship between neighborhood SES and involvement and penetration in covert behavior appears to be much the same as for the overt pathway.

Neighborhoods classified by familism

In contrast to what was the case for the overt pathway, the distribution of steps in the covert pathway was significantly different by neighborhood familism (Figure 12). Low familism areas had a lower proportion of boys with no covert behavior than high familism areas. Boys' in the low familism areas penetrated further into the pathway than boys' in the high familism areas. This pattern was clearer for the oldest sample (Figure 13). A possible explanation for this is that low familism, compared to high familism areas, are more often located near the city-centre

Figure 11. Distribution of the steps in the covert pathway by neighborhood SES. Low SES neighborhoods divided into inner-city and outer-city areas.Top figure;middle sample. Bottom figure; oldest sample. Per cent.

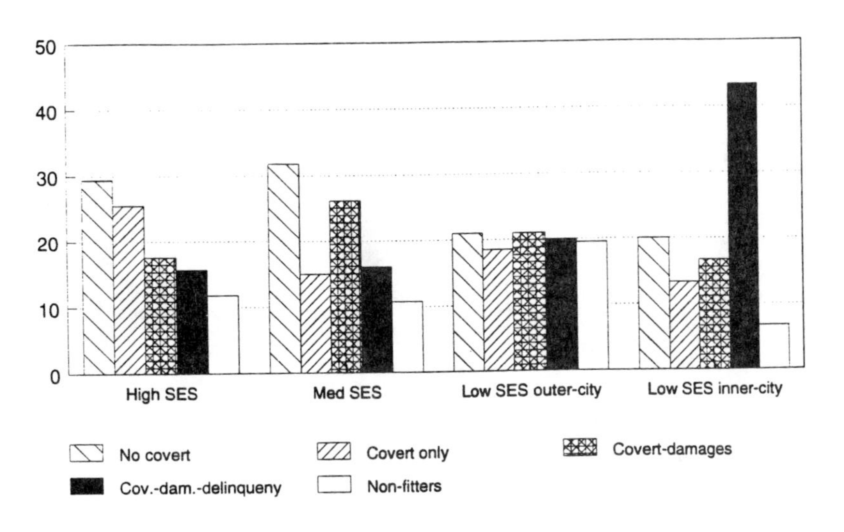

Chi-square 44,4 (df=12) prob.=0.000)

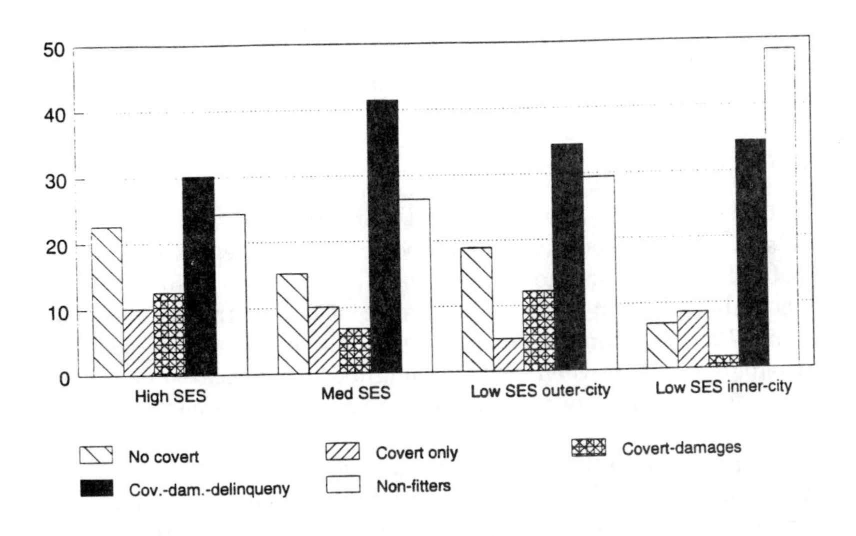

Chi-square 31,9 (df=12) prob.=0.001)

Figure 12. Distribution of steps in the covert pathway development by neighborhood familism. Middle and oldest sample combined. Per cent.

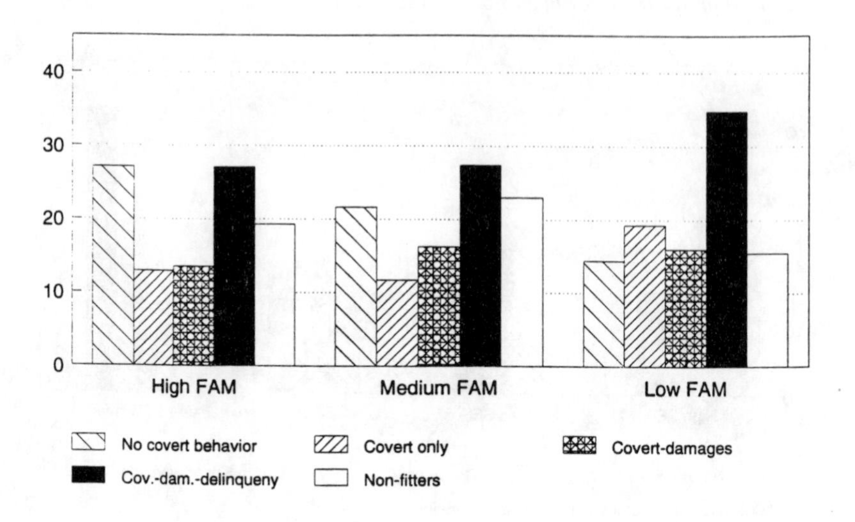

Chi-square 23,9 (df=8) prob.=0.002)

(see map 2 above) which have higher opportunities for covert delinquent acts. However, this is highly speculative.

Conclusion

In this chapter we have presented a preliminary analysis of the relationship between neighborhood residential segregation and individual's development of offending. We have also touched upon the question of the importance of opportunities close to home for the offending by juveniles which was addressed by distinguishing between low SES neighborhoods located near the city-centre of Pittsburgh and low SES neighborhoods located further out.

With all due caution, this being a first explorative analysis of the data, it holds some promise for future work. Although the neighborhood classification was cross-sectional and relatively crude it was sensitive enough to detect differences in the prevalence of boys' engaging in overt and covert behaviors and developmental differences in boys' penetration into overt and covert pathways. The general pattern, both for overt and covert behavior, was that the prevalence of boys' engaging in these behavior was higher in low SES neighborhoods. A novel feature of the present findings is that boys' penetration in to the overt

Figure 13. Distribution of the steps in the cover pathway by neighborhood familism. Top figure;middle sample. Bottom figure; oldest sample. Per cent.

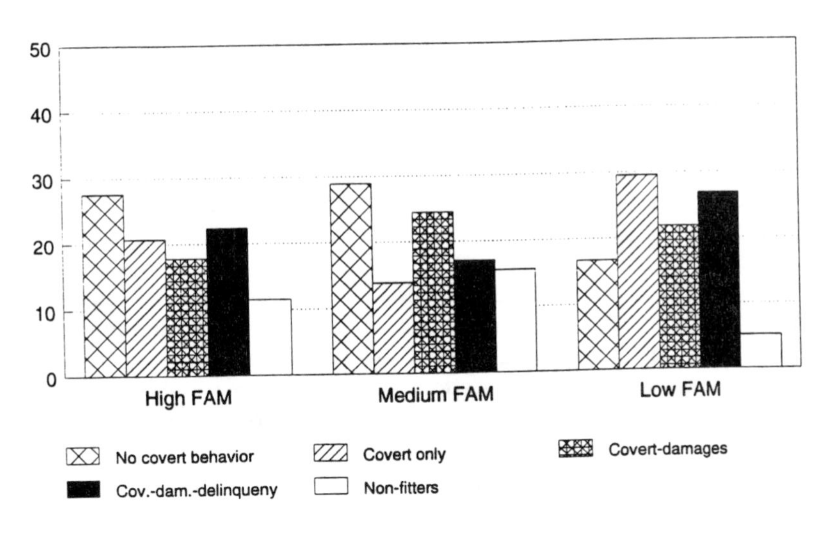

Chi-square 26,4 (df=8) prob.=0.001)

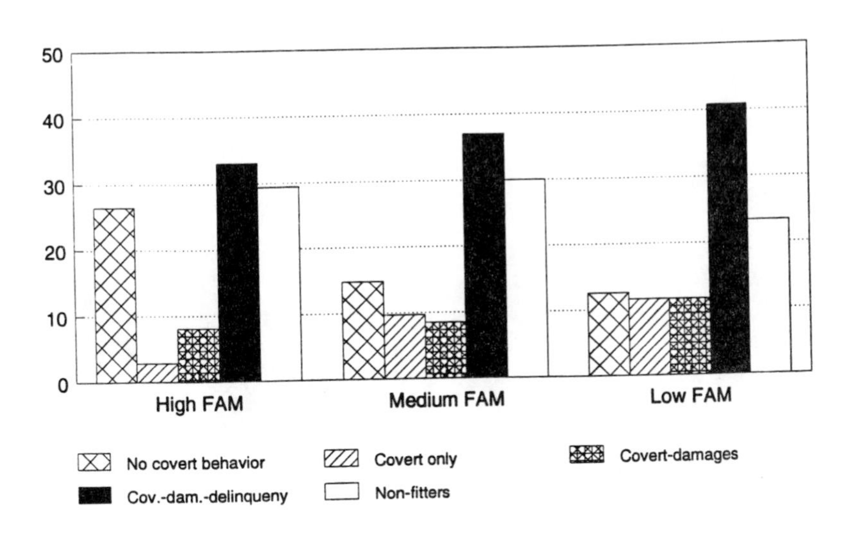

Chi-square 19,7 (df=8) prob.=0.012)

and covert pathways varied with the neighborhood in which they lived. Boys' living in low SES neighborhoods tended to advance further into a pathway than boys' living in high SES neighborhoods.

This may, or may not, be related to neighborhood differences in social control and opportunities for the commission of crime. Although some of the findings indicated that opportunity may play a role, it is premature to draw any conclusion about social control or opportunity differences as explanations of the findings presented here. We hope, in a later stage of this research, to be able to more closely elaborate on the lines of investigation started here.

One of the questions we also hope to be able to deal with is the question whether the youths reaching a specific developmental step in one neighborhood share the same individual characteristics as those reaching this step in other types of neighborhoods. This analysis, which we plan to do, but have not as yet have time to complete, will put some further light on the question of the relative importance of neighborhood contextual influences and individual characteristics for the development of offending. Further analyses will also need to address the types of neighborhoods which produce youth entering into multiple pathways rather than single pathways.

We anticipate that the current and planned analyses will enrich the formulation of theories of delinquency, and may, eventually, lead to the steering of resources to these neighborhoods which produces generation upon generation of youth engaging in serious crime.

References

Achenbach, T.M. & Edelbrock C.S. (1983). *Manual for the Child Behavior Checklist and Revised Child Behavior Profile.* Burlington Vt.

Barkley, R.A. (1989). Attention Deficit-hyperactivity Disorder. In eds. E.J. Mash & R.A. Barkley: *Treatment of Childhood disorders*. New York: Guilford press.

Behar, D. & Stewart, M.A. (1982). Aggressive Conduct Disorder of Children: The Clinical History and Direct Observations. *ACTA Psychiatrica Scandinavica 65* .

Belson, W.A. (1975). *Juvenile Theft; The Causal Factors.* London: Harper & Row.

Blalock, H. (1985). Contextual-effects Models: Theoretical and Methodological Issues. *Ann. Rev. Soc. 10.*

Blumstein, A., Cohen, J., Roth, J.A. & Visher, C.A. (1986). *Criminal careers and 'career criminals'.* Washington DC: National Academy of Science.

Bottoms, A.E., Claytor, A. & Wiles, P. (1992). Housing Markets and Residential Community Crime Careers: A Case Study from Sheffield. in (eds) Evans D.J., Fyfe N.R. & Herbert D.T.: *Crime, Policing and Place.* Routledge. London.

Braithwaite, J. (1979). *Inequality, Crime and Public Policy.* London: Routledge and Kegan Paul.

Brantingham, P.J. & Jeffery, C.R. (1981). Crime, Space and Criminological Theory. In eds. P.J. Brantingham & P.L. Brantingham: *Environmental Criminology.* Beverly Hills: Sage publ.

Brantingham, P.J. & Brantingham, P.L. (1984). *Patterns in Crime.* New York: Macmillan.

Costello, A.J., Edelbrock, C.S., Dulcan, M.K., Kalas, R. & Klaric, S.H. (1984). Report on the NIHM Diagnostic Interview Schedule for Children (DISC). Unpublished manuscript. Western Psychiatric Institute and Clinic. Pittsburgh PA.

Elliot, D.S., Huizinga D. & Ageton S. (1985). *Explaining delinquency and drug use.* Beverly Hills: Sage publ.

Farrington et.al. (1990). Advancing knowledge about the onset of delinquency and crime. In eds. B.B. Lahey & A.E. Kazdin: *Advances in Clinical Child Psychology* (vol 13). New York. Plenum.

Freud, A. (1965). The Concept of Development Lines. *Psychoanalytic Study of the Child 18.*

Frick, P.J., Lahey, B.B., Loeber, R., Tannenbaum, L., Van Horn, Y., Christ, M.A.G., Hart, E.A. & Hanson, K. (1993). Oppositional defiant disorder and condust disorder: A meta-analytic review of factor analyses and cross-validation in a clinical sample. *Clinical psychological review 13.*

Green, S.M., Loeber, R. & Lahey, B.B. (1991). Stability of Mothers Recall of the Age at Onset of their Child's Attention and Hyperactivity Problems. *Journal of the Academy of Child and Adolescent Psychiatry 30.*

Hamburgh, B.A., Kraemer, H.C. & Jahnke, W. (1975). Behavioral and attitudinal correlates of substantial drug use. *American Journal of Psychiatric 132.*

Harries, C.D. & Ullman, E.L. (1974). The Nature of Cities. In ed. K.P. Schwirian: *Comparative Urban Structure.* Lexington: D.C. Heath and Company.

Janson, C.-G. (1980). Factorial Social Ecology. An Attempt at Summary and Evaluation. *Ann. Rev. Sociol. 9.*

Johnstone, R.J. (1984). *City and Society. An Outline for Urban Geography.* London: Unwin Hyman.

Kandel, D.B. (1978). Convergence in prospective longitudinal surveys of drug use in normal populations. In ed D.B. Kandel. *Longitudinal Research on Drug Use.* New York: Wiley.

Kandel, D.B. & Faust, R. (1975). Sequence and stages in Patterns of Adolescent Drug Use. *Archives in General Psychiatry 32.*

Kazdin, A.E. (1992). Overt and Covert Antisocial Behavior: Child and Family Characteristics among Psychiatric inpatient children. *Journal of Child and Family Studies 1.*

LeBlanc, M. Cote, G., Loeber, R. (1991). Temporal Paths in Delinquency: Stability, Regression and Progression Analyzed with Panel Data from an Adolescent and a Delinquent Male Sample. *Canadian Journal of Criminology.*

LeBlanc, M. & Frechette, M. (1989). *Male Criminal Activity from Childhood to Adulthood: Multilevel and Developmental Perspectives.* New York: Springer verlag.

Loeber, R. (1985). Patterns and Development of Antisocial Child Behavior. In ed. G.J. Whithurst: *Annals of Child Development* (Vol 2). Greenwich CT: JAI Press.

Loeber, R. (1988). The Natural Histories of Juvenile Conduct Problems, Substance Use and Delinquency: Evidence for Developmental Progressions. In eds. B.B. Lahey & A.E. Kazdin: *Advances in Clinical Child Psychology* (Vol 11). New York: Plenum.

Loeber, R. (1991). Questions and Advances in the Study of Developmental Pathways. In eds. D. Cicchetti & S. Toth: *Rochester Symposium on Developmental Psychopatology III.* Rochester NY: Rochester University Press.

Loeber R., Green, S.M. & Lahey, B.B. (1990). Mental Health Professionals' Perception of the Utility of Children, Mothers, and Teachers as Informants on Childhood Psychopatology. *Journal of Clinical Child Psychology 19.*

Loeber R., Green S.M., Lahey B.B., Christ M.A.G. & Frick P.J. Developmental Sequences in the Age of Onset of Disruptive Child Behaviors. *Journal of Child and Family Studies 1.*

Loeber, R., Green, S.M., Lahey, B.B. & Stouthamer-Loeber, M. (1989). Optimal Informants on Childhood Disruptive Behaviors. *Development and Psychopathology 1.*

Loeber, R., Keenan, K., Giroux, B., Stouthamer-Loeber, M. & Van Kammen, W. (1992). *The Diffeential Role of Early Onset, Hyperactivity, and Substance Use in Boys' Pathways to Serious Dispruptive Behavior.* (unpublished manuscript). Western Psychiatric Institute and Clinic. University of Pittsburgh.

Loeber, R. & LeBlanc, M. (1990). Toward a Developmental Criminology. In eds. M. Tonry & N. Morris: *Crime and Justice 12*. Chicago: University of Chicago Press.

Loeber, R. & Schmaling, K.B. (1985a). Empirical Evidence for Overt and Covert Patterns of Antisocial Conduct Problems: A Meta-analysis. *Journal of abnormal Child Psychology 13.*

Loeber, R. & Schmaling, K.B. (1985b). The Utility of Differentiating Between Mixed and Pure Forms of Antisocial Child Behavior. *Journal of abnormal Child Psychology 13.*

Loeber, R. , Stouthamer-Loeber, M. & Green, S.M. (1991). Age at Onset of Problem Behavior in Boys, and Later Disruptive and Delinquent Behaviours. *Criminal Behaviour and Mental Health 1.*

Loeber, R., Stouthamer-Loeber, M., Van Kammen, W. & Farrington, D.P. (1989). Development of a New Meaure of Self-Reported Antisocial Behavior in Young Children: Prevalence and Reliability. In ed M.W. Klein: *Self-Report Methodology in Criminological Research.* Boston: Kluwer-Nijhoff.

Loeber, R., Stouthamer-Loeber, M., Van Kammen, W. & Farrington, D.P. (1991). Initiation, Escalation and Desistence in Juvenile Offending and Their Correlates. *Journal of Criminal Law and Criminology 82.*

Maguin, E. (1992). *Manual for Retrieving Juvenile Court Data Files from the Allegheny County Juvenile Court Files.*(unpublished manuscript). Western Psychiatric Institute and Clinic, School of Medicine. University of Pittsburgh.

Moffitt, T.E. (1992). *Adolescent-limited and Life-course-persistent Antisocial Behavior. A Developmental Taxonomy.* (unpublished manuscript). Dept of Psychology. University of Winconsin.

Radke-Yarrow, M., Campell, J.D. & Burton, R.V. (1970). Reliability of Maternal Retrospection: A Preliminary Report. In ed. K. Danziger. *Readings in Child Socialization.* Oxford: Pergamon.

Reiss, A.J. & Rhodes, L.E. (1961). The Distribution of Juvenile Delinquency in the Social Class Structure. *American Sociological Reveiew 26.*

Reiss, A.J. (1986). Why are communities important in understanding crime? In A.J. Reiss & M. Tonry (Eds.), *Crime and justice 8: Communities and crime.* Chicago: University of Chicago Press.

Reiss, A.J. & Tonry, M. (1986). *Crime and Justice, 8:* Commmunities and crime. Chicago: The University of Chicago Press.

Russo, M., Loeber, R. & Keenan, K. (1992). *Oppositional Defiant and Conduct Disorders: Validation of the Proposed DSM-IV Alternative Diagnostic Option.* (unpublished manuscript). Western Psychiatric Clinic and Institute. School of Medicine. University of Pittsburgh.

Schwirian, K.P. (1974). Some Recent Trends and Methodological Problems in Urban Ecological Research. In ed. K.P. Schwirian: *Comparative Urban Structure.* Lexington : D.C. Heath and Company.

Shannon, L.W. (1988). *Criminal career continuity.* New York: Human scienses press.

Shroufe, L.A. (1989). Pathways to Adaptation and Maladaptation: Psychopathology as a Development Deviation. in ed. D. Cicchetti. *The Emergence of a Discipline: Rochester Symposium on Developmental Psychopatology* (Vol 1). Hillsdale: Erlbaum.

Stewart, M.A., Copeland, L.E. & deBois, C.S. (1988). Age of Onset of Aggressive Conduct Disorder: A Pilot Study. *Child Psychiatry and Human Development 19.*

Theodorson, G.A. (1971). *Studies in Human Ecology.* Evanston: Row,Peterson and Company.

Timms, D.W.G. (1971). *The Urban Mosaic.* Cambridge: Cambridge University Press.

Tolan, P.H. & Guerra, N.G. (1992). *A Development Perspective on Adolescent Antisocial Behavior.* (Unpublished paper). University of Illinios at Chicago.

Tonry, M., Ohlin, L.E. & Farrington, D.P. (1991). *Human Development and Criminal Behavior: New Ways of Advancing Knowledge.* New York: Springer verlag.

Wallden, M. (1985). *Boendesegregering och social miljö.* Byggforskningsrådet.

Van Kammen, W., Loeber R. & Stouthamer-Loeber M. (1991). Substance Use, Antisocial, and Delinquent Behavior in Young Boys. *Youth and Adolescence 20.*

Wikström, P.-O. (1985.) Everyday violence in contemporary Sweden: Ecological and situational aspects. (BRÅ Report No. 15). Stockholm: Liber förlag.

Wikström, P.-O. (1990). Age and crime in a Stockholm cohort. *Journal of Quantitative Criminology, 6.*

Wikström, P.-O. (1991). *Urban Crime, Criminals and Victims.* New York: Springer verlag.

Wikström, P.-O. (1991b). Housing Tenure, Social Class and Offending. The Individual-level Relationship in Childhood and Youth. *Criminal Behavior and Mental Health 1.*

Wikström, P.-O. (1994). Preventing City-Centre Crime. (forthcoming) in Preventing Crime. Vol 19. *Crime and Justice.* eds M. Tonry & D.P. Farrington. Chicago: University of Chicago Press.

Modeling Individual and Community Effects on Deviance over Time: Multi-level Statistical Models

by Stephen W. Raudenbush

Research reported here was supported by grants from the John D. and Catherine T. MacArthur Foundation and the National Institute of Justice to the Program on Human Development and Criminal Behavior.

Abstract

Although the relationship between age and criminal behavior has a predictable functional form when data are aggregated across persons (Hirschi and Gottfredson, 1983), that relationship is much less predictable at the individual level. More knowledge is needed about factors that predispose children to different age-deviance trajectories and about how these trajectories are modified by interactions with the social environment. This paper considers a family of statistical models that can be tailored to study these questions. A two-level hierarchical linear model enables the investigator to characterize each individual's development in terms of a set of person-specific parameters; these parameters are in turn viewed as multivariate outcomes to be explained by background variables hypothesized to influence later development. When the subjects under study are nested within social contexts such as schools and communities, a three-level model facilitates specification of the effects of social context and person-context interactions. However, when some subjects migrate across contextual boundaries during the course of the investigation, a crossed random effects model is required to achieve the same goals. Each of these models can incorporate effects of time-invariant and time-varying covariates, and each allows missing data and unbalanced designs. Applications of the three models are illustrated via reanalysis of data from criminology and education.

Introduction

Researchers have come to view the relationship between age and crime as "one of the brute facts of criminology" (Hirschi and Gottfredson, 1983) but continue to debate its implications for research. Some have argued that criminological theories must account for the age-crime curve observed in many societies (Greenberg, 1979), and characteristics of "criminal careers" such as onset, persistence, frequency of offending, and desistance have become key outcome variables, apparently requiring longitudinal research for their explanation (c.f., Blumstein, Farrington, & Moitra, 1985).

Hirschi and Gottfredson (1983) have disputed this view (see also Gottfredson & Hirschi, 1987, 1990). They describe the shape of the age-crime curve as essentially invariant across cultures and demographic groups. Group differences in offending rates increase during adolescence and decrease during early adulthood, they claim, but remain invariant in proportion to one another. If so, group differences in age of onset, frequency of offending, and age of desistance are really just expressions of stable underlying, group differences in the relative likelihood of criminal involvement. Since these group differences can be observed cross-sectionally, the authors view arguments for longitudinal research on criminal careers as unpersuasive.

According to their general theory of crime (Gottfredson and Hirschi, 1990), stable individual differences in social control reflecting differences in early socialization account for the apparently stable group differences in propensity to offend manifest over the life course. Although the truth of this theory would appear to contradict the need for longitudinal research, Janson (1992) has argued persuasively that longitudinal research is necessary to test the theory. First, the theory requires measures of both early socialization and of later criminal involvement on each subject. Accurate measurement of early socialization cannot be obtained retrospectively (at the time crimes are committed) so that prospective data are required. Second, a credible demonstration of the links between early socialization, later social control, and later deviant behavior requires panel data on persons. Third, Gottfredson and Hirschi view social control as a trait anchored in early socialization, but the asserted stability of social control cannot be tested without panel data on persons. Ironically, Janson argues, "Gottfredson and Hirschi have provided us with the strongest incentive in years to try large scale protracted prospective longitudinal studies" (page 21).

Janson's arguments are sufficient to justify longitudinal research as a strategy for learning about the genesis and development of criminality. However, the tasks of longitudinal analysis can be clarified further by recognizing a characteristic weakness in our understanding of the age-crime curve: The asserted invariance of the age-crime curve is based on the aggregation of large numbers of individual cases within groups. As one moves closer to individual-level data, one will likely find that the age-crime curve is, at best, a rough approximation to the data. Indeed, if the age-crime curve were invariant at the individual level, one could make near-perfect predictions about future criminal activity from the observation of the frequency of very early criminal activity. Since no study demonstrates such predictive power at the individual level, one or both of the following assertions must be true:

1. The unique constellation of predisposing characteristics associated with a person at, say, age 10, predicts a unique age-deviance trajectory for that person over the next 20 or so years of development. The predisposing characteristics may include temperamental and cognitive orientations, personality traits, early social learning, moral development, physical capabilities, attractiveness, economic well-being, hormonal configurations, peer allegiances, community norms – and many other possible variables. Each of these and the entire package of them in interaction may affect the particular trajectory one moves onto in early adolescence. The invariant age-crime curve of which criminologists write is then the average of these unique trajectories taken over many such individual cases.

2. The uniqueness of each person's age-deviance trajectory from age 10 to 30 results not only from the uniqueness of that person's set of pre-disposing characteristics; it results also from the particular set of interactions that occur over time between that person's expressions of deviant activity and the responses of others, including agents of social control such as parents, neighbors, older siblings, school authorities, police, and courts, but also including rebellious victims, competing deviant persons, and admiring or condemning peers. The natural history of a person's deviant activity is therefore a history of reciprocal transactions in which a deviant act or an expression of deviant belief elicits a response which either increases or decreases the probability of further deviant acts; and further expressions of individual behavior either increase or decrease the probability of various types of environmental response. How the environment responds to any act has both a systematic and random component, increasing the unpredictability of age-crime curves at the person level. As in a chess game, outcomes remote in time are hard to predict because each action opens up new possibilities for reaction, giving rise to a great multiplicity of possible sequences. Once again, the smooth and seemingly invariant age-crime curves of the criminological literature represents the averaging of many thousands of jagged, often tortuous, and unpredictable personal histories.

It seems likely that both assertions (1) and (2) are true; that difficulty predicting personal development arises both because of the uniqueness of each person's constellation of predisposing characteristics; and because the many possible responses of the environment to a given deviant act give rise to many possible sequences of individual action and environmental reaction. If this reasoning is correct, then personal age-crime trajectories may be modified in one of two ways:

- by modifying a person's constellation of pre-disposing characteristics; and
- by modifying the response of the environment to deviant activity.

The seeming invariance of the age-crime curve has served as the basis for an argument in favor of cross-sectional research and against longitudinal research. However, the variability of personal age-crime curves appears to lend support to longitudinal research and to undermine the argument for major investment in cross-sectional research. In particular:

1. The field currently lacks knowledge about the predisposing characteristics that are critical in distinguishing among personal age-deviance trajectories later on. Although social control theory offers important hypotheses, the shape of personal age-deviance trajectories cannot be inferred from aggregated, smooth age-crime curves. For example, age-crime invariance at the aggregate level does not preclude the veracity of Moffitt's (1990) hypothesis that there exist adolescence-limited versus chronic and persistent offenders and that these types of offenders vary dramatically in terms of certain critical psychological variables early in life. A sound test of this hypothesis apparently requires a prospective study in which fairly a dense webb of psychological data gathered early in life are used to predict the shape of development later.
2. We know too little about how social environments such as the community and school shape others' responses to expressions of deviant and criminal behavior, thereby either reducing or increasing the probability of subsequent anti-social action.
3. Points (1) and (2) imply that it is not sufficient to understand either how a constellation of psychological predispositions affects later development nor to understand how social environments respond to pro- or anti-social behavior to shape subsequent development. The two sources of influence are likely correlated and may operate in statistical interaction with each other. For example, persons pre-disposed to anti-social development may have a propensity to reside in neighborhoods lacking social cohesion and control (correlation of individual and social influence); and the realization of potential for anti-social development may depend on the social setting (interaction between individual and social influence). Farrington's chapter in this volume offers a convincing demonstration of the need simultaneously to study individual and ecological correlates of change in anti-social behavior.

Implications for Statistical Modeling

How individual and social factors operate independently and jointly to shape development can apparently be adequately studied only the context of longitudinal research. The conception evolving from this analysis is that personal characteristics create propensities favoring certain kinds of developmental trajectories; but development is realized over time in a social context. An adequate conception of individual development must apparently take into account the main effects of age, as suggested in the literature on the age-crime curve; the main effects of both psychological and social-contextual influences; and interactions involving age, psychological variables, and social context descriptors. Individual-level developmental curves apparently depend on personal and social influences and their interaction; and neither the shape of these curves nor the influence of such variables on them can be inferred from cross-sectional data.

To render the discussion more concrete, we refer to Figure 1. The figure shows the fitted "age-crime curve" for a randomly sampled subject; specifically, the estimated probability that such a subject will commit serious theft during a year (vertical axis) as a function of age (horizontal axis) based on the National Youth Survey (Raudenbush, 1992).[1] Notice that the curve has exactly the age-crime characteristics described in the criminological literature: age of onset is captured by an accelerating rate early in adolescence; a decelerating trend occurs a little later, leading to a peak age and, finally, a rapidly falling rate ("desistance").

Figure 2 presents results from a more fine-grained model in which the age-crime curve is predicted by sex and ethnicity. Notice that sex differences are not just rate differences at differ-

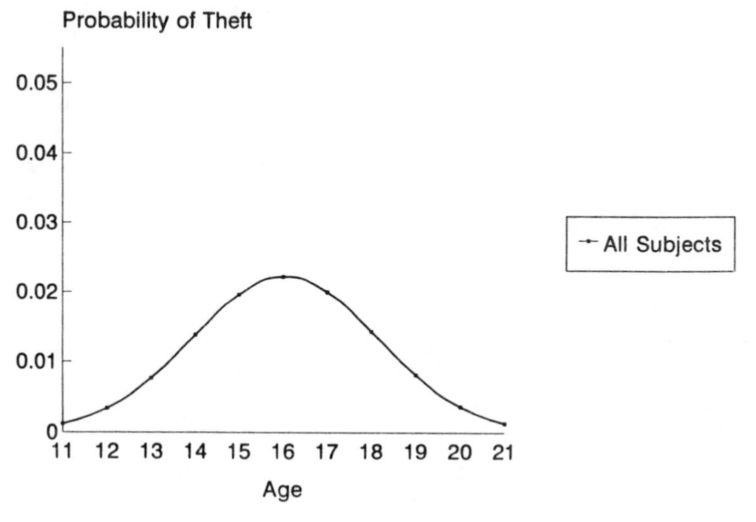

Figure 1. Expected rate of serious theft per year for a typical typical subject (vertical axis) as a function

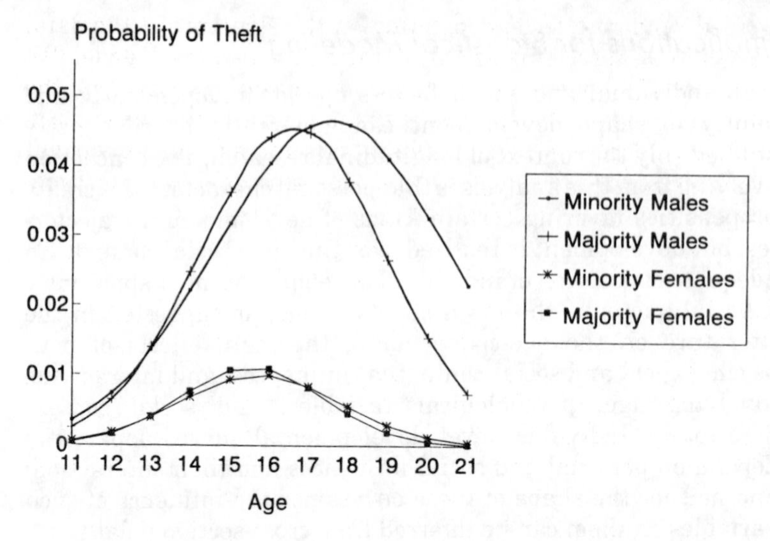

Figure 2. Expected rate of serious theft per year for a typical subject of a given gender and ethnicity (vertical axis) as a function of age (horizontal axis) based on the National Youth Survey.

ent ages. Moreover, ethnic differences are manifest not simply as rate differences. Indeed, the figure shows clear evidence of similar peak rates for minority and majority males; however, the rate of desistance is slower for minority than for majority males, giving rise to provocative hypotheses about how inequalities in social opportunity delay desistance.

This type of curve defines one of the most important objects of study in modern research on crime and deviance. In principle, every youth has a "personal" curve with respect to this kind of outcome, and it is each person's entire curve, including rate of acceleration early, rate of deceleration later, peak age, and rate of desistance, that require investigation. The parameters of each curve can be viewed as a vector of outcomes to be by predicted by early temperamental and family characteristics as well as by time-varying covariates (e.g., parental separation, arrest, incarceration). Moreover, we seek to understand how the organizational characteristics of schools and communities interact with the psychological characteristics of persons inhabiting them to influence the shape of each person's curve.

The conceptual framework we have constructed can be represented faithfully in terms of the parameters of a hierarchical linear statistical model, also referred to as a multilevel model or a covariance components model (Goldstein, 1987; Bryk and Raucenbush, 1992). In particular, the link between psychological predispositions and subsequent development can be represented by a two-level hierarchical model. Effects of the social contexts of communities and schools can be incorporated either as nested random effects in a three-level model or as crossed random effects, depending on the structure of the data. We begin by describing and illustrating the two-level model. We then consider how to incorporate effects of social context via the more elaborate models. Each of the models allows the investigator to represent predisposing factors as time-invariant predictors and environmental responses to deviance via time-varying predictors.

The Two-Level Model: Effects of Psychological Characteristics on Development

Laird and Ware (1982) and Strenio, Weisberg, & Bryk (1983), working independently, proposed essentially identical approaches to the analysis of repeated measures data, both employing maximum likelihood estimation based on the EM algorithm of Dempster, Laird, and Rubin (1977). In this approach, each subject's growth curve is characterized by a set of person-specific parameters. For example, in a linear growth model, the parameters might be a mean and a rate of growth. However, these parameters are themselves viewed as randomly sampled from a population of persons. Hence, the model may be viewed as having two levels: a within-subjects level and a between-subjects level. Laird and Ware (1982) refer to this kind of model as a "random effects model," though it differs from classical random effects models in allowing covariation between growth parameters. Hence, Dempster, Rubin & Tsutakawa (1981) referred to related models as "covariance components" models. Strenio, Weisberg & Bryk (1983) applied the term "hierarchical linear model" reflecting the important influence of Lindley and Smith (1972) whose pioneering work on hierarchical models inspired many of the subsequent developments.

Bryk and Raudenbush (1987) reconsidered decades-old dilemmas in the measurement of change from the standpoint of the hierarchical linear model. They showed how the model could be employed to assess the psychometric properties of an instrument for measuring characteristics of the growth curve such as the status of a subject at a time point, the linear rate of growth, or the rate of acceleration. They showed how to formulate and test alternative models for mean growth and how to assess the extent of individual variation around the mean growth curve. To assess correlates of growth, they conceived each set of individual growth parameters to a multivariate outcome to be predicted by measured characteristics of the person's background and environment. They viewed this work as building directly on the contributions of Rogosa, Brand, and Zimkowski (1982) and Rogosa & Willett (1985), who viewed the formulation of explicit models for individual growth as essential in understanding the problems of measuring growth or change.

Applications of hierarchical linear models to study individual growth in educational and psychological research include papers by Goldstein (1989), who refers to these models as "multilevel models," Willms and Jacobson (1989), and Bryk and Raudenbush (1988). Huttenlocher et al (1991) used this approach to shed new light on vocabulary development during early childhood. Francis et al. (1991) consider the potentially broad applicability of this approach in the context of clinical studies with an illustration from data on recovery from brain injury.

The estimation theory used in the examples here is based on the EM algorithm of Dempster, Laird, and Rubin (1977) and is discussed in detail in Raudenbush (1988) and in Bryk and Raudenbush (1992; Chapter 10). We shall not consider estimation theory in this paper.

Example: Changing Attitudes Toward Deviance During Adolescence

Raudenbush and Chan (1992) utilized a two-level hierarchical linear model to study growth in pro-deviant attitudes during adolescence based on the US National Youth Survey. Their analysis serves as a useful example for introducing the logic of the model.

For simplicity we focus on the youngest NYS cohort of 239 11-year olds sampled in 1976 and followed until 1980 so that subjects with complete data were observed on five occasions. The outcome variable for this analysis is a nine-item scale assessing attitudes favorable to deviant behavior. Subjects were asked how wrong they believe it is for someone their age to: cheat on school tests; purposely damage or destroy property that does not belong to him or her; use marijuana or hashish, steal something worth less than $5.00, hit or threaten someone without any reason; use alcohol; break into a vehicle or building to steal something; sell hard drugs such as heroin, cocaine, and LSD; or steal something worth more than $50.00. In each case, subjects were asked to choose one of four categories: "very wrong," "wrong," "a little bit wrong," or "not wrong at all." This scale was administered annually for five years. Of our total sample, 68.2% had complete data at all five points of data collection; 18.2% had data at four time points, 6.7% had three waves of data, 3.9% had two waves, and 3.0% had only one wave. Our analytic method utilizes any data available, so no subjects were eliminated. A logarithmic transformation of the outcome substantially reduced skewness. The descriptive statistics provided in Table 1 are in this logarithmic metric.

Predictors. Sex, race, income, cohort, and exposure to deviant peers were initially employed as predictors. However, race and

Table 1. Descriptive statistics for the log of attitude towards deviance and the log of exposure to delinquent peers by age, cohort and sex.

	Age	11	12	13	14	15	16	17	18
	Log of attitude towards deviance								
	Cohort 1								
Male	m	.24	.27	.36	.45	.49	–	–	–
N=122	sd	.21	.21	.28	.27	.27	–	–	–
Female	m	.19	.21	.29	.36	.40	–	–	–
N=117	sd	.17	.22	.25	.31	.33	–	–	–
	Cohort 2								
Male	m	–	–	–	.41	.51	.56	.55	.55
N=140	sd	–	–	–	30	.31	.30	.27	.28
Female	m	–	–	–	.36	.44	.46	.46	.51
N=105	sd	–	–	–	.27	.26	.26	.24	.27
	Log of exposure to delinquent peers								
	Cohort 1								
Male	m	.39	.36	.43	.48	.49	–	–	–
	sd	.29	.26	.32	.32	.32	–	–	–
Female	m	.20	.23	.31	.38	.41	–	–	–
	sd	.18	.22	.27	.32	.33	–	–	–
	Cohort 2								
Male	m	–	–	–	.52	.57	.60	.61	.61
	sd	–	–	–	.32	.34	.31	.33	.31
Female	m	–	–	–	48	.54	.56	.54	.53
	sd	–	–	–	.30	.32	.29	.26	.26

income proved unuseful in predicting deviance and so were dropped from the analysis. Sex (1 = female; 0 = male) and cohort (1 = cohort one; 0 = cohort two) are, by definition, time-invariant. "Exposure to deviant peers," was based on a nine-item scale that was administered every year and so is a time-varying predictor.

The scaling of exposure closely parallelled the scaling of deviance. Subjects were asked how many of their friends engaged in the nine activities mentioned above. Responses were coded on a five-point Likert scale (from "all of them" to "none of them"). Item responses were averaged (Cronbach's alpha = .80) and transformed into a logarithmic metric. Means and standard deviations appear in Table 1.

The analysis seeks to specify the appropriate shape of the mean and individual change functions, to take into account the effects of time-invariant covariates, and to take into account the effects of time-varying covariates.

Shape of the Mean and Individual Change Curves

Level-1 model. We begin with a simple linear model for individual change. According to this model, there is a tendency for the deviant attitude score of each subject to change at a steady rate from age 11 to age 15:

$$Y_{it} = \pi_{0i} + \pi_{1i}\,(AGE-13)_{it} + e_{it}, \quad (1)$$

where

Y_{it} is the deviant attitude score for subject i at time t, i = 1,...,239; t = 1,...,5;

$(AGE-13)_{it}$ is the age of subject i at time t minus 13 so that $(Age-13)_{it}$ is −2, −1, 0, 1, or 2 at ages 11, 12, 13, 14, and 15 respectively, corresponding to times t = 1, 2, 3, 4, and 5;

π_{0i} is the intercept of subject i, so that, given the coding of (Age−13), π_{0i} is the expected outcome of subject i at age 13;

π_{1i} is the expected rate of increase per year in the outcome for subject i;

and

e_{it} is the random within-subject error of prediction for subject i at time t, conditional on that subject's change parameters π_{0i}, and π_{1i}. These within-subject errors are assumed mutually independent and normally distributed with mean of zero, i.e., "$e_{it} \sim N(0,\sigma^2)$".

Level-2 model. Equation 1 characterizes each subject's trajectory from age 11 to 15 is by two parameters, π_{0i}, the subject's average level of deviant attitude during this period (corresponding to the expected outcome at age 13), and π_{1i}, that subject's rate of increase in deviant attitudes. Our current interest focuses on the inter-individual differences in the mean level and rate of increase in pro-deviant attitudes. We expect that the average rate of increase is positive during these early adolescent years, but that there will also exist substantial variation across subjects in these rates. To examine these hypotheses, we formulate a simple *level-2* model

$$\pi_{0i} = \beta_{00} + u_{0i}, \quad (2)$$
$$\pi_{1i} = \beta_{10} + u_{1i},$$

where

β_{00} is the grand mean deviant attitude score at age 13;

β_{10} is the grand mean rate of increase in deviant attitudes;

u_{0i} is the random effect of person i on deviant attitudes at age 13;

and

u_{1i} is the random effect of person i on the rate of increase in deviant attitudes.

The random effects (μ_{0i}, μ_{1i}) are assumed bivariate normal in distribution with zero means, variances τ_{00}, τ_{11}, and covariance τ_{01}. The regression coefficients β_{00} and β_{10} are termed fixed effects. When Equations 1 and 2 are combined, the resulting equation may be written

$$Y_{it} = \beta_{00} + \beta_{10}\,(AGE-13)_{it} + \varepsilon_{it}, \tag{3}$$

where $\varepsilon_{it} = u_{0i} + u_{1i}\,(AGE-13)_{it} + e_{it}$.

Two aspects of the error ε_{it} render Equation 3 inappropriate for estimation via ordinary least squares regression. First, these errors are correlated within subjects by virtue of the fact that every time-series observation for subject i shares random effects u_{0i} and u_{1i}; and the errors are heteroscedastic, given the dependence of their variance on $(AGE-13)_{it}$. Under these conditions, and with balanced data, ordinary least squares estimates of the fixed effects β_{00} and β_{10} would be efficient in the case of Equation 3 but the standard error estimates would not. When the data are unbalanced (as they are here) and/or when time-varying covariates are added to the model, ordinary least squares regression would yield inefficient estimates of the fixed effects as well.

Results. Let us first consider the results for the fixed effects (Table 2 Model 1). We see, first, that the mean growth rate β_{10} is estimated to be .063, t = 12.55, indicating a highly significantly positive average rate of increase in deviant attitudes during ages 11–15. In terms of the standard deviation of the outcome at age 11, this is equivalent to an expected increase of just under a third of a standard deviation per year.

This result certainly does not imply that every subject is increasing in deviant attitudes, and to assess the extent of variation in "growth rates" we need to learn more about τ_{11}, the variance of the growth rates. The results in Table 2 (Model 1) yield the estimate $\hat{\tau}_{11}$ = .0030, and the associated chi-square test is highly significant, implying that significant variation exists among subjects in rates of increase. The estimated standard deviation of the growth rates is $\sqrt{(.0030)}$ = .055, implying that it would neither be surprising to find subjects with no rate of increase nor to find subjects with rates of increase in excess of 2/3 of a standard deviation per year. The results also supply strong evidence that the base rates (π_{0i} = deviant attitudes at age 13) vary substantially across subjects (note the chi-square of 1504.8, df = 223, associated with $\hat{\tau}_{00}$ = .0345).

A test for quadratic effects. Equation 1 specifies that changes in deviant attitudes are strictly linear during ages 11–15.

Table 2. Hierarchical Linear Model Results for Cohort One.

a) Fixed Effects

Predictor	Model 1: No Covariates Coefficient	SE	t-ratio	Model 2: Sex as a Covariate Coefficient	SE	t-ratio	Model 3: Sex and Exposure as Covariates Coefficient	SE	t-ratio
For base rate, π_{0i}									
Intercept, β_{00}	0.329	0.013	—	0.3649	0.0179	—	0.3463	0.0150	—
Sex, β_{01}				–0.0741	0.0258	–2.88	–0.0311	0.0216	–1.44
For linear change, π_{1i}									
Intercept, β_{10}	0.063	0.005	12.55	0.0679	0.0069	9.84	0.0606	0.0062	9.74
Sex, β_{11}				–0.0112	0.0100	–1.12	–0.0230	0.0092	–2.50
For exposure effect, π_{2i}									
Intercept, β_{20}							0.2935	0.0316	9.28
Sex, β_{21}							0.0831	0.0508	1.64

b) Variance Components

Parameter[a]	Model 1: Estimate	Chi-Square	df	Model 2: Estimate	Chi-Square	df	Model 3: Estimate	Chi-Square	d
$Var(\pi_{0i}) = \pi_{00}$	0.0345	1504.8***	223	0.0333	1473.1***	222	0.0213	902.0***	219
$Var(\pi_{1i}) = \pi_{11}$	0.0030	469.8***	223	0.0030	468.7	222	0.0017	377.1	219
$Var(e_{it}) = \sigma^2$	0.0262			0.0262			0.0243		

Notes: *** $p < .001$ [a]Degrees of freedom are based on the number of persons with sufficient data for ordinary least squares estimation of person-specific parameters. All estimates are based on all the data, including persons with insufficient data for OLS estimation.

However, it could be that change is curvilinear. For example, it could be that a support for deviance is accelerating or decelerating on average during these ages; and it could be that rates of acceleration or deceleration vary across subjects. To study these possibilities, Equation 1 was elaborated to include a quadratic contrast. The results indicated, however, that there was no significant tendency for mean growth to be quadratic, and the estimated variance component for quadratic effects was very small. These findings suggest that a linear change or "growth" structure is adequate to describe change in deviance for cohort one.

Specification of a Between-Subjects (Time-Invariant) Covariate

Our results so far indicate substantial variation among subjects both in terms of base rates and rates of increase in pro-deviant attitudes, encouraging a search for differences in subject background that might account for this variation. In this illustrative analysis, we utilized race, income, and sex as predictors, but found that only sex was related to base rate or rate of change. Using the variable sex as an example, we now illustrate how time-invariant predictors ("covariates"), either discretely or continuously measured, may be incorporated in the model.

The level-1 model of Equation 1, which accounts for variation within subjects over time, remains unchanged. However, the level-2 model (Equation 2) is elaborated:

$$\pi_{0i} = \beta_{00} + \beta_{01}X_i + u_{0i}, \qquad (4)$$
$$\pi_{1i} = \beta_{10} + \beta_{11}X_i + u_{1i},$$

where
$X_i = 1$ if female, 0 if male;

β_{00} is now the expected level of deviant attitudes at age 13 for males;

β_{01} is the mean difference in deviant attitudes between females and males at age 13;

β_{10} is expected rate of change in deviant attitudes for males;

β_{11} is the mean difference in rate of change between females and males;

u_{0i} is the random effect of person i on deviant attitudes at age 13 after accounting for sex differences;

and

u_{1i} is the random effect of person i on the rate of increase in pro-deviant attitude after accounting for sex differences.

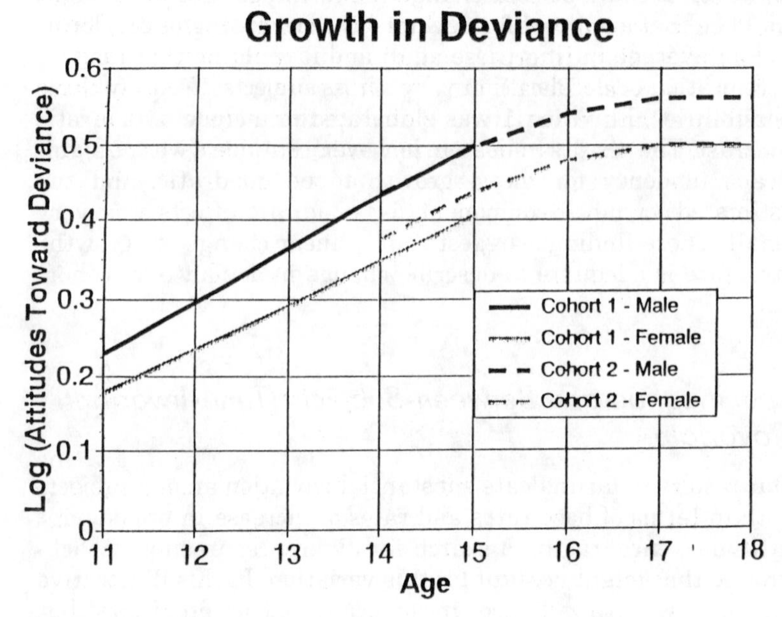

Figure 3. Expected logarithm of the attitudes toward deviance (vertical axis) as a function of age (horizontal axis) for cohort one (solid line) and cohort two (dashed line) based on separate analyses for each cohort.

The results (Table 2, Model 2) imply that females have significantly lower base rates at 13 in deviant attitudes, $\hat{\beta}_{01} = -.074$, t = −2.88. However, there is no significant sex difference in rates of increase, $\hat{\beta}_{11} = -.011$, t = −1.12. These results are graphed for males and females in Figure 3 (see solid lines above ages 11 through 15).

Specification of a Within-Subjects (Time-Varying) Covariate

The researcher may also wish to control for covariates that change with time. Examples might include changes in family status, movement to a new neighborhood, loss of a job, or incarceration. We shall utilize exposure to deviant peers which we expect to change over time. Of course, such exposure cannot be viewed as exogenous to pro-deviant attitudes because those who are initially high in pro-deviant attitudes may seek out deviant peers, and this new set of friendships may lead to further increases in pro-deviant attitudes. It is nonetheless interesting to discover whether controlling for exposure to deviant peers partially or even completely accounts for growth in deviant thinking between 11 and 15. If not, other mechanisms may be at work that explain interpersonal differences in rates of change.

Level-1 model. Recall that to incorporate between-subjects (time-invariant) covariates required elaboration of the level-2 model. In contrast, specification of within-subjects (time-varying) predictors requires elaboration of the level-1 model (Equation 1), which now becomes

$$Y_{it} = \pi_{0i} + \pi_{1i}\,(AGE-13)_{it} + \pi_{2i}\,(EXPOSURE)_{it} + \varepsilon_{it}, \qquad (5)$$

where $(EXPOSURE)_{it}$ represents the level of exposure to deviant peers of subject i at time t, π_{2i} is the partial effect of exposure, controlling for age, and both the intercept, π_{0i}, and the linear age effect (rate of change), π_{1i}, are adjusted for exposure.

Level-2 model. Three parameters (the π's) now characterize the trajectory of each subject. The level-2 model must now specify how those are viewed as varying across subjects. That model becomes

$$\begin{aligned} \pi_{0i} &= \beta_{00} + \beta_{01}Xi + u_{0i}, \\ \pi_{1i} &= \beta_{10} + \beta_{11}X_i + u_{1i}, \\ \pi_{2i} &= \beta_{20} + \beta_{21}X_i, \end{aligned} \qquad (6)$$

where X_i remains the indicator for sex (1 if female, 0 if male). Note that we have constrained the random effect of subjects on the exposure slope (u_{1i}) to be zero. A prior analysis revealed that the exposure random effect was quite collinear with age random effect, and it was difficult to estimate both random effects, so the exposure effect was fixed.

Results. Table 2 (Model 3) reveals several interesting results. First, we see that exposure is strongly and positively related to pro-deviant attitudes, $\hat{\beta}_{20} = .294$, $t = 9.28$. The causal status of this effect remains unclear, though, as mentioned, the relationship between exposure and pro-deviant attitudes is probably reciprocal. Second, once exposure is controlled, the mean difference in pro-deviant attitudes at age 13 between males and females become non-significant, $\hat{\beta}_{01} = -.031$, $t = -1.44$. Apparently males are more likely to be exposed to deviant peers and this higher propensity helps account for the higher rates of pro-deviant attitudes among males. Third, once exposure has been controlled, sex differences in rates of change become significant, $\hat{\beta}_{11} = -.023$, $t = -2.50$. If exposure is held constant, the rate of increase tends to be faster for males than for females.

Subsequent Analyses

Raudenbush and Chan (1992) replicated the logic of the analysis described above using data from a second cohort of youth who were 14 at the outset of the study (in 1976) and 18 at the termination of data collection (descriptive statistics for cohort 2 are listed in Table 1). Results for this older cohort were quite different from those for the 11–15 year-old cohort reported above. Specifically, a significant negative quadratic trend, manifest both for males and females, appeared in the 14–18 year old data. Such a trend may be interpreted as evidence of a deceleration in the rate of increase of pro-deviant attitudes during later adolescence. Figure 3 displays the mean trajectories by sex for the two cohorts. Cohort one, aged 11–15 (solid line) exhibits a comparatively rapid rate of increase in pro-deviant attitudes, and the relationship between age and the outcome during these early adolescent years is linear. In contrast, the rate of increase is slower in cohort 2's data (dashed line), and a curvilinear effect is apparent, with the rate of increase nearing zero at around age 17.

There are several alternative explanations for the differences between results for cohorts 1 and 2 displayed in Figure 3. First, the comparatively rapid increase in pro-deviance during early adolescence, followed by deceleration later in adolescence, could indicate an underlying developmental phenomenon in which deviant propensities increase rapidly during early adolescence and then decelerate later, achieving a peak in late adolescence and then declining during early adulthood. In contrast, it could be that demographic differences between the two cohorts interact with age, and that if we had data on cohort 1 from ages 14–18 we would see, for example, a continuing linear increase in pro-deviant attitudes. According to this explanation, the comparatively smaller rate of increase manifest in cohort two's data reflects the different personal backgrounds or experiences of that cohort and has nothing to do with their older age. Interactions between age and period could also arguably account for the different trajectories of the two cohorts.

To distinguish among these potential explanations, Raudenbush and Chan conducted a further analysis that linked the data from the two cohorts and tested for a cohort effect and an age-by-cohort interaction. If these effects were found null, the weight would fall on the developmental explanation. This kind of analysis is potentially important in longitudinal studies using an accelerated design in which subjects of varying age are sampled at a single time point and then followed for several years. The goal of such an analysis is to describe development over a comparatively long interval of the life course by collecting data over a comparatively short interval of time (Tonry, Ohlin, & Farrington, 1991). In the current example, one hopes to learn about development over nine years (between ages 11–18) even though data were collected on only five occasions, from 1976 to 1980. The two-level hierarchical linear model is well-suited to linking the data across cohorts because the model readily incorporates unbalanced data. We review Raudenbush and Chan's analysis below.

Linking Data From the Two Cohorts

Level-1 model. For every subject in both cohorts we now specify a growth model that allows for acceleration early and deceleration late in adolescence:

$$Y_{it} = \pi_{0i} + \pi_{1i}\,(\mathrm{LIN})_{it} + \pi_{2i}\,(\mathrm{QUAD})_{it} + \pi_{3i}\,(\mathrm{CUBIC})_{it} + e_{it}, \qquad (7)$$

where

Y_{it} is the outcome for subject i at time t, i = 1,...,484, t = 1,...,5;

$(\mathrm{LIN})_{it}$ is a linear contrast coefficient that depends on subject i's age at time t, t = 1, 2, 3, 4, and 5;

$(\mathrm{QUAD})_{it}$ is a quadratic contrast coefficient that depends on subject i's age at time t;

$(\mathrm{CUBIC})_{it}$ is a cubic contrast coefficient that depends on subject i's age at time t;

π_{0i} is the intercept of subject i, so that, given the coding of the contrast coefficients (see Table 3), π_{0i} is the expected outcome of subject i at age 14.5;

π_{1i} is subject i's linear effect of age, and, given the coding of the contrast coefficients, π_{1i} is the expected rate of increase in pro-deviant attitude for subject i at age 14.5;

π_{2i} is the quadratic effect of age for subject i, and, given the coding of the contrast coefficients, π_{2i} is proportional to the rate of "acceleration" in pro-deviant orientation for subject i at age 14.5;

π_{3i} is the cubic effect of age for subject i; and

e_{it} is the usual random within-subject error of prediction for subject i at time t.

Table 3 displays the coding of the linear, quadratic, and cubic contrast coefficients. It is vital that the "time" metric in the level-1 model be constructed so that both cohorts are located on the same age-related scale. If we had chosen occasion 1,...,5 rather than age as the underlying time metric for Equation 7, it would not have been possible to link the data in a developmentally meaningful way.

Level-2 model. Equation 7 characterizes each subject's trajectory from age 14 to 18 by three parameters, π_{0i}, π_{1i}, and π_{2i}. In the level-2 model, we would like to model these as a function of sex and cohort. However, given only two points of overlap between cohorts, we can model only two of the growth parameters as a function of cohort. We therefore model π_{0i} and π_{1i} as a function not only of sex, but also of cohort. If cohort is unrelated to these two growth parameters, we shall conclude that the two cohorts share the same expected levels of deviance and the same linear rate of change at age 14.5. We write the level-2 model as follows:

$$\begin{aligned}\pi_{0i} &= \beta_{00} + \beta_{01}X_i + \beta_{02}Z_i + u_{0i},\\ \pi_{1i} &= \beta_{10} + \beta_{11}X_i + \beta_{12}Z_i + u_{1i},\\ \pi_{2i} &= \beta_{20},\\ \pi_{3i} &= \beta_{30},\end{aligned} \tag{8}$$

where

X_i = 1 if female, 0 if male;

Z_i = 1 if cohort 1, 0 if cohort 2;

β_{00} is the expected deviance at age 14.5 for males in cohort 2;

β_{01} is the mean difference in deviance between females and males at age 14.5;

β_{02} is the mean expected outcome difference between cohorts one and two at age 14.5;

β_{10} is expected rate of change in deviance for males in cohort 2 at age 14.5;

β_{11} is the mean difference in rate of change between females and males at age 14.5;

β_{12} is the mean difference in rate of change between cohorts at age 14.5;

β_{20} is the expected quadratic effect for both males and females;

β_{30} is the expected cubic effect for both females and males; and

u_{0i} and u_{1i} are random effects for person i.

The assumptions are that the random effects (u_{0i}, u_{1i}) are bivariate normal with covariances $\tau_{pp'}$ for p,p' = 0,1. The reader will notice that the variable sex is used to predict the π_{0i} and π_{1i} but not the quadratic effect, π_{2i} or the cubic effect, π_{3i}. That is because an analysis not reported here showed no sex differences in these curvilinear effects. Also, the quadratic and cubic effects are constrained to have no variance (i.e., u_{2i} and u_{3i} do not appear in the equation). It was not possible to estimate the random effects variance for these curvilinear effects with an acceptable degree of precision. Data with longer time series per person and more overlap between cohorts would allow sufficiently precise estimation of these variances.

Results

Fixed effects. An important result is that no significant cohort effects were found on the deviance base rate, π_{0i}, or on the linear rate of change in deviance, π_{1i} (Table 3). This result implies that both the base rate in deviance and the rate of change in deviance at age 14.5 are not significantly different across the two cohorts.

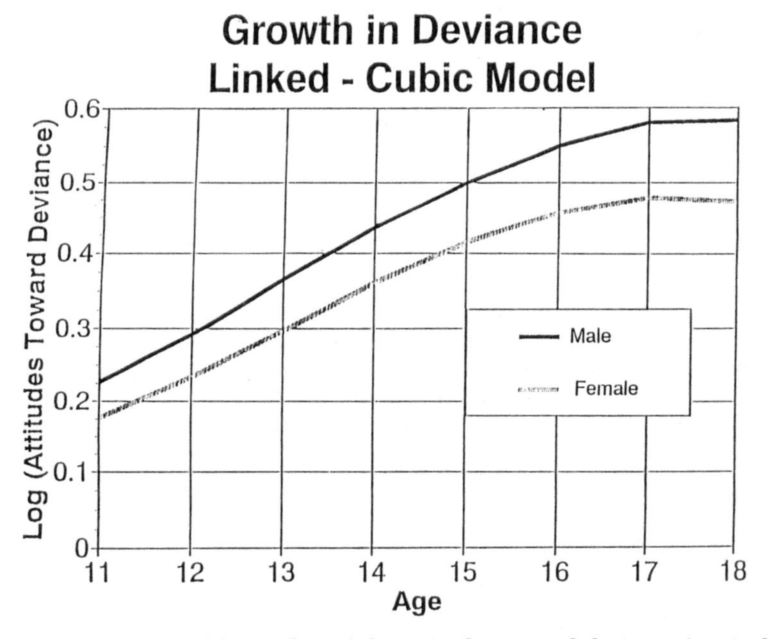

Figure 4. Expected logarithm of the attitudes toward deviance (vertical axis) as a function of age (horizontal axis) for all subjects in cohorts one and two, based on an analysis that links data from the two cohorts.

Moreover, there is reason to believe that the null hypotheses of no cohort effects were tested with reasonable power. Note, for example, that the standard error the estimate of the cohort effect on the base rate is .021, implying that, to be significant, the magnitude of the cohort effect would have to exceed about .042. Now suppose that the true cohort effect were .08, representing a mean difference of 25 percent of the standard deviation of the outcome at age 14 (see Table 1 which shows that the standard deviation at ages 14 and 15 is about .32). A standardized effect size of .25 is conventionally viewed as small but not trivial in social science research. Our analysis would appear to have power greater than .90 to detect such an effect.

Table 3 indicates significant linear, quadratic, and cubic effects; there are sex differences only on the base rate. Figure 4

Table 3. Hierarchical Linear Model Results for Linkage Between Cohorts One and Two.

a) Fixed Effects

Predictor	Coefficient	SE	t-ratio
For base rate, π_{0i}			
Intercept, β_{00}	0.4409	0.0217	—
Sex, β_{01}	–0.0796	0.0198	–4.01
Cohort, β_{02}	0.0071	0.0212	0.33
For linear effect, π_{1i}			
Intercept, β_{10}	0.0551	0.0084	6.54
Sex, β_{11}	–0.0002	0.0107	–0.02
Cohort, β_{12}	–0.0027	0.0147	–0.18
For quadratic effect, π_{2i}			
Intercept, β_{20}	–0.0048	0.0022	–2.12
For cubic effect, π_{3i}			
Intercept, β_{30}	–0.0016	0.0007	–2.23

b) Variance Components

Parameter[a]	Estimate	Chi-Square	df
$Var(\pi_{0i}) = \tau_{00}$	0.0401	2146.7***	468
$Var(\pi_{1i}) = \tau_{11}$	0.0095	781.2***	468
$Var(\varepsilon_{it}) = \sigma_2$	0.0312		

Notes: *** $p < .001$

[a] Degrees of freedom are based on the number of persons with sufficient data for ordinary least squares estimation of person-specific parameters. All estimates are based on all the data, including persons with insufficient data for OLS estimation.

Contrast Coefficients for the Analysis

Age	Linear Coefficient	Quadratic Coefficient	Cubic Coefficient
11	–3.5	7	–7
12	–2.5	1	5
13	–1.5	–3	7
14	– .5	–5	3
15	.5	–5	–3
16	1.5	–3	–7
17	2.5	1	–5
18	3.5	7	7

displays the expected growth curves for males and females based on this model. The two trajectories conform to theoretical expectation in that the rate of increase in pro-deviant attitudes is greatest during early adolescence and diminishes to zero in later adolescence. Using the coding scheme in Table 3, it is possible to calculate two interesting features of the growth curves.

The first is a point of inflection, that is, the age at which change in deviance begins to decelerate. This value is found by setting the second derivative of the growth function with respect to age equal to zero and then solving for age. The result for these data is that the inflection point occurs soon after age 13. Of course, this estimate is not precise given that growth is nearly linear during a broad interval of ages.

The second interesting feature of the growth curve is the "peak age," that is, the age at which deviance achieves a maximum. This value is found by setting the first derivative of the growth function with respect to age equal to zero and then solving for age. For our data, the typical peak age occurs at about 17.7 years of age. Note that given our inference that only the base rate and not the linear, quadratic, or cubic effects depend on sex, the expected inflection point and typical peak age are the same for females as for males. However, given our belief that linear rates of change vary across subjects, the peak age must also be presumed to vary. It is therefore possible to reparameterize the model so that the level of deviance at this peak becomes a characteristic of the trajectory under study. Interest might then focus on characteristics of personal background and experience that predict how deviant subjects' attitudes will be at their most deviant.

Incorporating the Effects of Social Context

To illustrate the incorporation of social-contextual effects, it will be necessary to rely on examples from educational research because the relevant data in criminological studies have not yet become available. Moreover, the examples use continuously distributed outcomes rather than discrete outcomes such as behavioral counts of interest in studying deviant behavior. Experience using hierarchical models is far more developed in the case of continuous outcomes than in the case of discrete outcomes.

What is essential in the following sections, however, are the designs and the models. The designs involve time-series data on persons who are members of social contexts (schools or communities). The models must therefore incorporate both inter- individual and inter-contextual variation in the shape of development. Pre-disposing characteristics of persons and contexts are represented in the model as time-invariant covariates. Responses of the environment over time are represented as time-varying covariates. Unpredictable components of variation at the personal and contextual level are represented as random effects. Extension to non-normal data and non-linear models is quite straightforward, and we consider this issue briefly in closing.

Suppose that during the course of the investigation, each subject is a member of one and only one social context such as a community. Then the design would involve time-series data collected on subjects nested within social context. A three-level hierarchical model is appropriate for such a design, and we describe application of this model below. However, in most settings, subjects will migrate across social contextual boundaries during the course of the investigation. In this case, subjects are crossed rather than nested within social context. We shall consider hierarchical models in which each time-series observation is nested within a cell created by the cross-classification of subjects and contexts. We begin, however, with the simpler three-level model for nested data.

Three-Level Models

Let us return to the curves plotted in Figure 4 that describe the characteristic relationship between age and pro-deviant attitudes for males and females in the US between 1976 and 1980. These plots represent estimated mean growth curves for males and females. However, Table 3 indicates that significant interpersonal variation exists; both the base-levels of the outcome and the linear rate of increase vary significantly from subject to subject. In essence, each subject has a personal growth curve and the plots in Figure 4 represent the average of these personal trajectories.

Let us suppose that the subjects of our study were nested within communities during the course of the investigation. Time-invariant community covariates could be used to predict the intercept, linear, quadratic and cubic change components in a way quite analogous to the use of sex as a covariate in Equation 4. Time-varying covariates measured at the community level could be incorporated in the same way as we incorporated exposure to deviant peers as a time-varying covariate in Equation 5. However, we need also to incorporate the unmeasured (random) effects of communities. To do so, we add a third level to the model.

Unfortunately, the NYS data do not include information about the membership of young people in ecologically meaningful community or neighborhood contexts, and so we turn to an example from educational research in order to illustrate application of the model.

Example: Growth of Children Nested Within Primary Schools

Bryk and Raudenbush (1988) analyzed a subset of the Sustaining Effects Study data (Carter, 1984) in which 618 students nested within 86 schools were followed during the first three years of primary school. Test scores in mathematics and reading were collected at five points: spring of grade one, fall and spring of grade 2, and fall and spring of grade 3. The California Tests of Basic Skills were the outcome measure. These have been equated across forms to reveal growth. The existence of an interval scale over the ages under study is a critical element in modeling change and we shall return to this issue in closing.

Level-1 model. Children's growth in math and reading tends to be well-described by a linear model during these grades; however, some accommodation must be made for the effect associated with their receiving no instruction during the summer. Hence, we formulate a model for change over time that includes an intercept, a linear rate of change, and the effect of a time-varying covariate indicating whether the previous period was the summer or the academic year:

$$Y_{tij} = \pi_{0ij} + \pi_{1ij}\,(\text{TIME POINT})_{tij} + \pi_{2ij}\,(\text{SUMMER DROP})_{tij} + e_{tij} \quad (9)$$

where

Y_{tij} is the outcome at time t for child i in school j;

$(\text{TIME POINT})_{tij}$ takes on values of 0,1,2,3, and 4 at the five time points, respectively;

$(\text{SUMMER DROP})_{tij}$ takes on a value of 1 in the fall and 0 in the spring;

π_{0ij} is the expected value of the outcome when both TIME POINT and SUMMER DROP are zero and, hence, represents the "initial status" of child ij, that is, the status of the child at spring of first grade;

π_{1ij} is the linear rate of increase in learning per time point;

π_{2ij} is the summer effect on the outcome for that subject; and

e_{tij} is a random error assumed independently normally distributed with variance σ^2, i.ε., $e_{tij} - N(0, \sigma^2)$.

According to the model, child i in school j will gain π_{1ij} in achievement and $\pi_{1ij} + \pi_{2ij}$ during the summer. Hence, three parameters describe the growth of each child: an initial status, π_{0ij} on average learning rate, π_{1ij}, and a summer drop-off effect, π_{ij}.

Level-2 model. Within each school, each of the three child-specific growth parameters π_{pij}, p = 0,1,2, is now modeled as varying around a school mean, i.e.,

$$\pi_{pij} = \beta_{p0j} + u_{pij} \quad (10)$$

where β_{p0j} is the mean value of growth parameter p within school j and u_{pij} is a random child effect. These child effects are assumed to have a trivariate normal distribution with variances $\mathrm{Var}(u_{pij}) = \pi_{xpp}$ and covariances $\mathrm{Cov}(u_{pij}, u_{p'ij}) = \pi_{xpp'}$, to be estimated. Thus, each school is characterized by a mean initial status, a mean growth rate, and a summer drop-off effect. Within each school children's growth parameters vary randomly. In fact, a preliminary analysis revealed little evidence that the summer drop-off effect varied much among children within schools and so this variance and the associated covariances were constrained to be null.

Level-3 model. The three β's that characterize typical growth within a school are now viewed as varying randomly across the entire population of schools according to the model

$$\beta_{p0j} = \Theta_{p00} + v_{p0j} \tag{11}$$

where Θ_{p00} is the grand mean of the growth parameter p, and v_{p0j} represents a random school effect for parameters p = 0,1,2. The three school effects are assumed to vary across schools according to a tri-variate normal distribution with variances $\mathrm{Var}(v_{p0j}) = \tau_{\beta pp}$ and covariances $\mathrm{Cov}(v_{p0j}, v_{p'0j}) = \tau_{\beta pp'}$.

Results. Figure 5 displays the mean growth curves in both reading and mathematics. The figure indicates that, for mathematics, as expected, there is a positive growth rate during the academic

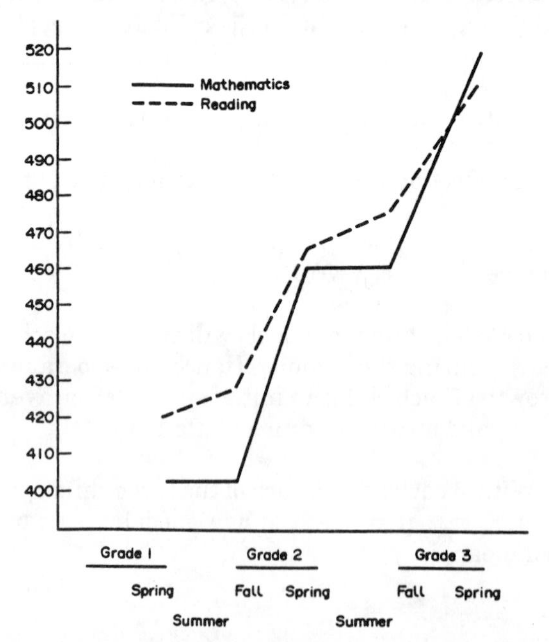

Figure 5. Expected growth functions in math and reading based on three-level model analysis of data from the Sustaining Effects Study.

year and essentially no growth during the summer. For reading the results are a bit different. There is some growth during summer, though certainly less than during the academic year.

Of course we assume that the growth curves vary from child to child within schools and from school to school. In essence, each child and each school can be characterized by a growth function of the type displayed in Figure 5, and, in fact, empirical Bayes methods can be used to estimate such functions for each of the 86 schools and each of the 618 children.[2]

Table 4. Three-Level Results from Sustaining Effects Data.

a) Fixed Effects

Predictor	Coefficient	SE	t-ratio
Average Initial Status, Θ_{000}	403.27	2.28	—
Average Learning Rate, Θ_{100}	28.51	0.62	46.05
Average Summer Drop, Θ_{200}	–27.78	1.23	–22.60

b) Variance Components

Parameter[a]	Estimate	Chi-Square	df	p
Level 1				
σ_2	613.10			
Level 2				
Inital Status, $\tau\pi_{00}$	1033.05	2148.80	532	.000
Learning Rate, $\tau\pi_{11}$	3.98	694.17	532	.000
Level 3				
Initial Status, $\tau\beta_{00}$	173.04	154.51	85	.000
Learning Rate, $\tau_{\beta 11}$	19.08	235.85	85	.000
Summer Drop, $\tau_{\beta 22}$	44.60	121.58	85	.000

Table 4 provides the results for the math outcome. The mean growth curve is described by the mean initial status, Θ_{100} = 403.27, the mean academic-year learning rate, Θ_{100} = 28.51, and the mean summer drop-off effect, $\Theta_{200} = -27.78$. Note that the mean summer learning are is $\Theta_{000} + \Theta_{100} = 28.51 - 27.78$ is near zero as indicated in Figure 5.

Perhaps more interesting are the variance component estimates. Variance components estimates for initial status are 1033.05 within schools and 173.04 between schools, implying that only 173.04/(173.04 + 1033.05) or 14.3 percent of the variation in initial status lies between schools. In contrast, the variance in growth rates between schools is estimated at 19.08, and the variance within schools at 3.97, implying that the lion's share of 82.8 percent of the variance lies between schools! The implication of these results for school effects research is potentially of great import. Most studies of school effects have compared schools by comparing the status of the students in them and found that school differences account for only a fraction of the total variance. Bryk and Raudenbush's (1988) results imply that if investigators study school differences in *learning rates* rather than status, especially in subjects learned only in school, such as mathematics, they are likely to discover much more significant effects of school differences than have previously emerged from school effects research. We caution that these effects would not appear as important as they are had we used *observed* learning rates as the criterion. The observed rates are likely to be highly fallible as a result of sampling and measurement error, which contribute much more to the within-school variation than to the between-school variation, leading to an under-estimate of the school contribution. The results presented in Table 4 are maximum likelihood estimates of variances of the "true" or "latent" learning rates, giving a larger and more realistic estimate of the importance of school differences than would appear had the observed rates been assessed.

Incorporating covariates. The model we have presented so far includes two time-varying predictors (TIME POINT and SUMMER DROP). However, it includes no child-level or school-level predictors. Such covariates can be readily included in the model. For example, the level-2 model could be expanded so that

$$\pi_{pij} = \beta_{p0j} + \Sigma\, \beta_{pqj} X_{qij} + u_{pij} \tag{12}$$

where each X_{qij} is a child-level predictor (e.g., sex, socioeconomic status, etc.). The school-specific coefficients β_{pqj} could be allowed to vary randomly over the population of schools, to be constrained to be equal across schools, or to be themselves predicted by school level covariates. Also, the level-3 model of Equation 11 can be expanded so that the school mean growth parameter β_{p0j} can be predicted by school-level covariates. The level-three model may therefore be written

$$\beta_{pqj} = \theta_{pq0} + \Sigma\, \theta_{pqs} W_{qsj} + v_{pqj} \tag{13}$$

for coefficients β_{pqj}, p = 0,1,...P and q = 0,1,...,Q where p indexes the growth parameters in the level 1 model and q indexes the child-level covariates used to predict a growth parameter. The variables W_{pqj}, s = 1,...,S_{pq} are school-level covariates that are hypothesized to influence the magnitude of the school-specific coefficient β_{pqj}. Bryk and Raudenubsh (1992) provide a thorough exposition on three-level models in general and on their application to the Sustaining Effects Data, including specification of child-level and school-level covariates.

Summary and extrapolation to the study of deviance. A three-level model is useful for studying the individual change of subjects nested within social contexts. The level-1 model specifies a change or growth function for each individual. At level 2, the individual change parameters vary across persons sharing the same social context as a function of context-specific parameters plus error. At level-3, the context-specific parameters vary across contexts as a function of population-wide parameters plus error. Time-varying covariates are specified at level 1, person-specific covariates at level 2, and context-specific covariates at level 3. The variance-covariance structure of the data is decomposed into variance-covariance structures within persons, between persons within contexts and between contexts.

The most obvious application of such three-level models in studying deviance involves formulating a model for change in anti-social behavior or attitudes over time for each person at level 1. The level-1 model would specify the outcome as a function of age and possibly time-varying covariates. That is, the level-1 model specifies the "age-deviance" curve for a particular subject as well as allowing the incorporation of time-varying environmental interventions that may modify that curve. At level-2, person-specific covariates are included. These may represent the investigator's theory regarding the constellation of predisposing characteristics that are viewed a shaping later development with respect to deviant behavior or attitudes. Time-invariant community-level predictors are specified at level 3. However, community characteristics that change over time may represent important environmental interventions. These will be specified as time-varying predictors at level 1. The social context need not be the community; in some cases school context may be more relevant. It is also possible to employ this model in studying the development of siblings nested within families or of married persons over time.

The Two-Way Crossed Random Effects Model

The three-level nested random effects model facilitates an elegant representation of individual development within a social context. Its application, however, is constrained by the assumption that each person under study will inhabit one and only one social context (e.g., community) during the course of the investigation. If, instead, subjects migrate across social context during the course of the study, a rigid adherence to the three-level model would require one of the following undesirable decisions: ignoring the migration; discarding the data of those who migrate; or ignoring the social context altogether. If the frequency of migration is small, it may make sense to treat the context of origin as the context throughout (ignoring migration). Discarding data is not to be recommended, and ignoring social context defeats the purpose of this paper.

A more generally satisfactory solution is to regard subjects as crossed with context. Each time-series observation is viewed as nested within a cell defined by the cross-classification of persons and social contexts. We formulate a model for individual development as in the level-1 models above. However, this model includes a series of indicator variables, one for each social context, conceived as time-varying covariates. In general there will be many such social contexts, and it will be unparsimonious to treat each context effect as a fixed effect in the model. Instead, we view the context effects as random realizations from a probability distribution, and we estimate the parameters of that distribution. As in the three-level model, the context effects are therefore random, though now they vary within subjects. This approach is illustrated in another example from research on cognitive growth, with results borrowed from Raudenbush (in press).

Example: The Effects of Teachers on Children's Growth in Mathematics

Studying teacher effects on children's growth during the primary grades yields the kind of data structure displayed in Figure 6 where each row represents a child and each column a teacher. The data constitute a sub-sample from the "Immersion Study" (Ramirez et al., 1991), a national evaluation of alternative programs for children in the US having limited English proficiency. The outcome measure is again the California Test of Basic

Each X indicates an Observation

Grade	Grade 1										Grade 2									Grade 3					Grade 4			
Teacher	1	2	3	4	5	6	7	8	9	10	11	12	13	14	15	16	17	18	19	20	21	22	23	24	25	26	27	Totals
Student																												
5003	X										X																	2
5005		X										X																2
5006	X																											1
5007			X										X															2
5009				X										X						X					X			4
5010				X							X																	2
5011	X										X									X								3
5013			X																									1
5014														X								X						2
5015					X												X					X						3
.																												.
.																												.
.																												.
5232										X																		1
5234						X							X										X					3
5236					X												X						X					3
5237			X								X																	2
5238				X								X																2
5241										X																		1
5242								X												X								2
5243	X																		X									2
5245								X											X									2
5246					X									X										X		X		4
Totals	5	13	15	18	14	15	13	13	10	7	2	9	10	11	13	4	6	15	11	12	12	3	3	2	11	2	1	Totals

Figure 6. Organization of Data in a Sub-Sample from the Immersion Study.

Skills. The investigators aimed to test each child during the spring of each year from grade 1 to grade 4. However, attrition was very high, and most children have fewer than four data points.

In Figure 6, the first row describes the data for child 5003 who was assigned teacher 2 during first grade and teacher 11 during grade 2 and was not available for testing during grades 3 or 4. The Figure gives the data pattern for the first and last ten of the 123 children who provided a total of 250 observations and encountered 27 teachers. The data are quite sparse for estimating both child and teacher effects. There are from one to four data points per child and from 2 to 18 data points per teacher. The analytic approach uses all of the data to estimate these effects, though inferences must be made with extreme caution given the likely non-randomness of the missing data.

A Two-Level Growth Analysis. We first consider how the data might be analyzed ignoring teacher effects. At level-1 (within-children) we would model the math outcome for each child via a linear regression

$$Y_{ir} = \pi_{0r} + \pi_{1r}a_{ir} + \varepsilon_{ir}, \varepsilon_{ir} - N(0, \sigma^2), \quad (14)$$

where

Y_{ir} is the math outcome for child r at time i, i = 1,...,4; r = 1,...,123;

a_{ir} = grade – 1, so that $a_{ir} = 0$ at grade one;

π_{0r} is therefore the expected outcome at first grade for child i;

π_{1r} is the expected gain per year for child r; and

ε_{ir} is a within-child error.

At level 2, we might view the intercept and rate of change of each child as varying randomly over the population of children, i.e.,

$$\pi_{pr} = \beta_{p0} + u_{pr} \quad (15)$$

where β_{p0}, p = 0, 1 are, respectively, the population mean outcome at grade one and the population mean rate of change; and the errors u_{pr} are viewed as realizations from a bivariate normal distribution defined on the population of children. In fact, results of estimation based on a two-level hierarchical linear model are displayed in Table 5, column 1.

Crossed random effects analysis. We now modify the level-1 model (Equation 30) to incorporate the effects of teachers as “time-varying covariates” via the model

Table 5. Modeling Results for Immersion Data

a) Fixed Effects	Model 1: Teacher Variance Ignored			Model 2: Teacher Variance Estimated			Model 3: Teacher Variance Predicted		
Predictor	Coefficient	SE	t-ratio	Coefficient	SE	t-ratio	Coefficient	SE	t-ratio
Expected First Grade Status,	256.54	2.51	—	257.53	1.71	—	257.66	1.86	—
Expected linear growth rate,	47.28	2.24	21.00	45.48	1.48	30.74	44.90	1.65	27.20
Effect of masters' degree,							5.37	3.62	1.48
b) Variance Components									
Parameter	Estimate			Estimate			Estimate		
Intital status: $Var(\pi_{0i}) = \tau_{00}$	484.22			442.82			437.04		
Growth rate: $Var(\pi_{1i}) = \tau_{11}$	133.58			94.63			90.74		
Covariance, initial status and growth rate: $Cov(\pi_{0i}, \pi_{1i}) = \tau_{01}$	28.02			92.87			92.37		
Teacher effect: $Var(v) = \delta^2$				79.49			68.71		
Residual error: $Var(e_{it}) = \sigma^2$	319.60			274.37			279.75		

$$Y_{ir} = \pi^{(1)}_{0r} + \pi^{(1)}_{1r} a^{(1)}_{1ir} + \sum_{c} \pi^{(2)}_{c} a^{(2)}_{cir} + \varepsilon_{ir}, \tag{16}$$

where $\pi^{(1)}_{0r}$ and $\pi^{(1)}_{1r}$ represent the intercept and rate of growth for child r but now $\pi^{(2)}_{c}$, $c = 1,...,27$ represent the teacher effects associated with the 27 teacher indicator variables $a^{(2)}_{cir}$, $c = 1,...,27$.

Variation between children is modeled exactly as in the previous level-2 model (Equation 15) except that superscripts "(1)" are added to each symbol to distinguish them from the teacher effects.

It would clearly be unparsimonious to estimate 27 regression coefficients, one for each teacher. Instead, we conceive of the teacher effects as varying randomly around a mean of zero:

$$\pi_c^{(2)} \sim N(0,\delta^2), \tag{17}$$

(see column two of Table 5). In a second analysis, we shall add teacher level of education as a predictor.

A comparison of results between the two-level model that ignores teachers and the crossed random effects model produces some interesting insights. Estimation of the teacher effect variance of = 79.5 is accompanied by reductions in the estimates of variance attributable to variation among children in intercepts (442.8 in column two versus 484.2 in column one), variance among children in slopes (94.6 versus 133.6), and variance within children (274.4 versus 319.6).

The addition of the teacher education indicator to the model (column 3) resulted in a small reduction in the teacher-level variance component from 79.5 to 68.7. The effect of higher education was in the expected direction, but non-significant, $t = 1.48$.

Comparison with two- and three-level models. Like the two- and three-level nested model, the two-way crossed random effects model begins with a model for individual change. However, because social context can vary within a person over time, social context effects are formulated as time-varying covariates. Because the social context effects are numerous and often are assumed to represent a large population, they are specified as random variables. These variables may have a mean of zero; or their means may depend on covariates defined at the context level. Although our example includes only random main effects of context, it is also possible to define regression coefficients that vary over context. For example, the effect of student aptitude on the outcome could be defined as randomly varying over teachers.

As in the case of the three-level nested model, the crossed-random effects model allows specification of covariates that are time-varying or time-invariant. The time-invariant covariates can be defined on persons or contexts. In fact, the crossed-random effects model can be shown to be more general than the three-level nested model in that any nested-model results can be reproduced by the crossed-random results. However, the crossed-random effects analysis is more computationally intensive, so that the nested analysis is preferable when justified.

Conclusions

Two-level, three-level, and crossed random effects models provide a reasonably flexible family of analytic approaches to modeling individual development and social context effects. Each of these models is founded on a model for individual change over time. Each person's development is described by a set of person-specific parameters, and these parameters, in turn, are viewed as varying randomly across the population of persons and, in the cases discussed here, social contexts. Time-varying or time-invariant covariates – and their interactions – may be incorporated at the appropriate levels. In general, the constellation of characteristics that predispose persons to deviance may be specified as predicting the entire trajectory of later development. Environmental responses to deviance may be incorporated as time-varying covariates.

Missing data, unbalanced designs, and unequal spacing of time points across subjects pose no difficulties for the analyses, though the investigator must carefully study the sources of attrition and imbalance to insure that these do not give rise to erroneous inference. The capacity of the methods to handle unbalanced data suits it well to application in accelerated longitudinal designs, as indicated in the example from the National Youth Survey.

The metric of the dependent variable is of critical importance in studies of quantitative change. In each of the examples illustrated in this paper, the dependent variable was measured on an interval scale having the same definition over time. It is on this scale that terms like "early acceleration" in deviant propensity, "peak age," and "rate of desistance" become meaningful. In the educational examples the concepts of "summer drop off" in learning rate and "proportion of variation in learning rates attributable to schools" similarly depend on the existence of a meaningful interval scale over the ages under study. The standardization of such dependent variables within ages or their transformation to percentile ranks are fatal to the characterization of development in these meaningful and dynamic terms.

The examples provided here have employed outcomes measured continuously and predicted by linear models with normal errors. Progress on non-linear, non-normal models for discrete outcomes is now rapid. Raudenbush (1992) has presented preliminary results based on this kind of model (see Figures 1 and 2), and a subsequent paper will consider their application to the study of individual development in a social context. What appears crucial in the non-normal case as well as the normal case is the formulation of explicit models that reflect the conceptualization of the psychological and ecological correlates of development and that are appropriate to the design of the data collection. It is clear, therefore, that the basic principles of modeling elucidated here will apply as well to a broader class of outcome measures.

Notes

[1] Seven overlapping cohorts of data spanning ages 11–21 were fitted. Each subject had five years of data, with the presence or absence of serious theft observed each year. A generalized linear model with random effects was estimated by means of maximum quasi-likelihood as suggested by Schall (1991).

[2] These empirical Bayes estimates are produced routinely by the computer software used in these examples (Raudenbush, Bryk, Seltzer, & Congdon, 1988).

References

Blumstein, A., Farrington, D.P., & Moitra, S. (1985). Delinquency careers: Innocents, desisters, and persisters. In Morris, M. & Tonry, M. (Eds.) *Crime and Justice: An Annual Review of Research,* Vol. 6. Chicago: University of Chicago Press.

Bryk, A.S. & Raudenbush, S.W. (1987). Application of hierarchical linear models to assessing change. *Psychological Bulletin,* 101, 1, 147–158.

Bryk, A.S. & Raudenbush, S.W. (1988). Toward a more appropriate conceptualization of research on school effects: A three-level hierarchical linear model. *American Journal of Education,* 97, 1, 65–108.

Bryk, A.S. & Raudenbush, S.W. (1992). *Hierarchical Linear Models: Applications and Data Analysis Methods.* Newbury Park, CA: Sage.

Carter, L.F. (1984). The sustaining effects study of compensatory and elementary education, *Educational Researcher,* 13,7,4–13.

Dempster, A.P., Laird, N.M. & Rubin, D.B. (1977). Maximum likelihood from incomplete data via the EM algorithm. *Journal of the Royal Statistical Society,* Series B, 39, 1–8.

Dempster, A.P., Rubin, D.B. & Tsutakawa, R.K. (1981). Estimation in covariance components models. *Journal of the American Statistical Association,* 76, 341–353.

Francis, D.J., Fletcher, J.M., Stubting, K.K., Davidson, K.C. & Thompson, N. M. (1001). Analysis of change: Modeling individual growth. *Journal of Consulting and Clinical Psychology,* 39, 1, 27–37.

Goldstein, H. (1987). *Multilevel Models in Educaitonal and Social Research.* London: Oxford University Press.

Goldstein, H. (1989). Models for multilevel response variables with an application to growth curves. In R.D. Bock (Ed.), *Multilevel Analysis of Educational Data.* New York: Academic Press.

Gottfredson, M. & Hirschi, T. (1987). The methodological adequacy of longitudinal research. *Criminology,* 25, 3, 581–614.

Gottfredson, M. & Hirschi, T. (1990). *A General Theory of Crime.* Stanford: Stanford University Press.

Greenberg, D.F. (1979). Delinquency and the age structure of society. In Messinger, S.L. & Bittner, E. (Eds.) *Criminology Review Yearbook.* Beverly Hills, CA: Sage.

Hirschi, T. & Gottfredson, M. (1983). Age and the explanation of crime. *American Journal of Sociology,* 89, 3, 552–584.

Huttenlocher, J.E., Haight, W., Bryk, A.S. & Seltzer, M. (1991). Early vocabulary growth: Relation to language input and gender. *Developmental Psychology,* 27, 2, 236–249.

Janson, C-G. (1992). *A Case for a Longitudinal Study.* Paper presented at the Freudenstadt Workshop, July 19–25.

Laird, N.M., & Ware, J.H. (1982). Random-effects models for longitudinal data. *Biometrika,* 65 (1) 581–590.

Lindley, D.V., & Smith, A.F.M. (1972). Bayes estimates for the linear model. *Journal of the Royal Statistical Society,* Series B, 34, 1–41.

Moffitt, T.E. (1990). Juvenile delinquency and attention deficit disorder: Boys' developmental trajectories from age 3 to age 15. *Child Development,* 61, 893–910.

Ramirez, D. Yuen, S., Ramey, R. & Pasta, D. (1991). *The Immersion Study: Final Report.* Washington. DC: US Office of Educational Research and Improvement.

Raudenbush, S.W. (1988). Educational applications of hierarchical linear models: A review. *Journal of Educational Statistics,* 13, 2, 85–116.

Raudenbush, S.W. (in press). A crossed random effects model for unbalanced data with applications in cross-sectional and longitudinal research. To appear in *the Journal of Educational Statistics.*

Raudenbush, S.W. (1992). *Statistical Models for Individual Change in Deviance.* Paper presented at the annual meeting of the American Society of Criminology, New Orleans.

Raudenbush, S.W. & Chan, W.S. (1992) Growth curve analysis in accelerated longitudinal designs. *Journal of Research on Crime and Delinquency,* 29, 4, 387–411.

Rogosa, D.R., Brand, D. & Zimowski, M. (1982). A growth curve approach to the measurement of change. *Psychological Bulletin,* 90, 726–748.

Rogosa, D.R. & Willett, J.B. (1985). Understanding correlates of change by modeling individual differences in growth. *Psychometrika,* 90, 726–748.

Schall, R.S. (1991). Estimation in generalized linear models with random effects. *Biometrika,* 78, 4, 719–727.

Sternio, J.L.F., Weisberg, H.I. & Bryk, A.S. (1983). Empirical Bayes estimation of individual growth curves parameters and their relationship to covariates. *Biometrics,* 39, 71–86.

Tonry, M., Ohlin, L.E. & Farrington, D.P. (1991). *Human Development and Criminal Behavior: New Ways of Advancing Knowledge.* New York: Springer-Verlag.

Ware, J.H. (1985). "Linear Models for the Analysis of Longitudinal Studies." *American Statistician,* 39 (2), 95–101.

Willms, J.D. & Jacobson, S. (1990). Growth in mathematics skills during the intermediate years: Sex differences and school effects. *International Journal of Educational Research,* 14, 157–174.

Methods of Studying Community Change in the Rate and Pattern of Crime

by Robert J. Bursik Jr. and Harold G. Grasmick

Introduction

Although there is some debate in the literature concerning the relative merits of cross-sectional and longitudinal data in criminology (see, for example, Hirschi and Gottfredson, 1983), the increasing allocation of federal and private funds for the collection and analysis of data over time reflects a widespread sentiment that the potential theoretical and practical benefits of longitudinal research warrant such an investment. One of the most important outcomes of this trend has been the resurrection of a research tradition that had lain dormant for quite some time: the examination of what have been called "careers" in crime and delinquency (see, for example, Blumstein, et al., 1986). While this term has typically been used to refer to developmental profiles of individual behavior over time, Reiss (1986, p. viii) has argued that such an orientation could also enhance our understanding of crime at the local community, or neighborhood, level.

A profile approach to neighborhood crime rates certainly is not new. McKay (1967), for example, estimated crude time series models for each of Chicago's neighborhoods in an attempt to highlight variation in long term delinquency trends.[1] Unfortunately, despite the statistical sophistication that has characterized recent longitudinal studies of community crime and delinquency rates, virtually all of this research has been characterized by a series of analyses of adjacent intervals in the overall period of observation (see Bursik, 1984, 1986; Bursik and Webb, 1982; Schuerman and Kobrin, 1983, 1986; Shannon, 1982, 1984, 1988). Therefore, these models have captured only a limited sense of the dynamics reflected in a longitudinal profile. This limitation has been due primarily to the reliance of these studies on some variant of regression-based structural equation models. Such models are neither suitable for the decomposition of the total variation within neighborhoods over the entire period of observation, nor for the analysis of this variation in terms of presumably related ecological dynamics. Yet this is exactly the approach that is needed if longitudinal datasets are to provide the information concerning long-term intra-community changes in crime and delinquency rates that are inherent to the notion of a profile in such activities. In this paper, we argue that the decomposition of within-community variation over time by means of a hierarchical linear model utilizing orthogonal polynomial contrasts provides measures of long-term profiles that overcome many of the limitations inherent to more traditional regression-based longitudinal models. The benefits and strengths of such an approach are illustrated in an analysis of the delinquency rates of Chicago's local communities from 1930 to 1970.

The Implications of a Community Profile Approach

Although career approaches to criminal behavior have been a central research focus of modern criminology since the publication of Delinquency in a Birth Cohort (Wolfgang, Figlio and Sellin, 1972), there appears to be no generally accepted definition of what constitutes a career in crime. Many studies simply define a career as a longitudinal sequence of crimes committed by an individual offender (see, for example, Blumstein et al., 1986: 12); others note that a criminal career involves a series of "stages, activities or positions" (Wanderer, 1984) without specifying what kind of series would reflect a career and what kind would not.

Conversely, at least three models of the empirical form of a neighborhood delinquency profile can be derived from the community literature. The traditional social disorganization approach of Shaw and McKay (1942) assumes that relative rates of delinquency should be more or less constant over time regardless of changes in the composition of the population residing in those areas since local areas maintain ongoing roles within the ecological system of a city. This appears to have been a fairly accurate description of at least Chicago prior to World War II (see Bursik, 1986). However, Bursik (1986) and Bursik and Webb (1982) have argued that since recent urban dynamics have led to important and unpredictable redefinitions of the ecological character of local communities, significant changes have occurred in the relative rates of delinquency experienced by urban neighborhoods, making the profile more chaotic than stable. McKay's (1967) study of Chicago reached similar conclusions. Finally, the arguments of Schuerman and Kobrin (1986) and Shannon (1986) suggest that there is a fairly orderly developmental sequence that leads to consistently increasing rates of crime and delinquency, or what Shannon has called the "hardening of the inner city".

Some of the differences in these orientations reflect the unique historical and economic dynamics which have characterized Chicago (Shaw and McKay, Bursik, Bursik and Webb), Los Angeles (Schuerman and Kobrin) and Racine (Shannon). Yet it also must be emphasized that all of these studies have noted significant variation in the types of change that have characterized neighborhoods in these localities. Thus, it is to be expected that elements of all three of these "ideal type" patterns will be present in a particular metropolitan area, and that this variation will be related to the differential involvement of urban neighborhoods in the ecological redefinition of the urban system in which they are imbedded. Any fruitful analysis of community profiles therefore must be able to detect variation in the nature of such longitudinal patterns as well as be able to facilitate an examination of the sources of such variation.

A Proposed Approach to the Identification of Community Profiles of Delinquency

The typical strategy used in the analysis of longitudinal studies of local community delinquency rates entails the estimation of a series of regression equations in which the delinquency rates at time t are regressed on a series of presumably associated, contemporaneously measured constructs as well as on constructs measured at earlier waves that are assumed to have a lagged effect on delinquency at time t.[2] However, the estimated beta weights of such models provide very little information concerning the dynamics of change that may underlie this process (see Rogosa et al., 1982; Rogosa, 1987). For example, consider the beta coefficient associated with a lagged delinquency rate in a simple, two-wave linear regression:

$$b = \frac{\Sigma_i (Y_{t,i} - \text{mean } Y_t) \quad (Y_{t\text{-}1,i} - \text{mean } Y_{t\text{-}1})}{\Sigma_i (Y_{t\text{-}1,i} - \text{mean } Y_{t\text{-}1})^{\ 2}}$$

The most straightforward indicator of change in a neighborhood's delinquency rate between these waves $(Y_{t,i} - Y_{t\text{-}1,i})$ appears nowhere in the formula. Rather, the coefficient simply represents the degree to which a neighborhood's deviation from the mean at time t can be predicted by its deviation at time t-1. This has two important drawbacks for the analysis of neighborhood profiles of change. First, the coefficient reflects the confounded effects of two very different longitudinal profiles: ongoing stability in the delinquency rate and predictable change in that rate (see Kessler and Greenberg, 1981).

Second, even if all the neighborhoods in the analysis experience a dramatic drop in their delinquency rates between the two waves, the beta coefficients will be positive if the rank ordering of the delinquency rates remains generally consistent, since a positive deviation at time t will be associated with a positive deviation at time t-1. Therefore, while standard regression-based models are powerful tools for the analysis of between neighborhood variation, they are of limited use in the derivation and analysis of longitudinal community crime profiles, which reflect within neighborhood variation over time.

One improvement to the traditional regression model of neighborhood change has focused on the analysis of residual change scores, which represent the difference between the observed delinquency rate at time t and the rate that would have been predicted on the basis of time t-1 (see Bursik and Webb, 1982; Bursik, 1986; Schuerman and Kobrin, 1986; Taylor and Covington, 1988). To create such a measure, one regresses the level of delinquency at time t on its level at time t-1. The residual for each neighborhood i is then used as the measure of change between time t-1 and t, i.e.,

$$\text{Res } Y_{i,t} = Y_{i,t} - t\,(a + b^{*}\, Y_{i,t-1})$$

Since this score represents the difference between the delinquency rate at time t and the rate that was predicted on the basis of time t-1, the measure is corrected for ongoing patterns that characterize the neighborhood; that is, it represents change that was "unexpected" given the dynamics which characterize the city in which the community is located (see Bursik, 1986, p. 43). These change scores are typically regressed on measures that have been similarly computed for the ecological variables presumed to be related to delinquency.

Residual change scores have been used fruitfully in ecologically-based research in which one is interested in the changing role of the neighborhood within the context of the entire urban system. For example, a residual change score of 0 indicates that the delinquency rate at time t is what one would expect given the prior level of delinquency, i.e., the ecological role of the neighborhood has been stable during this period. On the other hand, deviations from 0 are, in a sense, unexpected on the basis of the prior role of the neighborhood and suggest that the community is experiencing ecological redefinition (see Bursik, 1986, pp. 42–43).

While the residual change score provides a useful description of short-term ecological trends, they are very limited as general indicators of community profiles. Since the regression equation used to estimate the measure of change utilizes information from all the neighborhoods in the city under analysis, the residual change score is standardized in terms of the dynamics of these other areas. Therefore, a score of 0 provides no information about changes in the absolute rates of delinquency; such a score might occur in the context of dramatic increases or decreases in the delinquency rate as long as they are predictable. In addition, this approach is extremely cumbersome when multiple waves of data are analyzed. Thus, applications of this technique have generally focused on a series of two-wave trends, thereby providing a very truncated sense of the overall patterns of change experienced by the neighborhoods.

A potentially powerful resolution of the limitations of traditional regression-based approaches to change may be found in the field of educational psychology, in which a great deal of attention has been directed to the identification and analysis of individual developmental profiles (see the review of Rogosa et al., 1982). While these "growth" models have not been commonly used in the area of criminology, they have considerable promise for the analysis of change at the neighborhood level. Given the great popularity of LISREL for the analysis of structural equations, readers are perhaps most familiar with the simplex family of such models that have formed the basis of several of Karl Joreskog's illustrations of that software (1979; see also Rogosa and Willett, 1985).

$$Y_{i,t} = \eta_{i,t} + \varepsilon_{i,t}$$

represents the measurement model in which the observed score Y (such as a delinquency rate) at time t in neighborhood i is a function of the true score η for that period and measurement error $_{i,t}$. The simplex model assumes that the set of these scores over time can be represented by:

$$\eta_{i,t+1} = \beta\eta_{i,t} + \delta_{i,t+1},$$

where $\delta_{i,t+1}$ are independent disturbances and $\eta_{i,1}$ equals $\delta_{1,p}$.

It should be apparent that a simplex model of neighborhood profiles is identical in spirit to many commonly used time series models that incorporate a lagged value of the delinquency rate as an explanatory variable. The primary difference is in the limited number of time-based observations and the multiple units of analysis. Given the autoregressive structure of the model it is assumed that the partial correlation $\varrho_{\eta tj \eta tl \cdot \eta tk} = 0$, where $j<k<l$. Although the simplex model assumes that there is a common developmental profile shaped only by past levels of delinquency and random disturbances, it might seem to provide the basis for the simple test that longitudinal community profiles can be characterized by a single developmental pattern. However, Rogosa and Willett (1985, pp. 102–105) have presented the results of a simulation in which the simplex structure hypothesis could not be rejected even when the model was tested with data that severely violated the autoregressive assumption. Therefore, the conclusions that can be drawn on the basis of such models

concerning the longitudinal dynamics of delinquency rates are unclear.

A very attractive alternative to the simplex model is found in the two stage, hierarchical linear model (HLM) of Bryk and Raudenbush (1987). The HLM is one of a family of statistical techniques that have been developed for the estimation and analysis of growth curves (such as the mixed model analysis of variance, regression with random coefficients, James-Stein estimation, and covariance components models). In addition, it is essentially identical to the multilevel linear model of Mason, Wong, and Entwisle (1983) although that was developed for contextual, rather than growth, analysis. We have focused our discussion on the Bryk and Raudenbush formulation because we feel that its unique clarity makes it the most readily accessible presentation for criminologists interested in such models.

The first step of the estimation procedure entails the decomposition of the variation over k periods in the observed delinquency rates of each neighborhood. Under the assumption that the delinquency rate of neighborhood i at time t is a function of a systematic trend associated with time (T) plus a random error (Bryk and Raudenbush, 1987, pp. 148), regression procedures are used to model the growth curve of each community. While a variety of functional forms can be used to fit the data, Bryk and Raudenbush (p. 148) note that a polynomial model provides a convenient starting point. In the general case of a k-wave study, it is possible to estimate the parameters associated with all polynomials through the k-1th order. For example, with a two wave study design, one can estimate only the constant and linear parameters; in a four wave study, one could also obtain estimates of the quadratic and cubic coefficients.

We feel that a second-order polynomial growth curve is especially informative due to the relative ease with which its components can be interpreted, i.e.:

$$Y_{i,t} = \alpha_i + \beta_{1,i}T + \beta_{2,i}T^2 + \varepsilon_{i,t},$$

where $Y_{i,t}$ is the delinquency rate in community i at time t,a_i is the estimated constant, $\beta_{1,i}$ reflects the overall linear trend in these rates within community i (i.e., has the rate of delinquency increased or decreased over time?) and $\beta_{2,i}$ estimates the degree to which the sequence of delinquency rates in that neighborhood has a parabolic form (i.e. the extent to which the linear trend accelerates or decelerates over time). The longitudinal profile of each neighborhood is therefore summarized by this vector of three regression parameters.

Bryk and Raudenbush (p. 150) suggest that the community-specific regression parameters can be estimated through ordinary least squares techniques. This creates a serious problem, for the typical longitudinal study design found in criminological research often has as few as two waves and rarely more than five or six. As a result there will be very few degrees of freedom available for the estimation of the model. A solution to this problem is suggested by Bliss'(1970) use of orthogonal polynomial contrasts to derive trend parameters in a regression equation. Table 1 presents the coefficients used to estimate these parameters when five waves of data have been collected.[3]

Table 1. Orthogonal polynomial contrasts for five periods of observation.

	Constant	Linear	Quadratic
Time 1	1	–2	2
Time 2	1	–1	–1
Time 3	1	0	–2
Time 4	1	1	–1
Time 5	1	2	2

The polynomial regression coefficients for each community are computed by summing the products of each coefficient times the delinquency rate for the corresponding period of observation and dividing by the sum of the squares of the contrast coefficients (see Bliss, 1970, p. 3), i.e.,

CONSTANT = ((1*Del Rate Time 1)+(1*Del Rate Time 2)+(1*Del Rate Time 3) + (1*Del Rate time 4)+(1*Del Rate Time 5))/5

LINEAR = ((-2*Del Rate Time 1)+(-1*Del Rate Time 2)+(0*Del Rate Time 3) + (1*Del Rate Time 4)+(2*Del Rate Time 5))/10

QUADRATIC = ((2*Del Rate Time 1)+(-1*Del Rate Time 2)+(-2*Del Rate Time 3) + (-1*Del Rate Time 4)+(2*Del Rate Time 5))/14

Since the CONSTANT contrast simply computes the overall level of delinquency in a community during the period of observation, dividing the estimated parameter by the number of waves results in the average rate of delinquency. Therefore, the interpretation of the CONSTANT coefficient is very straightforward. Note that the LINEAR contrast defines a positive slope. A positive linear effect, therefore, would reflect a longitudinal profile with a generally increasing trend in the delinquency rate; a negative coefficient would reflect a decreasing trend. Finally, the QUADRATIC contrast defines a curve that is concave upward, i.e., accelerating in the rate of delinquency. A negative coefficient would therefore define a career trajectory that is concave downward, decelerating in the rate of that behavior.

Unfortunately, the interpretation of the LINEAR and QUADRATIC effects is not straightforward since they represent change in terms of the values of the orthogonal polynomial contrast coefficients. Luckily, Bliss (1970, pp. 4–5) presents a very straightforward set of equations that convert these coefficients into a deviational metric (i.e., T – TBAR) so that they can be interpreted in the same way as traditional regression coefficients:

$$\text{Constant} = a' = YBAR - (B2*I2(k**2 - 1))/12$$
$$\text{Linear} = b_1 = B1*I1/i*$$
$$\text{Quadratic} = b_2 = B2*I2/i*2,$$

resulting in

$$Y = a' + b1(T - TBAR) + b_2(T - TBAR)^{**2}.$$

YBAR is the average delinquency rate, T is the period of observation (such as the year), TBAR is the average period of observation (i.e., the average year), B1 and B2 are the linear and quadratic regression coefficients in the orthogonal polynomial metric, I1 and I2 are coefficients used in the computation of the orthogonal polynomial contrasts that ensure that they are whole numbers with no common divisor (which are noted in tables of these coefficients and which are both equal to 1 when there are five periods of observation), k is the number of periods of observation, and i* is the length of time between the periods.[4]

In the second stage of the HLM model of Bryk and Raudenbush, the focus switches from the analysis of within-community variation to the analysis of variation between communities in the size of the trend coefficients. That is, the parameters that were estimated during the first stage become the dependent variables in a second set of regressions. This is a key strength of the HLM approach, for it simultaneously exploits both the cross-sectional and longitudinal structures of multi-wave datasets.

Bryk and Raudenbush discuss several regression procedures for this second stage of estimation which have differing assumptions concerning the error structure. However, special complications arise in the specification of the exogenous variables related to community trends since the ecological characteristics that may be assumed to affect the shape of such trends also have a dynamic nature, i.e., they are not time invariant. Our proposed solution is to use the orthogonal polynomial coefficients to create trend parameters for the ecological dynamics, and use these parameters as the exogenous variables in the second stage of regressions.

The use of a traditional ordinary least squares model to estimate the regression parameters of the second stage is somewhat problematic because each of the coefficients estimated in the first step of the HLM procedure represents the sum of a "true" trend parameter and some unknown degree of "noise" that is reflected in the standard error. Thus, the values of the exogenous and endogenous variables used in the second stage are characterized by stochastic variation. While this would not represent a problem in regard to the estimation of the model if this were only the case for the dependent trend parameters, it can significantly complicate the situation when both the dependent and independent variables are stochastic measures (Johnston, 1972: 281).

Yet recall that our determination of the trend components in stage 1 did not entail statistical estimation per se. Rather, each parameter was computed on the basis of a straightforward nonprobabilistic mathematical transformation of the five observations for each community, rather than through the regression techniques proposed by Bryk and Raudenbush. Therefore, we propose that the estimated trends represent the computations of a "fixed" algorithm, and therefore can be treated as non-stochastic elements in the model. Our future research will investigate the relative effects of this strong measurement assumption on the estimation of the model.

Such a transformation suggests the estimation of three equations during the second stage. The first examines the strength of the relationship between the overall rate of delinquency and the hypothesized ecological causes; this would entail a regression of the delinquency-related CONSTANT term on the ecological CONSTANT terms and is analogous to cross-sectional ecological analyses. Second, we would be interested in the degree to which linear trends in the delinquency rate may be related to the dynamics of ecological change. Therefore, the LINEAR delinquency parameter would be regressed on the LINEAR and the QUADRATIC ecological trend coefficients. Finally, certain ecological dynamics may lead to an acceleration or deceleration of existing delinquency trends. This suggests the final regression of the QUADRATIC parameter of the delinquency rates on the LINEAR and QUADRATIC ecological terms. The strength of the proposed analytical strategy is worth highlighting. Traditional simultaneous equation models decompose only the between-community variation in delinquency rates. The suggested alternative based on the use of a hierarchical linear model and orthogonal polynomial contrasts results in a set of three equations that facilitate an examination of the variation within a community over time as well as variation in delinquency profiles between communities.

Trends in Chicago's Local Communities, 1930–1970

The method of the preceding section was used to examine trends in the rates of male referrals to the Cook County Juvenile Court on delinquency petitions in the 74 officially recognized local community areas in Chicago, Illinois between 1930 and 1970.[5] Figure 1 presents the average delinquency rate of these areas during this period, and is represented by the orthogonal polynomial regression:

$Y = 8.31 + 2.245T + 1.111T^2$.

Figure 1.

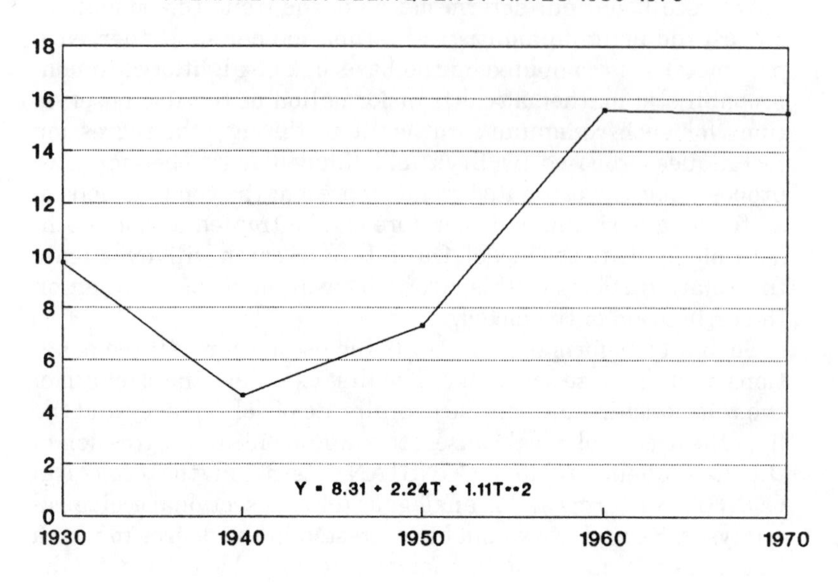

It is tempting to speculate why the average delinquency rate decreased around World War II only to increase and accelerate dramatically between 1950 and 1960. However, these trends should be considered with extreme caution for two reasons. First, significant modifications in the juvenile law of Illinois occurred during this period; thus, to an unknown extent, these changes represent the effects of changes in the definition of delinquency over time. Second, especially since 1960, major improvements in the technology of crime reporting have been implemented in most criminal justice agencies (see the argument of McKay, 1967, p. 114). Therefore, the increase between 1950 and 1960 may be more indicative of juvenile court practices than an actual rise in delinquency. Nevertheless, under the assumption that definitional and technological changes affected the reported delinquency rate in each of Chicago's local communities equally, Figure 1 provides a good baseline for the illustration of the orthogonal polynomial approach and the examination of neighborhood variation in delinquency rate trajectories.

By definition, since Figure 1 represents the average of all community profiles, the mean values of the estimated trend components for these areas are identical to those estimated for the city as a whole.

Table 2. Distribution of the trend coefficients.

	Mean	S.D.	Min	Max
CONSTANT	8.31	6.45	–1.69	29.98
LINEAR	2.25	3.11	–6.59	9.07
QUADRATIC	1.11	1.57	–2.92	4.95

However, as Table 2 indicates, there is a great deal of variation in the values of the trend components for these areas: the linear trajectories of some neighborhoods are represented by a consistent increase in the delinquency rate over time (e.g., one community generally increases its delinquency rate by over 9 referrals per 1,000 males each decade) while others are not (e.g., one community is represented by a decrease of over 6.5 referrals per 1,000 males each decade), and the rates of increase accelerate in some communities and not in others. To illustrate the degree to which the trend coefficients adequately capture the dynamics characterizing these communities, Figure 2 presents the delinquencyrates between 1930 and 1970 for two Chicago neighborhoods characterized by very different career trajectories.

Figure 2.

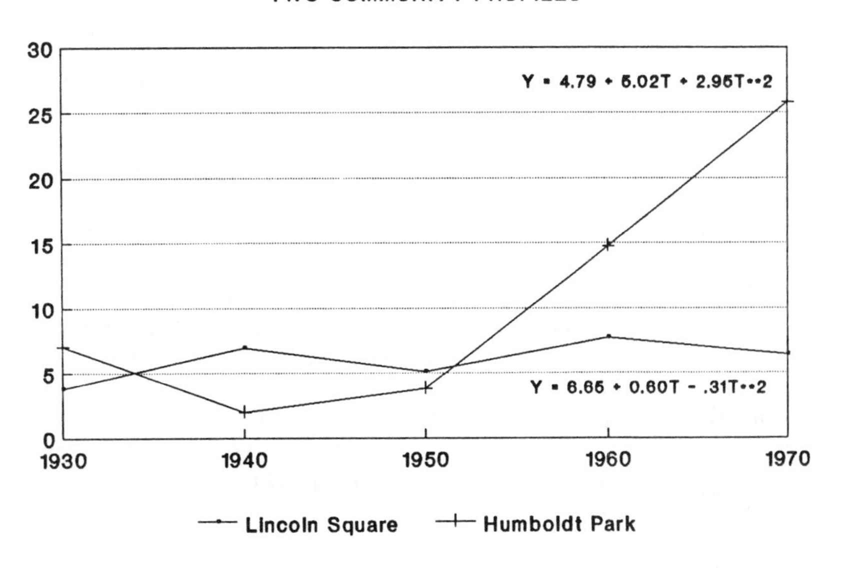

Lincoln Square is a relatively stable white ethnic community (German, Poles, Swedes and Russians) located on Chicago's North Side. Although it experienced a great deal of growth prior to 1930, the rate of growth slowed considerably between 1930 and 1960 and a slight decline in its population has occurred since then. As shown in Figure 2, while there was a very slight overall increase in its delinquency rate since 1930, it was been fairly negligible. The polynomial regression estimate of the career trajectory is:

$$Y=6.65 + 0.60T - 0.31T^2$$

which provides a good representation of the general stability of the delinquency rates in this area.

A very different situation characterizes Humboldt Park, which has experienced a rapid influx of Hispanics and blacks since 1950, accompanied by a mass out-migration of ethnic whites. Thus, between 1950 and 1970, it underwent a great deal of significant ecological redefinition. Concurrently, as seen in Figure 2, this was also a period of dramatic increases in the delinquency rates of the neighborhood and an acceleration in the rate of that increase over time. Again, we feel that the estimated polynomial regression provides an excellent depiction of these changes, i.e.,

$$Y=4.79 + 5.02T + 2.95T^2.$$

The preceding examples suggest that the orthogonal polynomial approach provides a simple and parsimonious representation of neighborhood crime profiles. However, far more central is the determination of the relationship between these patterns and the processes of ecological redefinition that characterize urban areas. The orthogonal polynomial contrasts were used to decompose the trends in measures of six community characteristics that were consistently measured and available for each of the five periods under analysis: nonwhite composition, the unemployment rate, the percentage of residents employed in professional occupations, the percentage of residents who own their own homes, the percentage of households with more than one person per room, and the median level of educational attainment in the community. The strong intercorrelations that exist among these six indicators at the neighborhood level make it nearly impossible to derive stable estimates of their individual associations with trends in the delinquency rate. Therefore, to facilitate the analysis of this paper, factor analyses with oblique rotations were conducted on each set of trend components to derive summary measures of Chicago's processes of ecological redefinition at the neighborhood level.

Table 3. Factor analysis of the ecological indicators: constant trend component. Oblimin rotation.

	Factor 1	Factor 2
Percent Nonwhite	.950	.113
Percent Unemployed	.849	–.228
Percent Professional	–.100	.916
Percent Owner Occupied	–.637	–.078
Household Density	.860	–.182
Median Education	.054	.896
Eigenvalue	3.644	1.430
Factor Correlation	–.343	

Two basic dimensions of community structure underlie the constant components of ecological structure. The first indicates that neighborhoods with relatively high levels of nonwhite composition also tend to be characterized by high rates of unemployment, high levels of household density, and low rates of owner occupancy. The second dimension, which is only moderately correlated with the first, reflects the tendency of communities with high rates of professional employment to also have relatively high median levels of education. Such findings are completely congruent with those of more traditional ecological analyses.

Table 4. Factor analysis of the ecological indicators: linear trend component. Oblimin rotation.

	Factor 1		Factor 2
Percent Nonwhite	.772		–.123
Percent Unemployed	.449		–.361
Percent Professional	–.637		–.061
Percent Owner Occupied	–.476		.135
Household Density	.998		.247
Median Education	.016		.622
Eigenvalue	2.914		1.085
Factor Correlation		–.293	

Of greater interest for the purposes of this paper are the findings of Tables 4 and 5. While Table 4 suggests that there are two weakly correlated dimensions of linear change in Chicago's neighborhoods, an examination of the factor loadings indicates that the second dimension primarily reflects the level of educational attainment in the community. Therefore, Chicago generally appears to be characterized by a single linear trajectory of ecological redefinition in which increases over time in the nonwhite composition, unemployment rate, and the level of household density are accompanied by concurrent decreases in the rates of owner occupancy and professional occupational status.

Table 5. Factor analysis of the ecological indicators: quadratic trend component. Oblimin rotation.

	Factor 1		Factor 2
Percent Nonwhite	.829		.290
Percent Unemployed	.334		–.802
Percent Professional	–.580		.304
Percent Owner Occupied	–.310		.029
Household Density	.589		–.564
Median Education	.031		.130
Eigenvalue	2.660		1.073
Factor Correlation		–.229	

Table 5 indicates that there have been two significant dimensions of acceleration underlying the ecological redefinition of Chicago. In neighborhoods in which the rates of increase in the levels of nonwhite composition and household density have accelerated over time, the rate of change in the level of professional

Table 6. Regression delinquency trend components on dimensions of ecological change.

	DELINQUENCY		
	Constant	Linear	Quadratic
Intercept	8.312	1.342	1.110
Ecological Constant–1	4.880*	—	—
(S.E.)	(0.547)		
Beta	0.740		
Ecological Constant-2	−0.363	—	—
(S.E.)	(0.553)		
Beta	−0.054		
Ecological Linear-1	—	1.792*	0.164
(S.E.)	(0.353)	(0.191)	
Beta	0.553	0.101	
Ecological Quadratic-1	—	1.407*	0.379*
(S.E.)	(0.343)	(0.185)	
Beta	0.407	0.218	
Ecological Quadratic-2	—	−0.248	0.928*
(S.E.)	(0.394)	(0.213)	
Beta	−0.074	0.546	
F	48.990	16.578	11.177
df	2,71	3,70	3,70
p	0.000	0.000	0.000
R^2	.580	.415	.323

* represents an effect at least twice the magnitude of the standard error.

occupational status has decreased. In addition, there is a second component of change in which a deceleration in the rate of change in the unemployment rate has been accompanied by similar processes in the levels of household density. Interestingly, the quadratic components for the unemployment rate and median educational level appear to development independently of these other ecological processes.

Table 6 presents the regression analyses of the delinquency rate trend components on the dimensions of ecological redefinition.[5] As noted in the analytic plan described in the preceding section, the first column represents the regression of the general rate of delinquency during this forty year period on the two summary indicators of the overall ecological structure. As was the case with the CONSTANT factor analysis, the findings are similar to those presented in many previous studies. High rates of delinquency are related to a composite CONSTANT-1 factor score of the nonwhite composition, unemployment rate, rate of owner occupancy, and level of household density, all of which have been suggested as indirect indicators of the level of social disorganization in a neighborhood (Bursik, 1988; Bursik and Grasmick, 1993). Likewise, as predicted by the social disorganization framework, the constant delinquency component is not related to the professional or educational characteristics of a neighborhood after controlling for the CONSTANT-1 factor.

The findings presented in columns 2 and 3 of Table 6 highlight the important dynamics that can be discerned through the hierarchical linear model. The composite linear ecological redefinition variable is strongly and positively associated with concurrent ongoing increases in the rate of delinquency, again as predicted by the social disorganization model. In addition, the rate of increase tends to be higher in neighborhoods characterized by accelerations in the nonwhite composition and level of household density and decelerations in the percent professional (QUADRATIC-1). Finally, although linear trends in ecological redefinition are not associated with accelerations in the delinquency rate over time, the quadratic delinquency component is significantly related to both quadratic dimensions of ecological change.

Discussion

We feel that our illustration has highlighted several analytic strengths of the HLM approach. First, it is true that we have not exploited the full capabilities of the HLM model, especially concerning the nature of "true" and random variation in the trend parameters. However, we have presented a justification for our assumption of fixed measurement on the basis of the orthogonal polynomial transformation which has been used. If researchers feel that this assumption is warranted in their own particular cases, the technique is a relatively simple one that can be utilized easily with virtually any available computer software and can readily be applied to most of the currently popular datasets that are used to examine the relationship between ecological dynamics and illegal behavior.

Second, the model is able parsimoniously to utilize information pertaining to the entire period of analysis, rather than being forced to focus on a series of sequential subperiods. As a result, the analyst is able to gain a much richer sense of the ecological dynamics that are associated with the changing relative spatial distribution of crime and delinquency in an urban area. Third, although offense-specific information is not available to us in the Chicago dataset, it would be relatively easy to use the HLM and orthogonal polynomials to analyze changes over time in the mixture of types of criminal activities that characterize neighborhoods.

Finally, it is worth noting that the utility of the proposed approach goes beyond community-based studies. For example, although multi-wave panel studies of delinquency (such as the National Youth Survey) have the potential ability to provide information concerning the dynamics of such behavior that is complementary (and in some ways superior) to that derived from the traditional official offense histories, this potential largely has been untapped. For example, the hierarchical linear model could be used to analyze the dynamic relationships between delinquency and those processes assumed to be related to its commission. Given these analytic and theoretical benefits, we hope that the HLM and orthogonal polynomial approach may become an important tool in future longitudinal criminological research of all types.

Notes

[1] Although the discussion of the paper is framed in terms of delinquency rates, this is primarily an editorial convenience to avoid the continual use of the clumsy "crime and/or delinquency" phrase. The themes to be addressed as well as the model to be developed in this paper are relevant to all research in which neighborhood rates of illegal behavior (whether committed by adults or juveniles) are analyzed over time.

[2] Our discussion of regression models is meant to reflect the entire class of such models, which includes cross-lagged correlations as well as the more general structural equation approach.

[3] These coefficients are tabulated in many multivariate statistics textbooks. (see, for example, Bliss, 1970, p. 586). Given the five waves of data, it is possible to estimate five different trend coefficients (i.e., the three that are noted as well as the cubic and quartic components). However, the interpretation of such higher order trends is neither straightforward nor especially intuitive. Therefore, for the purposes of this paper, we have restricted our attention to those which we assume to be most familiar.

[4] In the analysis to follow, the length of time between periods of observation has been specified as 1 to represent change between decades, and time (T) has been coded as 3, 4, 5, 6 and 7 to represent 1930, 1940, 1950, 1960 and 1970. 5. During this period there were 76 officially recognized areas. We have eliminated the central business district (The Loop) and the O'Hare airport area from the analysis since their small numbers of juveniles make the rates of delinquency computed for these areas very unstable.

[5] Since the second ecological linear component of change is fairly weak and primarily represents only educational attainment, we have restricted our attention only to the first dimension derived by the factor analysis.

References

Bliss, C.I. (1970). *Statistics in Biology,* Vol II, McGraw-Hill, New York.

Blumstein, A., Cohen, J. Roth, J.A. & Visher, C.A. (1986). *Criminal Careers and "Career Criminals."* Washington, DC: National Academy Press.

Bryk, A.S., & Raudenbush, S.W. (1987). Application of hierarchical linear models to assessing change. *Psychological Bulletin* 101: 147–158.

Bursik, R.J., Jr. (1984). Urban dynamics and ecological studies of delinquency. *Social Forces* 63: 393–413.

Bursik, R.J., Jr. (1986). Ecological stability and the dynamics of delinquency. In Reiss, A.J., Jr., and M. Tonry (eds.) *Communities and Crime.* University of Chicago Press, Chicago, pp. 35–66.

Bursik, R.J., Jr. (1988). Social disorganization and theories of crime and delinquency: problems and prospects. *Criminology* 26: 519–551.

Bursik, R.J., Jr. & Grasmick, H.G.(1983). *Neighborhoods and Crime: The Dimensions of Effective Community Control.* New York: Lexington.

Bursik, R.J., Jr. & Webb, J. (1982). Community change and patterns of delinquency. *American Journal of Sociology* 88: 24–42.

Hirschi, T. & Gottfredson, M. (1983). Age and the explanation of crime. *American Journal of Sociology* 89: 522–584.

Joreskog, K.G. & Sorbom, D. (1979). *Advances in Factor Analysis and Structural Equation Models.* Abt Books, Cambridge.

Kessler, R.C. & Greenberg, D.F. (1981). *Linear Panel Analysis: Models of Quantitative Change,* Academic Press, New York.

Mason, W.M., Wong, G.Y. & Entwisle, B. (1983). Contextual analysis through the multilevel linear model. In Leinhardt, S. (ed.), *Sociological Methodology 1983–1984,* Jossey-Bass, San Francisco, pp. 72–103.

McKay, H.D. (1967). A Note on Trends in Rates of Delinquency in Certain Areas in Chicago. In Task Force Report: *Juvenile Delinquency and Youth Crime.* The President's Commission on Law Enforcement and Administration of Justice, U.S. Government Printing Office, Washington, DC, pp. 114–118.

Reiss, A.J., Jr. (1986). Why are communities important in understanding crime? Pp. 1–34 in *Communities and Crime,* edited by A.J. Reiss, Jr. and M. Tonry. Chicago: University of Chicago Press.

Rogosa, D. (1987). Casual models do not support scientific conclusions: a comment in support of Freedman. *Journal of Educational Statistics* 12: 185–195.

Rogosa, D., Brandt, D. & Zinowski, M. (1982). A growth curve approach to the measurement of change. *Psychological Bulletin* 92: 726–748.

Rogosa, D. & Willett, J.B. (1985). Satisfying a simplex structure is simpler than it should be. *Journal of Educational Statistics* 11: 99–107.

Schuerman, L.A. & Kobrin, S. (1983). *Crime and urban ecological processes: implications for public policy.* Paper presented at the annual meetings of the American Society of Criminology. Denver.

Schuerman, L.A. & Kobrin, S. (1986). Community careers in crime. In Reiss, A.J., Jr., and Tonry, M. (eds.) *Communities and Crime.* University of Chicago Press, Chicago, pp. 67–100.

Shannon, L.W. (1982). *The Relationship of Juvenile Delinquency and Adult Crime To the Changing Ecological Structure of the City.* Executive Report, submitted to the National Institute of Justice.

Shannon, L.W. (1984). *The Development of Serious Criminal Careers and the Delinquent Neighborhood. Executive Report,* submitted to the National Institute of Justice and Delinquency Prevention.

Shannon, L.W. (1986). Ecological evidence of the hardening of the inner city. In Figlio, R.M., Hakim, S., and Rengert, G.F. (eds.), Metropolitan Crime Patterns. *Criminal Justice Press,* New York, pp. 27–53.

Shannon, L.W. (1988). Criminal Career Continuity, Human Sciences Press, New York.

Shaw, C.R. & McKay, H.D. (1942). *Juvenile Delinquency and Urban Areas,* University of Chicago Press, Chicago.

Taylor, R.B. & Covington, J. (1988). Neighborhood changes in ecology and violence. *Criminology* 26: 553–589.

Wanderer, J.J. (1984). Scaling delinquent careers over time. *Criminology* 22: 83–95.

Wolfgang, M.E., Figlio, R.M. & Sellin, T. (1972). *Delinquency in a Birth Cohort.* Chicago: University of Chicago Press.

Optimizing Data Quality of Individual and Community Sources in Longitudinal Research

by Magda Stouthamer-Loeber

Introduction

Very often large, longitudinal studies are undertaken to address serious problems that affect society as a whole, or, at least, large populations. Examples are the development of serious antisocial behavior, the long-term effect of smoking, the relationship of cholesterol and health, and the long-term effects of early intervention programs, such as Head Start or other programs that have followed it. Results of such studies may lead to public policy decisions and individual decisions that alter people's lives and may direct public and private financial spending.

Longitudinal studies, by their nature, are generally very expensive and it is the researcher's task to ensure that the study, which may often involve large sums of tax payers' money, is worth the expense. Therefore, although any research needs to be executed as best and as carefully as possible, this responsibility weighs more heavily in the case of large, longitudinal studies. One usually has (or wants) only one chance at executing a large, longitudinal project; whereas a flaw in a small research project can be remedied by redoing the study with a new group of subjects and some variation in the design, this is rarely the case in the kind of study under consideration here.

Although papers and chapters have been written on various aspects of conducting large scale longitudinal studies, this is not an easily accessible body of knowledge since it is scattered throughout journals that generally focus on the content of research rather than on the process. The 'how to do it' part is often learned the painful way or, otherwise transferred, like family lore, from one researcher to another, in hints, bits of advice, and anecdotes.

Unfortunately, at the planning stage and the initial phases of a large longitudinal study, researchers, by necessity, have the least experience when they need it most. It is at the initial stages that serious errors can be made in planning, budgeting and participant acquisition that may haunt a study from then on.

This paper has been written in the hope that others who start out on a large study may benefit from what we have learned in the process of conducting a number of studies. An earlier paper has outlined in detail some of our procedures (Stouthamer-Loeber, van Kammen, & Loeber, 1992). The present paper enlarges on some themes mentioned in the previous paper by discussing additional issues related to data quality.

This paper will mainly draw upon the experience gained from the Pittsburgh Youth Study, as well as from some smaller studies. The Pittsburgh Youth Study is an ongoing longitudinal study on the development of antisocial and prosocial behavior in inner city male students who were in grades 1, 4, and 7 when the study began. About 3,000 students were randomly selected from the rolls of public schools. 84.8% of the families consented to participate. After the initial assessment the 250 most antisocial boys in each grade sample were retained for the follow-up study along with a randomly selected equal number of boys from the remainder. This led to a follow-up sample of about 500 boys per grade sample, in total, 1517 participants.

Participation required, at each assessment, an interview with the boy, an interview with one of his parents, as well as a questionnaire completed by a teacher. Data are also collected from school records and court and police records. Assessments were initially done every six months, but are now done on a yearly basis. The samples have been assessed up to 10 times. The participation rate is still close to 90%.

The Pittsburgh Youth Study has been fortunate to have benefitted from the experience of David Farrington, co-investigator, and also Lee Robins and Joan McCord, advisors to our study. In addition, we have learned from Beverly Cairns, Terrie Moffitt, and from the staff of the Rochester Youth Development Study and the Denver Youth Study with whom we were associated for the first five years of the study. Furthermore, a stable cadre of key staff members have gained, over the years, an enormous amount of knowledge which is being applied to continue to improve the performance of the study.

General Principles

The ultimate goal of any study is to provide answers to the questions one had set out to address. This can only be done if the data that have been collected are to be trusted. The intermediate goal, then, is to collect reliable and complete data which are fully documented at all levels and, in addition, to accomplish this within a set time-frame and within a set budget. This sounds relatively simple but requires elaborate planning and continuous vigilance.

Planning. The planning for the actual execution of a study needs to take place at the time that the study is proposed, so that the design, time-line, and budget are in accordance with each other and are laid out in the greatest detail. The aim of the planning is to reduce uncertainty about what is feasible and to prevent unpleasant surprises as much as possible.

Errors resulting from insufficient planning may be an underestimation of start-up time, or an underestimation of the length of time it takes to assemble a sample, or even the feasibility of assembling a sample at all, and, almost certainly, an underestimation of the costs.

When working out a proposed budget there is always the fear that the project will appear to be too expensive to be funded, coupled with a great optimism that, somehow, the work can be done, if only one gets the grant. It is rare that this optimism is warranted; the more usual situation is a reduction in scope of the project because there is not enough money to execute the design as planned.

One of the ways by which we have tried to reduce uncertainties in the cost of a project is to reduce as many items in the budget to a unit cost. For instance, interviewers are not paid by the hour but are paid a *fixed* sum per completed interview. This fixed sum also includes a fixed remuneration for mileage, so that no extra paperwork needs to be processed.

One of the principal steps in the preparation for a study is of course, to conduct a pilot study in which participant selection, participant acquisition, instrument preparation, and data collection from participants and records are all tried out. This is particularly important if any of the procedures are unfamiliar to the investigators or if the cooperation from potential participants and the necessary agencies is in doubt. This may seem an irritating hold-up in the rush to acquire substantive knowledge, but it certainly helps to know beforehand that the study one contemplates will, most likely, be capable of delivering the information one is seeking.

Even with the best planning there will be surprises (e.g., budget cuts, changes in procedures imposed by agencies, neighborhoods that become less safe for interviewers) that force one to make adjustments in mid-stream, but whatever can be foreseen should be dealt with ahead of time. This allows one the energy to deal with the really unexpected crises.

Vigilance. To insure a high reliability and completeness of the data one has to set very high standards. It is unrealistic to think that the data collection of a large study will be entirely perfect, but it is essential to strive for something as close to perfection as one can make it. Therefore, if an interviewer has missed some questions, he/she needs to go back to the participant and ask the questions; if a participant can not be found easily, then find him/her anyway; if a person is too busy now, try later; if birthdays of different data sources do not match, call the mother, etc.

In an atmosphere where correctness and completeness of the data are valued highly, staff will take great pride in going to extraordinary lengths to do the best possible job.

The reason for the obsession with completeness and correctness is that in a longitudinal study, there is an accumulation, over phases, of participants with incomplete or no data. If, for instance, in every phase a random 2% of the participants have incomplete data on a particular set of questions (not considering the participants who have dropped out), then after five phases 9.6% of the participants may have to be left out of the analyses because of missing data. While 2% of participants with missing data does not sound too bad, almost 10% is not so good.

More serious than incomplete data is loss of participants. While incomplete data is more likely to be randomly distributed across participants, the literature generally asserts that the persons most likely to drop out of a study are those that are the most disturbed and disorganized or least educated (Jessor & Jessor, 1977; Nurco, Robins, & O'Donnell, 1977; Robins, 1963, Cordray & Polk, 1983). Thus, loss of participants may bias the results of the study and should be avoided as much as possible.

To exercise continuous vigilance about data quality and the process of data collection it is important to *make visible* in the form of reports on a *routine* and *ongoing* basis the status of all steps in the process. These status reports can be used by staff members for self-monitoring, and may direct their efforts. The reports also show supervisors how well staff members are doing, giving supervisors a frequent opportunity to recognize success, effort, and innovation. Also, such reports can give early warning about possible problems, or they can form the basis for brainstorming and decision making about an actual problem. This is particularly important if the window for finding and interviewing participants is narrow, as is generally the case when there are repeated assessments.

As part of the vigilance, at every step of the data collection and management process, procedures need to be in place to ensure the quality of the data. Just as one expects that car manufacturers check the proper installation of brakes and that pharmaceutical companies check that the dose of medication does not vary from pill to pill, one should expect that statements resulting from the study are not misleading because of sloppy data collection or handling. It is not enough to *believe* that one's staff would never be inattentive, take shortcuts, or cheat. It is better to have proof that this is, indeed, so. Knowing that a quality control system is in place will take away the temptation to compromise the integrity of the study.

Data Collection from Participants

Preparation of a community. Important early decisions that may affect the success of a study are whether to inform the community at large about an upcoming study, whether to enlist the support of community leaders, whether to form a board that can act as a facilitator if problems arise, or whether to keep a low profile and only involve those people directly necessary to conduct the study. It may seem a democratic and open thing to do to let everyone know about an upcoming study and to invite their input; however, there are risks that need to be taken into account.

Although there are no hard data to tell us what to do, common sense may guide us through at least part of the decision making process. Factors to keep in mind are:

1) How intrusive is the research design? Does it require an intervention that affects the whole or a large part of the community or a particular population, as in the case of random allocation to services, classrooms, or interventions? In that case the community needs to be involved, so that, ahead of time, it is clear that the study can be implemented.
2) How hostile is the community or the population of interest to the topic of study or to the persons conducting the study? Potential participants may feel very strongly that the *topic* is too sensitive or threatening, or they may feel that the *group* they represent is used for research purposes but does not benefit from it. If such feelings threaten the execution of a study, it is necessary to enlist the support of community or group leaders to endorse the study and explain the potential usefulness of the results.

The danger is always, however, that one *fails* to enlist support and, instead, organized opposition is created. This could be the case, for instance, when asking a teacher union to endorse teacher participation in a study not immediately related to working conditions of teachers. Or, in areas or times with strong racial tension minority leaders may, or may not, be swayed to endorse a study that is not seen as directly addressing their agenda.

Our strategy has been that if a study does not involve community interventions, is fairly non-controversial in topic, and one does not expect to encounter resistance beyond individual cases, it is safer to keep a low profile and only involve those persons necessary for the execution of the study. This prevents inviting possible negative publicity from disaffected persons whose disaffection may even be unconnected with the goal or execution of the study. Such unsolicited publicity may harm or even jeopardize the study. Thus, the pros and cons of seeking community support need to be weighed very carefully since a wrong decision may fatally affect the study.

Treatment of participants. Researchers need to ask themselves why potential participants would participate in a long-term study. Is it because the goals of the study are seen as important? Is it because of the financial reward (usually small)? Is it because they like to have someone to talk to? Is it because it is easier to say yes than to say no? Or is it because the interviewer is such a nice person? Usually it is some combination of the above. One can almost be sure, however, that, regardless of the loftiness of the goals of the study and almost regardless of the financial reward that most studies can offer, if the interviewer is not pleasant, reassuring and professional, the person will refuse to participate or will drop out. It is, therefore, of the utmost importance that interviewers and *all* other staff, including office staff who answer phone calls or who look after the participant payments, are trained to treat participants as valued experts and partners in the research enterprise. They need to be treated as one would like to be treated oneself.

To instill this in staff members it is important to make sure that this attitude permeates the entire project and is not only 'put on' in front of the participants. Apart from strictly enforcing the confidentiality rules, it is good practice to discourage staff members from referring to the persons participating in the study as subjects, which dehumanizes them somehow, and not to allow them to tell any funny or horror stories about participants just for amusement, even if names are omitted.

When participating in a study that continues over a long period of time and requires relatively frequent assessments, the novelty wears off and participants may begin to feel that they have done their duty towards society. At this point the main reason for staying in the study is generally because people have been treated well and feel appreciated. Considering the investment in each individual participant over time and the fact that he or she cannot be replaced, almost no effort is too large to ensure continued participation.

Interviewer selection and training. Having emphasized the important role of the interviewers in retaining participants it should be clear that good interviewers are absolutely crucial to a study. We have learned how to select street-wise, intelligent people who can read well, can follow skipping patterns, who are in need of money and have a pleasant self-assurance. However, we have not always been able to predict well whether a potential interviewer will produce a sufficient number of interviews, will creatively search for participants, and will be able to prevent refusals. For that reason, we always train a few more people than we need, and let them know that after one month their performance will be evaluated on a precise set of criteria, and those not reaching those criteria will be let go. The criteria that are used are the number of completed interviews, percent of errors, percent of refusals, missed mandatory contacts with the office, complaints from participants, and evidence of fraud. Over the years we have built up a cadre of interviewers who come back every phase, so that the uncertainty over how well the interviewers will do has been reduced considerably.

We have described our hiring and training procedures elsewhere (Stouthamer-Loeber, van Kammen, and Loeber, 1992), but the main points of the training are extensive exercises in how to treat participants, how to deal with reluctant participants, how to search for lost participants, how to administer the interview and complete all forms according to the rules, and what the exact job requirements are in terms of quality and quantity of work. Even veteran interviewers go through the whole training procedure at every phase so that no 'drift' takes place.

Progress of an interviewing phase. As was mentioned earlier, progress of an interviewing phase is carefully monitored by storing all information in a database system. This system is updated daily. Interviewers are required to call in daily and to come in for individual supervision once a week at a set time. The database system is capable of producing reports on numbers of interviews that have been completed, status of interviews to be done, number of errors made per interviewer, number of refusals, searches, participants for whom target dates are nearing, participants in institutions, out of state interviews, etc. These reports enable us to direct our efforts and attention to where it is most needed.

Quality of data. The quality of the data is checked in a number of ways. First, at the beginning of each phase interviewers are accompanied in the field by their supervisor who records the interview and gives feedback to the interviewer about his/her performance.

Since the majority of our interviewers have been with us for a number of phases, they know how to do an interview when their supervisor is present. That does not mean that the interviewers always conduct the interview in the same correct manner if the supervisor is not there. Recently, we have told the interviewers that they may, without knowing it, interview a 'phantom family' who is not really part of the study but who is in the participant pool to give us feedback on interviewers' performance.

We also randomly call about 10% of the families after the interview is completed to ask whether the interviewer was courteous as well as to check on some factual information to make sure that the interview was indeed done. The overwhelming amount of feedback is very positive, which is immediately relayed to the interviewers; however, it has also led to the firing of an interviewer (whom we had not suspected in the least) for fudging data.

Since the random calling may be the basis for dismissing an interviewer, it is very important that the questions on the calling form are standardized, that a number of the questions are about very factual information that does not change from day to day, and that the answers are recorded as carefully as possible. In other words, when it is necessary to confront an interviewer, the evidence should be so clear and plain that there can be no argument about it.

The point of all this checking is that the interviewers are aware of it, that they know how much we care about the correctness of their work, and what the consequences are if procedures are not followed.

The most successful procedure for obtaining complete data is that we pay interviewers a fixed price for a completed interview, but *only* after the interview has been data entered and found to be correct and complete by our standards. To not hold up interviewers' pay unnecessarily, data entry and checking is done within one week of submitting materials. If materials are not correct or complete, it is the interviewer's responsibility to make it so, which may mean that he/she needs to recontact the participant.

Participation. Various specific strategies for recruiting participants have been detailed by a number of researchers (Capaldi & Patterson, 1987; Green et al, 1992; Stouthamer-Loeber, van Kammen, & Loeber, 1992; Winett, Neale, & Williams, 1979) and these will not be repeated here. We will discuss some general principles and strategies for achieving a high participation rate.

As was mentioned earlier, the loss of participants because of refusals or the inability to find them, is likely to result in a biased sample. It is, therefore, important to keep the loss of participants to a minimum. In our study, where participant loss is relatively small, we have not found, over six data waves, any disproportionate loss with regard to delinquency status, SES, race, single parent status, and educational level of mother. We attribute this to the fact that not being able to locate a participant easily, having to contact and reschedule numerous times, and relatively gruff receptions do not discourage our interviewers to the point where they would stop trying.

To achieve a continued high participation rate, one should be prepared for the fact that the last 10% of the sample requires a very large part of the time over which an assessment period stretches and a very large part of the resources. In a small substudy of the Pittsburgh Youth Study it took a little over two weeks for an interviewer to complete an interview with 90% of the resident biological fathers; however, the completion of the remaining 10% took over seven weeks (Stouthamer-Loeber, van Kammen, Loeber, Miller, & Kumer, 1992). Looked at it in terms of number of contacts or attempts to contact, 90% of the sample required seven contacts or less, whereas the remaining 10% required up to 24 contacts or attempts to contact. Once one accepts that the natural course of an assessment wave is from easy to very difficult and one allows for sufficient time, then, if one can muster financial resources, creativity, persistence and good humor, it is possible to achieve high participation rates.

Creativity, persistence, and good humor are certainly necessary to keep the refusal rate low. Very often people refuse or are reluctant because it is a bad time to ask them to do anything; they are too busy, something is burning in the kitchen, there are upheavals in their lives, they just had a quarrel with their son and don't want to even think about him, etc. Interviewers need to understand these reasons and learn, first of all, not to take refusals personally. About half of the people who at one time say that they do not want to do an interview will, one or two months later, happily consent to be interviewed. It is, therefore, of the utmost importance that interviewers, when encountering resistance, always leave the door open for a future contact.

There is some evidence buttressing the impression that reluctance to participate or being hard to get in terms of number of contacts necessary before an interview is completed are more temporary phenomena than stable characteristics of a person. Green, Navratil, Loeber, and Lahey (in preparation), in a study of 96 clinic-referred boys and their families, were not able to distinguish a stable group of 'problem' participants who from phase to phase were always difficult to engage in an interview. Rather, participants were relatively unpredictable at each phase as to the effort necessary to complete the interview.

Searching for participants. In our study, from 15% to 20% of the participants moved between the half-yearly assessments. Very rarely have we lost a participant permanently because we could not find him. However, searching for participants takes time and money and one should be prepared for this. A number of papers have been written on how to find participants and readers are referred to these for long lists of suggestions (Farrington, Gallagher, Morley, St Ledger, & West, 1990; Green, Navratil, Loeber, & Lahey, 1992; Navratil, Green, Loeber, & Lahey, 1992; Robins, 1963; Stouthamer-Loeber, van Kammen, & Loeber, 1992). Over time and from country to country these techniques vary because of the changing access or lack of it of certain sources of information (Robins, 1977). Lately computerized data bases have been added to the list of tools for finding persons.

Three general principles are important, however. It is necessary to prepare access to certain sources of information about a participant's whereabouts ahead of time. For instance, for school-age children schools are an excellent source of information since school records are generally sent from one school to the next when a child moves. Therefore, the 'old' school is frequently in a position to give the name and address of the 'new' school. The 'new' school will release address information more readily if a signed consent for this purpose can be shown. The same applies to obtaining information from relatives, friends, employers, organizations of which the participant is a member, and various government agencies.

The second point sounds terribly simple: collect as much and as often as possible identifying information. Seemingly factual information such as names, birthdays, addresses, social security numbers and other ID numbers as well as grade in school and family relationship sometimes, however, turns out to be surprisingly inaccurate or fleeting. We have learned to collect this kind of information at every phase so that we can determine who is the biological mother, which is the correct spelling of the name, the correct grade, birthday, etc. After several phases when we cannot figure out which of the conflicting pieces of information is correct, we have called mothers to find out which was the correct information.

Participants may also have a bewildering variety of names and aliases. A child may be listed on his birth certificate as Napoleon Augustus Jones, but Mr. Jones Sr. may have disappeared soon after Napoleon's birth and the child may have used as last name the mother's maiden name, and a variety of last names of mother's boyfriends. Or, he may hardly know what his real name is since everybody calls him Skinny Beanstalk, or EsBe for short. We try to keep up to date with all names and aliases since the official name may be almost irrelevant.

The final principle for finding participants is even simpler than the previous one: when every method for finding a person has been tried without success, start all over again. A relative may have heard about the family in question in the meantime; a probation officer may know now that the participant is in jail, or a school may now have a new address. The point is not to give up.

It should be clear that these heroic efforts at finding participants and at completing interviews should be duly recognized and applauded, and staff engaging in these activities should receive the moral and actual support that makes it possible and rewarding to do the best possible job.

Data Collection from Community Sources

In addition to information specifically collected from the participant or other persons, existing records may be used as source of information. The sources may be courts, schools, medical agencies, etc. Information from such sources may be an important part of the study and access to the data contained in them needs to be carefully prepared before the study begins. Just because records exist does not mean that a researcher has access to them, or, if the researcher has access, that the records will be useful.

If the records are not public, in the sense that one could walk in off the street and look things up, then the first hurdle is to convince agency personnel that one's request is legitimate, that it serves an important purpose, and that it will not cost a large amount of agency time and money to accomplish one's purpose.

Second, once there is some agreement in principle about access to the records, the details need to be pinned down. Who will search the records, agency personnel, or research staff, or a combination of both? If agency personnel, is there a cost attached to this, and what is a realistic time-line? If research staff, when are they allowed to do the work and is there a space where they can do the work? If the permission to search records has been given very reluctantly, one may find out that, particularly when no agreements have been made about the details, the project will be stalled or various objections will surface when the work needs to be done.

It is very important to find out exactly what is in the records and in what form. Agencies keep records for a variety of purposes, such as fiscal, legal, or year-end reporting. Their reason for keeping records may not require them to have their records in a particular order, to keep records beyond a certain period, or to be careful about the completeness and correctness of the information. Therefore, one may find that records are erased after a year, that there is no discernable system for identifying persons except by reading all of the records, that system-specific ID numbers are re-used and not unique, that the same subject may be found under different names, or that information is haphazardly recorded. For instance, juvenile court records may be kept under a family ID since they are often part of the Family Court. The question is, what last name has been used to classify a youngster; his own last name, his mother's last name, his grandmother's with whom he has really lived most of his life? An example of records that are less complete than one would wish may be achievement test results from schools. Weak students, including habitually truant students may stay away on the day of testing and schools might not mind that so much since it will increase their average if weak students are absent. These are just two simple examples of the problems that one may encounter which show how crucial it is to have a good look at the records before a study starts.

Often access to the records is restricted, in that agency staff identify and retrieve the files from which the research staff then extracts information. In this case it is very important to supply agency personnel with as much identifying information as possible. Knowing that 'factual' information such as date of birth or name is far from fool proof, it may be necessary to try and induce the agency person to search in different ways, e.g., by all names and aliases *and* by date of birth, or by address *and* by social security number. This is a delicate matter and may be more easily done if the researcher pays for the work involved. Even then, agency staff is generally doing the work on top their ordinary duties and may not relish extra work.

It is, of course, a researcher's dream to find an agency where everything is beautifully computerized. Visions of hassle-free tapes or floppies float before the eye. However, the accuracy of the data so received revolves again around the identifying information that has been used to select the persons from the database. Is ID number 00005 really your John Smith, or someone else altogether? To be certain that the information one receives from an outside source matches the participants, it is good practice to ask for a piece of additional identifying information, not provided by the researcher, in the data base, such as a birth date or an address. One can then check against one's own records and sort out the discrepancies to make certain that one has correct matches. This may seem excessive caution but is necessary if one is dependent on others for the correctness of information without being able to check it. Even with the best precautions, errors may creep in. For years we have been confounded by a set of twins whose first names differed by just one letter. Although we have always interviewed the right boy, we have consistently received data from school records for his twin, since we had the twin's school ID number in our files.

Worse than false inclusion (which can usually be sorted out) are exclusions of subjects because the person searching the records did not search for all possible names, did not read the files carefully, or knew that there should be a record but could not find it or considered it too much trouble to retrieve it. It is therefore important to check if all cases known to the investigator from other sources are represented in the agency records. For instance, all participants who have reported to have been arrested should be found back in the police records. This checking is possible if one wants to use agency data on an individual level. If one wants to use agency data for aggregating over some community unit, however, the possibilities for checking the accuracy of the records are reduced. Even less control and opportunity for checking exists if data are used that have been aggregated by an agency, such as neighborhood profiles, or school achievement test data by school or district. It may take a lot of ingenuity to devise a way to estimate the accuracy of such data.

A very delicate problem arises when one finds that the record keeping is completely inadequate for one's purposes. If one is interested in prospective records, can one suggest a better record keeping system? The chances of success of such a suggestion are better when it is clear that the agency would benefit from it in terms of time-saving, money, or information that they would like to have. Sometimes it may be possible to point out that even if the agency does not benefit directly from a better record keeping system, the results of the study utilizing these better records may be of importance to them. Another possible solution is to place a research person in the agency to keep the records for them. This may be appealing since it may possibly reduce the workload for staff members, but on the other hand, an 'outside' person may be in the way and require information that previously was not gathered. Whatever the situation is, it is clear that when cooperation is needed it is necessary to have time to prepare an agency, to find out what is possible and what is not, and to develop a working relationship that is to the benefit of both the agency and the researcher.

One final point should be made before leaving the topic of outside data sources. One of the most common complaints from agencies, and, possibly, a reason for their sometimes less than enthusiastic cooperation is that previous researchers took what they needed, never thanked them, and never gave them any feedback or papers that had resulted from their data. Just as participants are to be treated courteously, so are agency personnel, from the director to the secretary who clears off a desk on which to work.

Management and Use of a Data Base

Once the raw data have been collected as correctly and completely as possible, a new set of challenges presents itself. How are data to be stored, documented, and analyzed? With frequent assessment waves one may feel overwhelmed and certain routines need to be instituted to ensure that data are managed in such a way that use can be made of them. In addition, researchers need to feel secure that no errors or omissions have crept in during the data entry, data cleaning, data reduction and analysis stages.

Shapiro and Charrow (1989) have reported deficiencies in data management (quality control, documentation and archiving) in more than 20% of routine data audits done on research conducted under the aegis of the Food and Drug Administration in the United States. Other researchers have also noted an alarming number of instances of data mismanagement (Prud'homme, Canner, & Cutler, 1989; van der Putten, van der Velden, Siers, & Hamersma, 1987). This does not refer to intentional deception in scientific research, but generally to unintentional errors and carelessness in, or lack of documentation of, raw data, variables, and analyses on which papers are based. The term "audit worthiness" has been coined to stand for good housekeeping in data management and analysis (Freedland & Carney, 1992). The larger the data set and the more researchers working on it, the more difficult it will be to impose accountability and to set uniform standards for data and analysis management, but the more necessary it is.

Large studies should, ideally, have a data librarian whose sole function it is to keep track, log in, back up, and distribute raw data and variables. Unfortunately, such a position is often seen as a luxury that few studies can afford. As with data collection, information on how to manage data and analyses is not easily accessible and most large research projects develop their own ways of preventing chaos or crawling out from under initial chaos as they go along. Following are some of the steps in our data management efforts.

Data entry. As was mentioned, we do data coding and data entry immediately as materials come to the office. The immediate data entry does not only benefit the interviewers whose pay is dependent on it, but also allows for orderly storage of booklets and keeping the data entry room as clean as possible. Data is entered twice, and discrepancies are resolved, so we are fairly sure that our data files reflect the answers in the booklets.

All coding is done before data entry. It may sometimes be tempting to postpone some coding to later; however, the effort to retrieve and store booklets, code, enter, and combine files is very large and should be prevented as much as possible.

At the end of each data collection phase an audit is held comparing an actual count of the booklets, data files, the file tracking the interviewer progress, interviewer payment file, and the participant payment file. This is done as an extra precaution to make sure that everything balances and no booklets or files have gone astray in the office.

Data cleaning. The process of data cleaning serves to insure that invalid values have been corrected and that skipping patterns have been followed. After data cleaning, frequencies are printed out and put in a binder together with the instrument and the coding scheme if any was used. The cleaned raw files can then be used by data analysis staff. However, if further changes in the raw data files are still necessary, this should ideally be done by one person who documents the date of the changes and who can check which data users need to be informed of the change.

Documentation of variables. We have set up a rigid format of data reduction which documents every step in the creation of variables by keeping as a computer file and as a hard copy all SPSS commands, from selecting particular items from raw data files, combining items from different data files, recoding, treatment of missing data, etc. These files, and the variables resulting from them are kept on one computer and are logged into a DBase system that allows us to search for variables in a variety of ways. A hard copy of all the information on a variable or a particular set of variables goes into a binder which contains the frequencies of the raw items, a copy of the instrument(s), the structure file for creating the variable(s), any intermediary analyses such as correlations or Cronbach's Alpha, and frequencies of the new variable. All variables are named in such a way that it is apparent which samples and phases were used and who made the variable.

Analyses. Each analysis project receives a project number. All printouts have reasonably intelligible headings and are put into binders. All SPSS commands for running the analyses are saved and eventually printed out and added to the binder. Over time we have added more and more comments to our command files and made use of indexes for the analyses in the binders.

When variables finally make it into papers, it is good practice to add a page to the office copy listing the variable names used and the project number, so that if anything needs to be looked up, it can be done.

This may all sound very tedious and time-consuming, which it is. However, anyone who, at times, has indulged in a quick, undocumented, burst of analyses will agree that it is even more tedious and time-consuming trying to retrieve or reconstruct inadequately documented variables or analyses at a later date.

Data back-up. Every three months all data and important programs are backed up and a copy is taken out of the building. In addition, all data entry files in progress are always backed up on diskettes. Backing up data is, again, a tedious procedure, but one needs only a small mishap to convince one of the necessity of this procedure.

Data sharing. Documentation is important, even if only one person works on the data, but it becomes absolutely essential when more people (some of them possibly not on site) share a data set. It is often necessary to give the collaboration some structure in the form of procedures to follow and rules to abide by.

One of the first concerns is to make sure that everyone works with the latest, most error-free files. So, a record needs to be kept of who is using which data in order to be able to provide updates if necessary.

Another concern is that all researchers are working on non-competing projects. It is, therefore, good practice to require brief written summaries of intended projects before they are started, so that all researchers know what has already been "claimed".

Good collaboration is also shown in agreement on core variables. When new variables are being contemplated, a researcher should be able to look up what variables are already in existence in a particular area, to prevent a waste of effort and confusing publications, that have slightly different variables to measure similar concepts.

Projects in which data are shared with people outside of the primary research group have an additional layer of etiquette. It is the donor's responsibility to provide all documentation to make the data understandable. If the data have been released to a *particular* person for a *particular* set of analyses only, as detailed in the written summary, the user should abide by these conditions. Data sets have been known to travel from one person to another (with or without documentation) and to have been put to unauthorized use. This is not to say that data should not be shared or used by different researchers. On the contrary, important data sets should ideally be used by researchers with different points of view or different analyses techniques. However, some rules should be observed to ensure responsible and collaborative use.

In using data collected by other researchers, it is not only courteous, but often very beneficial to share the results of the analyses with the donor before publishing them. Sometimes another interpretation may be immediately apparent to the donor because of his/her greater familiarity with the data and the data collection process, thereby rescuing the user from errors.

The main point about data and analyses management is that even the most meticulously collected data can quickly turn into something impenetrable if some simple rules are not observed. In these days when budget cuts are the rule, the first thing that researchers, understandably, protect from cuts is the data collection process. This leaves the data management and analysis side often understaffed and vulnerable to chaos. This is all the more reason to develop clear and efficient procedures for data and analysis management and collaboration.

Conclusion

Researchers who envision undertaking large-scale longitudinal research as conceiving of an idea for research and then, after a blank interval, writing important papers will be disappointed. Such research cannot, in my opinion, be undertaken by staying in one's ivory tower and considering the day-to-day activities of data collection and management as the concern of the 'hired hands'. The researcher needs to be familiar with every step in the process, not only to ensure that the right decisions are made, but also to understand what the eventual variables used in analyses stand for. Although some parts of the operation may become somewhat routine after a few phases, new situations, questions, and decisions continue to crop up requiring input from the investigator.

In addition, the conduct of a longitudinal study requires extraordinary effort, persistence, and inventiveness from the staff and the investigator needs to be able to recognize and encourage this. Staff needs to hear frequently how important their work is and how every little bit of effort counts.

This kind of involvement of the investigator takes, of course, time away from analyses and writing. However, it should be the investigator's first responsibility to ensure that everything is done to produce the best possible data set and to understand exactly its possibilities and its limitations. Without this, the next steps in the process, data analyses and report writing become relatively fruitless.

Acknowledgments

This chapter contains part of the collective wisdom acquired over the years by our research group. Particular thanks are due to Rolf Loeber, Welmoet van Kammen, Dianne Miller, Rosemary

Costanzo, Matt Cronin, Barbara Kumer, Susan Jones, Bruce Giroux, Joyce Thompson, Phen Wung, JoAnn Koral, and many others, including all interviewers, who have all worked with great dedication to make the Pittsburgh Youth Study a success.

The work in this chapter was supported by grant No. 86-JN-CX-0009 from the Office of Juvenile Justice and Delinquency Prevention, Office of Justice Programs, U.S. Department of Justice, and by a grant from the Pew Charitable Trusts, and NIMH grant MH48890, as well as a sub-contract with the Program on Human Development and Criminal Behavior, School of Public Health from Harvard University. Points of view or opinions in this document are those of the author and do not necessarily represent the official position or policies of the U.S Department of justice.

References

Capaldi, D. & Patterson, G.R. (1987). An approach to the problem of recruitment and retention rates for longitudinal research. *Behavioral Assessment,* 9, 169–178.

Cordray, S. & Polk, K. (1983). The implications of respondent loss in panel studies of deviant behavior. *Journal of Research in Crime and Delinquency,* 20, 214–242.

Farrington, D.P., Gallagher, B., Morley, L., St Ledger, R.J. & West, D.J. (1990). Minimizing attrition in longitudinal research: Methods of tracing and securing cooperation in a 24-year follow-up study. In D. Magnusson and L. Bergman (Eds.), *Methodology of longitudinal research.* Cambridge: Cambridge University Press.

Freedland, K.E. & Carney, R.M. (1992). Data management and accountability in behavioral and biomedical research. *American Psychologist,* 47, 640–645.

Green, S.M., Navratil, J.L., Loeber, R., & Lahey, B.B. (1992). *Retaining research subjects in a longitudinal study of deviant behavior:* I. Quantitative data. In preparation.

Jessor, R. & Jessor, S.L. (1977). *Problem behavior and psychosocial development: A longitudinal study of youth.* New York: Academic Press.

Navratil, J.L., Green, S.M., Loeber, R. & Lahey, B.B. (1992). *Retaining research subjects in a longitudinal study of deviant behavior:* I. Qualitative data. In preparation.

Nurco, D.N., Robins, L.N. & O'Donnell, J.A. (1977). Locating respondents. In L.D. Johnston, D.N. Nurco, & L.N. Robins (Eds.), *Conducting follow up research on drug treatment programs* (pp. 71–84). Washington, DC: U.S. Government Printing Office.

Prud'homme, G.J., Canner, P.L. & Cutler, J.A. (1989). Quality assurance and monitoring in the Hypertension Prevention Trial. *Controlled Clinical trials, 10* (Suppl.), 84S-94S.

Robins, L. N. (1963). The reluctant respondent. *Public Opinion Quarterly,* 27, 278–286.

Robins, L.N. (1977). Problems in follow-up studies. *American Journal of Psychiatry,* 134, 904–907.

Shapiro, M.F. & Charrow, R.P. (1989). The role of data audits in detecting scientific misconduct: Results of the FDA program. *Journal of the American Medical Association,* 262, 2505–2511.

Stouthamer-Loeber, M., van Kammen, W. & Loeber, R. (1992). The nuts and bolts of implementing large-scale longitudinal research. *Violence and Victims,* 7, 63–78.

Stouthamer-Loeber, M., van Kammen, W., Loeber, R., Miller, D. & Kumer, B. (1992). *Contacting and Interviewing Subjects.* Report prepared for the Program on Human Development and Criminal Behavior, Harvard School of Public Health.

van der Putten, E., van der Velden, J.W., Siers, A. & Hamersma, E.A.M. (1987). A pilot study on the quality of data management in a cancer clinical trial. *Controlled Clinical Trials,* 8, 96–100.
Winett, R.A., Neale, M.S. & Williams, K.R. (1979). Effective field research procedures: Recruitment of participants and acquisition of reliable, useful data. *Behavioral Assessment,* 1, 139–155.

Prevention of Adolescent Delinquency, an Integrative Multilayered Control Theory Based Perspective

by Marc Le Blanc

Introduction

Reviewers of the prevention of delinquency literature would certainly agree that criminologists, psychologists, sociologists, social workers, and others professionals have been very creative. An infinite number of prevention programs have been experimented in Occident during this century. However, any specialist of delinquency prevention would conclude that no program stands out as a definitive solution to the problem of adolescent delinquency. Prevention specialists do not have a great confidence in any of the particular programs because evaluations, when they exist, are rudimentary or they suffer from various methodological weaknesses (see for example the reviews of Wright and Dixon, 1977; Finckenauer, 1982; Lundman, 1984).

Withstanding this difficulty, even if we accept that many programs are promising (Wilson, 1987), it is also evident to prevention specialists that none of the existing programs are sufficient and that their effects are, at most, mitigated. As a consequence of the limited impact of each particular program, the prevention of adolescent delinquency cannot be equated to one program. In many instances specific prevention programs have been presented as a panacea. Contrary to that point of view, prevention should to be conceived as an comprehensive and integrated set of complementary programs. Coordination and dialogue between various agencies and levels of government is then absolutely essential.

If we accept that premise, then the principal question becomes how can we decide which of the infinite number of prevention programs should be considered in a comprehensive and integrate preventive action. To decide which program should be used to prevent adolescent delinquency, three options are represented in the delinquency prevention literature: the classificatory, the empirical and the theoretical perspectives. The classification point of view, such as the Lorion et al (1987) paper among others, proposes programs according to the a division between primary, secondary and tertiary prevention or relative to institutions, such as school, family, and so on. The empirical point of view looks for scientifically identified risk factors and select programs that can limit their impact, Farrington (Farrington et al, 1986; Farrington, 1992) and Le Blanc (1991) adopt such a pragmatic perspective. The theoretical point of view chose the programs according to a theory, Weis and Hawkins (1979, see also Hawkins et al, 1992) social development model is of such nature.

In this paper, we will follow this last avenue. A theory will be chosen because of its applicability to the various levels of definitions of crime, it is a multilayered integrative control theory. Such a theoretically based perspective is scientifically and practically sound. From a scientific point of view, every criminologist would certainty accept that no risk factor is a necessary and sufficient cause of the participation or of the continuation of a criminal career. As a consequence, the prevention of adolescent delinquency cannot rest on a program that attack only one specific risk factor. If no factor is a necessary and sufficient condition of offending, only a theory can stack risk factors under the umbrella of constructs related by a common philosophy. Contrary to the classificatory and the pragmatic perspectives, the theoretical point of view maximizes the selection of appropriate programs because of the inherent logic of the constructs of the theory and their interactions, it should then be easier to attain unity in a comprehensive set of programs.

From an applied criminology point of view, it seems more pedagogical and practical to adopt a theoretical perspective then the other two perspectives for the development of a comprehensive delinquency prevention action aimed at adolescents. The theoretical point of view is highly pedagogical because it is then easier to explain the content of the objectives of the various programs to peoples that have to intervene in coordination. In addition, this perspective is practical because a common language will certainty favor dialogue between programs and persons that implement them.

This paper is composed of three sections: 1) we discuss the levels of definition and explanation of the phenomenon of crime; 2) we propose a mutilayered integrative control theory; 3) and, finally, we identify the prevention programs that are congruent with this theory. Our work will suffer some limits. The set of preventive programs proposed will be targeted only to delinquency even if many of the proposed actions can be helpful for other problem behavior. Our definition of delinquency, as in our previous work (Le Blanc and Fréchette, 1987, 1989) will be legal, the infractions to the criminal code. The term delinquency will also involve another limit, only the period of adolescence will be considered even if we will sometimes propose preventive actions that focus on antecedent ages periods. Finally, the major shortcoming of this paper is that it will be only an outline of the theory and of the comprehensive prevention program because of space limitation.

Levels of Definition and Explanation of the Phenomenon of Delinquency

The objective of this section is to specify the levels of definition and explanation of the phenomenon of delinquency that a multi-layered integrative criminological theory must be able to compose with. The French criminologist Jean Pinatel (1963), in a masterly effort to define the bases of criminology, was the first to propose that criminologists should distinguish between three levels of definition of the criminal phenomenon, namely the criminality, the criminal and the crime, each level having its own perspectives, its own rationales and its own methods. Figure 1 sketches these levels of definition and explanation of delinquency.

He defines the first, criminality, as the sum of infractions committed at a given time and place, influenced by demographic, economic or political factors and which occur on a societal scale. The terms criminality and *delinquency* will be used in this paper to refer to that level of definition and it should not be confused with the use of the term criminality to indicate an individual criminal propensity as do Gottfredson and Hirschi (1990) and others. At that level of definition, the dependent variable is the rate of delinquency for a particular geographical and social unit and for a specific time period. The independent variables are indicators of the state of a society (differential social organization in Sutherland terns, Sutherland and Cressey, 1960), characteristics of a community (social disorganization in the Chicago school terms, Shaw and McKay, 1969), indicators of the functioning of an institution (school organization characteristics for example, Gottfredson and Gottfredson, 1985).

The second level, the criminal or the *delinquent*, is centered, for Pinatel, on the transgressor himself and proceeds to a study of his personal characteristics as well as of the factors that influence the formation and evolution of his personality. This level of definition of the phenomenon of delinquency refers to the expression individual offending, as suggested by Blumstein et al (1986). The dependent variable is any descriptive indices of the criminal career, participation, frequency, onset, duration, and so on or any developmental measures, such as the processes of activation, aggravation or desistance (Le Blanc and Fréchette, 1989). The independent variables are personal characteristics of an individual, such as his biological capacity and his personality, or social indicators such as his relationship with his environment, his bond to society in Hirschi's terms (1969), his social class, and so on.

The third level of interpretation, that of the crime or the *delinquent act* itself, is only as a small part of the life or of the criminal career of the subject. It is considered as an event that has a beginning, a development and an end and the task of criminology is to

Figure 1.

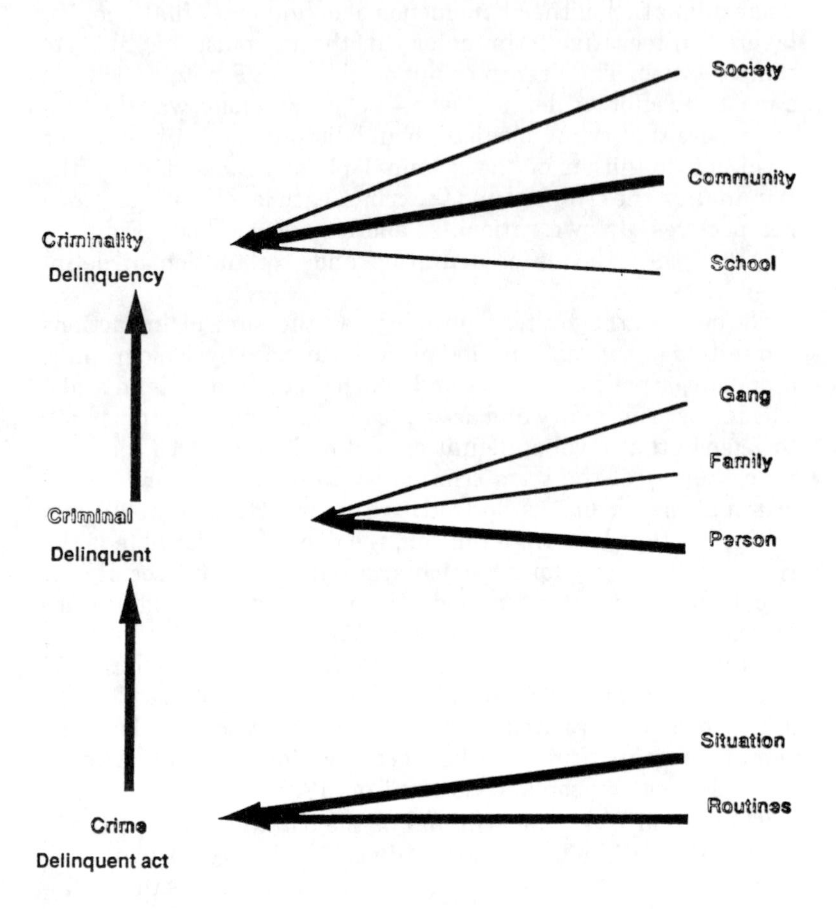

ascertain the factors or mechanisms that cause its appearance. At that level the dependent variable is any characteristics of specific offenses. The independent variables are characteristics of the situation, such as routine activities or other variables of the rational choice model of Cusson (1983) or Clarke and Cornish (1985).

This basic criminological rule, that there are three levels of definition matched with three levels of explanation, was rediscovered by American criminologists recently but the emphasis has been mainly on two levels, crime and criminality (Hirschi, 1979, 1989; Short, 1985, 1989) just like Sutherland had suggested much earlier (Sutherland and Cressey, 1960). It should also be pointed out that this basic rule is far from being followed up in the discourse of criminologists since they very often used the term delinquency when vaguely referring to all three levels of definition (Matza, 1964, Muchielli, 1965). Others formulated their theory without specifying the level they were addressing (Mailloux, 1971, and Lemay, 1973) while others expressed a concept of delinquency that did not correspond to the level concerned in their analysis (thus Cohen, 1955, and Cloward and Ohlin, 1960, used a definition of delinquency that referred to the conduct but in fact they were formulating a theory of the delinquent career or of the delinquent role). However, a number of more recent authors, from Hirschi (1969) to Cusson (1981), Arnold and Brungardt (1983), Pearson and Weiner (1985), Short (1989), Cullen (1985), and Hirschi and Gottfredson (1987), to cite only these few, take into account the need to specify the level of definition when elaborating their theoretical proposition for the explanation of the criminal phenomenon.

Accepting that there are three levels of definition of the criminal phenomenon implies that there are corresponding levels of explanation that are distinct and that are matched to them. Psychologists tends to distinguish three levels of explanation of behavior: the milieu, the person and the situation, while sociologists refer mainly to the society, the community and the institutions. As shown in Figure 1, these levels of explanation can be matched with the levels of definition of the criminal phenomenon, each level of explanation is principally pertinent to a particular level of definition. And, to respect the logic of the ecological fallacy principle, explanatory variables of one level cannot be used to explain the dependent variable of an other other level.

Societal variables may affect the person and his milieu, however only person variables can influence directly individual offending and person variables cannot affect the rate of delinquency directly. The same logic applies to the delinquent act and the delinquency levels of definition. Figure 2 also implies also that the levels of definition and explanation may have some relationships with each other. Delinquent acts are constituent parts of the delinquent while individual offending is included in delinquency. Figure 2 also states that the explanatory variables are constantly interacting and, it is also implicit from a developmental point of view, that levels of definition and explanation do influence each other over time along a spiral. At a specific point in time, the characteristics of a person and of his environment, associated with previous behavior, will partially determined subsequent behavior which, in turn, will modify the characteristics of the person and his relationships with his environment.

Figure 2.

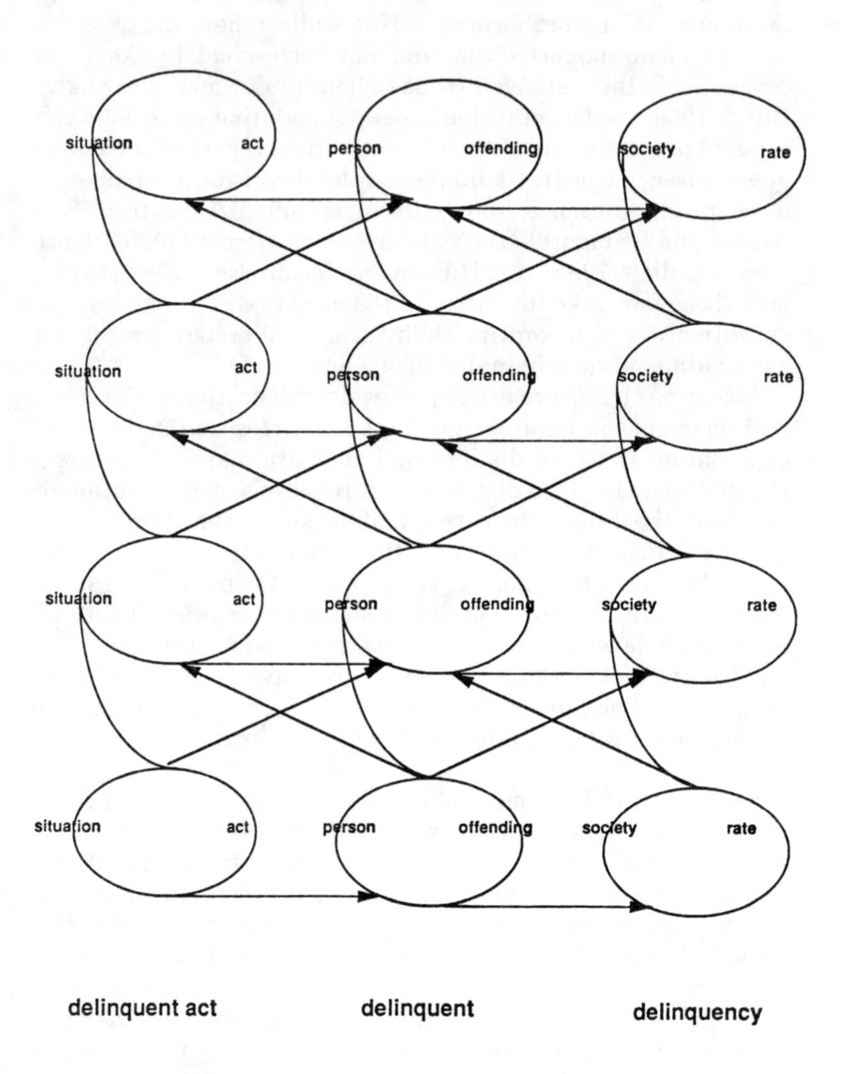

Integrative and Elaborated Control Theory

From the levels of definitions and explanation of the phenomenon of delinquency presented in Figure 1, there can be at least eight layers in the explanatory control theory. In this paper, we will limit our-self to three stratum: the community, the person, and the act. Before identifying the constructs that are pertinent to each layer, it is fundamental to define the term integrative.

During the sixties, the term integrative was used in criminology to designate an integration of theoretical perspectives or the simultaneous consideration of data from the disciplines of sociology and psychology. This definition of integration was the consensus among scholars in North America and Europe; this position was supported by Mannheim (1965), Wolfgang and Ferracuti (1967), and Szabo et al (1968) among others. Two decades later, the term integrative was no more referring to an interdisciplinary integration for American criminologists, its scope was reduced to an integration of sociological theories by Johnson (1979) and Elliott et al (1985) and this tendency was confirmed by the Albany Conference (Messner et al, 1989). Because of this unfortunate change in the meaning of the term theoretical integration, it is now necessary to distinguish clearly between types of theoretical activity. In criminology, there are three major types of theoretical activities that have been performed. These types of theoretical development are elaboration, integration and modeling.

Elaboration is a development, an expansion of an existing theory. Hirschi's bonding theory possesses all these characteristics in relation to Durkheim initial statement of the importance of the bond to society (1895, 1934). He even cites from Durkheim (Hirschi, 1969), then he specifies the four elements of the bond. Elaboration has been most often empirical in contemporary criminology, it we refer to the numerous studies verifying Hirschi's theory that Kempf (1993) reviews, rarely it is formal (see Gibbs 1985, Le Blanc and Caplan 1992), and sometimes it is discursive (Bernard 1987, Catalano and Hawkins 1986, Le Blanc and Caplan 1992, Thornberry, 1987). Theoretical elaboration can also take the form of a multilayered theory as defined by Lenski (1988), a general theoretical statement from which special theories are derived; we have proposed this type of elaboration for bonding theory under the denomination of middle range family, school and peers control theories (Le Blanc and Caplan, 1993).

Integration is the second type of theoretical activity, it is the formulation of a theory that incorporates separate concepts into a new whole. In criminology, and particularly concerning bonding theory, we can distinguish theoretical activities that can be classified in three different kinds of integrations: unification, combination and incorporation. Integrative unification concerns the levels of explanation of the phenomenon considered, a common conceptual frame is proposed for the micro and macro levels of explanation, for example crime and criminality; Pearson and Weiner (1985) propose a social learning unification while Gottfredson and Hirschi (1990) develop a social control one with the constructs of bond and self-control. Integrative combination involves the amalgamation of different orienting theoretical strategies such as social control, social learning, labeling, or any assimilation of these theories or others; there are numerous such combination of social control theory with other unit theory, most of these amalgamations concern social learning or differential association (Conger 1976, Matsueda 1988, Catalano and Hawkins 1986, Reid 1989) and the most comprehensive attempt was realized by Elliott et al (1985, 1989) using social control, social learning and strain theories. Integrative incorporation use concepts from different disciplines, biology, psychology, sociology, to formulate a new theory; constructs of control theory have been affiliate with biological and/or psychological constructs by Arnold and Brungardt (1983), Denno (1985), Udry (1988) and Le Blanc et al (1988).

Modeling is the third type of theoretical activity, it has become prevalent during the last few decades. Concerning social control theory there is a multiplication of such models, most of the verifications of Hirschi's theory reviewed by Kempf (1993) are of that nature. Many of the elaborations and integrations cited above are also presented as models. Each model distinguishes himself by the constructs involved and/or by their measurement and/or by the type of sample used. No model is replicated on different sets of data. The mere existence of these numerous models correspond to the situations of theory proliferation, theory competition and theory variation describe by Wagner and Berger (1985).

The multilayered integrative control theory that we propose is integrative in the classical sense, it uses constructs originating from different disciplines, sociological, biological and psychological criminology. It is also an elaboration of bonding theory into a more comprehensive control theory following a formalization (Le Blanc and Caplan, 1993) and the construction and verification of middle range control theories of the family system, the school experience and the constraints domain (Le Blanc et al, 1992a, b, Le Blanc, 1992a, b).

A Multilayered Integrative Control Theory

Lenski (1988) defines a multilayered theory as a family of theories that provides covering principles derived from a broadly inclusive general theory. Our general theory states that, **in a favorable context, controls will be tighter and they will develop in harmony with expectations, and, as a consequence, conformity will result and will be maintained over time**. Conversely, in an unfavorable context, when the controls are loose and insufficient, the criminal phenomenon of will manifest and maintain itself.

In our theory, there are numerous personal, family, school and other factors that are interacting to constitute four categories of control processes, bonding, maturating, modeling and constraining. These processes are modulated by two types of contexts, the social and cultural and the physical and biological contexts. This theory is systemic in the sense that there is a structure, a sequence between the components, as well as reciprocal and directional relationships between the components and also feedbacks, as illustrated in Figures 3 to 6. It is also a developmental theory because over time there is stability and change within the components as well as because of there mutual influences.

In a multilayered theory, the components have to be present at all the levels of definition and explanation of the criminal phenomenon. It is not our intention to fully develop our multilayered theory in this paper, what we want to show is that there are isomorphic constructs in the criminological literature for the various levels of definition and explanation. And, from there, to identify a pertinent comprehensive strategy for the prevention of adolescent delinquency from programs describe in the literature. Let us formulate the integrative control theory a the level of individual offending because our theory is more thoroughly developed at that level. Then we will present a sketch of the theory at the other level of definition of the criminal phenomenon.

An Integrative Control Theory of Individual Offending

Over the last forty years, criminology did not witness any significant theoretical invention. Social disorganization (and its variants strain and control), cultural deviance, labeling and radical theories had been formulated in rudimentary form for some times. And, even then they were theoretical elaborations of ideas of nineteen century theorists such as Quetelet, Durkheim, Marx, Tarde, and others. Control theory is traced back to the 19th century idea that the family is the cause of delinquency by Empey (1978) and it can be linked to Quetelet (1842, p.95) statement that "This fatal propensity appears to be developed in proportion to the intensity of the physical power and passions of man ... The intellectual and moral development ... subsequently weakens the propensity to crime ...". Kornhauser (1978) sets the origin of a more elaborated version of control theory with Trasher and Shaw and McKay, while Empey (1978) emphasizes Freud psycho-dynamic formulation. Nevertheless, much of the recent literature forgets about formulations that preceded Hirschi's statement.

Precursors and followers of Hirschi would probably agree with Empey's statement of the content of control theory (1978,.207): "... their emphasis upon the idea that delinquent and conformist behavior is a function of the ability of the child to control his anti-social impulses. They start from the assumption that children require training if they are to behave socially. Delinquent behavior will result either if a child lacks the ability for effective training or because he has been trained badly." This statement fits particularly well the last version of control theory that introduces the notion of low self-control (Gottfredson and Hirschi, 1990).

Our initial elaboration of control theory also involves psychological variables (Le Blanc and Biron, 1980), while our most recent version incorporates the six components enumerated earlier on: bonding, modeling, maturating, constraining, social structures and biological capacities (Le Blanc et al, 1988; Le Blanc and Caplan, 1993). The theory is abstracted in Figure 3. It assumes that **adolescent's** *conformity* to conventional standards of behavior is obtained when *allocentrism* is installed, when his *bond* to society is solid, when *constraints* are firm, and when he is exposed to strong *pro-social influences*. This personal and social governance of conformity is conditional on the biological capacity of the individual and on his position in the social structure. From a developmental point of view, the allocentrism and the bond will develop if, in one hand, the individual has minimum biological capacities and if he is in a favorable social position and, in an other hand, if constraints are appropriate and models pro-social. Alternatively, delinquency happen and continue when egocentrism persist, when the social bond is tenuous, when constraints are insufficient and deviant influences are present. These causes of delinquency will be more effective when the individual has some biological deficiencies and when comes from a lower social class. *Delinquency*, in this theory, is defined by acts, the detection of which are thought to result in sanctions by agents of the larger society.

Social structure. The position of the individual in the social structure is the first contextual condition that affects the development of the bond to society and the exposition to pro-social influences (Hagan, 1988, is the most prominent recent proponent of that position). It has been constantly documented in criminology that, if the adolescent lives in a deteriorate community and if his parents are of low socioeconomic status, his probability of becoming delinquent and of having a criminal career is much higher (Blumstein et al, 1986). The impact of belonging to specific ethnic or racial groups is similar. It is also well known that in these milieus there exist various subcultures of deviance that support deviant patterns of behavior and more occasions are present for offending in these communities (see for example Cloward and Ohlin, 1960). Such social conditions are indirect causes of delinquency, as shown in Figure 3, and this situation is particularly well documented by studies about the impact of the family system on self-reported and official delinquency (see for example Laub and Sampson, 1988, and Le Blanc, 1992a).

Figure 3.

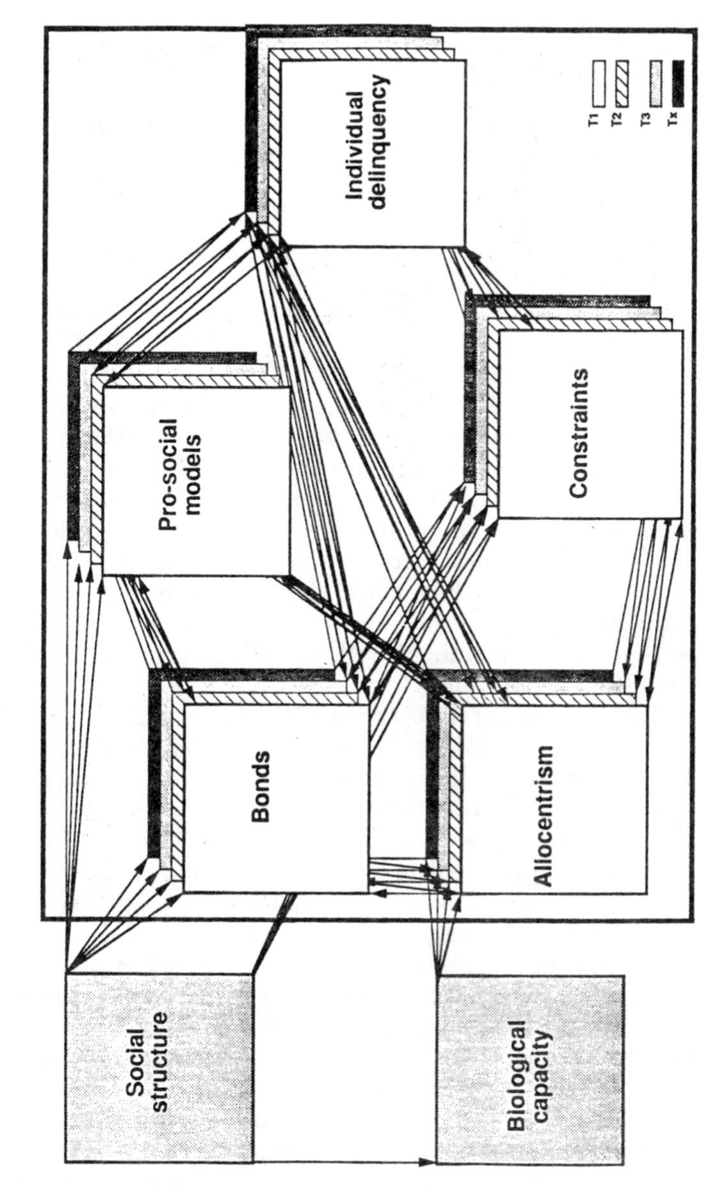

Control theory at the level of individual delinquency
Individual delinquency
Pro-social models
Constraints
Bonds
Allocentrism
Social structure
Biological capacity
T1
T2
T3
Tx

Biological capacities. Arnold and Brungardt (1983) were the first to introduce the construct of biological capacity in a control theory of adolescent delinquency. It is also documented that biological deficiencies (nature of the functioning of the central nervous system, and so on) (Hodgins, 1985; Moffit, 1990) and a difficult temperament are conditions that limits the possibilities for the development of the personality of the individual (Wilson and Herrnstein, 1985). It is expected that such deficiencies will affect the development of the allocentrism of the person and, in particular, it should affect the cognitive development of the individual (IQ and moral development). The egocentric and cognitively primitive individual will be more likely delinquent and will likely persist in offending. Such factors are indirect causes of delinquency as shown in Figure 3.

The bond to society. Following Hirschi (1969) and the numerous replications of his theory (Kempf, 1993), it can be stated, after formalizing his theory (Le Blanc and Caplan, 1993), that an individual's *bond* to society is manifested towards several institutions constituting the different spheres of the adolescent's world. Three institutions are emphasized for the age group considered: family, school, and peers. The adolescent is related to these institutions via three avenues: attachment to persons, commitment to institutions, and involvement in conventional activities. The development of the bond to society may be more difficult when the adolescent and his parents are subjected to adverse socioeconomic conditions and when he and/or they are highly egocentric and less able cognitively.

The most important element of the bond to conventional society is the individual's *attachment to persons*. The importance of this element lies in the number of persons in society that can lead to an individual's attachment. There are three categories of such figures: parents, peers, and persons in positions of impersonal authority. Attachment to persons is situated within the framework of the social norm that states what ought to be. It is assumed that if a person is sensitive to the opinions of others, then he is to that extent bound by the norms. Consequently, the internalization of norms depends on the individual's attachment to persons and the attachment to persons favors the acceptance of societal constraints such as parental discipline, school sanction, and protects against formal sanctions. Attachment to conventional persons acts as a major deterrent to the commission of delinquent acts in that the stronger this tie, the more likely it will be considered by the adolescent when and if he considers committing a delinquent act. This attachment to persons also counters the impact of criminal influences: a weak or broken attachment to persons increases the susceptibility to deviant and criminal influences. The theory defines the process through which attachment to persons works against the commission of delinquent acts and the criminal influences. That is, the adolescent's level of attachment to parents determines his level of attachment to peers and to persons in positions of impersonal authority. The cumulative impact of these attachments protects the adolescent against criminal influences and discourages occasional and persistent offending.

The second element of the bond is the *commitment to institutions*. The adolescent commitment to institutions could develop towards school, religion, work or success, and so on, but because of the nature of adolescence it is postulated that the most important institution that is involved in the development of the adolescent's commitment is school. Commitment refers to an attitude of acceptance of an institution, an affective investment in education, religion, and so on. Conversely, deviant behavior is considered a cost. Therefore, when an adolescent is faced with the temptation to commit a delinquent act, he must evaluate the costs of his delinquent behavior in relation to the investment he has made. The assumption underlying the idea of commitment to institutions is that the attitudinal investment of most adolescents would be seriously affected if they were to commit delinquent acts. Commitment is viewed as a constraint on delinquency and as a protection against criminal influences since they would jeopardize the adolescent's possibility of realizing the fruits of his investment. That is, it is suggests that the adolescent is committed to conformity not only by his present investments but also by what he hopes to achieve.

Involvement in conventional activities is the third element of the bond of the individual to society. The involvement process states that the greater the involvement of the adolescent in conventional activities, the less time he has to engage in deviant acts and the less chance there is that he could be exposed to criminal influences. When defining delinquency as an activity, the emphasis should be placed on the nature of the conventional activity as opposed to the quantity of conventional activities. With this position, four types of activities are presumably important. These activities center around the family, the peers, the school, and the work. These types of activities are important since school-related activities inhibit delinquent activities, whereas participation in work is positively related to the commission of delinquent acts. The other two types of involvements, activities with parents and peers (particularly if they are conventional), are viewed as a protection against the commission of delinquent acts.

The allocentrism. A comprehensive and an integrative perspective for the explanation of delinquency cannot immediately ruled out individual differences. The importance of individual differences in the emergence and the development of individual offending has also been sufficiently documented in the criminological literature (Feldman, 1978; Kornhauser, 1978; Wilson and Herrnstein, 1985; Fréchette et Le Blanc, 1987), and is worth consideration in an integrative control theory. If there is a large variety of psychological theories, there is only one that has a common set of postulates with social control theories. As shown by Empey (1978), it is the psycho-dynamic perspective. This perspective was initially developed by Freud that postulates that children were originally antisocial, and that socialization proceeds through successive stages toward maturation.

Allocentrism is the movement away from the natural egocentrism of the individual, it manifest itself by the genuine consideration of what surrounds a person, it is the disposition to be concerned by others and to behave in relation to them. This major axe of the development of humans (see Lerner, 1986) is used to synthesized the personality dimensions that have been associated with offending. We have proposed this construct to represent the personal control (Le Blanc and Biron, 1980; Le Blanc et al, 1988) in complement to Hirschi's social control theory and in accordance with a classic conception of the explanation of delinquency which stresses the importance of psychological variables (Wolfgang and Ferracuti, 1967, among others). In their recent book, Gottfredson and Hirschi (1990) propose such an integrative conception with their notion of low self-control, which is in our view a limited specification of the possible psychological traits of an individual that can support individual offending.

A review of the literature in this domain convinced us that two major lines of complementary thoughts should be integrated in our integrative control theory (Fréchette and Le Blanc, 1987). The first stems from psycho-dynamic theory and lead us to consider the level of psychic development, which means that the child is progressing from a certain level of primitivity toward a rich psychic life manifested by a certain level of allocentrism. The second line of research made it possible to identify a great number of personality traits that have been associated with delinquent conduct. We synthesized them under the concept of the egocentric personality, a deficient psychological functioning. The egocentric personality has four distinguishing traits: hyposociality (inability to cope with the demands and constraints of social life), negativeness (hostile attitude toward others), insecurity (malaise and strong feelings of discomfort) and primitivity (rudimentary manner of functioning; giving strict priority to personal needs). This cohesive structure constitutes the framework for the psychic support of individual offending. Personal isolation emerges as the main characteristic of serious delinquency; in other words, the most determining negative influence is withdrawal from intimate human contact. The isolation is immediately supported by a multidimensional structure that involves hyposociality, which seems to be the most powerful element, and negativeness in massive doses; these two components are then strengthened by insecurity and primitivity.

Figure 3 indicates that the normal development of the allocentrism favors the establishment of a solid bond to society, the receptivity to social constraints and pro-social influences, and, finally, the conformity to conventional standards of behavior.

However, the levels of allocentrism and cognitive development are dependent on the individual biological capacity. Allocentrism is expected to improve over time and then counter the continuation of individual offending.

The constraints. Following Durkheim (1895, 1934) classic distinction between norms, defined as rules of law and moral values, and discipline, characterized as monitoring and punishment, we can propose that there are two major sources of restrain when an individual envisages a delinquent act, internal and external constraints (see the full elaboration of the constraint component in Le Blanc, 1992b).

External constraints are of two categories, formal and informal. The *formal external constraint* perspective has been more fully elaborated by labeling theorists (see Shoemaker, 1990), while the informal social reaction point of view is developed by bonding theorists (see Le Blanc and Caplan, 1993). Labeling theory states that the imposition of the official label of delinquent, following criminal activity, favors the development of a delinquent self-image and the emergence of new and more serious forms of criminal activities. Bonding theorists concentrate on *informal external constraints*. They recognize that very low and very high levels of parental control are least effective, as well as both strict and punitive and lax and erratic disciplines are related to conduct problems. When the attachment to parents and the family context (family structure, marital relations, parental deviance, and so on) are statistically controlled, the direct parental control variables (supervision and discipline) are significantly related to delinquency during adolescence (Le Blanc, 1992a). In the school domain, contrary to the family domain, external constraint, as compared to bonding, is the best explanation of adolescent delinquency and adult criminality (Le Blanc, 1992c).

The notion of internal constraint has been elaborated by bonding theorists under the notion of beliefs (Hirschi, 1969) and by deterrence theorists under the notion of perceived certainty and severity of sanctions (see Paternoster, 1987). The first notion refers to the adolescent's *belief in conventional standards of behavior*, that is, the extent to which he believe he should obey the rules of society. The adolescent's belief acts as a moral obstacle to the commission of delinquent acts. The less an adolescent believes he should obey the rules of society, the greater the probability that he will commit delinquent acts. However, there is variation in the adolescents attitude of respect toward the rules of society; many persons feel no moral obligation to conform. Four types of belief are potentially important: acceptance of the normative system, use of neutralization techniques, legitimacy of rules imposed by parents and of controlling institution (Le Blanc and Caplan, 1992). Perceptual deterrence theory postulates an inverse relationship between *the perceived certainty and severity of sanctions* and self-reported offending.

Empirical test of this hypothesis are numerous but the results are still inconclusive (Le Blanc, 1992b).

As represented in Figure 3, the individual receptivity to social constraints depends on the quality of the adolescent bond to society, the level of development of his allocentrism and on the presence of strong pro-social influences. It is one of the last protection against individual offending. When constraints are inappropriate to the age of the adolescent, erratic or absent, they are direct and proximal causes of individual offending as shown in our previous studies (Le Blanc et al, 1988; Le Blanc, a, b, c).

The pro-social influences. Tarde (1924) introduced the modeling explanation of delinquency which was elaborated later on by Sutherland (Sutherland and Cressey, 1960) and which has been shown to be an important cause of adolescent delinquency (see Elliott et al, 1985, 1989; Thornberry et al, 1990). A central assumption of control theories is that companionship with delinquents is an incidental by-product of the quality of the bond to society. This assertion suggests that the relationship between delinquent companions and delinquency is spurious. However, after testing this hypothesis with his data, as confirmed by numerous studies, Hirschi (1969) revises his bonding model to state that delinquent companions has a direct or causal impact on the commission of delinquent acts. Furthermore, after formalizing Hirschi's theory we proposed that a weak or broken bond to society leads to the acquisition of delinquent friends as well as having a direct effect on the level of delinquency (Le Blanc and Caplan, 1993). In the last revision of bonding theory, Gottfredson and Hirschi (1990) suggest that low self-control leads to an important street life and to the membership in a deviant group and then individual are more likely to offend more frequently.

The delinquent friends represents, in part, the adolescent's *exposure to criminal influences*. An adolescent, however, can also be exposed to criminal influences through the nature of the deviant subcultures that are present in his community, television programming and videos viewing, parental deviance and criminality, the adolescent out of the home routine activities, and so on. Figure 3 states that the adolescent receptivity to criminal influences depends on the nature of his community, the quality of his bond to society, the development of his allocentrism and the tightness of the constraints that are imposed by himself or others. Thus the receptivity to criminal influences is a direct and proximal cause of individual offending as shown by numerous criminological studies (see particularly Elliott et al, 1985, 1989; Thornberry et al, 1990).

Criminal activity. The criminal career paradigm attained a prominent status with Blumstein at al (1986) work and it as been elaborated to a developmental criminology paradigm by Loeber and Le Blanc (1990). Our study shows that offending develops through three mechanisms: activation, aggravation and desistance (see Le Blanc and Fréchette, 1989). In our theory,

Figure 4.

Control theory at the level of community delinquency

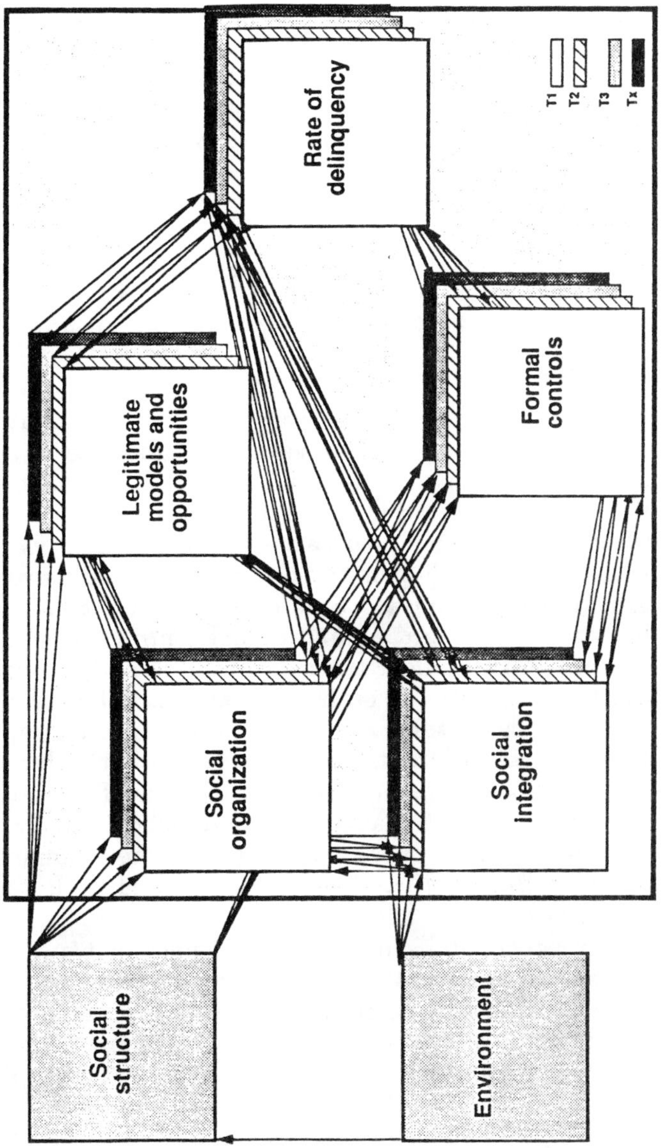

Social structure

Environment

Social organization

Social integration

Legitimate models and opportunities

Formal controls

Rate of delinquency

T1
T2
T3
Tx

offending is activated because of criminal influences, insufficient constraints, egocentrism, and bonding deficiencies. It is expected to aggravate when social and personal controls are weak and it does disappear when such controls are created or reinstalled (Le Blanc, 1992d; Ouimet and Le Blanc, 1993).

Figure 3 indicate that our theory of adolescent offending is interactional, because of the reciprocal relations between the constructs, and developmental, because of the change over time that is represented by the superposed boxes. With this theory of the individual offending in mind, we will propose its isomorphic counterparts at the other two levels of definition and explanation of the criminal phenomenon.

An Integrative Control Theory of Community Delinquency

Figure 4 represent our theory at the level of explanation of the community. The dependent variable is the rate of adolescent delinquency in a particular community at various points in time, it could be expressed in terms of an overall rate or of rates of specific types of delinquent acts. The independent variables, as in the individual offending theory, comprise six constructs: social structure, environment, social organization, social integration, legitimate opportunities, and formal control. These constructs represent the bonding, the modeling, the maturating and the constraining processes of the general control theory, as well as the social and cultural and the physical and biological contexts. Most of these constructs were introduced by the Chicago school or the ecology of delinquency school. Some of these constructs have been elaborated at a micro and macro level by Sampson (1991) and the intervening dimension of the community social organization constructs has been explicated by Bursik (1988) among others.

Our community control theory assumes that **a high rate of** *conformity* to conventional standards of behavior is obtained when *social organization* and *social integration* are sufficient, when *formal controls* are efficient and deterrent, and when there are enough *legitimates opportunities*. This regulation of conformity is conditional on the *environment* and on the position of the community in the *social structure*. Alternatively, a high rate of delinquency will exist when social disorganization and isolation are persistent, when formal controls are insufficient and when deviant subcultures and opportunities are present. These causes of a high rate of delinquency in a community will be more efficient when the environment is deteriorated and when the social status of the community is low. The rate of conformity will vary over time and between communities according to changes in the levels of social organization, social integration, formal controls and legitimate opportunities. Lets outline the content of each of these community constructs.

Social structure. The social structure context, what Fiueira-McDonough (1991) call the population dimension and Wikström (1990a) the urbanization dimension, is defined by such characteristics as poverty, mobility, ethnicity, it parallels the social structure of the individual level theory. Since the seminal studies of Shaw and McKay (1969) it is well documented that the rates of delinquency are higher in communities that display a lower social status and poverty and that these communities are more often composed of immigrants. Figure 4 states that a disadvantage social context favors social disorganization and social isolation, the presence of illegitimate opportunities and inappropriate formal control (see also Wikström, 1990a). The indirect impact of the social structure on the rate of delinquency through the social organization dimension is documented by Sampson in this volume. A change in the position of the community in the social structure may also affect formal and informal social controls and the rate of delinquency in that community (Bursik and Grasmick, 1992).

The environment. The environmental context is the isomorphic construct to the biological capacity at the level of the delinquent. It is defines traditionally in criminology by the density and crowding dimensions (Fiueira-McDonough, 1991) and by the physical deterioration of the inner city of the Chicago school. It could now also involve such characteristics as the level of pollution by lead or any other substances. The impact of the physical environment has long been documented (Shaw and McKay, 1969) and it can be stated that the structural and environmental characteristics of the community are contexts that favor or disfavor community control over delinquency. Figure 4 states that a physically deteriorated environment encourages social disorganization and social isolation, the presence of gangs and criminal organizations and often involves repressive formal control. An environmental change could also indirectly modify the rate of delinquency over time.

Social organization. Social disorganization traditionally refers to the weakness of informal networks, it is the loss of community control over its members and the erosion of informal networks (see Sampson, 1988, 1991). It is the inability of organizations, groups and individuals members of a community to solve their common problems collectively (Shoemaker, 1990). This is a sort of bonding, ties between the members of a community that are in nature similar to the individual bonding as in the previous level of explanation of the phenomenon of delinquency. Figure 4, in accordance to lower-class theories (Cohen, 1955; Cloward and Ohlin, 1960), states that when social disorganization is high various deviant sub-cultures exist in the community. It is also expected that there will be more social isolation, more cultural conflicts and less appropriate formal controls (see also

Fiueira-McDonough, 1991) and greater opportunities for crime (Wikström,1990a) in such a situation. Variations in social organization over time should also affect the rate of delinquency.

Social integration. The distinction between structure and culture as long been established in sociology, particularly by Parsons. Following that direction and drawing on Sutherland (Sutherland and Cressey, 1960) constructs of economic and political individualism and on Sellin (1938) notion of culture conflict, we can propose a strong continuity between the egocentrism-allocentrism continuum at the level of the individual and individualism and culture conflict at the level of the community. The Merton (1957) anomie construct and the Angel (1947) social integration notion (cultural, normative, communicative) could be complement or alternative denominations of this construct to social integration. Figure 4 proposes that social disorganization and isolation will increase in deteriorated environment and in low social status community. From existing ecological data, it can be sustained that social disorganization and isolation are reciprocally related. Social disorganization and social disintegration will support the emergence of various subcultures and they will encourage the development of formal social control (Figueira-McDonough, 1991, reports that there is an inverse relationship between social disorganization and formal control). Over time, changes in social integration should produce changes in opportunities and formal control, but also changes in the rate of delinquency.

Legitimate opportunities. In a deteriorated environment and a low socioeconomic status community, various deviant models and numerous illegitimate opportunities will be available to adolescents, such as the retreatist, the criminal and the violent subcultures (this situation is masterly describe by Cloward and Ohlin, 1960). These subcultures and the corresponding black markets (stolen goods businesses, undeclared work, prostitution, and so on) will offer deviant models and they will constitute appropriate opportunities for adolescents living in such a community. In addition, in these communities the resources for conventional activities are insufficient, such as work, playgrounds, sport organizations, art classes, and so on. The existence of these subcultures and illegitimate opportunities will encourages repressive formal control and they will sustain a high rate of delinquency as illustrated in Figure 4. Changes in the level of such opportunities over time should correspond to equivalent changes in the rate of delinquency.

Formal control. Figueira-McDonough (1991) concludes from her review of the literature that social disorganization is a central cause of delinquency necessitating, in turn, the intervention of formal controls or the transfer of many control functions from primary groups to formal organizations. In such a case, law enforcement agencies will be more present and repressive, and in these communities there will also be a proliferation of agencies

Figure 5.

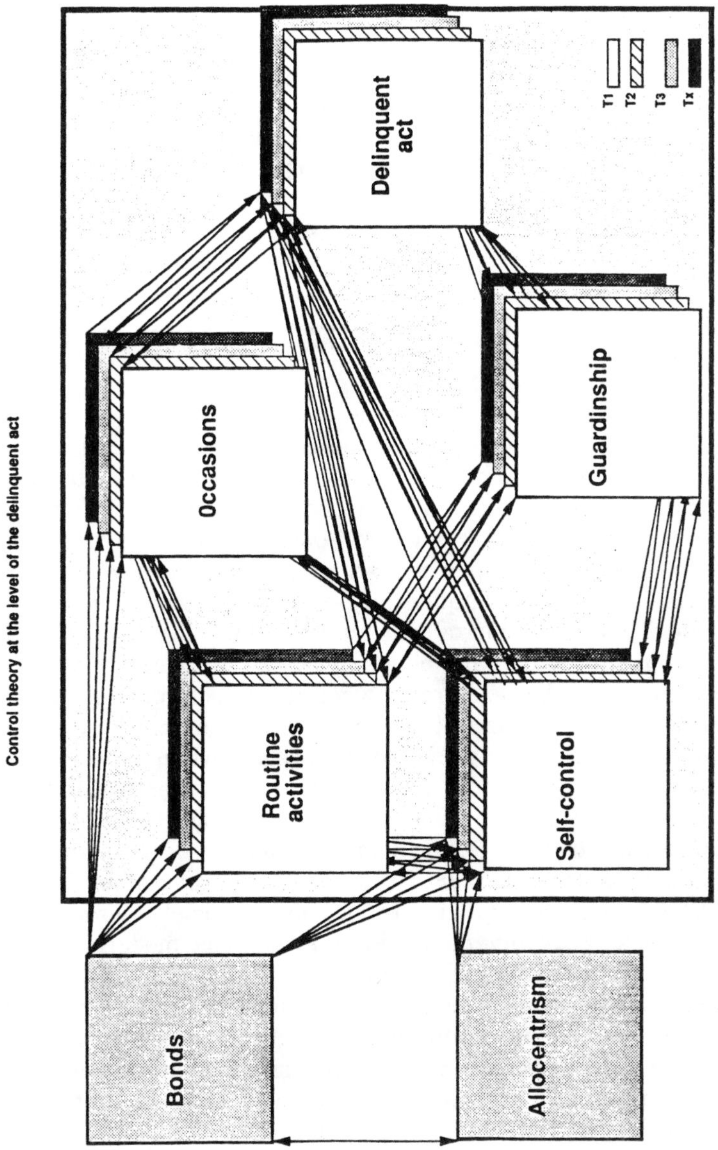
Control theory at the level of the delinquent act
Delinquent act
Occasions
Guardinship
Routine activities
Self-control
Bonds
Allocentrism
T1
T2
T3
Tx

and programs in the domains of the school, the personal counseling, the professional training, the health services, and so on. Figure 4 states that formal control is a proximal cause of the rate of delinquency and that it is reenforced by the presence of various subcultures and illegitimate opportunities.

Figure 4 also indicates that this theory is developmental and interactional. Development in shown by superpose boxes. Interaction is represented by reciprocal and directional arrows. Community control will not only determine the rate of delinquency, it will have a significant impact on family control and indirectly on individual offending as shown by Sampson in this book.

An Integrative Control Theory of the Delinquent Act

Moving to the micro level of definition and explanation of the delinquency phenomenon, the delinquent act, our theory can be state in the following way. Offense control theory assumes that **acting out** is difficult when *routine activities* are supervised by adults, when *self-control* is high, when there is *no occasion* for the commission of a delinquent act, and when *guardianship* is reliable. This regulation of conformity is conditional on the person *allocentrism* and on his *bonds* to society. Alternatively, a delinquent act will be perpetrated when the person self-control is low, when his routine activities are out of the home, when there are numerous occasions to commit crimes and when possible targets are not well protected. These causes of the perpetration of an offense will be more efficient when the ties of the individual to society are tenuous and when the adolescent is egocentric, what Cornish and Clarke (1986) would call background factors. Felson (1986) also refers explicitly to the bonds to society (commitments, attachments, involvements) in his synthetical model of the delinquent act as the handle-unhandle potential offender. Over time, a delinquent act is committed or not depending on the variations in the offense control mechanism. Figure 5 presents our theory.

The dependent variable is the particular criminal offense with its various characteristics (nature of the delinquent act, the mechanic of the perpetration: planning, instrument, accomplices, and so on, the psychological reaction during and after the crime) (see Le Blanc and Fréchette, 1989). The explanatory constructs are isomorphic with the constructs of the other two levels of definition and explanation of the delinquency phenomenon. It is expected that routine activities will be away from the family and the household when the adolescent bond is tenuous and when he lives in a social disorganized community. It expected that self-control will be low if the adolescent is egocentric and if he lives in a community where anomie, cultural conflict and individualism, and social isolation are high. It is expected that occasions to commit a crime will be more frequent if the adolescent is receptive to deviant influences and if he lives in a community where illegitimate opportunities are present and numerous. Finally, it is expected that protections against crimes will be insufficient and that victims will be more vulnerable when formal control is the dominant mode of control and when the adolescent is weakly constrained to conformity.

Our delinquent act control theory relies greatly on Felson (1986) discussion of the relationships between criminal choices, routine activities, informal control, ecology and social control theories. Figure 5 also represent the relationships in a developmental point of view, the superposed boxes, and in an interactional perspective, the bi-directional arrows. The bonding and the maturing processes have been discussed earlier on and they will not be the object of comments in this section.

Routine activities. The individual life-style or the daily activity patterns that disperse the adolescent away from his family (Felson and Gottfredson, 1984) and the household situation (Cohen and Felson, 1979) are highly criminogenic situations. According to routine activity theory, these activities will bring the adolescent in contact with numerous targets or occasions for the commission of a delinquent act, and, particularly, the adolescent will be in contact with targets that are unguarded. Figure 5 states that such routines activities will increase the contacts with unguarded targets and this in proportion to the individual bond to society and in relation to his level of self-control. Changes in routine activities may also modify the probability of the commission of a delinquent act or a transfer from one type of criminal activity to another type of offense.

Self-control. Gottfredson and Hirschi (1990, p. 87) define self-control as "the idea that people differ in the extend to which they are vulnerable to the temptation of the moment" and Cornish and Clarke (1986) introduce similar notions with what they call the previous experiences and learnings and the reactions to chance event. The egocentric person is also describe as impulsive (Fréchette et Le Blanc 1987). Figure 5 indicates that low self-control will persist when the adolescent bonds to society are tenuous and when he is egocentric. The adolescent will then be more likely to prefer routine activities out of the home that offer excitement and thrill, which will, in turn, increase the occasions for the perpetration of a delinquent act.

Occasions. The Chicago school teaches criminologists that in delinquent prone communities there are numerous occasions for the commission of delinquent acts. Cohen and Felson (1979) routine activities theory is using the construct suitable targets to represent the possibilities to commit a delinquent act. The individual makes a rational choice about the suitability of the target (the degree of effort involve, the amount and immediacy of the reward, the likelihood and severity of punishment, and the moral cost involve according to Clarke and Cornish, 1985). The more a target seems suitable, the higher the probability of the commission of the offense, particularly if the adolescent self-control is low and his bond to society weak. Figure 5 also states that the presence of numerous suitable targets in a community is a proximal cause of the commission of a delinquent act by an adolescent.

Guardianship. In Cohen and Felson (1979) routine activity theory, three elements are necessary for the commission of a delinquent act: a likely delinquent, a suitable target, and the absence of a capable guardian against crime. A capable guardian can be a person, a physical protection devise or a specific situation. Figure 5 indicates that the absence of guardianship is a proximal cause of a delinquent act and that a situation is more likely evaluated as such when the adolescent bond to society is weak, his self-control low and when there are suitable targets.

The Three Layered Isomorphic Model

We have outline our integrative control theory for three layers of the delinquency phenomenon, the rate of delinquency, the delinquent, and the delinquent act. Figure 6 presents some of the relationships between these stratums. There are six categories of factors that are represented at each level of definition of the phenomenon of delinquency: the grounds (environment, biological capacity, cognitive and personal development), the milieus (social structure of the community, structural factors, social ties), the objectives of the development of maturity (social integration, allocentrism, self-control), the social conditions (social organization, social bonds, routine activities), the restraints (formal social control, internal and external constraints, guardianship), and the situation (legitimates opportunities, pro-social influences, occasions).

These factors are also sequenced according to their proximity to the dependent variables, they are the predisposing factors (grounds and milieus), the precipitating factors (objectives of development and conditions) and triggering factors (restraints and situations). The model in Figure 6 also implies that there exist some relationships that are not of the isomorphic type. For example, social disorganization may affect the level of guardianship of the suitable targets. In a deteriorated and polluted environment there are higher probabilities that the biological capacity of individuals will be deficient. For example, Wikström (1990a) postulates that urbanization will imply a weaker social control, greater opportunities for crime, more motivated offenders and more criminal events. Sampson (in this book)

Figure 6.

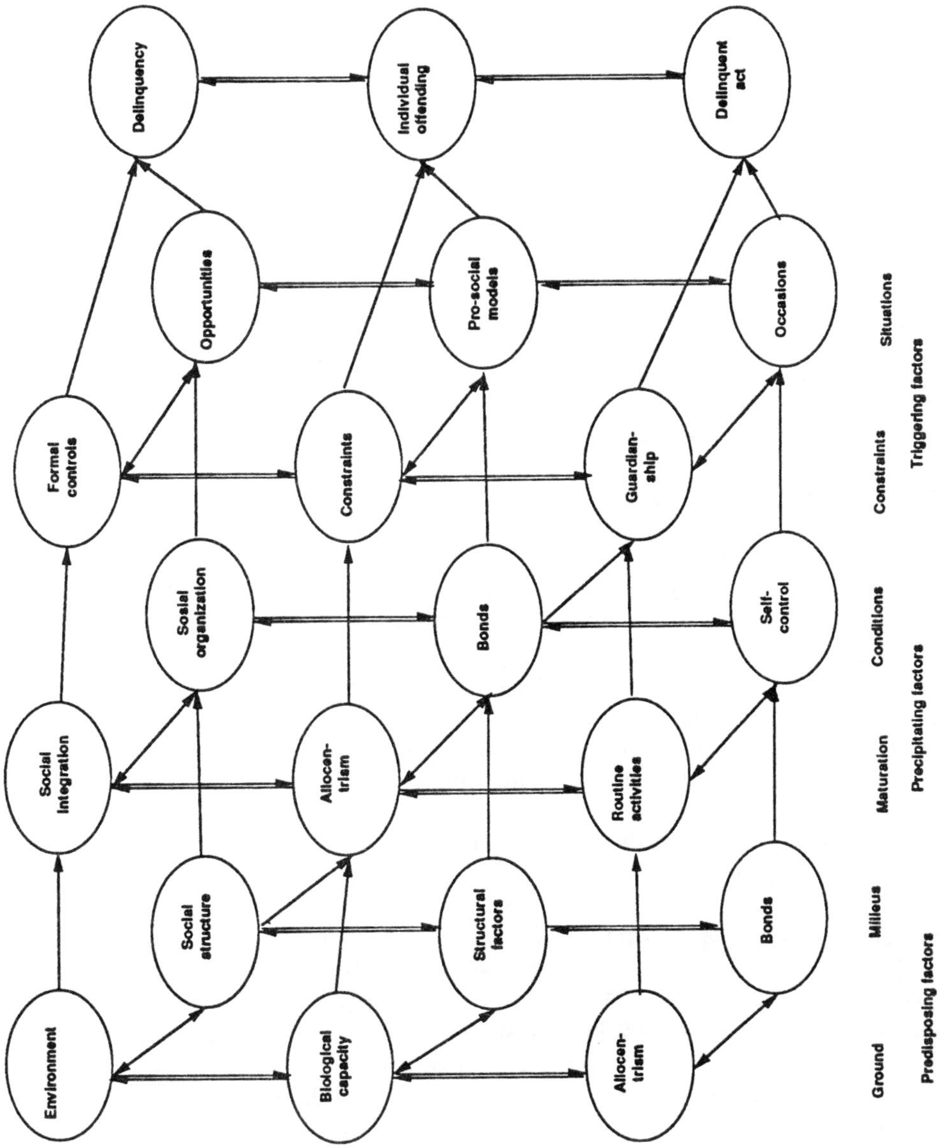

The multilayered integrative control theory

shows that community-level differences in social cohesion and informal control have significant effects on individual-level variations in offending, deviant attitude and association with delinquent peers through family management techniques. There are numerous such relations that could be stated and documented by the literature, however it is not the purpose of this paper to develop to that point the multilayered integrative control theory.

Prevention of Adolescent Delinquency

We have sketched a three layered integrative control theory of adolescent delinquency composed of eighteen explanatory constructs. Each of these constructs represent a set risk factors that implies objectives for prevention programs. These objectives must be addressed to try to limit the negative effect of the risk factors. From the programs describe in the scientific literature, we will select the ones that seems more appropriate in relation to the constructs and the objectives that they involve. We will not use the three layers, the community, the delinquent and the delinquent act, for the following reason. The factors at the level of the delinquent act cannot be treated independently of the factors at the other two levels.

The criminological literature tells us that the occasions to commit a delinquency act and the guardianship of the targets have to be prevented by community level programs and we cannot think of any special reasons to change that point of view. For example, environmental design measures and community surveillance actions are necessarily implemented at a community level. The literature on prevention also indicates that bond and self-control, for their part, can be prevented only by programs focusing on the individual, while routine activities prevention can benefit from actions at the levels of the individual and the community. For example, adolescent routine activities can be affected by actions on parental involvement in conventional activities with their adolescent and by the availability of adult supervised activities in a community. As a consequence of these past experiences, our comprehensive prevention scheme for the prevention of adolescent delinquency will involve a strategy which coordinate two categories of programs, community and individual actions.

Comprehensive prevention strategies have been proposed by the Katzenback report (Burns and Stern, 1967) and the National Advisory Commission on criminal Justice Standards and Goals (1973) in the United States. In Canada, a social development strategy is suggested by Waller and Weiler (1984) and in Quebec by the Bouchard report (1991). There are probably such reports in other countries. However, these propositions are empirical scheme based on inventories of risk factors rather then a theoretically based strategy such as the one proposed by Weis and Hawkins (1979).

The comprehensive prevention strategy outlined in this paper is not intended to be exhaustive, we will only illustrate the consequences of using an multilayered integrative control theory to design a global strategy for the prevention of adolescent delinquency. However, we will indicate for each construct the program objectives that are essential, this independently of the fact that certain programs have been classified as primary, secondary or tertiary by other authors.

Community Prevention of Adolescent Delinquency

The objective of community delinquency prevention is to reduce the rate of delinquency in a particular community or the rate of a specific aspect of the delinquency phenomenon, such as gangs for example. As indicated by Hawkins et al (1992) and Farrington et al (1986), many of the programs that will be suggested are also useful for the prevention of adolescent drug use or other conduct problems such as early pregnancy, school dropout, and so on.

Social structure. Under the construct position of the community in the social structure, the objective is to reduce inequalities between citizens. More often the preventive actions will be generalized governmental programs rather then specific actions in a particular community. They are not directed at the adolescent but toward their parents or other adults in the community.

The social structure dimension has been defined by three main dimensions: poverty, mobility and ethnicity. The impact of poverty can be limited by such programs as guaranteed minimum earnings, particularly a special attention should be given one parent families, and, specially by the development of work opportunities for these populations. Mobility can be influences by suitable and quality subsidized housing and easy access to appropriate health, social, recreational, and educational services, particularly schools of very good quality (physical, services, curriculum, personnel, social climate, and so on) and appropriate day nursery and early kindergarten services to support a more successful integration to primary school (see a successful experiment, Schweinhart et al, 1987). One objective of urban renewal could also be a mix of housing projects targeted at different socioeconomic status groups. Relative to the ethnicity dimension, actions are essential to avoid the constitution of huge ethnic ghettoes, incentives to multi-ethnic housing are to be experienced.

Environment. The low quality of the physical environment is a characteristic of communities with a high rate of delinquency. The density of the population can be reduce by urban planning, particularly when there are some urban renewal with a mix of social and other types of housing. Crowding can be reduce in social housing by constructing apartments of appropriate size. What is more difficult is to limit the physical deterioration of a community because owners do not live in that community and because there are no pressures on city politicians to invest in such a disadvantage community. Community mobilization on that theme is often efficient. These inner city disadvantage communities are often adjacent to old industries and the impact of lead or other types of pollution is important and sometimes very serious. Since we know that lead and other substances can affect significantly the development of children, attention should be given to these problems. To attain these objectives there is a need for the simultaneous involvement of the community and the support of governmental antipollution regulations and programs.

These actions are directed at the rate of delinquency in a community, they can also be concerned with the commission of specific delinquent act (burglary, mugings, and so on). The environmental design perspective proposed by Newman (1972) should be coordinated with the previous environmental actions. It involves redesign of streets and intersections, improved street lighting and transportation, building of appropriate playgrounds, and so on (see for example Lavrakas and Kushmuk, 1986, positive results with environmental design actions).

Social organization. The community organization actions, develop by the Chicago school, have long proven their usefulness to reinstall informal controls in a disorganized community. Sorrentino (1977) elaborates this intervention for the redevelopment of the neighborhood and Curtis (1987) proposes recent examples. In these recent prevention programs, as in the Fagan (1987) example, there are multiple components that are directed at various problems: work, lodging, nutrition, school success, revitalization of the environment, and so on. One component that is often forgotten in these community organization program is the integration of immigrants, this elements is important considering the changing nature of immigration in most northern countries (such as Islamic and undeveloped countries immigrants).

Concerning adolescents directly, participation in the community and in the school organization has to be important objects of attention in these communities. Community organization actions must involve adolescents and youths not only adults and should also be be directed at their specific problems (looking for a job, parenting, and so on). And, we now know which actions have to be taken to increase the quality of the schools (better physical facilities, more qualified personnel, pro-social climate, adapted programs, better moral and civic education), to favors school success (prevention of dropout, peer tutoring, special services, early identification of learning problems), and to prevent school delinquency and vandalism (see Gottfredson and Gottfredson, 1985; Côté et al, 1988; Le Blanc and Janosz, 1992; for comprehensive sets of school improvement programs).

The improvement of informal control in the disadvantage communities must also involve actions at the level of the commission of the delinquent act. Facilities for sports, social, and artistic activities and opportunities to meet and discuss significant problems (such as youth centers) must be available to adolescents. However, if we follow Felson and Gottfredson (1984) observations concerning routine activities, these and other pro-social activities should be in the presence of adults and, particularly, activities outside the household should be supervised by adults. Loitering in group and away from home is a particularly important target for the prevention of delinquent acts during adolescence.

Social integration. Anomie, individualism and culture conflict are pointed out as important risk factors for high rates of delinquency. Community organization will reduce disorganization and social isolation. However, there is a need for actions that will facilitate the contacts and the understanding of various racial, ethnic, religious, and social groups with the intention of reducing culture conflicts. Adolescents and youths must be directly involved in the development and operation of social organization and integration actions that concern them. School, recreational, and other activities must involve the participation of adolescents from diverse social and ethnic groups. Civic and moral education is probably a pertinent way for reducing anomie. It is difficult to distinguish a specific actions that do not have a simultaneous impact on social disorganization as well as on culture conflict, anomie and individualism. Increase informal control encourages social integration and the reverse. Community organization seems the major instrument for the reduction of social isolation and the increase of informal control.

Legitimate opportunities. In disadvantage communities, opportunities for conventional activities are often rare and the presence of deviant and delinquent subcultures is often significant. Three convergent types of actions are necessary in these communities to increase the prosocial influences. First, sports and cultural facilities for children and adolescent have to be optimally developed, part-time and full time work have to be available for adolescents, and social facilities have to be sufficient (youth clubs, scout groups, and so on). Second, strong repressive actions have to be undertaken, relative to prostitution, drugs, organized crime, marginal business, and so on, to limit the significance of illegitimate models and the presence of illegitimate opportunities. Third, specific delinquency prevention programs must exist concomitantly: suppression of retreatist, conflict and criminal youth gangs; street worker programs, prevention clubs, individual support for ex-gang members, and so on (see Spergel et al, 1990).

Not only does a comprehensive strategy must include the reduction of these macro-opportunities for the delinquent, but it must also incorporates actions on occasions for the commission of delinquent acts. Clarke and Mayhew (1980) call the reduction of these possibilities the hardening of targets (stronger materials, locks, bars, and so on) and the removing of targets (eliminating the target, such as coin boxes in telephone kiosks, or the means to commit the crime, such as arms in planes) (see also Rosenbaum, 1986, for other examples of such programs). Another example of an important of objective would be the reduction of the availability of drugs in school and in the community (Hawkins et al, 1992).

Formal controls. In the disadvantage communities, the formal control has to be transferred from agencies to the community, from formal agencies to informal group through the community organization actions. However, deterrence must be stronger. Community policing may be a mean of increasing the certainty of law enforcement (see Rosenbaum, 1986, for community policing experiments), there is also a need to increase the promptness of the administration of justice and the assurance of an appropriate sentence.

Deterrence must also be increase at another level, the stratum of the commission of specific delinquent acts. Informal and formal surveillance and protection of the community against crime must be increased (see Rosenbaum, 1986, for examples of such programs)

Individual Prevention of Adolescent Delinquency

In this section, we will focus mainly on the adolescent period, however we will identify objectives that have to be addressed earlier on in the life of these individuals if society wants to have a fair chance of reducing chronic delinquency, not only occasional delinquency during adolescence. Again in this section, we do not have the pretension to be exhaustive, we will focus our attention on the essential preventive actions according to the integrative control theory.

Structural factors. The main structural factors that have been showed to be pertinent for the regulation of adolescent delinquency (Kempf, 1992; Le Blanc and Caplan, 1993) are the age, the sex, the social class, and the type of family. If there are appropriate programs against poverty and mobility in disadvantage communities, as describe at the previous layer, the essential actions at the level of the delinquent is to make sure that these programs against poverty are targeted at the right families, particularly most specialists would now agree that they should be concentrated on one parent families, and, specifically, adolescent mothers (Bouchard, 1991).

Biological capacity. Since it is well known that the biological capacity of the child is affected by the mother health before and after birth, all prevention programs directed to that problem in disadvantage communities are essential (Bouchard, 1991). These educational and support programs have to be extended to families that have older children since sleeping and eating habits are often deficient in these communities, particularly many children do not eat before going to school or do not bring a lunch to school when they should. In addition of these and other health care actions, there is a need for the detection of neuropsychological and other dysfunctions and to limit the impact of these risk factors (see for example Moffit, 1990).

Bonds. There are three categories of bonds to society for the adolescent: the attachment to parents and to other persons in authority, the commitment to institutions, particularly school, and the involvement in conventional activities. The main problems with the bonds is that they are created from birth on for the attachment to persons and from six years old on for the commitment to education. As a consequence, when adolescence arrives it is difficult, without a long therapy, to restructure these bonds completely.

Attachment to parents, which is the best family predictor of adult criminality (Le Blanc, 1992a), needs early family support programs with home visiting and parenting counsel (see Hawkins et al, 1992). During adolescence, the attachment is manifested in two ways, communication and recognition. Programs that will help parents of adolescents to communicate adequately with them and to recognized their worth may be an effective preventive action since we have showed that this attachment construct mediate the impact of the other family variables on the monitoring-management dimension which is the proximal factor of adolescent offending (Le Blanc, 1992a). Since family conflict often support a tenuous attachment between the adolescent and his parents (Le Blanc, 1992a), services should be available to the parents in their community to resolve these problems before a divorce. In a mother based family, a male figure could be a significant element (such program as Big brothers and others) since it is a major factor of the continuation of delinquency (Fréchette and Le Blanc, 1987). It is also possible that the development of an attachment to persons in authority, a teacher, a coach, and so on, could serve as a compensatory mechanism, some delinquents increase their attachment to conventional adults during late adolescence (Le Blanc, 1993).

For the adolescent, the most important commitment is relative to education. Since this commitment is builded on school success

(Le Blanc et al, 1992b), there is a need for early childhood education programs, parent involvement in school work supervision all along schooling, interactive teaching, classroom management and cooperative learning, and tutoring by older successful peers (see Hawkins et al, 1992). And, if these actions are complemented by shared decision making, student services, academic innovations, higher education expectations, and curriculum restructuring it has been showed that the commitment to education increases and dropout diminishes (Gottfredson and Gottfredson, 1985; Le Blanc and Janosz, 1992).

Concerning the involvement in conventional activities, we have indicate the necessity for these opportunities at the community level. We should particularly stress here the importance of such activities with parents and, specifically with fathers since it has been showed that it is an important factor in the continuation of delinquency (Fréchette and Le Blanc, 1987, Farrington, 1991).

Allocentrism. The objectives of the preventive actions relative to the personality of the adolescent is the development of his allocentrism, of his cognitive capacity and of his level of self-control. Once again the roots of the egocentric personality and of the impulsivity are long and solid since this personality profile is present as early as ten years old (Le Blanc et al, 1991) and it could probably be traced back to the difficult temperament children (Wilson and Herrnstein, 1985)//.

The treatment of the egocentric personality has not been very effective. Ross and Fabiano (1985) are proposing an interesting congnitive-behvioral interpersonal social skills training that could be applied to early adolescent whit an egocentric personality. There are also some other treatment programs that could be used as a preventive measure: eliciting and changing values, social skills training and self-esteem enhancement (see McGuire and Priestley, 1991). There are also various promising cognitive behavioral interventions with aggressive children and adolescent (Holin, 1990; Goldstein et al, 1989). These preventive actions could start much earlier on with children with a difficult temperament since it is documented that difficult temperament children are more often delinquents (see Wilson and Herrnstein, 1985). Programs of parental support are also experienced with these children (Bouchard, 1991).

From the point of view of the commission of a delinquent act, self-control is particularly important. Numerous authors are proposing that at risk children and adolescent be involved in training programs to increase self-control, that help to avoid risk-taking behavior, and to learn problem-solving skills (McGuire and Priestley, 1991, Goldstein et al, 1989, and Holin, 1990, are proposing repertories of such trainings; see also Hawkins et al, 1992, for programs relative to the avoidance of smoking and alcohol and drug use).

Prosocial influences. Withstanding that there are actions on deviant subcultures, illegitimate opportunities and crime occasions, at the level of the delinquent the anti-social influences can be of many types. The principal ones for adolescent are parental models, mass media messages, and peer models.

Parental alcohol and drug use and criminality are enduring correlates of adolescent delinquency (Wilson and Herrnstein, 1985; Farrington et al, 1986). Whatever the mechanism by which modeling happens, it is important that mental health, alcohol and drug abuse programs are available to parents and that they are encourage to follow them.

The type of television viewing by suggestible children is associated with aggressive behavior (see Wilson and Herrnstein, 1985) and it is also possible that other media (videos, and so on) can produce the same effect on aggression and sexual activity. It should be a prevention target at the levels of the community and the individual. Programs that involve the control of television viewing by parents, development of the imaginative life and other skills have been experimented with promising results (Tremblay and Charlebois, 1988).

Peer drug use and delinquency are associated with the adolescent own drug use and delinquency (see Elliott et al, 1985, 1989). Two strategies are proposed to counter the influence of deviant peers, insert potential delinquent in prosocial groups (Feldman et al, 1983) and train adolescent to resist peer pressure (Tobler, 1986; Hawkins et al, 1992). Peer rejection in elementary grades is associated with delinquency (Coie, 1992) and social skills training does have a positive impact on interpersonal behavior but not on subsequent deviance (Hawkins et al, 1992). Positive peer culture in school and in the community is another mean of increasing the impact of conventional peers (Vorrath and Brendtro, 1974).

Constraints. External constraints such as regulations, supervision and discipline are imposed by the family, the school and other social institutions. These constraints can take the form of internalized norms such as the beliefs in the moral validity of the law and the form of the perception of the risks of an arrest or of any other penalty (Le Blanc, 1992b).

Family management practices are highly associate with adolescent delinquency (Loeber and Stouthamer-Loeber, 1986; Le Blanc, 1992a). And, Patterson (1982) proposes a behavioral training scheme to show the appropriate monitoring and discipline of children to parents. The results are positive (Loeber, 1987) but with children rather then with adolescent (Reid, 1983). Parental management training can then be an effective preventive action during childhood.

Concerning the beliefs in the moral validity of the law and the external control by the various institutions and the perceptual deterrence, these factors are not usually the object of preventive actions. However, the techniques for eliciting and changing values reviewed by McGuire and Priestly (1991) could be used for the purpose of understanding social reaction. School (Le Blanc et al, 1992a) and criminal justice (see Farrington et al, 1986) labeling are controversial factor of adolescent delinquency. Diversion from criminal justice is also a controversial preventive measure (Kobrin and Klein, 1983).

Conclusion

In 1764, Cesare Beccaria wrote: "Il vaut mieux prévenir les crimes que de les punir; tel est le but principal de toute législation, laquelle est l'art de rendre les hommes les plus heureux possible ..."[1] (1965, p. 74). In 1987. James Q. Wilson stated: "our knowledge of delinquency prevention is not sufficient to permit us to do more than sketch some possibilities. The value of the suggested interventions must be further assessed, and the complex problems of institutional structure and targeting clients must be solved in the light of practical experience. Despite all the uncertainties and unanswered questions, ignoring the promising leads that exist would be a mistake, as would rushing ahead with large-scale programs as if the uncertainties and questions did not exist." (p. 308).

Today, no criminologist needs to be convinced that the prevention of adolescent delinquency is necessary. The period since Beccaria, and particularly since Powers and Witmer (1951) classic experiment, should have been sufficient to do so. Now, we know that many prevention programs are promising, but it is too early to favour any or to apply any of them to the whole population of adolescent because results are never clear-cut. There is no risk factor that is a necessary and sufficient condition of adolescent delinquency and there is, consequently, no panacea for its prevention. In this paper, we have taken the position that there is a need to experiment a new strategy for the prevention of adolescent delinquency.

A strategy by which a set of prevention programs is put together, a set that is comprehensive and coordinate. Not a set based on an inventory of risk factors, but a set bounded together by a multilayered integrative control theory. A theory of delinquency, of the delinquent, and of the delinquent act which imposes that actions be taken at all these level simultaneously. Such a theory, from a practical point of view, maximizes the coordination between the various preventive actions.

The multilayered integrative control theory also proposes isomorphic constructs that delimit the objectives for preventive actions. The constructs are the position in the social structure and the environment or the biological capacity as contexts in which control mechanisms are operating. These control mechanisms are the bonding, the maturating, the modeling and the constraining processes. These constructs assure the comprehensive character of the prevention strategy. In addition, they offer the advantage of avoiding the habitual situation when programs are targeted at one level of the definition of the delinquency phenomenon without any actions at other levels. For example, the situation of a community where there are programs to diminish the occasions for the commission of delinquent acts and where there are no concurrent action to eliminate illegitimate opportunities or to neutralize deviant models or gangs. Or, for example, the situation when there is an intervention on parental monitoring and discipline without any intervention on parental deviant models, parents conflict, family bonds, parents difficult living situation.

A theory is then a useful instrument for the coordination of various preventive actions and it is a major way to foster comprehensiveness in the prevention of adolescent delinquency. It is also a sound scientific devise, since control theory is the dominant criminological theory with the capability to be elaborated in such a way that it is pertinent to all the levels of definition and explanation of delinquency. Control theory also offers the possibility to incorporate most of the basic criminological theoretical constructs. It is expected that a comprehensive strategy for the prevention of adolescent delinquency, such as the one proposed in this paper, will be more successful than any specific prevention programs. However, it has to be experimentally demonstrated and the components of the global strategy have to be further developed. The theory is also far from completely elaborated. In this paper, we only illustrated the directions it should take without thoroughly operationalizing such a global strategy for the prevention of adolescent delinquency.

If a theory is for us a necessary instrument for the conception of a comprehensive and coordinate prevention strategy, there is another essential condition. This condition is the adaptation of the prevention strategy to the characteristics of the community and its particular adolescent delinquency problem. A theoretically based comprehensive prevention strategy can be elaborated only after a careful study of the particular situation of a community. In a specific community, some risks factors may be inoperative while others may be more significant and it is for this reason that some epidemiological and descriptive studies have to be undertaken before the strategy is finalized in a particular community. Empirical data and an integrative theory are the two essential prerequisite to any action of prevention of adolescent delinquency. Wikström (1990b) proposes a working model in which a set of surveys is done before the suggested actions are definitely chosen and in his model the preventive actions are also evaluated, then modified, then reevaluated, and so on. The Stockholm project (Wikström, 1990c) has some features of an integrated comprehensive prevention strategy: it covers the three levels of definition of delinquency, many criminological constructs are present, theories are outlined, empirical surveys are undertaken before the elaboration of the preventive strategy. However, many constructs of control theory are absent, the integration between the sub-projects is not always evident, the community perspective is more developed then the individual point of view. Withstanding these limits, it is to our knowledge the most ambitious prevention project undertaken until now.

The major objective of a comprehensive prevention strategy is to advance toward a fair society, particularly for adolescents from disadvantage communities. However, it is not expected that a theoretically based strategy will eliminate delinquency. It should facilitate action of governments and voluntary organizations and it should be more efficient then an uncoordinated and a fragmented strategy of prevention of adolescent delinquency.

Notes

[1] Translation of the author: "it is better to prevent than to punish crime; this is the main objective of laws, which is the art giving as much as possible happiness to men"

References

Angel, R.C. (1947). The social integration of American cities of more than 100,000 population. *American Sociological Review,* 12: 335–342.

Arnold, W.R. & Brungardt, T. (1983). *Juvenile Misconduct and Delinquency.* Boston, Houghton Mifflin.

Beccaria, C. (1965). *Des délits et des peines.* Genève, Librairie Droz.

Bernard, T.J. (1987). Structure and control: Reconsidering Hirschi's concept of commitment. *Justice Quarterly,* 4 (3), 409–424.

Blumstein, A., Cohen, J., Roth, J.A. & Visher, C.A. (1986). *Criminal career and "career criminals".* Washington: National Academy Press.

Bouchard, C. (1991). *Un Québec fou de ses enfants.* Rapport du groupe de travail pour les jeunes. Québec, Ministère de la santé et des services sociaux.

Burns, V.M. & Stern, L.W. (1967). *The prevention of juvenile delinquency.* Task force report: Juvenile delinquency and youth crime. The President's Commission on Law Enforcement and Administration of Justice. Washington, U.S. Government Printing Office.

Bursik, R.J. (1988). Social disorganization and theories of crime and delinquency, Problems and prospects. *Criminology,* 26: 519–552.

Bursik, R.J. & Grasmick, H. (1992). Neighborhoods and crime: A systemic approach. Lexington, Heath.

Catalano, R.F. & Hawkins, J.D. (1986). *The social development model: A theory of antisocial behavior.* Paper presented at the Safeco lectureship on crime and delinquency, University of Washington.

Clarke, R.V.G. & Mayhew, P. (1980). *Designing out crime.* London, Her Majesty's Stationary Office.

Clarke, R.V. & Cornish, D.B. (1985). Modeling offender's decisions: A framework for research and policy. In M. Tonry and N. Morris. *Crime and justice: An annual review,* 6. Chicago, University of Chicago Press.

Cloward, R.A. & Ohlin, L.E. (1960). *Delinquency and opportunity: A theory of delinquent gangs.* New York: Free Press.

Cohen, A.K. (1955). *Delinquent boys:* The culture of the gang. New York: Free Press.

Cohen, L.E. & Felson, M. (1979). Property Crime Rates in the United states: A Macrodynamic Analysis 1947–1977, with ex ante Forecasts for the mid – 1980. *American Journal of Sociology,* 86: 90–118.

Coie, J.D. (1992). Toward a theory of peer rejection. In S.R. Asher, J.D. Coie. *Peer rejection in childhood.* New York, Cambridge University Press.

Conger, R. (1976). Social control and social learning models of delinquency: a synthesis. *Criminology,* 14 (1), 17–40.

Cornish, D. & Clarke, R. (1986). Introduction. In D.B. Cornish and R.V. Clarke. *The reasoning criminal.* Rational choice perspectives of offending. New York, Springer-Verlag.

Côté, G., Le Blanc, M., Ouellet, G. & Pronovost, A. (1988). *Violence et délinquance à l'école: inventaire de mesures préventives.* Montréal, Commission des écoles catholiques de Montréal, Service des études.

Cullen, F.T. (1985). *Rethinking crime and deviance theory: the emergence of a structuring tradition.* Ottowa, Rowman & Allanheld.

Curtis, L.A. (1987). Policies to prevent crime: Neighborhood, family, and employment strategies. *The Annals of the Academy of Political and Social Science,* 494.

Cusson, M. (1983). *Delinquency, why?* Toronto, University of Toronto Press.

Denno, D.H. (1985). Sociological and human development explanations of crime: Conflict and consensus. *Criminology,* 23: 711–741.

Durkheim, E. (1895). *Les règles de la méthode sociologique.* Paris: Presses universitaires de France.

Durkheim, E. (1934). *De l'éducation morale.* Paris: Presses universitaires de France.

Elliott, D.S., Huizinga, D. & Ageton, S.S. (1985). *Explaining delinquency and drug use.* Beverly Hills: Sage publications.

Elliott, D.S., Huizinga, D. & Ménard, S. (1989). *Multiple Problem Youth: Delinquency, Substance abuse, and Mental health problems.* New York: Springer-Verlag.

Empey, L.T. (1978). *American delinquency.* Homewood, Dorsey Press.

Fagan, J. (1987). Neighborhood education, mobilization, and organization for juvenile crime prevention. *The Annals of the Academy of Political and Social Science,* 494: 54–70.

Farrington, D.P. (1991). Childhood aggression and adult violence: Early precursors and later life outcomes. In D.J. Pepler and K.H. Rubin. *The development and treatment of childhood aggression.* Hillsdale, Lawrence Erlbaum.

Farrington, D.P. (1992). Career criminal research: Lessons for crime prevention. *Studies on Crime and Crime Prevention,* 1, 1: 7–29.

Farrington, D.P., Ohlin, L.E. & Wilson, J.Q. (1986). *Understanding and controlling crime: Toward a new strategy.* New York, Springer-Verlag.

Feldman, M.P. (1978). *Criminal behavior: a psychological analysis.* New York, John Wiley & Sons.

Feldman, R.A., Caplinger, T.E. & Wodarski, J.S. (1983). *The St-Louis conundrum: the effective treatment of antisocial youths.* Englewood Cliffs, Prentice Hall.

Felson, M. (1986). Linking criminal choice, routine activities, informal control and criminal outcomes. In D.B. Cornisk, & R.V. Clarke (Ed.), *The reasoning criminal: Rational choice perspectives on offending* (pp.119–128). New York: Springer-Verlag.

Felson, M. & Gottfredson, M. (1984). Social indicators of adolescent activities near peers and parents. *Journal of Marriage and the Family,* 46: 709–714.

Finckenauer, J.O. (1982). Scared straight and the panacea phenomenon. Englewood Cliffs, Prentice Hall.

Fiueira-McDonough, J. (1991). Community structure and delinquency: A typology. *Social Service Review,* 65, 1: 68–91.

Fréchette, M. & Le Blanc, M. (1987). *Délinquances et délinquants.* Montréal, Gaétan Morin.

Gibbs, J. (1985). The methodology of theory construction in criminology. In R. F. Meier (Ed.), *Theoretical Methods in Criminology* (pp.23–50). Beverly Hills: Sage Publications.

Goldstein, A.P., Glick, B., Irwin, M-J, Pask-McCartney, C. & Rubana, I. (1989). *Reducing delinquency, Intervention in the community.* New York, Pergamon.

Gottfredson, G.C. & Gottfredson, D.C. (1985). *Victimization in schools.* New York: Plenum Press.

Gottfredson, M.R. & Hirschi, T. (1990). *A general theory of crime.* Stanford, Stanford University Press.

Hagan, J. (1988). *Structural criminology.* New Brunswick, Rutgers University Press.

Hawkins, J.D., Catalano, R.F. & Miller, J.Y. (1992). Risk and protective factors for alcohol and other drug problems in adolescence and early adulthood: Implications for substance abuse prevention. *Psychological Bulletin.*

Hirschi, T. (1969). *Causes of delinquency.* Berkely: University of California Press.

Hirschi, T. (1979). Separate an unequal is better. *Journal of Research in Crime and Delinquency,* 16 (1), 34–38.

Hirschi, T. (1989). Exploring alternatives to integrated theory. In Messner, S.F., Krohn, M.D., Liska, A.E. *Theoretical integration in the study of deviance and crime: Problems and prospects.* Albany, State University of New York Press.

Hirschi, T. & Gottfredson, M.R. (1987). The distinction between crime and criminality. In T. Hartnagel, & R. Silverman (Ed.), *Critique and explanation* (pp.55–69). New Brunswick: Transaction Books.

Hodgins, S. (1985). Biological factors implicated in the development of criminal behaviors. In R. Linden. *Criminology, A Canadian perspective.* Toronto, Holt, Rinehart, Winston.

Holin, C.R. (1990). *Cognitive-behavioral interventions with young offenders.* New York, Pergamon Press.

Johnson, R.E. (1979). *Juvenile delinquency and its origins: An integrated approach.* Cambridge: Cambridge University Press.

Kempf, K. (1992). Hirschi's theory of social control: is it fecund but not yet fertile? *Advances in Theoretical Criminology,* 4.

Kobrin, S. & Klein, M.W. (1983). *Community Treatment of Juvenile Offenders:* The DSO Experiments. Beverly Hills, Sage Publications.

Kornhauser, R.R. (1978). *Social sources of delinquency: An appraisal of analytic models* . Chicago: University of Chicago Press.

Laub, J.H. & Sampson, R. (1988). Unraveling families and delinquency: A reanalysis of the Gluecks' data. *Criminology,* 26: 355–380.

Lavrakas, P.J. & Kushmuk, J.W. (1986). Evaluation crime prevention through environmental design: The Portland commercial demonstration project. In D. P. Rosenbaum. *Community crime prevention, Does it work?* Beverly Hills, Sage Publications.

Le Blanc, M. (1991a). La prévention de la délinquance chez les adolescents, une approche globale, intégrée et différentielle. In *Recueil des études commandées par le Groupe de travail pour les jeunes.* Québec, Ministère de la santé et des services sociaux.

Le Blanc, M. (1992). Late Adolescence Deceleration of Criminal Activity and Development of Self and Social Control: Concomitant Changes for Normative and Delinquent Samples. *Studies on Crime and Crime Prevention,* 1,1.

Le Blanc, M. (1992a). Family dynamics, Adolescent Delinquency and Adult Criminality. *Psychiatry,* 55: 236–253.

Le Blanc, M. (1992b). The relative importance of internal and external constraints in the explanation of late adolescence delinquency and adult criminality. J. McCord. *Coercion and punishment in long-term perspectives.* London, Cambridge University Press.

Le Blanc, M. (1992c, submitted). *Family, School, Delinquency and Criminality, The Predictive Power of an elaborated Social Control Theory for Male.*

Le Blanc, M. & Biron, L. (1980). *Vers une théorie integrative de la régulation de la conduite délinquante des garçons.* Montréal, groupe de recherche sur l'inadaptation juvénile, Université de Montréal.

Le Blanc, M. & Caplan, A. (1993) Theoretical formalization, a necessity: the example of Hirschi's bonding theory. *Advances in Theoretical Criminology,* 4: 239–343.

Le Blanc, M. & Fréchette, M. (1989). *Male Criminal Activity, from childhood through Youth: Multilevel and developmental perspectives.* New York, Springer-Verlag.

Le Blanc, M., Ouimet, M. & Tremblay, R.E. (1988). An integrative control theory of delinquent behavior: a validation 1976–1985. *Psychiatry,* 51: 164–176.

Le Blanc, M., Vallières, E. & McDuff, P. (1992a). Adolescents' school experience and self-reported offending: A longitudinal test of a social control theory. *International journal of Youth and Adolescence,* 8: 197–247.

Le Blanc, M., Vallières, E. & McDuff, P. (1992b, submitted). *School experience, self-reported delinquency, and adult criminality.* The predictive power of a social control theory for male adolescent.

Le Blanc, M., McDuff, P., Charlebois, P., Gagnon, C., Larrivée, S. & Tremblay, R.E. (1991). Social and psychological consequences, at 10 years old, of an earlier onset of self-reported delinquency. *Psychiatry,* 54, 1: 133–147.

Lemay, M. (1973). Psychopathologie juvénile: les désordres de la conduite chez l'enfant et l'adolescent. Paris, Fleurus (2 vol.).

Lenski, G. (1988). Retinking macrosociological theory. *American Sociological Review,* 53: 163–171.

Lerner, R.M. (1986). Concepts and Theories of Human Development. New York, Random House.

Loeber, R. (1987). What policy makers and practionners can learn from family studies of juvenile conduct problems and delinquency. In Wilson, J.Q. & Loury, G.C. *From children to citizens, Volume III:* Families, schools, and delinquency prevention. New York, Springer.

Loeber, R. & Le Blanc, M. (1990). Toward a developmental criminology. In Tonry, M. & Morris, N., *Crime and justice: an annual review,* 12: 373–473. Chicago, The University of Chicago Press.

Loeber, R. & Stouthamer-Loeber, M. (1986). Family factors as correlates and predictors of juvenile conduct problems and delinquency. In Tonry, M. & Morris, N., *Crime and justice: An annual review.* 8 Chicago, University of Chicago Press.

Lorion, R.P., Tolan, P.H. & Wahler, R.G. (1987). Prevention. In H. C. Quay. *Handbook of juvenile delinquency.* New York, John Wiley & Sons.

Lundman, R.J. (1984). *Prevention and control of juvenile delinquency.* New York, Oxford University Press.

Mailloux, N. (1971). *Jeunes sans dialogue.* Paris, Fleurus.

Mannhein, H. (1965). *Comparative criminology* (Vol. II). London, Routledge and Kegan Paul Ltd.

Matsueda, R.L. (1988). The current status of differential association theory. *Crime and delinquency,* 34: 277–306.

Matza, D. (1964). *Delinquency and Drift.* NY: John Wiley & Sons Inc.

McGuire, J. & Priestley, P. (1991). *Offending behavior: Skills and stratagems for going strait.* London, B T Batsford.

Merton, R.K. (1957). *Social theory and social structure.* New York: Free Press.

Messner, S.F., Krohn, M.D. & Liska, A.E. (1989). *Theoretical integration in the study of deviance and crime: Problems and prospects.* Albany, State University of New York Press.

Moffit, T.E. (1990). The neuropsychology of juvenile delinquency: A critical review. In Tonry, M. & Morris, N., *Crime* *and justice: An annual review,* 12. Chicago, The University of Chicago Press.

Muchielli, R. (1965). *Comment ils deviennent délinquants: genèse et développement de la socialisation et de la dissocialité.* Paris, Éditions sociales françaises.

National Advisory Commission on Criminal Justice Standards and Goals (1973). *Community crime prevention.* Washington, U.S. Department of Justice, U.S. Government Printing Office.

Newman, O. (1972). *Defensive space: crime prevention through urban design.* New York, MacMillan.

Ouimet, M. & Le Blanc, M. (1993). Événements de vie et poursuite de la carrière criminelle au cours de l'âge adulte. *Revue internationale de criminologie et de police technique.*

Paternoster, R. (1987). The deterrent effect of the perceived certainty and severity of punishment: A review of the evidence and issues. *Justice Quarterly,* 4: 173.

Patterson, G.R. (1982). *Coercive family process.* Eugène, Castalia.

Pearson, F.S. & Weiner, N.A. (1985). Toward an Integration of Criminological Theories. *The Journal of Criminal Law and Criminology,* 76: 116–150.

Pinatel, J. (1963). *Traité de criminologie.* Paris, Dalloz.

Powers, E. & Witmer, H. (1951). An experiment in the prevention of delinquency: The Cambridge-Somerville youth study. New York, Columbia University Press.

Quetelet, A. (1835). *Sur l'homme et le développement de ses facultés, ou essai de physique sociale.* Paris, Bachelier.

Reid, J.B. (1983). *Home-based treatment for multiple offending delinquents.* Eugène, Oregon Social Learning Center.

Reid, L.D. (1989). A path analytic examination of differential social control theory. *Journal of drug education,* 19: 139–156.

Rosenbaum, D.P. (1986). *Community crime prevention, Does it work?* Beverly Hills, Sage Publications.

Ross, R.P. & Fabiano, E.A. (1985). *Time to think.* A cognitive model for delinquency prevention and offender rehabilitation. Johnson City, Institute for social sciences and arts, Inc.

Sampson, R. (1988). Local friendship ties and community attachment in mass society. *American Sociological Review,* 53: 766–79.

Sampson, R. (1991). Linking micro and macrolevel dimensions of community social organization. *Social Forces,* 70: 43–64.

Schweinhart, L.J. (1987). Can preschool programs help prevent delinquency? In Wilson, J.Q. & Loury, G.C. *From children to citizens,* Volume III: Families, schools, and delinquency prevention. New York, Springer Verlag.

Sellin, T. (1938). *Culture conflict and Crime.* New York, Social Science Research Council.

Shaw, C.R., McKay, H.D. (1969). *Juvenile delinquency and urban areas* (2th edition). Chicago, University of Chicago Press.

Shoemaker, D.J. (1990). *Theories of delinquency: An examination of explanations of delinquent behavior.* New York, Oxford University Press.

Short, J.F. (1985). The Level of Explanation Problem in Criminology. In R.F. Meier. *Theoretical Methods in Criminology.* Beverley Hills, Sage Publications.

Short, J.F. (1989). Exploring Integration of the Theoretical Levels of Explanation: Notes on Juvenile delinquency. In Messner, S.F., Krohn, M.D., Liska, A.E. (1989). *Theoretical integration in the study of deviance and crime: Problems and prospects.* Albany, State University of New York Press.

Sorrentino, A. (1977). *Organizing against crime: Redeveloping the neighborhood.* New York, Human Sciences Press.

Spergel, I.A. (1990). *Youth gangs: Problem and response.* Chicago, School of Social service administration, University of Chicago.

Sutherland, E. H. & Cressey, D.R. (1960). *Principles of criminology* (6th edition). Chicago, Lippincott Co.

Szabo, D., Le Blanc, M., Deslauriers, L. & Gagnée, D. (1968). Interprétations psycho-culturelles de l'inadaptation juvénile dans la société de masse contemporaine. *Acta criminologica,* I: 9–134.

Tarde, G. (1924). *La criminalité comparée.* Paris, Alcan.

Thornberry, T.P. (1987). Toward an interactional theory of delinquency. Criminology, 25(4), 963–892.

Thornberry, T.P., Lizotte, A.J., Korhn, M.D. & Farnworth, M. (1990). *The role of delinquent peers in the initiation of delinquent behavior.* Washington, Annual meetings of the American Sociological association.

Tobler, N.S. (1986). Meta-analysis of 143 adolescent drug prevention programs: Quantitative outcome results of program participants compared to a control or comparison group. *Journal of Drug Issues,* 16: 537–567.

Tremblay, R.E. & Charlebois, P. (1988). *La prévention du développement de comportement antisociaux chez les jeunes garçons agressifs, effets observés à la fin de l'intervention.* Montréal, Groupe de recherche sur l'inadaptation pychosociale chez l'enfant, Université de Montréal.

Udry, J.R. (1988). Biological predisposition and social control in adolescent sexual behavior. *American Sociological Review,* 53: 709–722.

Vorrath, H.H. & Brendtro, L.K. (1974). *Positive peer culture.* Chicago, Aldine.

Wagner, D.G. & Berger, J. (1985). Do sociological theories grow? *American Journal of Sociology,* 90: 697–728.

Waller, I., Weiler, D. (1984). *La prévention du crime par le développement social.* Document de base et de référence. Ottawa, Conseil canadien de développement social.

Weis, J.G. & Hawkins, J.D. (1979). *Preventing delinquency: The social development approach.* Seattle, Center for law and justice, University of Washington.

Wikström, P-O.H. (1990a). Delinquency and the urban structure. In P.-O.H. Wikström. *Crime and measures against crime in the city.* Stockhom, National Council for Crime Prevention, Sweden.

Wikström, P.-O.H. (1990b). The Stockholm project: An introduction. In P.-O.H. Wikström. *Crime and measures against crime in the city.* Stockhom, National Council for Crime Prevention, Sweden.

Wikström, P-O.H. (1990c). *Crime and measures against crime in the city.* Stockhom, National Council for Crime Prevention, Sweden.

Wilson, J.Q. (1987). Strategic opportunities for delinquency prevention. In Wilson, J.Q. & Loury, G.C. *From children to citizens,* Volume III: Families, schools, and delinquency prevention. New York, Springer Verlag.

Wilson, J.Q. & Herrnstein, R.J. (1985). *Crime and human nature.* New York, Simon & Schuster.

Wolfgang, M.E. & Ferracuti, F. (1967). *The subculture of violence.* London, Tavistock Publications.

Wright, W.E. & Dixon, M.C. (1977). Community prevention and treatment of juvenile delinquency. *Journal of Research in Crime and Delinquency,* 14, 1: 35–67.

Individual and Community Influences on Victimisation and their Implications for Crime Prevention

by Ken Pease

It is contended that the distinction between individual and community influences is unhelpful for many of the purposes of crime prevention, and that community crime influences are always mediated through individual perceptions and actions, and may be addressed at that level. Crime prevention actions vary in the number of individuals whose perceptions or acts are simultaneously influenced. Choice of crime prevention measure should be biased towards those of least generality in the first instance, for civil liberty considerations primarily, but also to prevent waste and overreach. The same wish to be as precise as possible in targetting crime prevention argues strongly for the prevention of repeat victimisation to be chosen as a strategy for crime prevention generally.

Individual Crime Prevention: The Development of Research

The beginning of significant research attention to primary crime prevention in the UK can be dated fairly precisely at 1976. That year saw the publication of Home Office Research Study No 34, "Crime as Opportunity" (Mayhew et al 1976). The research there reported was inspired by data from quite a different area, that of suicide. The observation was that when toxic town gas was substituted by natural gas in British homes, the suicide method of preference, gas poisoning, ceased to be available. In fact, the total number of suicides decreased. This meant that people to whom a suicidal method of preference was denied did not necessarily choose an alternative. Some chose not to take their lives at all. This pattern of incomplete substitution of suicide method reasserted itself when US regulations on catalytic conversion were introduced. (see Clarke and Mayhew 1988 for an account of both effects). Ron Clarke, formerly of the Home Office Research and Planning Unit opined that if this were true of a decision so fundamental as suicide, might it not also be true of the decision to commit crime? If some reduction in suicide could be effected by removing some of the opportunities to kill oneself, could not some reduction in burglary or cheque fraud be effected by removing some of the opportunities to commit such crime? This led to a great deal of research focussing upon opportunity reduction as the means of crime prevention. The first work in this tradition, published in the seminal 'Crime as Opportunity' referred to above, included research on the prevention of car theft by the introduction of steering column locks (Mayhew et al 1976).[2] It was shown that the compulsory fitting of steering column locks to all cars in West Germany led to a reduction in the theft of cars, a reduction which was sustained over at least a decade. The compulsory fitting of steering column locks to all *new* cars in the UK led to a reduction in the proportion of stolen cars which were new.

This research was quickly followed by other work stemming from the same group in the Home Office Research Unit and elsewhere. Very substantial successes have been achieved in crime control by primary prevention (see Clarke 1991). Sometimes these can be serendipitous, such as the effects on motorcycle crime of introducing the legal requirement for motorcycle riders to wear helmets (Van Straelen 1978, Mayhew 1991). However, more often they have been deliberate, and in the aggregate, the scale and variety of successful crime prevention enterprise is becoming impressive.

The advantage of opportunity reduction approaches is that they tend to be clear in purpose, swift in implementation and clear in evaluation required. Their drawback is that they are specific to a range of contexts. Target hardening can only work if someone responds. If no-one does, it is worthless. In some areas, no-one will come.

Community Crime Prevention?

Most of the other contributions to this volume have been informed by the theoretical perspective offered by Shaw and McKay. To oversimplify, insofar as they deem social disorganisation to be criminogenic, crime prevention would operate through community organisation. Such a view, expressed in other terms and with different theoretical origins, has re-emerged strongly during the last decade.

Alongside the opportunity reduction studies collected in 'Designing Out Crime' (Clarke and Mayhew 1980) was one by Sheena Wilson, which identified child density as a determinant of levels of vandalism. This implicated the policy of housing departments (it being a British study, with high levels of public housing) in the allocation of people to homes. This has also been emphasised in studies performed in Sheffield by Tony Bottoms,

Paul Wiles and their colleagues (see Bottoms et al. 1989, Bottoms and Wiles 1992). They contend

> *"In order to understand and explain offending behaviour by residents of particular areas, it is vital to consider who lives in these areas; how they came to live there in the first place; what kind of social life the residents have created; how outsiders (including official agencies) react to them; and why they remain in the areas and have not moved" (Bottoms and Wiles 1991a, p 122).*

The re-emphasis of social factors in crime prevention has taken many forms. King (1989) emphasises the role of social crime prevention through local democratic channels, as in France, and contrasts this approach with the individualistic approach to crime prevention "a la Thatcher". Bottoms and Wiles (1992) regard the neglect of people dynamics as a fault of Anglo-American criminology in general.

Perhaps the most trenchant critique of a primary prevention tradition is offered by Currie (1988). He distinguishes two visions (phases) of community crime prevention. Phase 1[1] thinkers

> *"envision the community exerting its moral authority over bad people who seem to appear from nowhere, and who will surely take over if we don't wave the wand of traditional values at them – through tough policing, among other means" (p282).*

and contends that at its worst, Phase 1 thinking

> *"can slide into a kind of nostalgic voluntarism that exhorts shattered communities to pull themselves up by their own bootstraps, without help – and without money .... Phase 1 is no longer very impressive as a strategy against serious crime .... The overselling of Phase 1 ideas has tangible and disturbing consequences: it diverts resources away from other things we might do, while offering facile but easily dashed hopes that quick solutions will stop crime" (p 284).*

Phase 2, by contrast,

> *"is more complicated in its understanding of crime and how communities might combat it. But .... it is also far more promising, especially as a strategy for preventing serious crime, not merely reducing fear or taming neighbourhood incivilities. It is also, it is suggested, far more attuned to deeper and more fruitful criminological traditions" (p 282).*

It seems to the writer that Currie caricatures (or is unaware of) the kinds of research done under Phase 1 traditions. Not all crime takes place in the kinds of shattered community whose image he evokes. There are many ways and places in which simple measures can be fruitful. Even in shattered communities, it is far from clear that simple measures do not represent a toehold on order on the basis of which a nucleus of community organisation may be formed. It is a commonplace of change programmes that the first step should be the one most easily implemented, so that some experience of success may form the hub of more ambitious efforts at change. For these reasons, Currie's dismissal of Phase 1 thinking is not persuasive.

The Allocation of Crime Prevention Effort

It is perhaps in the allocation of effort and resources that community crime prevention appears to have occupied the moral high ground. Putting locks on the doors of houses in shattered and deprived communities seems insulting. Indeed it may be, but scarcely more so than seeking to foster community ties in communities which are already closely knit.

The finding which acted as a spur to consider allocation was that the proportion of police force complement which was given over to crime prevention was inversely proportional to the force area's recorded crime rate (Harvey at al. 1988). This is not plausibly regarded as an indication of the success of police crime prevention departments. It is almost certainly that crime prevention personnel are appointed predominantly in areas not consumed by the needs of reactive policing. It stimulated consideration of the proper match between crime prevention effort and crime incidence within police forces. There was reason to suppose that the match was not precise. The average crime prevention officer's day in England will be taken up with talks to civic groups, surveys of either public buildings or private dwellings whose occupants have requested such a service, and the like. In one case observed by my colleague Penny Grimshaw (see Harvey et al. 1988), a crime prevention officer helped assemble exhibits at a local museum as part of his working day, not for any security reasons, but because (it was explained later) the museum was important to the local tourist industry. Most of the pressures on crime prevention officers operate to move them away from high crime areas. The impression of mismatch is reinforced by reading the Home Office's periodical 'Crime Prevention News'. This official account of the work of crime prevention officers and others is a pot-pourri of school quizzes, property marking and sports activities, preponderantly in rural areas. Much of what it reports has only a tangential relevance to crime prevention, and a much more obvious relevance to good public relations.

With the idea that, at least in this instance, it was not the squeaky wheel of crime prone-ness that was getting the grease, the next relevant project in which we became involved was the Kirkholt Burglary Prevention Demonstration Project (Forrester et al. 1988). In this, we had to dispense crime prevention measures across a limited number of dwellings. We found that the best single predictor of burglary victimisation was past burglary victimisation. Not only were the police in the area unaware of that fact, but we have since found that police statistical systems are generally established in ways which make it impossible readily to identify patterns of repeat victimisation. While some of the aspects of repeat victimisation have been known for a long time (see Sparks et al. 1976, Fienberg 1980, Reiss 1980, Sparks 1981), they have not been put to work in the attempt to prevent crime.

Table 1 provides illustrative data on the excess of repeat victimisation relative to expectation. It depicts the results of fitting a simple Poisson distribution to the occurrence of non-domestic burglaries in Lisburn, Northern Ireland during a two year period, and I am grateful to Fiona Bloomer for permission to use the data, which are as yet unpublished. It will be seen that the expected frequency of places burgled four or more time is less than one, but the observed frequency is 39. Considering the data another way, 16% of the burgled premises (1% of all premises) accounted for 40% of all burglaries.

Table 1. Observed and Expected (Poisson) Distribution of Non-Domestic Burglaries, Lisburn 1990–1992. (N premises = 2464).

Number of Burglaries	0	1	2	3	4+
Expected Frequency	2166	278	20	1	<1
Observed Frequency	2273	121	39	21	10

At this point, the implications of repeat victimisation for the allocation of crime prevention resources began to be recognised by our group. If what was required was a basis for the allocation of crime prevention resources, and if victimisation was a good indicator of future victimisation, and if this were true across areas afflicted by different rates of victimisation, there would be some attractions in the prevention of repeat victimisation as a crime prevention strategy generally.

What Do Differences in Community Crime Rates Mean?

The practical question implicit in what has been written to this point concerns whether crime prevention effort is best channeled to individuals at risk or communities at risk. This formulation implies that the notion of a community at risk is unproblematic. Yet our Kirkholt experience suggested that communities had high rates of crime in large part because a limited number of homes within the area were repeatedly victimised, rather than because a uniformly high rate of victimisation was experienced throughout the area.

The fundamental question to be addressed was whether community or areal differences in rates of victimisation are differences in rates of repeat victimisation (concentration) or proportion of citizens victimised (prevalence). Indeed it astonished us that we could find no previous research addressing this point. Area differences may be a function of the proportion of people victimised and/or the number of victimisations per victim. Clarifying the basis of area differences in these terms is important for crime control policy and practice. Let us take the two implausible extremes. If area differences turn out to be a function exclusively of victim prevalence, crime control activity must be spread throughout the community, since people who have not yet been victimised remain at substantial risk of victimisation. At the opposite extreme, if area differences were to be purely a function of the number of victimisations per victim, crime control should concentrate upon those already victimised, since they are the group at heightened risk in high crime areas. Some result intermediate between these extremes would make the crime prevention response a matter of judgement, but there would be some considerations tending towards the choice of the prevention of repeat victimisation. Notably, the prevention of repeat victimisation offers a more focussed strategy of crime prevention, and avoids the disproportionate suffering of a few people in the community.

The decomposition of area differences in crime incidence into their components, prevalence (proportion of people victimised) and concentration (number of victimisations per victim) was attempted by Trickett et al. (1992). This paper divided the sampling points used in the 1982 British Crime Survey according to their crime incidence, ranking them and classifying them into deciles by crime incidence. Areas were thereby classified from the 10% with the lowest crime incidence to the 10% with the highest. The way in which the areas so classified varied in terms of prevalence and concentration were then examined. The most dramatic difference was found in the prevalence of crimes against the person, which rose from 2% in the lowest decile to 18% in the highest. At the same time, while there were 1.2 victimisations of this kind per victim in the lowest crime areas, there were 3.8 victimisations per victim in the highest crime areas. As for property crimes, while the prevalence for the lowest crime areas was 13%, the prevalence for the highest was 51%. The number of property victimisations per victim in the lowest crime areas was 1.3, and in the highest crime areas 4.0. In short, Trickett et al (1992) showed that area contrasts were a function of both prevalence and concentration differences. How surprised one is by the pattern will depend upon preconceptions about high crime areas. While the ninefold difference by area in the prevalence of crimes against the person, and the fourfold difference in the prevalence of property crime are both notable, a point of great interest is the very large extent to which area variation reflects differences in the concentration of victimisation. Considering property crime in the highest crime decile, half of the interviewees had not been victimised at all. The other half had been victimised an average of four times each. There was plenty of crime to go around – everybody could have been victimised twice. The pattern suggests that there is substantial scope for crime control policies based upon the prevention of repeat victimisation. The purpose of the next few paragraphs is to check the accuracy of the Trickett et al. paper using some refinements of method, to establish changes over time in how area differences have changed, and to determine how these changes are constituted.[2] Data from the first three sweeps of the British Crime Survey are used, from 1982, 1984 and 1988. As in Trickett et al. (1992), the unit of analysis is the sampling point. Unlike the Trickett paper, only property and personal crime victimisation will be detailed. The analysis of all crime will be omitted. Its pattern tends to be similar to that of property victimisation, because of the proponderance of that type of crime. Another difference is that here the deciles are calculated separately for property and personal crime. The method adopted in the earlier paper was to calculate deciles for total crime, and to look at the incidence, prevalence and concentration of property and personal crimes separately for those deciles. This method is potentially misleading, because of the preponderance of property crime. This means that the deciles which formed the basis of the property crime analysis were more appropriate than those for personal crime. A final problem with the earlier study was that it counted among property crimes events which were not necessarily tied to the place concerned. Notable among such crimes is theft of and from motor vehicles, which could have happened anywhere. It was felt that the exclusion of such crimes gave a purer pattern of area differences. Such crimes are excluded from the present analysis.

1982 to 1988 represents a period of special interest because it spans a time in which the Conservative Government of Prime Minister Margaret Thatcher held power. Thatcher first came to power in 1979 and was removed from office in 1990. Her administration is one which embraced the virtues of self-reliance, in which the levels of social support were eroded. In general, intuition would suggest that indices of inequality generally would increase during the period. In the century before the 1980s, British society became less unequal, only to widen again in the 1980s. Similar evidence of increasing inequality has been adduced in relation to employment and health (Walker and Walker 1987) and in terms of the effects of taxation (Hills 1988). Which of the crime indices of inequality would change most markedly, prevalence or concentration, is difficult to speculate upon.

The general pattern of results for 1982 from Trickett et al. holds up using the modified method. The basic picture of the relationship between area crime incidence, prevalence and concentration yielded by Trickett et al. (1992) seems soundly based. Not necessary to the flow of the argument, but of much interest, is whether the pattern has changed over time, as revealed by the three sweeps of the British Crime Survey. This is calculated as the Gini coefficients for incidence, prevalence and concentration for each of the three years. It will be recalled that the Gini coefficient can vary between 0 and 1. 0 indicates a state of affairs in which victimisation is spread evenly across the sampling points surveyed. 1 indicates a situation in which victimisation is maximally concentrated. For the three measures the calculation is somewhat different. The Gini for incidence indexes the number of victimisations per respondent; that for prevalence indexes the number of victims per respondent; that for concentration indexes the number of victimisations per victim. In the present context the Gini for prevalence refers to the distribution of victims per constituency across constituencies; that for incidence refers to the distribution of crimes per constituency across constituencies; and that for concentration refers to the distribution of crimes per victim across constituencies. For clarity of exposition, one method of calculation is used for the set of coefficients presented, although it has been determined that the results are robust across methods of calculation.

The pattern of change in crime victimisation revealed is one in which the variation among areas in level of crime victimisation has increased. The high crime areas are characterised by increasingly more property crime victimisation than the low crime rate areas as time passes. Inequality amongst areas has increased. This applies to a lesser extent to crimes against the person, where the pattern of change is less starkly clear. However, the difference in the probability of victimisation by area has not increased. The areas have remained roughly as unequal in 1988 as they had been in 1982. What has changed is the difference between areas in the number of victimisations per victim. The importance of this finding is that any enterprise which seeks to reduce area inequality at least to the levels of 1982 must primarily be directed at the control of repeat victimisation, since it is this which has, alone, caused the increase in area inequality in victimisation, during the 1980s.

Clearly, then, victimisation concentrates not just upon particular groups, but upon particular individuals. The rates of repeat victimisation are highest in areas with high crime incidence. The way in which areal inequality has changed in England and Wales has reflected a change in victim concentration rather than a change in victim prevalence. Therefore, a strategy of crime prevention to which repeat victimisation is central would automatically be directed to those areas most beset by crime.

Repeat Victimisation by Crime Type, and Time Course

Farrell (1992) provides an excellent recent review of the data on repeat victimisation and it is from this work that much of what follows is adapted. For some kinds of crime, repeat victimisation clearly occurs. These include domestic violence (almost by definition), embezzlement (where the employer-employee relationship is a necessary condition of the offence) and many kinds of fraud, including computer and cheque fraud (Levi and Pease, in preparation). For these kinds of offence, it is self-evident that the prevention of repeat victimisation would prevent most crime of the type. For some crimes where repeat victimisation rates are substantial, the fact is less self-evident. The effect has been shown to occur in commercial burglaries (Bloomer 1992), domestic burglary (Polvi et al 1990), racial attacks (Sampson and Phillips 1992), and serious property crimes against schools (Burquest et al 1992).

The phenomenon of repeat victimisation appears solid across crimes and across methods of determination, being evident in both victimisation surveys and statistics of crimes reported to the police. Nonetheless its utility for crime prevention is limited unless enhanced risk is transient. Otherwise necessary precautions would have to remain in place indefinitely. Fortunately for the purposes of crime prevention, there is a very marked reduction in the rate of repeats over short periods of time after a first victimisation. This is true for all the studies listed above where time course has been examined, both where the phenomenon of repeat victimisation is self-evident and where it is not. The point is illustrated in Figure 1 by domestic break and enter victimisations in the city of Saskatoon, Saskatchewan. It will be seen that the rate of repeat calls for service diminishes to a very low level after a period of a few weeks of a first. This is not an artefact of telescoping in recall, since the curve is based upon data of crimes recorded by the police. Neither is it an artefact of the mode of presentation, since when absolute numbers of offences are recorded the same pattern emerges. Neither can it be an artefact of widespread demolition of burgled houses. (While this seems fanciful, it is the only alternative explanation which is sustainable). The pattern of declining risk is also evident during the first month after a burglary, since repeats cluster in the first half of the first month.

The meaning of repeat victimisation statistics will be discussed later. Whatever the meaning is, the practical significance is that, given that the period of elevated risk is quite closely circumscribed, special precautions can be taken over that time without an unrealistic, semi- permanent deployment of resources.[3] The prevention of *repeat* victimisation may thus prove to be a cost-efficient strategy of crime prevention generally, and some small developments in that spirit are already under way, involving the loan of silent alarms to people recently victimised, either by assault or burglary, (see below). The other advantages of the strategy, adapted from Pease (1990, 1991) are as follows:

- because it is based on a careful examination of the individual circumstances of a crime, it will tend to involve all the appropriate measures, social and physical, for the prevention of repeat victimisation;
- preventing repeat victimisation protects the most vulnerable social groups, without having to identify those groups as such, which can be socially divisive. Having been victimised already probably represents the least contentious basis for the claim to be given crime prevention attention;
- repeat victimisation is highest, both absolutely and proportionately, in the most crime-ridden areas, which are also the areas that suffer the most serious crime (Pease 1988). The prevention of repeat victimisation thus *automatically* directs attention to the areas which need it most, rather than the converse, as is now the case (Harvey et al. 1988);
- the rate of victimisation offers a realistic scheduling for crime prevention activity. Preventing repeat victimisation is a way of 'drip-feeding' crime prevention;
- at least in England and Wales, the strategy addresses the way in which inequality of victimisation rates has changed during the period covered by the British Crime Survey.
- a high enough rate of victimisation would tend to convert attention to repeat victimisation into a wider initiative, with the advantage over conventional community approaches of being rooted in real events suffered by citizens.

A brief description of some of our present work based on the prevention of repeat victimisation may help clarify the principles involved.

The Liverpool Project

The analysis of police incident logs (calls to the police from the public) for the area in question revealed a distinct pattern of repeated domestic violence. A large proportion of all calls to domestic violence came from a small proportion of all households to which the police were repeatedly called. As noted above, the prevention of *repeat* domestic violence was the concept underlying the project, based upon previous research by the Manchester group. We know that

(1) there exists a 'heightened risk period' for repeat domestic victimisation – when a person has called the police she is more likely to call them again within a short period of time.

In summary, a household with one call to the police for a 'domestic' incident has a probability of 0.8 of another within one year. The typical period between incidents is much less than a year. After a first incident, 35% of households suffer a second incident within five weeks of the first. After a second incident, 45% of households suffer a third incident within five weeks of the second.

(2) The approach to any crime by a single method is a kind of tokenism.

(3) Domestic violence programmes which are unbalanced will surely fail, and safety plans must be individually developed for their victims.

One of the advantages of the time course of repeat victimisation is that it is realistic to think of special precautions for a limited time – precautions which would be unrealistic if they were maintained over a long period, and which allow a little hardware to go a long way. One of these precautions could be an alarm. This could form *part* of a general approach to reducing repeat victimisation. One part of the presenting problem in Liverpool (and this is almost certainly true elsewhere too) was violence which people, almost always women, suffered in their homes at the hands of ex-spouses or partners. Sometimes an injunction was in force, sometimes it was not. With colleagues in the Merseyside Police and DC Terry Fieldsend of South Yorkshire, an acknowledged national authority on alarm systems, we settled upon some criteria for alarms to be used in this circumstance. They should be very portable, not rely on British Telecom lines if possible, and be capable of being issued very quickly after an incident. The solution came through seeking existing products whose adaptation met the requirements of the enterprise. One of the companies contacted, Tunstall Telecom, was prepared to form a working group to explore ways of linking their equipment with other proprietary products. Tunstall specialises in alarms for the elderly, so that if an old person, for example, falls down and is unable to move, pressing a button on a pendant around their neck dials Tunstall's central station from the unit in the home, and a voice link is opened. Even if the elderly person is unable to speak, the origin of the call is evident to Tunstall at the point of reception. The Tunstall product of interest was the Solo II. In some cases in which the equipment would be used, it was deemed preferable to avoid British Telecom lines, both because of homes without such lines, and because a determined assailant could cut lines outside the house, which would give only a (useless) warning to the victim. Thus, the notion was to link the Solo to a cellular network. This was achieved by the use of a FAX interface. The Solo system and the first cellular phone and interface (supplied by Unicar of Leeds) was delivered to Merseyside Police in April 1992 and the first alarm was issued on April 27th. Although the bulk of units issued have been linked to a British Telecom line, the cellular phone connection may eventually be the more common arrangement. In recognition of this, we have taken to calling the arrangement a cellularm in what follows.

In general terms, the cellularm has considerable advantages over more traditional set-ups. It can be installed in minumum time because it does not need to be hard-wired. It offers a more advanced and cost-effective technology to replace Home Office alarms. The prospect exists of it being raised from an inert state, thus offering the lowest possible power consumption. It allows swift central police control of placement according to extant priorities. It opens a voice channel, so that officers can hear what is happening and give verbal reassurance that help is on its way. This also aids the confirmation of activations as non-accidental. At the time of writing, thirteen such units are on current loan to people in C Division of Merseyside Police. They can be triggered either from a neck pendant or from a button on the equipment itself. Triggering the alarm activates the central alarm system in the police Divisional Control Room (DCR), automatically recalling the address history and information to the computer screen. The alarms receive a priority response from the police. The alarms in our scheme are offered to those who have obtained a court injunction against their ex-partners, *and/or* where there is a history of violence at the address and they are vulnerable to attack. It is important to stress that the option is available to people who have not got injunctions, but whom police judgement suggests are in danger. They are issued for a limited time, in the first instance for thirty days, offering a period during which other means of ensuring a person's safety can be developed. It is crucial that the loans are temporary. The pattern of repeat victimisations means that a limited number of alarms will suffice for the needs of a whole police division, and that the alarms will not not develop into an open-ended, ever-expanding commitment on police resources.

DC Fieldsend spelled out the possibilities within his own force, and a scheme was launched by South Yorkshire Police on May 28th. using the system for a wider range of purposes, including burglary prevention. Further development has resulted in an ability to incorporate 'wire-free' low power radio linked movement detectors in order to provide protection in premises subjected to repeated burglary. Upon activation of detection equipment, police control room staff are able to assess the validity of the activation by listening to events inside the protected premises via the audio channel, thus facilitating a flexible and effective deployment of resources. This feature is currently available only in a minority of the more sophisticated commercially installed intruder alarm systems. This is the first use of the device in its wider application.

Criticisms

The anticipated criticisms of the approach advocating the prevention of repeat victimisations are that it is mechanistic and naive. In defence, it should be restated that the eschewal of the distinction between individual and community prevention is not an eschewal of the relevance of factors which simultaneously operate on many people (the preferred characterisation of community influences). The housing market is relevant to both offence (and particularly offender) rate differences between areas. However, it operates, as Bottoms et al. 1992 show), via perceptions and expressions of preference. The housing market is a shorthand for a series of individual decisions. Even in the most lawless places with which I have had contact, what residents say they want is very specific. It is the eviction of people living in a particular house, the disruption of a drug market in a shopping precinct, the effective boarding up of empty houses which may be set ablaze. These are issues which can be addressed by very specific measures. They may fail, in which initiatives of more general impact are called into play. Prior consignment of a set of crimes into a 'community' arena consigns them to treatment which carries a set of reformist baggage which may or may not be appropriate. Norval Morris' principle in regard to sentence was that sentences should not be longer than they would be if reform were not one of their purposes. Perhaps we could adapt the ukase to read "intervention in the name of crime prevention should not be more extensive than it would be if other social change were not one of its purposes".

The Meaning of the Time Course of Repeat Victimisation

The steeply declining rate of repeat victimisation over time needs to be explained. There are three possible explanations:

1. Repeats merely flag pre-existent risk differences;
2. The same offenders are responsible for the repeats;
3. Those who committed the first crime tell others, who commit the repeats.

The first point to be made is that whatever the explanation (or combination of explanations), the phenomenon does offer a plausible scheduling of crime prevention effort. So although the issue is (in my view) one which should be addressed with some urgency, many implications for crime prevention do not have to await its resolution. For what it is worth, all the evidence so far suggests that the second possible explanation is of enormous importance. but that the explanation will differ across crime types. For domestic violence, the identity of the perpetrator is usually not at issue, and the problem is clearly one of repeat offences by the same person. For plastic fraud and embezzlement, it is almost equally clear that the same person is responsible for repeated offences. For burglary, unpublished Dutch research (cited in Winkel 1991) suggests that around one-third of domestic burglars return to the same house. Unpublished work in Merseyside by Michael Barron also suggests that the risk of repeat victimisation is not contagious to one's immediate neighbours. Work in progress by Natalie Polvi at Warkworth Institution, Ontario, will clarify the picture. The Barron work cited and the steep time course curve in repeat victimisation both argue against the first alternative explanation for repeat burglary victimisation.

Assuming issues of meaning are resolved, and that repeat victimisation is deemed to be attributable primarily to the same offenders doing it again, the next phase of a research strategy would be to draw explicit and extensive parallels between criminal careers are victim careers. Are the more active offenders those who repeat against the same targets? Is the length and seriousness of 'victim careers' determinable? What is the relationship between community and individual victim lambdas? Perhaps the last question in particular may help clarify the relationship between individual and community crime victimisation.

Acknowledgements

My thanks go to Tony Bottoms for his very helpful comments on a previous draft of this paper, and to my colleagues in the Quantitative Criminology Group at Manchester for their partnership in much of the work reported.

Notes

[1] The exemplar of Phase 1 thinking which Currie uses is the work of James Q. Wilson and George Kelling rather than Ron Clarke's group, but it is clear that most of the work of that group and others reviewed in the primary prevention section above would be characterised by Currie as exemplifying Phase 1 thinking.

[2] A consolidated version of these analyses will be published under the joint authorship of Alan Trickett, Dan Ellingworth and Ken Pease.

[3] The above time course analyses incorporate a single crime type, but Reiss (1980) and Feinberg (1980) have shown the tendency amongst all crimes for repeats to be of the same type more often than would be expected. Thus the prevention only of repeat crimes of the same type may make a disproportionate impact on all victimisation.

References

Bloomer, F. (1992). Repeat Victimisations by Commercial Burglary in Lisburn. *Howard Journal submitted.*

Bottoms, A.E., Mawby, R.I. & Xanthos, P. (1989). A Tale of Two Estates. In D. Downes, (ed) *Crime and the City*. London: Macmillan.

Bottoms A.E. & Wiles, P. (1992). Explanations of Crime and Place In D.J. Evans, N.R. Fyfe & D.T. Herbert (eds) *Crime, Policing and Place: Essays in Environmental Criminology* London: Routledge.

Bottoms A.E., Claytor, A., & Wiles, P. (1992). Housing Markets and Residential Community Crime Careers. In D.J. Evans, N.R. Fyfe and D.T. Herbert (eds) *Crime, Policing and Place: Essays in Environmental Criminology*. London: Routledge.

Burquest R., Farrell, G., & Pease, K. (1992) *Lessons from Schools Policing* 8, 148–155.

Clarke, R.V. (ed) (1991). *Situational Crime Prevention: Successful Case Studies*. New York: Harrow and Heston.

Clarke, R.V., & Mayhew, P.M. (1988). The British Gas Suicide Story and Its Criminological Implications. In N. Morris and M. Tonry (eds) *Crime and Justice: An Annual Review of Research*. Vol 10. Chicago: University of Chicago Press.

Currie, E. (1988). Two Visions of Community Crime Prevention. In T. Hope and M. Shaw (eds) *Communities and Crime Reduction*. London: HMSO.

Farrell, G. (1992). Multiple Victimisation: Its Extent and Significance. *International Review of Victimology* 2, 85–102.

Fienberg, S.F. (1980). Statistical Modelling in the Analysis of Repeat Victimisation. In S.E. Fienberg and A.J. Reiss (eds) *Indicators of Crime and Criminal Justice: Quantitative Studies*. Washington DC: Bureau of Justice Statistics.

Forrester, D.P., Chatterton M.R. & Pease, K. (1988). *The Kirkholt Burglary Prevention Demonstration Project*. Crime Prevention Unit Paper 13. London: Home Office.

Harvey L., Grimshaw P., & Pease, K. (1988). The Work of Crime Prevention Officers. In R. Morgan and D.J. Smith (eds) *Coming to Terms with Policing*. London: Routledge.

Hills, J. (1988). *Changing Tax*. London: CPAG.

King, M. (1989). Social Crime Prevention a la Thatcher. *Howard Journal* 28, 291–312.

Mayhew, P.M. (1991). Displacement and Vehicle Theft: An Attempt to Reconcile Some Recent Contradictory Evidence. *Security Journal* 2, 233–239.

Mayhew, P.M., Clarke, R.V., Sturman, A. & Hough, J.M. (1976) *Crime as Opportunity*. Home Office Research Study No. 34. London: HMSO.

Mayhew, P.M., Clarke, R.V., Sturman, A. & Hough, J.M. (1976) Steering column locks and car theft. In P.M. Mayhew, R.V. Clarke, A. Sturman and J.M. Hough (1976) (eds) *Crime as*

Opportunity. Home Office Research Study No. 34. London: HMSO.

Pease, K. (1988). *Judgements of Offence Seriousness: Evidence for the 1984 British Crime Survey*. Research and Planning Unit Paper 44. London: Home Office.

Pease, K. (1990). Preventing Burglary on a British Public Housing Estate. *Security Journal* 2, 73–77.

Pease, K. (1991). Preventing Burglary on a British Public Housing Estate In R.V. Clarke (ed) *Situational Crime Prevention: Successful Case Studies*. New York: Harrow and Heston.

Polvi, N., Looman, T., Humphries, C. & Pease, K. (1990). Repeat Break-and-enter Victimisation: Time Course and Crime Prevention Opportunity. *Journal of Police Science* 17, 8–11.

Reiss, A.J. (1980). Victim Proneness in Repeat Victimisation by Type of Crime. In S.E. Fienberg and A.J. Reiss (eds) *Indicators of Crime and Criminal Justice*. Washington: Bureau of Justice Statistics.

Sampson, A., & Phillips, C. (1992). *Multiple Victimisation: Racial Attacks on an East London Estate*. Crime Prevention Unit Paper xx. London: Home Office.

Sparks, R.F. (1981). Multiple Victimisation: Evidence, Theory and Future Research. *Journal of Criminology and Criminal Justice* 72, 762–78.

Sparks, R.F., Genn, H., & Dodd, D. (1976) *Surveying Victims*. London: Wiley.

Trickett, T.A., Seymour, J, Osborn, D. & Pease, K. (1991). What Is Different about High Crime Areas? *British Journal of Criminology*.

Van Straelen, F.W.M. (1978). Prevention and Technology In J. Brown (ed) *Cranfield Papers*. London: Peel Press.

Walker, A. & Walker, C. (1987). *The Growing Divide: A Social Audit 1979–1987*. London: CPAG.

Wilson, S. (1980). Vandalism and 'defensible space' on London Housing Estates. In R.V. Clarke and P. Mayhew (eds) *Designing Out Crime*. London: HMSO.

Winkel, F.W. (1991). Policing, Victims, and Crime Prevention: Some Research-based Recommendationson Victim-orientated Interventions. *British Journal of Criminology 31*, 250–265.

Key Issues in the Integration of Individual and Community Explanations of Crime and Criminality

by Albert J. Reiss, Jr.

Introduction

This chapter draws attention to some key issues in the theoretical integration of individual and community explanations of crime and criminality. It begins by observing that a central problematic in criminology is to identify the major sources of variation in crime and criminality and how each contributes to explaining that variation. It then focuses attention on a rationale for studying the effect of two of these major sources of variation–community and individual–on the development of criminal behaviors. The chapter concludes by drawing attention to several neglected explanatory issues linking individual and community explanations of delinquent and criminal behaviors.

Sources of Variation in Rates of Crime and Criminality

That there is enormous variation in crime and criminality among societies is well established. Violent crime rates in the United States, for example, are far greater than those in Sweden and its homicide rates far exceed those in any other industrialized nation (Reiss & Roth, 1993:52–53). There likewise is considerable secular variation in crime rates within societies that is not easily explained. In the United States, for example, the homicide rate peaked twice in the twentieth century. There was a substantial increase in homicide from 1900 to 1930 followed by a substantial decline in the next 30 years to a low in the early 1960's. A rise in the 1960's and 1970's peaked in 1980 followed by a brief period of decline to 1985 and a rise since then to near its peak for the century by 1993 (Reiss & Roth: 1993:50).

Within a society, there is considerable variation in crime rates among its communities and substantial changes in rates within many communities in short periods of time (Reiss & Roth,

1992:79–88; Bursick, 1993). This temporal variation within communities is too great to be accounted for by the aging of birth cohorts or even, in most cases, changes in the composition of the population. Accordingly, other explanations have been offered. More than a half century ago Shaw and McKay (1931; 1942:177–83) linked community variation in juvenile delinquency rates in Chicago to their differential social organization. More recently, Wikström (1991:191–213) links variation in violence, vandalism, residential and nonresidential burglary and theft rates among Stockholm communities (1991:191–213) to the city's patterns of residential segregation and mechanisms for housing allocation.

There also is considerable variation in patterns of criminality within families with male more likely than female children to be delinquent or criminal. Even though participation in offending is increased if parents or siblings have criminal records, most delinquents in unbroken families have non-delinquent sibs (Visher & Roth, 1986:279). Finally, individuals show considerable variation in prosocial and antisocial behaviors and there is considerable variation in rates of offending within criminal careers (Blumstein, et. al, 1986:4–5),

Given this considerable variation in rates of crime and offending among and within societies, communities, and families as well as intra-individual variation over time, one of the key issues is how each contributes to the explanation of variation in rates of crime and criminality.

Criminologists have long recognized and documented substantial variation and change in crime and criminality among and within societies, communities, families, and individuals. Typically, however, their explanations focused upon explaining either individual/family or community variation and changes in rates–changes in either individual or community crime careers, for example–rather than on the integration of these explanations. No contemporary theory links variation in individual rates of delinquency and crime to variation in these rates within societies and their communities.

Not only must criminological theories integrate explanations of the considerable variation in rates of crime among and within societies and their communities with their constituent family and individual members, but any explanation must be consistent with the fact that there are substantial changes in these rates over relatively short periods of time. A first key issue then is to integrate society, community, peer, family and individual level explanations of variation and change in crime and criminality.

Because individuals grow up largely within a single society, it is difficult to investigate the effect of societal culture and organization on individual development and to isolate its effect independent of community, family, and peer group effects. One way of doing so is through cross-societal investigations which require either an elaborate cross-national design for a single study or the replication of a single design across different societies. Such designs are logistically complex in their implementation and costly. Yet dynamic heterogeneous societies offer approximations to cross-societal comparisons. One approximation is to investigate the development of immigrant children to a society and the other is to investigate variation among ethnic groups within a single society.

Much of modern history is characterized by the migration of populations to settled societies. Family or ethnic migrations from one society to another offer quasi- experimental conditions for investigating how children develop in different societies, much as Pauline Young demonstrated in her study of the effects of migration on the children of Russian Molokan families to Los Angeles (Young, 1932). Young compared the socialization and deviance histories of boys and girls from the same families born in Russia prior to migration with those of their siblings born immediately following migration and those born on the average some five years later. Demonstrating important differences in the deviance histories of the three cohorts with those last born in America having the highest rates of deviance, she also concluded that the contrasting cultures of Russia and America affected the adult adaptation of the girls brought up in America more than it did that of boys.

At the present time, there is substantial movement of legal and illegal immigrants to western cities. They are often residentially segregated in communities of the city. Berlin, London, Paris, Stockholm, New York, Chicago, Los Angeles and most major western cities have such ethnic enclaves which maintain major elements of their common culture, including the linguistic socialization of their children. These ethnic communities of recent immigrants and their children provide opportunities to study the effect of growing up in two different cultures. More generally, the residential settlement patterns of ethnic or religious subcultural groups within a society provide opportunities to investigate community and subcultural effects on human development within a society.

Rationale for Studying Both Individual and Community Effects on Individual Development

There are several theoretical and empirical traditions explaining delinquency and criminality. One of these focuses on individual differences, such as differences in intelligence and temperament. Another focuses on the effects of primary groups such as those of families and peers on the social learning of deviance. And a third focuses on explaining behavior in terms of the differential social organization of communities and societies. Earlier (Reiss, 1986b:25–29), I argued that a key issue is to resolve the explanatory power of the variables in these different theories. Longitudinal studies that simultaneously investigate individual and community explanatory factors are a critical way of resolving contradictory explanations in these competing theories and a means for integrating them. There are several reasons why it is important to undertake longitudinal studies that simultaneously investigate individual and community effects on the development of delinquent and criminal behavior within any given society.

The first reason is that the *main effects* of individual and community differences on delinquent and criminal behavior *are confounded* in all previous research (Reiss, 1986b; Tonry, et. al., 1991). The development of **individual** delinquent and criminal careers–their onset, continuation or persistence, and desistance–is ordinarily explained in terms of individual and related family differences. Communities and their properties, if they enter at all into the explanatory model, are treated simply as properties of individuals–as contextual explanatory variables. Analogously, the development of **community** delinquent and criminal careers is ordinarily explained in terms of the differential social organization (Shaw & McKay, 1942: 177–183) of communities or the growth and differentiation of the urban community (Burgess, 1925) and individual level variation is disregarded.

We may illustrate the potential for confounding main effects in conclusions about violent crime. Studies have variously shown that individuals with a propensity to aggression are more likely to commit violent crimes while others show that individuals who live in areas with high violent crime rates are more likely to commit a violent crime. Are aggressive individuals or high crime neighborhoods responsible for high violence rates? Do aggressive individuals migrate to high violence neighborhoods and the less aggressive persons leave them or do high violence neighborhoods lead individuals to be aggressive and then commit violent crimes?

A second reason for investigating individual development in different communities is that there are reasons to expect *interaction effects* between individual or family behaviors and community structure and organization. Several studies posit such interaction effects although they have not been systematically investigated.

One set of studies hypothesizes that neighborhoods affect the economic and social attachments of residents independent of their social class. Wilson, for example, (1991:10–12) hypothesizes that poor economic position leads to weak labor force attachments, weak family structure, and crime and other illegal activities by residents only when people are concentrated and socially isolated in ghetto neighborhoods. When poor people live in neighborhoods that provide avenues to social mobility, they develop a greater sense of collective efficacy and are more likely to be socially mobile.

Another set of studies provides evidence that the socialization practices of black parents varies with the race composition of communities. Black mothers who live in neighborhoods that are equally divided between black and white residents are more likely to socialize their children in race matters than are mothers in homogeneous black communities (Thornton, et al., 1990:407). There is evidence also that black parents in racially heterogeneous neighborhoods are more likely to socialize their children into assuming a black identity and consciousness than are parents in all black neighborhoods (Banks, 1984; Tatum, 1987).

A third reason for investigating the development of delinquent conduct in different kinds of communities is that one can expect reciprocal causal effects between community structure and delinquent behavior. Skogan (1992), for example, concludes that crime leads to a spiral of decay in urban neighborhoods causing the stable residents to move out and legitimate businesses to vacate their premises. This selective exodus leads to further deterioration and collective inefficacy with a concomitant increase in crime. One can similarly hypothesize that the weaker the social control structure of a neighborhood over adolescent behavior, the greater the opportunities for adolescents to engage in delinquency. The resulting increase in delinquency may further weaken the neighborhood control structure that again leads to further increase in delinquency.

A fourth reason for investigating delinquent and criminal development in communities is that like individuals *communities are dynamic entities.* Community changes may come about due to internal or external dynamic forces that alter community structure, patterns of organization, and means of formal and informal collective control. These changes in communities can affect individual development either directly or by reciprocal causation.

Although the central focus of criminological research tends to be on the development of *individual delinquent and criminal careers*, there are relatively few investigations of *community crime careers*. Exceptions are the work of Bursick and Webb (1982), Bursick (1986), Bottoms and Wiles (1986), McDonald (1986), and Schuerman and Kobrin (1986). No study, however, links the development of individual crime careers to changes in community crime careers or to changes in community structure and processes (Reiss, 1986b:17–21).

Dynamic changes in the structure and social organization and control of communities can substantially affect the composition and extent of crime in a community. One way that dynamic change occurs in communities is through selective in- and out-migration of its population of persons and organizations. There can be a spiral of such changes set off by either selective migration of persons or of organizations, e. g., a new ethnic group moves into a community or a major employer leaves the community. Ethnic replacement can be particularly consequential as it often has direct effects on relations between those who stay and those who move in. Rieder (1985), for example, has shown that ethnic change in a community can contribute substantially to intergroup conflict that gives rise to violent crimes of assault and mass collective disturbances.

Selective in- and out-migration also can affect the social integration of a community. The socially mobile who leave for job opportunities in other communities often leave behind the underachievers and less competitive, especially when the local community loses its infrastructure of economic opportunity. Those left behind, as Wilson observes, increasingly have a sense of collective inefficacy. The selective migration sets off other changes. Lacking an infrastructure of legal opportunities, illegal ones such as drug markets, arise. These neighborhoods, moreover, attract a disproportionate number of the dispossessed, addicted, homeless and transient persons that further contributes to lessened collective efficacy. Wilson (1991:11) suggests that these beliefs of inefficacy are transmitted as part of the concentration effects of urban poverty so that growing up in these neighborhoods is a substantial disadvantage.

There is a fifth reason for simultaneously studying individual and community development and change. Understanding where, when, and by what means changes occur provides critical information on where, when, and how to intervene to change the course of individual and community development. Currently, most interventions focus on individual technologies and only a relatively few focus on changing communities. Yet in neither case do the technologies of intervention take account of the relationships among them. Research focusing on developing and changing individuals and communities should provide valuable information on the appropriate targets of intervention–individual, community level factors, or both–and the critical times, situations, and technologies for intervention.

Some Neglected Key Issues for Integrating Individual and Community Explanations of Crime and Criminality

Attention has been drawn to the fact that few attempts have been made to theoretically integrate individual and community explanations of crime and criminality. Likewise, two substantial empirical literatures have grown up, one testing only the effect of individual and family differences on the development of delinquent and criminal behavior and the other testing only the effect of the differential social organization of communities on the prevalence of delinquency and crime in communities. As Farrington (1993) concludes, no individual, family, or neighborhood influences on offending have been conclusively demonstrated because they have not simultaneously measured individual, family, peer, and community influences. There is a need, therefore, to develop critical tests of these different influences.

Previous research has placed little emphasis on a number of issues that loom as important in understanding the separate effects of individual and community influences on the development of delinquent and criminal behavior or for integrating theories linking individual and community influences. Four such issues are identified and discussed below.

Selection Effects of Communities

There is a growing body of evidence linking selective migration among communities within a metropolis to community patterns of crime and criminality. The nature of these selection processes is not well understood and a key issue for integrating theories of individual, family, peer, and community influences on criminality is to understand them.

Two general patterns of selective migration have been documented for American cities. The first pattern is movement out of high crime rate to low crime rate communities. Skogan (1992) concludes that the fear of crime generated by increasing crime in a community leads residents to move from high crime central city to low crime suburban communities. This exodus is selective, however. The exodus from major American cities has been characterized as "white flight" since in the cities where it has been documented the crime rate of inner city blacks is high. The effect of this selective internal migration is to reinforce patterns of race and class segregation. The inner city consequently is increasingly comprised of communities with high crime rates and low income minority persons who cannot afford to migrate out of the inner city. A much different pattern of residential settlement and movement prevails in large cities of some European countries where in-migrants, immigrants, and underclass families are located in outer city communities and there is diurnal movement to the central city to offend (Wikström 1991; 1993).

A secondary pattern of exodus occurs from low income ghetto communities with high crime rates to other, largely city, communities. Wilson (1987; 1991) characterizes this as a selective migration of socially mobile minorities from disadvantaged underclass ghetto areas to communities that offer greater opportunities for employment. One result of this selective exodus is that urban ghetto communities come to be occupied by a relatively permanent underclass who have few legitimate opportunities in their community for making a living. Consequently, they turn to illegitimate opportunities. Their underclass ghetto areas become havens for illegitimate and illegal activities such as marketing illegal drugs, guns, or stolen property, and street prostitution.

Paralleling this selective migration out of inner city communities is a selective migration into them. Some communities become the residence of newly arrived legal and illegal immigrants. Others are substantially devastated physically and economically and the marginal and poor are over represented in them. These communities disproportionally attract others who cannot afford regular housing such as the unemployed, the homeless, the mentally ill, those with criminal records, and those who become drug dependent. Some of these communities develop subcommunities for particular deviant populations, such as the so-called Skid-rows that are havens for alcoholics and drug addicts. Other communities have public or council housing areas that disproportionally house problem households and problem youths. Government housing policies can be responsible for this concentration when they assign a substantial proportion of the units to families with problem and delinquent youths (Baldwin and Bottoms, 1976; Bottoms and Wiles, 1986). The structure of local housing markets and policies of tenant associations may also account for such differential concentration (Wikström, 1991:181–84).

These processes of selective in and out-migration to inner city ghetto areas and the creation of community areas whose residents are poor and dispossessed are not well understood. Several matters lend themselves to further investigation.

One matter inviting further investigation is to determine whether the structure of illegal activity in a community is primarily a consequence of selective migration of persons who engage in illegal activity to a community or, rather, to changes in the economic and social organization of a community resulting from out-migration and larger external forces. Do communities have substantial illegal activity because of their attraction to migrants seeking illegal enterprise or is the activity simply a result of the residual concentration of those who develop such opportunities when left behind.

To better understand the concentration of illegal activity in some urban communities, we also need to know more about the extent to which high crime rate communities are disproportionally made up of resident probationers and released offenders. Moreover, to what extent is their concentration in some neighborhoods more than others the result of a return of released offenders to their former place of residence and the release of probationers to their homes, of the selection of these communities by released offenders, or a continuing selective migration of offenders to communities where other offenders reside? Paralleling these investigations should be ones to learn how likely it is that released offenders or probationers are placed in, or move to, low crime rate communities and whether such differential placement or moves affects their subsequent rate of offending?

Unfortunately, there is only one study examining neighborhood effects on recidivism of incarcerated offenders. Steve Gottfredson and Ralph Taylor (1987) examined the effects of a neighborhood's economic composition on recidivism rates. They found that household income, percentage of workers with white-collar jobs, and housing prices in neighborhoods affected neither the likelihood of rearrest or the seriousness of the crime with which they were charged. Given their small samples in neighborhoods, their study lacked sufficient statistical power to detect neighborhood influence. Moreover, their measures of neighborhood influence did not include measures of differential social organization and control, measures of community that may have a more important effect on recidivism. Studies with a broader range of community measures and larger samples following released offenders for longer periods of time, perhaps using hazard models, are needed to determine whether there are separate neighborhood effects on recidivism.

Only two studies (Reiss & Rhodes, 1961; Johnstone, 1978) have ever investigated whether there are separable effects of neighborhood and individual socioeconomic status on an individual's delinquency rate. The results from these two studies are contradictory. The Nashville study of white male teen-agers (Reiss & Rhodes, 1961) concluded that low socio-economic status youths had a lower rate of delinquency when attending high than low socio-economic schools; correlatively, the delinquency rate of middle socio-economic status youth was highest when attending low socioeconomic status schools. The Chicago study of primarily black youths (Johnstone, 1978) provided some contradictory results. Although living in a poor neighborhood increased the likelihood of middle class youths committing crimes, it reduced the likelihood that low socio-economic status youth reported committing such crimes. Clearly research is needed to resolve this contradiction by separating community and school effects on delinquency from individual socio-economic status effects. Also needed are studies that investigate whether the movement of families in and out of poor neighborhoods affects youth's delinquency behavior. Similar studies should be undertaken for adult criminals.

Although there is a growing body of studies on the place of residence of offenders and the places where they offend, more studies explaining these patterns of movement are needed such as the study by Baldwin and Bottoms (1971) linking male offender residence in Sheffield, England to community housing types. They concluded that government housing policy was critical to understanding patterns of offender residence in the United Kingdom and demonstrated that the journey to other communities to commit crimes was crime specific. A recent review by Wikström (1991:213–215) of the relationship of offender residence patterns and the places where they commit crimes draws attention to the role that the differential distribution of crime opportunities in communities plays in accounting for offender journeys to commit crimes.

A closely related problematic is to understand the structure of social networks in these communities and their processes of recruitment and replacement. These include understanding how community networks facilitate recruitment of individuals into illegal activities, the conflicts that develop over control of illegal market territories within communities, and community processes of recruitment and socialization into patterns of offending.

A more general problematic worthy of investigation is to understand how community information enters into search behavior of individuals. Little is known about the search behavior of persons seeking a place to live or move. How do they acquire information and to what extent do they seek information about communities when seeking to move? What role do social networks play in informing persons of places to which to move and to what extent is their search behavior governed by information on housing, employment, and illegal markets in communities?. Little also is known about how intelligence about communities enters into the search behavior of offenders. How, for example, do they acquire their information on places to offend and to choose their victim targets?

Moral Development and Moral Orders

A much neglected issue in the development of prosocial and antisocial behavior is the integration of theories of moral development in individuals with theories of normative development in societies and communities. Theories of moral development in individuals usually take a moral order as a given and focus on how families, small groups, and larger institutions facilitate that moral development. Typically the theories do not consider how variation in moral orders among communities and societies shape individual development.

Correspondingly, theories about the moral or normative order of communities focus upon the ways that particular orders shape individual moral behavior through collective norms and sanctions, ignoring variation in individual moral development. The emphasis in these theories falls on accounting for community differences in sanctioning individual departures from collective norms rather than upon understanding how such collective norms come into being and change. To cite but one example, recent decades have witnessed considerable change in norms governing sexual conduct with profound implications for changes in family structure and individual moral development. Cohabitation represents not only a substantial change in family structure but a corresponding change in sex norms and sanctioning. Unanswered is the extent to which these changes are a function of changing individual behaviors, changes in sanctioning patterns, or changes in the moral order itself and how changes in any one of these affects changes in others.

Some recent formulations show promise for integrating these different explanations of moral behavior. One promising formulation is based on integrating explanations of how different forms of capital affect development and change in individual and organizational forms of behavior. Differences in resource, or physical capital, human capital, and social capital (Coleman, 1990:304) have been used, for example, to explain differences in school achievement. They presumably can be used to explain differences in the development of prosocial and antisocial behavior in individuals and communities as well.

Resource capital is made up of those physical resources that individuals or organizations can mobilize to facilitate development. Human capital consists of those attributes that inhere in individual persons such as their temperament, intelligence, skills, knowledge, and personality. And social capital consists of those resources that exist in relationships among persons such as trust and forms of collective action. A special form of social capital are prescriptive norms (Coleman, 1990:311) or what might be identified as moral capital.

One of the key issues, then, is how to explain individual outcomes in terms of the acquisition, mobilization, and changes in these forms of capital and the effect of their differential availability in communities. Particularly lacking are ways to link individual moral development–a form of human capital–to the moral capital of families, communities, and societies. A related key issue is to isolate the mechanisms that underlie their formation and change.

Effect of Sanctions on Behavior

Specific theories of deterrence posit that negative sanctions on deviant conduct are a deterrent to future individual misconduct. The certainty, celerity, and severity of individual punishments are hypothesized as deterrents, though empirical support for their separate effects on deterring different kinds of illegal behaviors is quite mixed (Nagin, 1978). Theories of formal and informal social control posit that general deterrence is a function of the type and rate of local formal and informal sanctions. There is some empirical support for this hypothesis for variation in formal sanctions. Sampson (1986), for example, demonstrates that local official sanctions of arrest and incarceration affect community robbery and homicide rates when population composition is taken into account. No studies have attempted to examine the specific (individual) deterrence hypothesis in communities with varying formal and informal sanctioning rates. A key issue then is to investigate their separable effects under different rates of formal and informal community sanctioning.

To my knowledge, tests of specific deterrence of delinquent and criminal behavior are based on calculating individual rates of sanctioning for a criminal career. The tests do not take into account the temporal relationship of formal and informal sanctions to offending. What is more, there are diverse interventions in the delinquent or criminal career that qualify as treatments or training rather than as punishments. The temporal deterrent effect of these different kinds of interventions, including punishments, is never investigated for their effect on subsequent offending. Moreover, deterrence theory is usually cast in terms of desistance from future offending rather than deceleration of the rate of offending. Parenthetically we note that tests of deterrence theory usually occur only for desistance in truncated careers rather than for life histories of offending behavior and ordinarily for the application of formal sanctions only. Deterrence theory preferably should be tested by combining offending and intervention histories, temporally ordering offending and informal as well as formal sanctions. Such tests should also account for acceleration and deceleration in rates of offending as well as desistance.

The issue of deterrence is further complicated by whether deterrence is primarily a function of individual punishments for specific acts or individual perceptions or expectations of punishment were they to commit those acts. Tests of the perceptual hypothesis rest on collecting information on perceptions of sanctioning rates. But since much individual offending is with co-offenders, their future behavior may depend upon how their co-offenders were sanctioned rather than upon some general perception about sanctions. For offending persons, their expectations presumably are a function not only of their own offending and sanctioning experiences but those of their co-offenders as well. Individuals may be deterred when not punished if they know their co-of fenders were punished for the offense in which they participated. Or, correlatively their future behavior may be affected by the knowledge that some of their co-offenders were not detected and punished.

Because individuals vary considerably in their rate of committing offenses with others, understanding individual deterrence depends not only upon knowing their sanctioning experience and that of their co-offenders but also upon knowing what is the sanctioning history of the offenders in their co-offending network (Reiss, 1980:13–15; 1986a:137–152; 1988;143–49 Farrington & Reiss, 1991). Knowledge of the sanctioning experiences of others in one's co-offending network may be more determinative of a persons future offending career than more general perceptions of sanctioning rates. It seems likely that acceleration, deceleration, and desistance in individual rates of offending is a function not only of one's own sanctioning experience but also of **knowledge** of the sanctioning experiences of one's immediate co-offenders and others in one's offending network. Moreover, offender perceptions of sanctioning rates may depend more upon this knowledge of punishments of co-offenders and of other offenders in one's network than upon a general sense of the rate of punishment for others in a community. Additionally, perceptions may vary more with one's own sanctioning experience and knowledge of that of other offenders than with the actual rate of punishment in a community. Hypotheses about the deterrent effect of expectations of punishment for a given delinquent or criminal offense, therefore, should be tested under varying conditions of actual punishment of offenders in offending networks of a community.

Communities and Development of Identities

It has long been observed that the sex ratio of criminality varies among communities with the crime rate of females closer to that of males in large American cities than in small towns or rural areas (Sutherland, 1947:99–102). The sex socialization of boys and girls seems to vary with the cultural and formal social organization of communities, although studies reaching such conclusions control neither for the differential organization of criminal opportunities in communities nor for differences in informal and formal social control over behavior. Although culture appears to exercise a profound effect on sex socialization into deviant behavior, it remains unclear whether and to what extent the cultural organization of communities has an independent effect.

Likewise, there is an older body of evidence on nativity and delinquency and crime that indicates that certain crimes or groups of crimes are characteristic of certain national groups (Sutherland, 1947:125). The types of crime committed by immigrant groups parallels that of their country of origin (Sutherland, 1944:125). Moreover, variation in delinquency and crime rates of second generation immigrants appears related to the cultural isolation of the immigrant group from the surrounding cultures (Sutherland, 1947:127). Country of origin rates persist to the degree a local community is isolated from those of cultures in close residential proximity.

These and similar findings are related on the individual level to the development of a cultural identity, raising the question of the extent to which the development of a sex, national, or other cultural identity depends upon the community in which one grows up and whether and in what ways such identities are linked to particular delinquent and criminal behavior. To what extent, for example, does an ethnic emphasis on a macho culture lead to the development of a male identity that approves the use of violence to resolve conflicts among males only whereas in other national groups an emphasis on macho culture may approve the use of violence towards both males and females. Moreover, to what extent is the development of cultural identities facilitated by the cultural homogeneity of a community and its isolation from frequent social and cultural contact with other communities? How are such patterns of cultural transmission in communities linked to patterns of delinquent and criminal behavior in them? Understanding the development of cultural identities and their transmission and support within communities is a neglected and key issue in understanding patterns of crime and criminality.

Summary and Conclusions

This chapter has identified a number of key issues in integrating individual and community explanations of crime and criminality. It first drew attention to the fact that there is considerable variation in crime among societies and within communities, families, and individuals within societies. It drew attention to the fact that each of these levels invites its own explanation and pointed to the difficulty of separating societal and cultural sources of variation from those within a society. It was suggested that investigating the development of persons who move to societies or of different ethnic communities within a society can provide some understanding of the role of culture and societal organization in the development of offending.

Using communities as the prototype of extra-individual organization we went on to show that unless one studies individual development within different communities, and study both as they change, we will be unable to separate the contribution of either individual or community explanatory variables in the development of delinquent and criminal behavior.

We turned in the latter part of the chapter to a number of neglected theoretical and empirical issues in integrating individual and community explanations of delinquent and criminal behavior. Four critical explanatory issues were singled out.

Because communities are dynamic entities, the structure of communities is the residual effect of selective in- and out-migration. The first issue, therefore, focused on the ways in which selective migration affects the structure and opportunities for offending in communities and on linking community structure to individual propensities and possibilities to move in and out of communities. The second issue poses the problem of linking individual moral development with the moral or normative structure of communities. The third issue raises questions about how the informal and formal sanctions exercised over individuals are linked to patterns of community sanctions. And the final issue begins with the observation that there is considerable difference in the criminality of persons based on their sex and/or their ethnic identity. Because individual identities, especially in the pre-adolescent years, are formed within communities, the problem becomes one of determining the effect of community sex and ethnic socialization patterns on individual development of identities and the linking of those identities to patterns of offending.

Methodologically, a longitudinal design in which one investigates individual development in different communities as they change is a requisite for separating individual from community effects. Such longitudinal studies also should provide a better understanding of the links between individual development and community structure and change, thereby leading to a theoretical integration of individual and community effects on criminal behaviors. The theoretical integration will be aided by a study of micro- as well as macro-processes of development and change. Methodologically, field ethnographies in communities can enhance our understanding of these micro-processes.

References

Baldwin J. & A. E. Bottoms (1976). *The Urban Criminal; A Study in Sheffield.* London. Tavistock Publications.

Banks, J. (1984). Black Youths in Predominantly White Suburbs: An Exploratory Study of their Attitudes and Self-Concepts. *Journal of Negro Education,* 53:3–17.

Bottoms, Anthony E. & Paul Wiles (1986). Housing Tenure and Residential Community Crime Careers in Britain. In *Communities and Crime* edited by Albert J. Reiss, Jr. and Michael Tonry. Chicago: University of Chicago Press.

Burgess, E. W. (1925). The Growth of the City. In *The City* edited by R. E. Park and E. W. Burgess. Chicago: University of Chicago Press.

Bursick, R.J., Jr. (1986). Ecological Stability and the Dynamics of Delinquency. In *Communities and Crime* edited by Albert J. Reiss, Jr. and Michael Tonry. Chicago: University of Chicago Press.

Bursick, R.J., Jr. (1993). Methods of Studying Community Change in the Rate and Pattern of Crime. In *Integrating Individual and Ecological Aspects of Crime* edited by David P. Farrington, Robert J. Sampson and Per-Olof Wikström. National Council for Crime Prevention Sweden.

Bursick, R.J., Jr. & Webb J. (1982). Community Change and Patterns of Delinquency. *The American Journal of Sociology* 88: 24–42.

Coleman, J.S. (1990). *Foundations of Social Theory.* Cambridge: Belknap Press of Harvard University Press.

Farrington, D. (1993). Have any Individual, Family or Neighborhood Influences on Offending been Demonstrated Conclusively? In *Integrating Individual and Ecological Aspects of Crime* edited by David P. Farrington, Robert J. Sampson and Per-Olof Wikström. National Council for Crime Prevention Sweden.

Gottfredson, S.D. & Taylor R.B. (1987). Community Contexts and Criminal Offenders. In *Communities and Crime Reduction* edited by T. Hope and M. Shaw. London: Her Majesty's Stationary Office.

Johnstone, John W. C. (1978). Social Class, Social Areas, and Delinquency. *Sociology and Social Research* 63:49–72.

McDonald, Scott C. (1986). Does Gentrification Affect Crime Rates? In *Communities and Crime* edited by Albert J. Reiss, Jr. and Michael Tonry. Chicago: University of Chicago Press.

Nagin, Daniel (1978). General Deterrence: A Review of the Empirical Evidence. In *Deterrence and Incapacitation: Estimating the Effects of Criminal Sanctions on Crime Rates* edited by Alfred Blumstein, Jacqueline Cohen and Daniel Nagin. Washington, D. C.: National Academy of Sciences.

Reiss, Albert J. (1980). Understanding Changes in Crime Rates. In *Indicators of Crime and Criminal Justice:* Quantitative Studies edited by Stephen E. Fienberg and Albert J. Reiss, Jr.. U. S. Department of Justice: Bureau of Justice Statistics. Washington, D. C.: U. S. Government Printing Office, pp. 11–17.

Reiss, Albert J. (1986a). Co-Offender Influences on Criminal Careers. In *Criminal Careers and Career Criminals* edited by Alfred Blumstein, Jacqueline Cohen, Jeffrey A. Roth, and Christy Visher. Washington, D. C.: National Academy Press, pp. 121–1660.

Reiss, Albert J. (1986b). Why are Communities Important in Understanding Crime? In *Communities and Crime* edited by Albert J. Reiss, Jr. and Michael Tonry. Chicago: University of Chicago Press.

Reiss, Albert J. (1988). *Co-Offending and Criminal Careers.* Crime and Justice: A Review of Research 10:117–170. Chicago: University of Chicago Press.

Reiss, A.J., Jr. & Farrington D. (1991). Advancing Knowledge About Co-Offending: Results from a Prospective Longitudinal Survey of London Males. *Journal of Criminal Law and Criminology* 82:360–395.

Reiss, Albert J., Jr. & Rhodes A.L. (1961). The Distribution of Juvenile Delinquency in the Social Class Structure. *American Sociological* Review 26:720–732.

Reiss, A.J., Jr. & Roth A.J. (1993). *Understanding and Preventing Violence.* Washington, D. D.C.: National Academy Press.

Rieder, J. (1985). *Canarsie: Jews and Italians of Brooklyn Against Liberalism.* Cambridge: Harvard University Press.

Sampson, R.J. (1986). Crime in Cities: The Effects of Formal and Informal Social Control. In *Communities and Crime* edited by Albert J. Reiss, Jr. and Michael Tonry. Chicago: University of Chicago Press.

Schuerman, L. & Kobrin S. (1986). Community Careers in Crime. In *Communities and Crime* edited by Albert J. Reiss, Jr. and Michael Tonry. Chicago: University of Chicago Press.

Shaw, C.R. & McKay H.D. (1931). *Social Factors in Juvenile Delinquency,* Vol. II of Report on the Causes of Crime. National Commission on Law Observance and Enforcement, Report No 13. Washington, D. C.: U. S. Government Printing Office.

Shaw, C.R. & McKay H.D. (1942). *Juvenile Delinquency and Urban Areas: A Study of Rates of Delinquents in Relation to Differential Characteristics of Local Communities in American Cities.* Chicago: University of Chicago Press.

Skogan, W. (1992). *Disorder and Decline: Crime and the Spiral of Decay in American Neighborhoods.* Berkeley: University of California Press.

Sutherland, E.H. (1947). *Principles of Criminology.* Chicago: J.B. Lippincott, Fourth Edition.

Tatum, B. (1987). *Assimilation Blues.* Westport, CT: Greenwood Press.

Thornton, M., Chatters, L., Taylor, R.J. & W. Allen (1990). Socio-demographic and Environmental Correlates of Racial Socialization by Black Parents. *Child Development* 61:401–09.

Tonry, M., Ohlin, L.E. & Farrington, D.P. (1991). *Human Development and Criminal Behavior: New Ways of Advancing Knowledge.* New York: Springer-Verlag.

Visher, C. & Roth J.A.(1986). Participation in Criminal Careers, Appendix A in Alfred Blumstein, Jacqueline Cohen, Jeffrey A. Roth and Christy Visher (eds.) *Criminal Careers and Career Criminals.* Washington, D. C.: National Academy Press.

Wikström, P.-O. H. (1991). *Urban Crime, Criminals, and Victims: The Swedish Experience in an Anglo American Comparative Perspective.* New York: Springer Verlag.

Wikström, P.-O. H. (1993). Preventing City-Center Street Crimes. Forthcoming in *Preventing Crime. Vol 19, Crime and Justice,* edited by Michael Tonry and David P. Farrington. Chicago: University of Chicago Press.

Wilson, W.J. (1987). *The Truly Disadvantaged: The Inner City, The Underclass, and Public Policy.* Chicago: University of Chicago Press.

Wilson, W.J. (1991). Studying Inner-City Social Dislocations: The Challenge of Public Agenda Research. *American Sociological Review* 56: 1–14.

Young, P. (1932). *The Pilgrims of Russian Town.* Chicago: University of Chicago Press.

Reports published in English by the National Council for Crime Prevention (BRÅ)

No 1	Non-Institutional Treatment – a preliminary evaluation of the Sundsvall experiment. *Eckart Kühlhorn* 1975
No 2	General Deterrence. A conference on current research and standpoints June 2–4. *Carl Johan Cosmo and Gösta Carlsson* 1975 (out of print)
No 3	Labeling Theory – a critical examination. *Johannes Knutsson* 1978
No 4	Deprivation of Freedom and the Police – an evaluation of the temporary custody act. *Eckart Kühlhorn* 1978
No 5	A new Penal System. Ideas and Proposals. *Erland Aspelin and Sten Heckscher* 1978
No 6	Police and the Social Order – Contemporary Research Perspectives. *Johannes Knutsson, Eckart Kühlhorn and Albert Reiss Jr* 1979
No 7	Non-Institutional Treatment and Rehabilition. An evaluation of a Swedish correctional experiment. Shortened version. *Eckart Kühlhorn* 1980
No 8	Computer Technology and Computer Crime. *Artur Solarz* 1981 (out of print)
No 9	Crime Prevention. *Eckart Kühlhorn and Bo Svensson* 1981
No 10	Drug Criminality and Drug Abuse in Sweden 1969–1981. *Jan Andersson and Artur Solarz* 1982 (out of print)
No 11	Current Swedish Legislation on Narcotics and Psychotropic Substances, 1984 (out of print)
No 12	Crime and Criminal Policy in Sweden, 1984 (out of print)
No 13	The Swedish Penal Code, 1984 (out of print)
No 14	Operation Identification – a way to prevent burglaries? *Johannes Knutsson* 1984
No 15	Everyday Violence in Contemporary Sweden. Situational and Ecological Aspects. *Per-Olof H. Wikström* 1985
No 16	The Swedish Code of Judicial Procecdure 1985 (out of print)
No 17	Predicting Social Maladjustment Stockholm Boys Grown up 1. *Jerzy Sarnecki and Stefan Sollenhag* 1985
No 18	Economic Crime - programs for future research. *Dan Magnusson* 1985 (out of print)
No 19	Crime and Criminal Policy in Sweden, 1985 (out of print)

1986:1 Delinquent networks. *Jerzy Sarnecki*
1986:2 The Swedish Penal Code
1986:3 Econometric Analysis of Crime in Sweden. *Perry Shapiro and Harold L. Votey jr*
1989 Juvenile Delinquency in Sweden. *Jerzy Sarnecki*
1990:1 Crime and Criminal Policy
1990:2 Current Swedish Legislation on Narcotics and Psychotropic Substances
1990:3 The Swedish Penal Code
1990:4 Crime Trends in Sweden 1988. *Editor: Lars Dolmén*
1993:1 Integrating Individual and Ecological Aspects of Crime. *Editors: David P. Farrington, Robert J. Sampson and Per-Olof H. Wikström*

Reports published by the Stockholm Project

1990:5 Crime and Measures against Crime in the City. *Editor: Per-Olof H. Wikström*
1991:3 Skola, livsstil och brott. *Lars Dolmén & Peter Lindström* (Swedish)
1991:5 Sociala problem, brott och trygghet. *Per-Olof H. Wikström* (Swedish)
1992:1 Familj, uppväxt och brott. *Peter L. Martens* (Swedish)
1993:2 School and Delinquency in a Contextual Perspective. *Peter Lindström*